(En) Gendering Knowledge

———

Feminists In Academe

Edited by
Joan E. Hartman
and
Ellen Messer-Davidow

1991

The University of Tennessee Press / Knoxville

Library of Congress Cataloging in Publication Data

(En)gendering knowledge:feminists in academe/
edited by Joan E. Hartman and Ellen Messer-Davidow.
— 1st. ed. p.   cm.
ISBN 0–87049–700–6 (cloth: alk. paper)
ISBN 0–87049–701–4 (pbk.: alk. paper)
  1. Feminist theory.   2. Feminist criticism.
3. Knowledge, Theory of.   4. Women scholars.
I. Hartman, Joan.   II. Messer-Davidow, Ellen, 1941–
HQ1190.E64   1991
305.42′01 — dc20   90–26492   CIP

Contents

Introduction

A Position Statement

Joan E. Hartman and Ellen Messer-Davidow

> Once upon a time, less than a generation ago, the place of feminist intellectuals
> was in the movement. When we worked with activist groups in the 1960s and
> 1970s, we were part of a mass political struggle. We helped to write position
> statements that analyzed the historical moment in which a revolutionary group
> found itself and that set forth strategies to bring about social change. . . . [The
> authors] were not making statements about "objective knowledge of true pro-
> positions about all women." They addressed a constituency to be organized, not
> a category to be described. They wrote in the mode of "knowing how," not
> "knowing that"; they had political know-how, not simply academic knowledge.
> — Kathryn Pyne Addelson and Elizabeth Potter, "Making Knowledge"

When we planned *(En)Gendering Knowledge: Feminists in Academe*, we expected to consider how feminists had altered academic knowledge. Taking the position that feminist research in the various disciplines formed a coherent inquiry, we outlined an epistemology that would bring feminists together across the disciplinary boundaries that were separating them. In retrospect, we see this volume as a search for another position in and on the academy, an alternative not only to poststructuralist critiques of knowledge but also to the present forms of our academic institutionalization. The position we assert now is that we feminists must rejoin what we put asunder in the early days of the Second Women's Movement: our intellectual inquiry and our social activism.

Originally, we designed this volume to problematize the segmentation of academic knowledge. As feminists working in, across, and against the disciplines, we wanted to question not only traditional knowledges, but also the division of academic knowledge into disciplines and the separation of the intellectual cores of these disciplines from their social contexts. We hoped to devise a feminist "social epistemology" that would cross the boundaries erected within and around academic knowledge. Social epistemology, according to Steve Fuller, who coined the term, is a socially situated inquiry into knowledge that requires knowers to ask such questions as: How are knowledges organized and produced? Who participates in organizing and producing them? What are the social relations of the producers? What are the social consequences of the knowledges?[1] Social epistemology is also a normative inquiry, because knowers ask these questions in the ethical as well as the empirical register: How should knowledges be organized and produced? Who should participate in organizing and producing them? What should be the social relations of the producers? What should be the social conseqences of the knowledges? By viewing the production of knowledge as social practice, we were then obliged to consider the available social explanations—for instance, empiricist, rational choice, hermeneutic, new realist, Marxist, and social constructionist. While most of these models privilege either agents or social structures in explaining the production of knowledge, social constructionism emphasizes their mutual constitution. A feminist social epistemology that employed it would view the production or transformation of academic knowledge as practice that constitutes both knowers and the institutions that enable and constrain them.

We invited as contributors feminists who were already taking stock of their disciplines. We asked them to emphasize the constitution of their disciplinary knowledge and the sex-gender categories that structured it. As a consequence, all of the contributors question the inadequate presence of women both as agents and as subjects of inquiry.[2] They challenge the gendering of discipines, the use of sex-gender ideologies to justify things as they are, and the harm caused by knowers who disclaim responsibility for the consequences of the knowledge they produce. In their programs for feminist knowledge and their critiques of traditional knowledge, these contributors reveal knowers as social agents, knowing as social practice, disciplines as social formations, and knowledge as productive of social consequences. Doing so, they also reveal the differences their own race or sexuality, class or gender have made in the knowledge they produce. Thus the design of the volume allows a play of disciplinary and social variables to illuminate four epistemic issues—*agency, perspective, value judgment,* and *selection.*

Agency, for us as for Anthony Giddens, "refers to doing."[3] Agents act and monitor their actions. What makes them agents is their capacity (not their intention) to act and, moreover, to act otherwise, to intervene in the world, to have an effect. Knowers exercise their agency not only when they devise facts and theories, but also when they attempt to transform the disciplines or even when they choose a different voice. As editors, we translated the epistemic issue of agency into a stylistic one, querying our contributors when they wrote in the agentless passive, "*whose* transactions do you report?" and "for *whose* purposes?" The identification of authorship (especially in the sciences) is a step toward subverting disciplinary authority, which is constituted in part by the anonymity of professional discourse.

Perspective has been defined visually as the function of positioning a person and a scene. The viewer's location and the configuration seen elicit the angle of vision, and, conversely, the viewer's location and the angle of vision determine the configuration seen. Intellectually, *perspective* may be defined as the function of relatively positioning a knower and a subject of inquiry. What positions knowers in society are their social circumstances: (1) affiliations with a gender, race, class, sexuality, and other cultural categories; (2) technical training, which differs not only across but also within disciplines; (3) personal histories; and (4) critical reflection on the ways these circumstances organize inquiry. Insofar as these circumstances are diverse, knowers' perspectives diverge. Most knowers acknowledge that they vary their perspectives according to research goals and methods but not that they do so according to cultural and personal circumstances. The contributors, however, foreground the ways being black or white, heterocentric or anticlassist, complacent or self-defining, shape the knowledge produced.

Through this social positioning, we acquire the *values* that draw us to certain disciplines, which in turn codify the values that influence our disciplinary *judgments* about subjects to investigate, methods to employ, knowledge to produce, and uses to which that knowledge should be put. Of course, disciplinary practitioners do not identically construct value or even individual values. Traditional humanists, Barbara Herrnstein Smith reminds us, separate facts from value but retain both within their disciplines. The production of facts is the business of scholars who locate, restore, and describe cultural artifacts, and the discrimination of value is the business of critics. "By virtue of certain innate and acquired capacities" (such as taste and sensibility), she writes, critics are "specifically equipped" to detect value as a "determinate property" of these cultural artifacts.[4] By contrast, positivist-empiricist scientists separate facts from values and banish the latter from their disciplines. They are specifically equipped to discriminate facts by virtue of their ability to exclude values (such as aesthetic preferences and social concerns) from their work. Both humanists and scientists proceed as if they have detached value from the values of knowers; instead they have reified it as a property of disciplinary objects. While humanists "find" value in artifacts and scientists "find" it in facts, feminist knowers, the essays in this volume reveal, affirm the value of our own values in the production of knowledge.

Cumulatively, the values of knowers guide their judgments, which in turn organize the disciplines.[5] The judgments that knowers make about their inquiry constitute a process of *selection* that produces the paradigms and canons they use to guide research, training, and teaching. Knowers' judgments, regularized and institutionalized, organize both the cognitive and the practical aspects of inquiry: on the one hand, the subjects, methods, and theories; and, on the other hand, the activities of producing knowledge and knowers. Conversely, the resulting selection continues to enable and constrain the knowers by determining (in a possibilistic sense) the selections they can make in the future. Thus, the range of selections is already defined; it is implicit in the organization of the discipline — how hegemonic its culture and how closed its borders to neighboring disciplines.[6] The contributors to this volume explicitly link disciplinary selections to the social positioning of knowers and the social relations that organize their work.

We asked the contributors to take one of these epistemic issues as a point of departure for their essays but to recognize its links with the others. Precisely because they are linked, the issues mediate agents and structures. Thus, we may view them as functions of agency, because knowers *have* perspectives, *acquire* values, *make* selections, and over time *constitute* (as they are constituted by) the institutions of knowledge. And we also can view them as functions of social structure, because institutions — families, schools, government agencies, media — constitute (as they are constituted by) agentic perspectives, values, and selections. At this historical moment, both views are required. Our emphasis on agency is an overdue response to poststructuralist proclamations of the death of the author and the subjection of subjects issued just when women began to exercise their agency as academics and activists.[7] Our emphasis on social structure is a timely response to conservative declamations against the newly institutionalized critical inquiries — women's studies, African-American studies, gay studies, Marxism, deconstruction — that disclose the politics of knowledge.[8]

We assign agency to the opening essay because disciplinary perspectives, value judgments, and selections are instantiated by agents and also because the disciplines variously construe agency as, for example, "objectivity" in biology, "participant observation" in sociology, and "pluralism" in literary studies. For each of the remaining issues we constructed a grid consisting of three disciplinary essays — selected from the natural sciences, social sciences, and humanities — and a philosophical essay theorizing them. This scheme permits us to consider the effects of disciplinarity on each epistemic issue: how traditional and feminist perspectives appear in sociology, classics, and literary studies; how values are refracted by biology, anthropology, and literary studies; and how disciplinary selections are made in the physical sciences, art history, and literary studies.[9] While a few of the essays criticize disciplinarity as Foucault has done, together they show the extent to which it continues to organize feminist inquiry.

The philosophical essays in each section address the commonalities of the disciplinary essays and extend their ideas on perspectives, values, and selections. These essays are more focused on the ethical and political than the historical considerations of producing knowledge. Appropriately, their authors are feminists who divide their academic homes between departments of philosophy and programs in women's studies. The concluding essay on knowhow moves from agency to social structure. It problematizes the institutionalization of feminist knowledge and recommends that we use the academic apparatus we have built to make feminist social change.

Feminist intellectuals, as Addelson and Potter observe in the quotation that precedes this introduction, once were engaged in political struggles. But when we situated ourselves "in" the academy, we divided our intellectual inquiry from our social activism. Feminism was not simply dichotomized; it was balkanized. We multiplied ourselves academically by bringing feminists into the disciplines and by establishing some six hundred women's studies programs. These different forms of institutionalization had different effects. In the disciplines we dispersed centrifugally into specializations, while in women's studies programs we moved centripetally to crossdisciplinary research and teaching. Meanwhile, the terrain, wherever we located ourselves on it, became increasingly fractured by the positivist, structuralist, and poststructuralist assumptions that began to divide feminist and nonfeminist academics. These disciplinary practices and epistemic allegiances compounded the differences that race, class, sexuality, ethnicity, and nationality made in an increasingly heterogeneous academy. The cultural fault lines ran deep, and we did not always acknowledge them; some feminists effaced differences as often as others inscribed them.

At the same time, we became adept at meeting the professional demands that earned us success as well as tenure. By the end of our second decade in the academy, the *Chronicle of Higher Education* observed that "the growth of women's studies is one of the success stories of American higher education."[10] Feminist inquiry, it pronounced, had become extremely sophisticated and influential — but, many of us suspected, at a price. With academic work consuming our energies, few of us sustained our political activism. We consoled ourselves with the thought that changing the academy was our contribution to the feminist revolution. And perhaps it has been. But the ascendancy of conservativism in politics and culture should remind us that academic feminism has not been sufficiently instrumental in the making of social change. We have produced brilliant cultural analyses but not political actions. Analyses, however, are an inadequate response to conservatives who express their opposition to feminism not only in public debates but also in Supreme Court decisions and government funding of academic research, art, and social programs.

Yet the contributors to this volume do not long nostalgically for the days when feminist intellectuals were movement activists. They look realistically at the present situation of feminist intellectuals in a contested academy and a conservative country, and they ask how academic knowledge can be used to advance the struggle now. Framed in this way, the question suggests an answer — that we evaluate academic knowledges with respect to agency and particular models of agency with respect to the distance they allow between inquiry and action. Doing so, feminists would join other poststructuralists in rejecting traditional models of knowers, stripped of cultural particularity and moral commitment, who discover knowledge but disclaim responsibility for its consequences. And we would reject the accompanying reification of knowledge as truth: knowledge represented as if it were antecedently *there* to be discovered and reported by intellectualized knowers rather than made by practical ones. But we would also be wary of poststructuralist models of knowers, whether Althusserian interpellation or deconstructive subject-positioning, because they neutralize agency and thereby planned social change.[11] And we would criticize their imperialism in equating all kinds of knowledge with discourse: knowledges represented as no more than effects of discourse, discourse as the social system that constructs subjects, subjects who can speak only as they have been spoken. Whereas the poststructuralist models feature a structure that produces a subject's "consent" or "resistance" to a particular knowledge or course of action, the traditional models feature a hyperindividualism that occludes structure as an object of knowledge and action. Both diminish us as agents of knowledge and social change.

In contrast to such models of agency, feminist social constructionism emphasizes both agent-initiated and system-imposed change. The practices of knowers, regularized and repeated across time and space, constitute the structures of both knowledge and the institutions that produce it. In turn, the routine institutional decisions — about awarding research grants and departmental budgets, allocating equipment and information, and employing personnel — produce a template that enables and constrains the knowers and thereby structures the knowledge they produce. These knowers and their academy, imbricated with other complex social practices, yield to informed interventions. As conservative political interventions are reminding us once again, academic autonomy is not an actuality but an ideology maintained by the academy. To reiterate the ideology, as liberals do in the face of increased political regulation of the academy, is to mystify the actuality, for the insularity promulgated by the one masks the control imposed by the other. Feminists, having successfully situated ourselves "in" the academy, need to recognize the dangers of academic knowledge as it is presently constituted. We need to redeem fully our capacity as agents to act as well as to know otherwise, to intervene in the world as well as the academy, to have an effect. A feminist social constructionism does not guarantee that we will act successfully in all of these ways, but it does underline our capacity — and responsibility — to rejoin feminist inquiry and social activism.

Notes

We are enormously grateful to Larry T. Shillock for his insight, care, and unfailing good cheer in helping us to prepare this volume. Ellen Messer-Davidow is pleased to acknowledge a Grant-in-Aid of Research from the Graduate School, University of Minnesota, which was awarded in part to support her work on this project.

1. Steve Fuller, *Social Epistemology* (Bloomington: Indiana University Press, 1988).

2. We use the term *agents* in order to stress the capacity of knowers for action (to make knowledge, to intervene in its production, to transform the conditions of reproduction generally), rather than the term *subjects*, which connotes the subjection of knowers to discourse and the principle of social determinism. We use the phrase *subjects of inquiry* to denote the matters that knowers construct and investigate, and we reserve the phrase *objects of inquiry*, with its connotations of objectification and objectivity, for the matters constructed by post-Cartesian investigations.

3. Anthony Giddens, *The Constitution of Society* (Berkeley: University of California Press, 1984), 10; also see 5–16.

4. Barbara Herrnstein Smith, *Contingencies of Value: Alternative Perspectives for Critical Theory* (Cambridge, Mass.: Harvard University Press, 1988), 19.

5. For an account of the ways in which values enter into scientific inquiry, see Helen E. Longino, *Science As Social Knowledge: Values and Objectivity in Scientific Inquiry* (Princeton, N.J.: Princeton University Press, 1990).

6. See Jennifer Milliken, "Travelling Across Borders," in "Symposium on Crossdisciplinarity," ed. Ellen Messer-Davidow and David R. Shumway, *Social Epistemology* 4, no. 3 (July–Sept. 1990): 317–21.

7. For two essays originally published as the Second Women's Movement began to spread, see Roland Barthes, "The Death of the Author" (1968), in *Image-Music-Text*, trans. Stephen Heath (New York: Hill and Wang, 1977), 142–48; and Michel Foucault, "What Is An Author?" (1969), in Foucault, *Language, Counter-Memory, Practice: Selected Essays and Interviews*, ed. Donald F. Bouchard, trans. Donald F. Bouchard and Sherry Simon (Ithaca, N.Y.: Cornell University Press, 1977), 113–38.

8. One of the most recent declamations is Roger Kimball, *Tenured Radicals: How Politics Has Corrrupted Our Higher Education* (New York: Harper and Row, 1990).

9. The matching of disciplines and epistemic issues — why, for example, sociology is assigned to perspectives, anthropology to value judgments, and physical science to selections — came about through a combination of our hunches about the concerns in disciplines and the interests of the contributors. The three literary essays reflect, in part, our own training in literature and, in part, our desire to demonstrate rather than gesture toward the paradigmatic diverstiy so notable in the literary studies disciplines now. With unlimited space, we could have included essays by a physicist or an astronomer, an economist or a political scientist, a musicologist or a film theorist. Given the limits of a single volume, we hope the disciplinary essays we include, by their stereoscopic focus, will provide readers with the illusion of completeness accompanied by a convincing density of exemplification.

10. Karen J. Winkler, "Women's Studies After Two Decades: Debates Over Politics, New Directions for Research," *Chronicle of Higher Education*, 28 Sept. 1988, A4–A7 (quotation on p. A4).

11. See John Mowitt's critique in "Forward: The Resistance in Theory," in Paul Smith, *Discerning the Subject* (Minneapolis: University of Minnesota Press, 1988), xiii; as well as Smith's analysis of the Derridian project to deconstruct philosophical, juridical, and textual subjects and why it fails to recognize agency (41–55).

Part I

Agency

1

Telling Stories: The Construction of Women's Agency

Joan E. Hartman

"Sir, a woman's preaching is like a dog's walking on its hind legs. It is not done well; but you are surprised to find it done at all."[1]

"Did you say teaching, Miss Hartman?", a (male) student asked, his eyes brimful of mischief. His question took me aback. My mind was on Boswell's *Life of Johnson*, not the war between the sexes. But I decided his question was personally benign, not a first shot in the war. Grudgingly I managed to appreciate his word-play and remarked that Johnson would have been as surprised to find me in a college classroom teaching as he was to hear of a Quaker woman preaching.

My Boswell/Johnson story I've told and retold; it's a telling story. At the time of the interchange, I was a young instructor (with a master's degree) teaching a survey course in British literature. I'd been talking about Johnson's magisterial pronouncements and quoted the one about a woman preaching (not included in the anthology we were using) from memory. It was tellingly present to me, and not just for its wit—though, as I recollect, I appreciated Johnson's discordant yoking of wordish women and performing dogs even as I was stung by its misogyny. In a world of pedestrian insults to women, his verbal acrobatics have class.

Now my response would emphasize Johnson's misogyny and its consequences, for my Boswell/Johnson story is embedded in a different narrative. For one thing, then I'd read only Virginia Woolf's canonical fiction; now I've read *A Room of One's Own*. Inventing William Shakespeare's sister, the talented Judith whose creative potential is as great as her brother's, Woolf mockingly attributes the original of Johnson's pronouncement to Nick Greene, the actor-manager who told her (before seducing her) that "a woman acting put him in mind of a dog dancing."[2] Greene's inability to conceive of a woman acting marks an imagination bounded by the conventions of the Elizabethan stage, where boys played women's roles. Woolf felt Johnson's pronouncement as a rebuff to herself, to women painters (like her sister Vanessa Bell), and to women composers (like her friend Dame Ethel Smyth); she bridles to think that "again in this year of grace, 1928," Cecil Gray, in *A Survey of Contemporary Music*, could apply it to Germaine Tailleferre.

For another thing, now I've spent more time as a college teacher—walking on my hind legs, so to speak—and I've been bruised by the discrimination that pronouncements like Johnson's legitimate. I still find it witty, even as I no longer relish its wit, because I recognize its abrasive consequences for me, for women who teach, and for women students. My Boswell/Johnson story still appears in the narrative of my development, my *bildungsroman*, but my understanding of who I am has altered my interpretation of it. I've learned to attend to the politics of gender and to employ a hermeneutics of suspicion.

We construct our selves as agents by piecing together our telling stories, by *emplotting* the events of our lives (to use Hayden White's term) in narratives that have explanatory power. White's comments apply to the stories we relate to ourselves, to our friends, and sometimes to our therapists. "And when he"—for White's *he*, the reader of histories, I substitute ourselves, simultaneously authors and auditors of our telling stories—when he "has perceived the class or type to which the story that he is reading belongs, he experiences the effect of having the events in the story explained to him. He has at this point not only successfully *followed* the story; he has grasped the point of it, *understood* it."[3] The conventions of autobiographical narratives are familiar to us: because we have encountered them elsewhere, we not only recognize their classes or types but also experience their power to make our selves and our lives coherent and comprehensible. If we do not create the conventions that govern and make comprehensible our telling stories, we nevertheless select among them, revising, emending, and even scrapping the materials we have on hand to shape our plots.

As we make our narratives our own, we apprehend ourselves as agents: we become conscious of ourselves as makers of our lives as well as makers of narratives about our lives. We are, to be sure, discursively constrained as we live, interpret, and emplot our stories, and we can deconstruct the conventions that constrain us. But if we *only* deconstruct them, if we fail to acknowledge that we also select among them to construct and reconstruct narratives and lives—by making sense of our telling stories through embodying them in narratives; by producing narratives sufficiently comprehensible to secure our assent and the assent of others; by acting in the world even as we are acted upon by it—then we disperse our selves wantonly.

When Ellen Messer-Davidow and I planned *(En)Gendering Knowledge: Feminists in Academe*, we designated agency as one of its four epistemic categories. These four we saw as points of divergence among our feminist social epistemology, traditional positivist-empiricism, and deconstruction. Exploring them, we hoped to further the development of feminist inquiry. In this volume we insist on the agency of knowers in order to emphasize our active roles in making and remaking knowledge. We subscribe neither to agent-centered explanations that discount social systems in order to endow agents with limitless power, nor to system-centered explanations that neutralize agency as a discursive or institutional effect. We hold that agents and systems — in *(En)Gendering Knowledge*, systems like disciplines, professions, and academic institutions — are mutually constitutive.

Agency is more disputed now than it was when we planned *(En)Gendering Knowledge*, inasmuch as it has become a point of divergence within feminist inquiry itself, as deconstructive feminists subscribe to system-centered explanation. Their interrogation of discursive categories dissolves "the subject" into multiple and evanescent intimations, imprisons agency in language, and leads to a theory subversive of practice itself.[4] At least two of our contributors assess the unfortunate consequences of deconstruction for feminist revision of disciplinary practices: Joyce A. Joyce for Black literary studies (see "Black Woman Scholar, Critic, and Teacher: The Inextricable Relationship Among Race, Sex, and Class"), and Sandra Harding for philosophy (see "Who Knows?: Identities and Feminist Epistemology").

Agency, as Anthony Giddens puts it, "refers to doing"; it also "implies power."[5] The stories women knowers tell are almost uniformly emplotted in narratives of thwarted agency that point, at least immediately, to the ways educational institutions fail women by constraining what they do and denying them power. If changes in the production and institutionalization of knowledge are not the only changes I and the other contributors to *(En)Gendering Knowledge* want, they are nevertheless desirable changes; moreover, they are changes that academic feminists, given the present scope of our agency and power, can hope to accomplish. Educational institutions perform what Ellen Messer-Davidow calls "structuring mediations between those who constitute them and the system of multiple oppressions that orders our culture" (see her essay in this volume, "Know-How"). They can also "perform restructuring mediations beween ourselves as feminist agents and the system we want to change." Within educational institutions we want epistemological change, disciplinary change, pedagogical change, and demographic change (that is, the inclusion of more women, a greater range of women, and women in a greater range of disciplines). These changes will empower women as agents, outside of as well as inside educational institutions — for our aims go beyond educational to social change.

In the rest of this essay, looking at women's experience of education in a variety of disciplinary, academic, and social contexts, I focus, first, on constraint, and second, on change. In "Ironic Engagement" I look at academic women who completed their graduate education in the 1960s and 1970s and entered (or attempted to enter) their respective disciplines as credentialed professionals. In "Knowing Women" I look at undergraduate women. In "Knowing, Teaching, and Power" I look at traditional and new pedagogies. And in "New Plots" I argue that academic feminists now possess both theories and practices that are distinctively ours and must remain ours if we are to create new plots for women — actually create them, rather than select among conventions always already there — by transforming disciplines, professions, and academic institutions and by using them to make feminist social change.

Ironic Engagement

Academic women are "outsiders within" (to quote from the title of Patricia Hill Collins' essay in this volume, "Learning from the Outsider Within: The Sociological Significance of Black Feminist Thought"), and our situation generates disabling contradictions. Education instructs us in the stances approved for inquiry: an "objective" or unsituated stance, marked by agentless passive prose ("it can be seen that . . . "), and a normative or reified stance, marked by consensual prose ("*we* see that . . . "). Academic women succeed by learning to adopt them, by renouncing our particular selves for displaced, ostensibly generic selves, and begin to be academic feminists by recognizing them as male and acknowledging how, in order to join the ranks of knowers, we feigned, adopted, and even internalized them. But identifying the "fit" between approved stances and academic institutions, a fit that enhances male security and makes us misfits, only raises our consciousness; it does not remedy our situation.

Two recent works gather stories, telling stories, about women's education and emplot them. One, by Mary Field Belenky, Blythe McVicker Clinchy, Nancy Rule Goldberger, and Jill Mattuck Tarule (hereafter, Belenky et al.), is *Women's Ways of Knowing: The Development of Self, Voice, and Mind* (1986); another, by Nadya Aisenberg and Mona Harrington, is *Women of Academe: Outsiders in the Sacred Grove* (1988).[6] Belenky et al. studied primarily undergraduate women, Aisenberg and Harrington women with doctorates; together they illuminate the undergraduate and graduate experiences that homogenize academic women, whatever the personal histories and cultural circumstances that diversify us. Both sets of authors gathered their stories through interviews that were lengthy, informal, and loosely structured; insofar as they could, they left their subjects room to emplot their own narratives. They were self-reflective ethnographers sensitive to differences in power between those who provide information and those who interpret it (for a discussion of power differentials in ethnography, see Micaela di Leonardo's essay in this volume, "Contingencies of Value in Feminist Anthropology"). They then worked through their interviews to discover plots they hoped were their subjects' rather than their own.[7]

Women of Academe is a study of women who were sufficiently unconstrained by gender to enter and complete graduate school and who found their agency thwarted when they tried to enter academic institutions as credentialed professionals. Those studied regard themselves ironically, interpreting their expectations as unrealistic and so distancing themselves from failure as well as from modest success. Their irony is a form of collaboration with the very disciplines, professions, and academic institutions that thwarted them.

Women of Academe is a study that in some sense misfired, for Aisenberg and Harrington began by looking for differences between tenured women securely inside the academy and "deflected" women intermittently and precariously inside, holding temporary, non-tenure-track, and part-time appointments. They found few differences among them with respect to credentials, disciplinary socialization, and professionalism.[8] Those they found involved publication: the women who scrambled for part-time jobs and taught service courses lacked time and support to amass a bibliography. None of the women they interviewed were Black or Third-World. None identified themselves as lesbians; aware that some were, Aisenberg and Harrington nevertheless accepted their definitions of themselves (for a discussion of one lesbian's experience as a knower and teacher, see Bonnie Zimmerman's essay in this volume, "Seeing, Reading, Knowing: The Lesbian Appropriation of Literature"). The majority of them entered the job market in a decade of expansion, the 1960s, and a decade of contraction, the 1970s; while expansion did not appreciably enlarge their opportunities, contraction shrank them.

Their distribution is representative of the disciplines women choose (and are chosen by): 37 in the humanities, 19 in history and the social sciences, and 6 in the natural sciences.[9] When I speak of women's choosing and being chosen by humanistic disciplines, I gesture toward the tracking and self-tracking that discourages them from scientific disciplines: "A life I didn't choose/chose me," as Adrienne Rich puts it.[10] Such is the force of tracking that women continued to enter the lower-paying humanities in the contracted marketplace of the 1970s and 1980s, when they offered fewer opportunities for full-time tenure-track employment than the higher-paying sciences.

Aisenberg and Harrington's analysis transmutes social formations into literary ones: that is, they identify "two distinct social patterns" with "two distinct dramatic conventions — the marriage . . . plot, which outlines the old norms, and the quest . . . plot, which by extension of its classic form, outlines the values and attributes of the public life to which women now aspire."[11] The women these authors interviewed encountered contradictions because they cast themselves and were cast as protagonists in (at least) two different — and oppositional — plots. In retrospect they recognized the contradictions and their costs. Few of them, however, would have done other than they had: they had managed to perform in the plot they wanted more, the marriage plot, while muddling through the plot they wanted less, the quest plot.

The marriage plot, as Aisenberg and Harrington use it, begins at birth; marriage is but its dénouement. The reproduction of mothering in the family and gendered expectations in childrearing, education, and the media — these contribute to the production of female subjects suited to the domestic rather than the public sphere. The marriage plot prescribes connectedness, love, deferral, and submission; it subverts women's agency by schooling their desires. Academic institutions enforce it by limiting women's opportunities and constraining their power.

The quest plot, as Aisenberg and Harrington use it, conflates two plots, a quest plot that begins with women's decision to work toward a doctorate and a profession plot that begins when, fully credentialed, they enter the job market. Aisenberg and Harrington call women's choice of the quest plot a "transformation": beyond the excitement of venturing forth, it promises to alter and expand identities already limned by the marriage plot. For, while the women they interviewed valued the connectedness, love, deferral, and submission prescribed by the marriage plot, they also hankered after the solitude, independence, dedication, and authority the quest plot promised or seemed to promise. Women, supporting players in the marriage plot, star in the quest plot and initiate their own adventures. The quest plot is defined by its opposition to the marriage plot: foreign rather than domestic, strange rather than familiar. The women Aisenberg and Harrington interviewed report a keen sense of their agency as they launched themselves on the quest plot, and their excitement apparently foreclosed their scrutiny of it.

Looking back on their questing selves, off to find the Grail, these women describe themselves as "naive" and "innocent" of the profession plot that the quest plot shades into. The tenured, moreover, were no wiser than the deflected about its entrepreneurial dimensions. I remember a venerable graduate-school professor larding his Grail remarks with corporate wisdom. As literary scholars our study was (in Wordsworth's resonant words) "the breath and finer spirit of all knowledge"— the quest plot was not Aisenberg and Harrington's invention. We were also to play golf with junior faculty, who would one day be our professorial colleagues, rather than with senior faculty. All of us, women and men, professed to be amused by his juxtaposition of the exalted and the mundane. (I'd have been better off taking it seriously, instead of looking back on it and myself ironically.) Among the circumstances accounting for women's naiveté, some are generational.[12] Our (male) graduate professors, however kind, neglected to mentor us because they did not think of us as serious professionals; often we did not think of ourselves as serious professionals. Perhaps these professors would have felt uncomfortable or even compromised mentoring young women. Women already married, often with children, trundled from class to library and laboratory to home, without time to develop camaraderie with other (mostly male) graduate students. Some unmarried women continued to play out the marriage plot; others covertly played out lesbian plots.

Aisenberg and Harrington's analysis emphasizes oppositions between the marriage plot and the quest plot more than oppositions between the quest plot and the profession plot; the first, the quest plot, supplies an ideological gloss to the second, the profession plot. The quest plot prescribes knowledge and authority as its goals, the profession plot tenure, rank, salary, and teaching as few students as possible. The quest plot leaves routes to its goals improvisatory; the profession plot prescribes a route whose turns are precisely marked and whose speeds are strictly enforced. It calls for a fast-track career, that is, a career with full-time employment and high productivity. The women Aisenberg and Harrington interviewed were pushed into slow-track careers in the 1960s by their limited mobility, in the 1970s and 1980s by the contracted academic marketplace. Above all, they were pushed into slow-track careers by their gender: teaching is an occupation the entrepreneurs of the profession plot are only too willing to leave to women. The women they interviewed liked teaching; nevertheless, when they found themselves shunted between non-tenure-track full-time and part-time teaching, they felt oppressed by their exploitation and by having reached the dead end of a quest to which they had been drawn by intellectual possibilities and commitments.

Aisenberg and Harrington conclude *Women of Academe* with complete narratives of four women humanists.[13] One, in philosophy, is tenured but slow-track; one, in American studies, hanging in without full-time employment; one, in Romance languages and literature, about to quit the profession after a series of temporary appointments; and one, in English literature, saved (in an editors' note) from quitting the profession by the last-minute reprieve of a tenure-track position that nevertheless will put her on a slow track because of her irregular career. All four exaggerate their innocence of professionalism in ways that may seem both excessive and self-willed — unless we recognize the importance of irony to the emplotment of their narratives.

The first narrative I see as comedy: after mishaps, a happy ending. Its protagonist produces a dissertation on an unfashionable subject, neglects to revise it for publication in a timely fashion, and then writes a book on philosophy of science for high school students and a book on women and philosophy that is neither popular nor scholarly; yet she receives tenure. This narrative's generic alternative is epic, in which a purposeful protagonist undertakes momentous deeds. What keeps the first narrative comedy is its narrator's inability to represent either her agency or her accomplishments as serious. The second and third narratives I see as satires. The narrators represent their accomplishments more seriously than the first narrator and with more corrosive irony; their plots, however, end inconclusively. Their generic alternative is tragedy: both narrators, like the protagonists of tragedy, are constrained by oppressive circumstances. What precludes tragedy is that, with hindsight, they mute their anger against the system and blame themselves for folly. The fourth narrative is a satire that, in view of its narrator's unexpected reprieve, needs reemplotment, probably as a comedy.

In short, all four narrators accept their thwarted agency and fault themselves for innocence rather than faulting the professional plot that constrains them. Aisenberg and Harrington are complicit with them in declining to acknowledge the extent to which professionalism constrains women's power. *Women of Academe* has been criticized, I think justly, for turning "sociopolitical questions into psychological ones,"[14] because its authors' analyses are agent-centered rather than system-centered, insufficiently critical of disciplines, professions, and academic institutions. What they envisage for their subjects is what many of their subjects wanted for themselves — slow-track careers.[15] They advise academic women to disabuse themselves of the illusions of the quest plot and recognize the realities of the profession plot in order to succeed as professionals; then they can fine-tune academic institutions to humanize them and ameliorate the lot of women. Aisenberg and Harrington might better have problematized systems than accommodated to them agents who then regard their disempowerment ironically. Systems are not changed by those who ironically accept their constrained agency.

Knowing Women

Most of the women Aisenberg and Harrington interviewed had distanced themselves from traditional modes of disciplinary inquiry. They preferred cross-disciplinary to discipline-bound inquiry and were more likely to study unformulated subjects at the edges of disciplines than sharply defined ones at their centers. They questioned oppositions between reason and feeling and between "objective" and "subjective"; they were tolerant of ambiguity. While most of them earned their doctorates before the development of academic women's studies, they were attracted to such programs because these reflect their perspectives and practices. Aisenberg and Harrington warily sketch a typology of women's intellectual work, for they resist — and rightly — the notion of separate spheres. Separate spheres are never equal. Moreover, the perspectives women bring to inquiry can be identified with the marriage plot. In a society where male is the norm and female the submissive (or aggressive) exception, these perspectives are devalued by the academy, whatever its claims to be exempt from vulgar prejudice.

In *Women's Ways of Knowing*, Belenky et al. also present a typology of women's intellectual work. The impetus to their study was the self-doubt that troubles undergraduate women whose success qualifies them for the graduate study they are often unwilling to undertake. Belenky et al. wanted to discover if traditional pedagogy, developed by male teachers for male students, is intellectually empowering for women. Their subjects came from what they call "invisible" colleges (that is, social agencies) as well as from elite and non-elite colleges.[16] And these researchers left their subjects room to plot their own stories, though most of them were not narrators as practised as the women Aisenberg and Harrington interviewed.

What Belenky et al. "found" are gendered variants of a plot worked out by William G. Perry, Jr., in his study of Harvard undergraduates privileged by class and culture as well as gender.[17] Their and his definitions of successful knowers are consonant with the social constructionist paradigm articulated in *(En)Gendering Knowledge:* because knowledge is historically, socially, and personally contingent, knowers must be critically aware of the processes by which they and others construct it and in turn are constructed by it. All agree that knowers move from patience to agency, from suffering to doing, and from insecure and dependent selves to secure and self-reliant ones. But Belenky et al.'s female version of Perry's male plot is shaded in ways that his is not and more littered with casualties. Some of these ways may be attributed to class. Most are attributable to gender, to the marriage plot that prescribes patience and dependence to women.

Belenky et al.'s plot involves five ways of knowing, four of which can be aligned with Perry's. They add (prior to his four) *silence*, in which women experience themselves as "mindless, voiceless, and subject to the whims of external authority."[18] This way of knowing appears inextricably linked with class, inasmuch as the women who experienced it all came from "invisible" and non-elite colleges (for a discussion of class, gender, and silence, see the essay in this volume by Angelika Bammer, "Mastery"). I link silence with authoritarian families in which power, not persuasion, determines behavior. "You do what I say; I'm boss around here" is a writing prompt that elicits moving narratives from male as well as female students at the urban public institution where I teach. Nevertheless, tacitly or explicitly, powerful fathers of any class provide models for the agency of their sons, submissive mothers for the agency of their daughters.

Belenky et al.'s remaining ways of knowing are *received knowledge, subjective knowledge, procedural knowledge,* and *constructed knowledge.*[19] From *silence* women move to *received knowledge:* while they recognize themselves as mindful rather than mindless, what they know is only the knowledge dispensed to them by others, not their own capacity to know and to make knowledge. Received knowers, both male and female, are depen-

dent. Nevertheless, because the authorities who dispense knowledge are ordinarily male, men can identify with them, whereas women's identification
is blocked. Instead of looking forward to emulating those who produce and
transmit knowledge, women learn to defer to them.

When women move to *subjective knowledge,* they know themselves as
knowers but experience their knowledge as warranted only to themselves by
themselves. The catalyst in their moving beyond *received knowledge* to *subjective knowledge* is often a failure of male authority. When it fails, women,
thrown back on themselves, learn to trust themselves as knowers capable of
producing at least that "low-grade" knowledge called intuition. To an extent
that Belenky et al. did not expect when they began their interviews, the
failure of male authority is connected with sexual abuse: incest, rape, or
seduction by fathers, uncles, teachers, doctors, clerics, bosses. Its frequency
shocked them.[20] Violence colors women's experience as knowers, and women
may move from received to subjective knowing in revulsion against male
betrayals. In contrast with the self-confident subjective knowers in Perry's
study, even the most advantaged subjective knowers in Belenky et al.'s study
were cautious and self-protective.[21] Moreover, they constituted almost half
the women interviewed, and, as Belenky et al. put it, "[i]n a world that emphasizes rationalism and scientific thought, there are bound to be personal
and social costs of a subjectivist epistemology."[22]

Women's moving beyond *subjective knowledge* to *procedural knowledge*
appears to be connected with, though not a necessary result of, college
education, inasmuch as all but one of the procedural knowers interviewed
were either college students or college graduates. One of Belenky et al.'s
most arresting points is that, while procedural knowing ultimately strengthens
women, the transition from subjective to procedural knowing means putting
their agency at risk: "Procedural knowers feel like chameleons; they cannot
help but take on the color of any structure they inhabit. In order to assume
their own true colors, they must detach themselves from the relationships
and institutions to which they have been subordinated."[23] Subjective knowing, intimately connected with the self, is self-affirming; procedural knowing, separate from the self, requires justification. Belenky et al. expatiate on
women's resistance to procedural knowing, for it is here in their development that women, measured against men, may *seem* deficient. In consequence, while they identify the challenges women encounter in their move
beyond subjective to procedural knowing, they are particularly concerned
to identify the supports (for a discussion of the psychological and social conditions that "fit" men for procedural knowing, see Denise Fréchet's essay in
this volume, "Toward a Post-Phallic Science").[24]

Few of the women Belenky et al. interviewed had moved beyond *procedural knowledge* to *constructed knowledge — Women's Ways of Knowing* som berly documents the failures of their education. The women who had moved beyond procedural knowledge managed to reclaim the agency they felt they had renounced to become procedural knowers and reconcile that agency with the procedures they had learned to employ. They reclaim their agency, but critically, with

> a heightened consciousness and sense of choice about "how I want to think" and "how I want to be." They develop a narrative sense of the self — past and future. They do not want to dismiss former ways of knowing so much as they want to stay alert to the fact that different perspectives and different points in time produce different answers. They begin to express an interest in personal history and in the history of ideas.[25]

Their agency strengthened by analysis, especially in the context of auto-biography ("a narrative sense of the self"), they move to a critical scrutiny of others' investigative procedures, along with their own, and possess complex criteria for evaluating knowledge. In addition, the history of ideas demonstrates to them that all knowledge, not just their own, is situated and contingent.

Equally somberly, the three constructionist knowers whose narratives appear in *Women's Ways of Knowing* acquired a social epistemology when they removed themselves from the sites of formal instruction, one to work for the A&P, another to work as a counselor, and another to work as a cook. They attribute their acquisition of a social epistemology to personal as well as intellectual needs — for identity, for moral criteria to determine rights and responsibilities, for a more adequate epistemology. These needs were not met by their formal instruction. While it assuredly contributed to their development, it ought to have contributed more fully and directly by including the personal, affective, and value-laden aspects of knowing rather than deferring them or regarding them as extracurricular.

Constructed knowing, Belenky et al. argue, has its own procedures, though they have not been codified like those for procedural knowing and may resist codification. They distinguish between "the effortless intuition of subjectivism (in which one identifies with positions that feel right) and the deliberate, imaginative extension of one's understanding into positions that initially feel wrong or remote" that is constructionism.[26] For them, procedural knowing, with its obliteration of agents, stands prior to constructed knowing, with its inclusion of them — *necessarily prior* and *necessarily transitional* between subjective and constructed knowing. I do not agree. The contributors to *(En)Gendering Knowledge* begin to codify procedures for constructed knowing in a variety of disciplines: they describe knowers self-consciously implicated in procedures and sensitive to contexts, careful neither to decontextualize subjects of study nor to disengage from them for the sake of straight-forward inquiries and conclusive results. Belenky et al.'s constructed knowl-edge is attained by complex, variable, and self-reflective procedures that can be taught along with the uniform and replicable procedures of disen-gaged knowledge.

Belenky et al.'s developmental plot (like Perry's) still reflects traditional positivist-empiricist epistemology: they maintain distinctions between em-pirical and hermeneutic knowing and give priority to empiricism. To re-fashion knowledge in the ways the contributors to *(En)Gendering Knowledge* propose requires refashioning their plot by eliminating procedural knowing as a discrete and necessary developmental stage for all knowers, male as well as female. This refashioning also will transform women's intellectual work into mainstream intellectual work and remove (some of) the stigma of sepa-rate spheres. With this refashioning, we predict that women, sharing with men a social epistemology, will be less strung out *cognitively* among the mar-riage plot, the quest plot, and the profession plot, however they remain strung out *practically* between the timetables of the marriage plot and the profession plot. Moreover, women at all stages of their education, and not just women in college, will be constituted by an epistemology more self-referential than the one that constitutes them at present and consequently will be more likely to come into possession of their agency as knowers. Educa-tion ought to counteract women's disempowerment, not replicate it. It can at least enlarge their agency while they are in academic institutions, as well as teaching them both to analyze the familial and social arrangements that constrain their agency elsewhere and to plan for familial and social change.

Knowing, Teaching, and Power

The transmission of knowledge tends to obscure its construction. Francis Bacon (as long ago as 1605) included among the errors inhibiting the ad-vancement of learning "the manner of the tradition and delivery of knowledge, which is for the most part magistral and peremptory and not ingenuous and faithful; in a sort as may be soonest believed and not easiliest examined."[27] Belenky et al. advocate a pedagogy in which teachers make visible for ex-amination their own agency and, through history of ideas, the agency of others; that is, they want teachers to present knowledge as emerging from processes that are both individual and collective, often flawed, and corrected by critical reflection and self-reflection. When teachers put themselves and their knowledge up for examination, they doff at least some of their authority and alter the dynamics of the classroom, for differences between the authority of teachers and students create for some students an unbridgeable gap, and the dynamics of the classroom produce students who are "stupid" as well as students who are "smart." In addition, Belenky et al. advocate a pedagogy that encourages students to make visible their own agency. They, like the academic women Aisenberg and Harrington interviewed, prefer discussion to lecturing.[28] Lecturing, which embodies the post-Cartesian objectification of knowledge, dispenses information about knowledge, not knowledge itself. More time-consuming modes of instruction are necessary to provide students opportunities to make visible their own acquisition and production of knowledge and to make them cognizant of their agency as knowers.

Belenky et al.'s constructionist pedagogy is allied with two other pedagogies, collaborative learning and feminist pedagogy; all three are (to adopt Paulo Freire's title[29]) "pedagogies of the oppressed," in which teachers, recognizing classrooms and academic institutions as political arenas in which students' agency is denied, alter their own behavior in order to alter their students' behavior.[30] Collaborative learning and feminist pedagogy came into being in response to extra-academic political situations during the early 1970s and, like Belenky et al.'s constructionist pedagogy, aim to alter power relations in the classroom. They are more explicitly *social* than Belenky et al.'s pedagogy, wider in that they attend to educational institutions as sites where *social* relations are reproduced.

Collaborative learning developed in response to the extension of higher education to students who, by background and economic status, previously had been excluded from it. Kenneth Bruffee, one of its theorists, traces interest in it (in America, rather than in Great Britain, where it originated) to difficulties encountered by these students in "adapting to the traditional or 'normal' conventions of the college classroom."[31] Some were poorly prepared, some, at least on the evidence of their high-school grades, well enough prepared. Ordinary remedial measures derived from the classroom model were not helpful to them; peer tutoring, often improvised in desperation, seemed to work. Differences in authority between tutors and students are small, and tutors, though they sometimes mimic the authoritarian stances of their teachers, have no professional investment in aggrandizing their authority. Collaboration with peers, both tutors and other students, demonstrates the social as well as the personal grounding of knowledge. When students are confronted with teachers' agentless and authoritative pronouncements, they learn either to mimic them or to retreat (silently and resentfully) to their own intuitive sense of things. Among peers, they put their perspectives into circulation and learn to find arguments in support of and strategies to persuade others to understand them; they also learn that others may understand them even while disagreeing with them. In addition, they learn (importantly) that they themselves are competent knowers; their recognition of their agency alters both their sense of themselves and their behaviors.

Feminist pedagogy developed in response to the Second Women's Movement: academic women, having experienced the authority of teachers and (usually male) professors, saw that authority as an extension of patriarchy, one that they had the power to dismantle, at least in their own classrooms. Women's studies began as a refashioned pedagogy; refashioned disciplinary practices followed. When students speak out to represent a range of experiences, they reveal consensual pronouncements ("*we* see that . . . ") as imperial. When they bring their diverse experiences to discussions, they become self-reflective about the personal and social positioning of their knowledge and the constitution of themselves as knowers. (I have also learned how particularly difficult it is for me, as a feminist, to resist my own imperial *we* in a class of women students.)

To enlarge the agency of women in educational institutions, the constructionist pedagogy of Belenky et al. and the *social* constructionist pedagogy of collaborative learning must be modified by feminist pedagogy. For, while the oppressed include *all* women and *most* men, men nevertheless are likely to oppress women in mixed communities of learners — that is, in classrooms — even when outnumbered by them. The classroom behavior of self-assured Harvard men who have learned that "everybody is different, everybody has opinions, and the business of the classroom is to express loudly what you believe and feel" stands in contrast to the classroom behavior of privileged college women cautious in revealing their opinions because they fear criticism and attack.[32] When they do reveal them, they frequently preface them with a diffident "It's *just* my opinion."

At my institution, where I teach less privileged students, I encounter diffidence regardless of gender, and I need to empower men as well as women. Collaborative learning is important for all my students. But collaboration too often signifies entering the conversation of *man*kind (Michael Oakeshott's phrase, repeated by Kenneth Bruffee[33]), and, when it does, my intervention is required to silence the men, who bring the authority of their gender into the classroom, in order to provide the women with space and encouragement to speak. Traditional expectations are so strong that, even when women outnumber men (as they often do in humanities courses at an institution like mine, where they constitute over half the student body), the predominance of women's voices unnerves both women and men. Sooner or later I have to see to it that they discuss their expectations and the experience of having them overturned. While the women come to earn their space and the men come to extend to them the encouragement and approbation all learners want and need, I do not think women should have to *earn* their space any more than men do. The social construction of knowledge, whatever its epistemological virtues, imports into the academy the inequitable distribution of power that prevails in society, so that, as women produce knowledge, men in turn pronounce judgment on it.

The hazards to women of a social constructionist pedagogy unmodified by feminism are attested to by the different educational experiences of women in coeducational and single-sex institutions. The communities of women I encountered as an undergraduate at Mount Holyoke and as a teacher at two similarly privileged women's colleges, Wellesley and Connecticut (when the latter was Connecticut College for Women), were valuable to me. Mount Holyoke was less competitive than the coeducational high school from which I graduated; at Mount Holyoke I learned to collaborate with other knowers as diffident as I about their authority, and I acquired a sense of my own agency. When I began to teach women rather like myself in communities of women, I was, I own, impatient with their diffidence; as I came to recognize the social contexts of their knowledge and my own, I was able to reinterpret my own diffidence and theirs.

Belenky et al. note the distaste with which college women regard agonistic positions, even when they are capable of taking them. Contests with professors with whom they disagree they see as unequal and probably futile, contests with professors with whom they substantially agree as artificial, and contests with friends as damaging. They select (to load my description with values) the complexities of collaborative synthesis rather than the simplicities of victory or defeat. Investigating the writing strategies of students in college composition classes, Sarah D'Eloia Fortune and Susan Osborn discovered analogous preferences. Fortune found that women organize their essays by recapitulating the processes through which they arrive at positions, instead of enunciating their positions and then marshalling arguments to support them and to refute counterarguments. Osborn found that women typically avoid the argumentative strategies prescribed in rhetorical handbooks in favor of participatory and dialogic forms.[34] If women value persuasion over argument, their social deference, sometimes taken as a sign of intellectual deficiency, should in fact be taken as a source of intellectual strength.

My Mount Holyoke classmate Lee Tidball has shown that women's colleges have provided two times as many "achieving" women (she defines their achievement by their being listed in *Who's Who in American Women*) as coeducational institutions; up to four times as many doctorates, particularly in science; and two times as many entrants into medical schools. Not all the women's colleges she surveyed are elite; she emphasizes communities of women, rather than communities of women segregated by class.[35] Her research indicates that communities of women, in and of themselves, foster women's intellectual development and empower them in subjects not traditionally studied by women, such as science and (in former years) medicine.

In addition, where female faculty are present in substantial numbers, they set the institutional tone; in consequence, Tidball shows, male faculty at women's colleges are more supportive of women's intellectual endeavors than male faculty at coeducational colleges and research universities. Women's colleges thus are more likely than coeducational institutions to provide "benign authorities" who enable women to acquire a sense of themselves as knowing agents.[36]

If Mount Holyoke failed me, it did so only by presenting knowers and knowledge as ungendered. I learned little about women and virtually nothing about patriarchy and its effects. While we celebrated Mount Holyoke's past (as a seminary it was the oldest of the Seven Sisters) and heard of the intrepidity and determination of its founder Mary Lyon, we did not hear much about the intrepidity and determination of twentieth-century women, and might not have listened if we had been told—it's knowledge some women still resist. We also heard a lot about the men who supported Mary Lyon. Deacon Porter had a dormitory and a dessert named after him, and once a year we ate steamed pudding and sang "Now on Mary Lyon's birthday/We eat Deacon Porter's hat." We knew that the appointment of the first male president of Mount Holyoke in 1937 had been and still was controversial, but we did not understand the position of the faculty still rumored to oppose him, and they did not try to make us understand.[37] The women faculty, virtually all of them, were single (I graduated in 1951), and the male faculty, virtually all of them, married. Somehow I never noticed.

My undergraduate education—as a collection of autobiographical essays called *Working It Out: 23 Women Writers, Artists, Scientists, and Scholars Talk About Their Lives and Work* (1977) attests—was fairly typical for women of my generation who went on to become academics. In educational institutions that treated us more or less benignly as apprentices, we acquired an individualistic sense of our own agency.[38] Twenty of the autobiographical narratives of *Working It Out* are by college-educated women, ten of them by academics. Most of these ten did their graduate work in the 1950s and 1960s, as I did; all who name their undergraduate institutions attended elite colleges, some as scholarship students, and many of them attended women's colleges.[39]

After Mount Holyoke, I went first to Duke for an M.A. in English and then, having stopped to teach for two years, to Radcliffe for a Ph.D. After Mount Holyoke I never again was taught by a woman. Yet the discrimination I encountered was muted and my capacity to ignore it immense: that women enrolled at Harvard through Radcliffe was a fact I looked around rather than at, even though I recognized I was there because Radcliffe women had raised the money that enabled me and other women to attend Harvard.[40] My professors were gentlemanly and kind. One of the few times I felt taken less than seriously because I was a woman, a professor advised me to write my term paper on women in the eighteenth-century novel. I took his advice as patronizing—I never had been asked to write about women before—and I think it was. Nevertheless, for want of a more compelling topic, I wrote on women in the novels of Defoe and Fielding. Recently I reread my paper and found his comment on it just: "Occasionally the women are forgotten and the general question of technique takes the floor." Technique, not representations of women under patriarchy, was what I knew how to discuss.

For some of the scientists and scholars who contributed to *Working It Out*, alienation and the diminution of their agency began in graduate school, but largely as a result of the disciplines they entered rather than the institutions they attended. Humanities predictably were the most hospitable, natural sciences the least, and social sciences betwixt and between, all in direct relation to the disciplines' respective alliances with hermeneutics or empiricism.[41] Among the women who did their graduate work at Harvard—Pamela Daniels, Evelyn Fox Keller, Sara Ruddick, Naomi Weisstein, and Marilyn Young—Young in history and I in literature felt most welcome. Daniels (who had a woman mentor in political science) taught in Erik Erikson's course on human life cycles and wrote an interdisciplinary dissertation. Ruddick in philosophy felt herself an observer in a masculine discipline but nevertheless wrote a dissertation; later she turned to literature. Weisstein in experimental psychology and Fox Keller in physics were most alienated, even reviled; the masculinist prestige of science made their abilities threatening to male graduate students. For Fox Keller, the animosity of her peers caused her to doubt the evidence of both her understanding and her grades that she could indeed "do" physics.[42]

Most of the academics who contributed to *Working It Out* married (not all their marriages lasted) and had children. Those who left graduate school to follow their husbands felt themselves dwindling into wives and mothers, bereft of agency; some were able to write dissertations under these conditions, others not. All eventually completed dissertations and managed to fashion personally rewarding work lives, a few in fast-track but most in slow-track careers. Perhaps because they entered the job market in a decade of expansion, albeit before affirmative action, they were better able to establish themselves than the women Aisenberg and Harrington interviewed; on the other hand, they may not be representative of their generation, inasmuch as Ruddick and Daniels solicited essays only from women who were working (it out). The experiences that enlarged their agency and enabled them to emplot their stories as *bildungsromane*, however, were connected to their experience of making social change in the Civil Rights Movement, the antiwar movement, and the Second Women's Movement.[43]

Academic change, though less convulsive than social change, is difficult to make, especially during a conservative hegemony. Disciplines and academic institutions changed during the 1960s and the 1970s in response to political movements; during the 1980s, conservatives, organizing on every front, began to recuperate both social and academic practices. The possessive individualism characteristic of the academy constitutes each course and each classroom as an arena for change or resistance to it. Academic feminists are sufficiently ensconced in educational institutions to make change in our own classrooms. But not in our colleagues' classrooms, nor yet in disciplines, professions, and educational institutions, and certainly not while we are relegated — at best — to slow-track careers. Enhancing our agency and the agency of women students, problematized by contradictions among the marriage, quest, and profession plots, thus becomes a legitimate feminist concern. We desperately need to make change, to invent new plots for women, for we have yet to encounter *bildungsromane* in which the agency of female protagonists is as generously constituted as the agency of male protagonists.

New Plots

The women who contributed to *(En)Gendering Knowledge* are not alone in viewing knowledge as historically, socially, and personally contingent. We can call on powerful allies: philosophers like Richard Rorty, who sets pragmatism against foundational knowledge and "objective" certainty; philosophers of science like Thomas S. Kuhn, who situates the "great discoverers" in scientific communities and institutionalized research traditions; and historians and sociologists of knowledge like Michel Foucault, who emphasizes the institutional matrices of knowers and knowledge. Their work, like ours, is revisionary. But we are the ones who need new plots. Gender figures prominently in our intellectual lives, inasmuch as we carry on our inquiries in institutions and research traditions that have been the exclusive precincts of men. To insist on our agency, produce feminist knowledge, and make academic and social change, we must attend to our power. If we look to male knowers to validate it, they, not we, interpret our stories. If they emplot feminist theory in their narratives of poststructuralism and feminist practice in their narratives of collaborative learning, what then is left to us? "I would not be thee, nuncle," says the fool to Lear; "thou hast pared thy wit o'both sides, and left nothing i' th' middle" (*King Lear* 1.4.203–205). Unless we are suspicious and resistant, not much.

Feminist theory, Paul Smith told us (in a session called "Men in Feminism" that he organized for the 1984 convention of the Modern Language Association), "is not easily separable from the general theory that has worked its way into studies in the humanities over the last ten or twenty years," situated as it is "within the array of poststructuralist discourses with which many of us [i.e., himself and other theoretical men] are now perhaps over-familiar."[44] I do not propose to rehearse the backings and fillings of the original papers, the responses to them, the responses to the responses, and the supplementary papers now in print. Rather I shall put the broadest and lowest interpretation on the papers that emplot academic feminists. Feminism, their authors tell us, has arrived, has indeed, like *post*structuralism, become *post*feminism. We are, they assure us, important to *their* narratives. They have learned from us, and we should come together, or perhaps already have come together, whether we recognize it or not — the language Smith uses to describe our conjunction exfoliates into metaphors whose sexual import is inescapable.[45] The alternative, that we emplot these theoretical men in *our* narratives, seems never to occur to them.[46]

As important to us as keeping our theory and practice feminist, however, is joining them, linking one side of our wit and t'other. If we oppose theory to practice — calling one elitist and obscure, the other egalitarian and honest — we diminish women's agency. Our theory does not fulfill Adrienne Rich's dream of a common language: it is abstract, technical, difficult to read, sometimes unreadable. The women with doctorates Aisenberg and Harrington interviewed find theory ascetic,[47] and almost half the women Belenky et al. interviewed mistrust "logic, analysis, abstraction, and even language itself" as "alien territory belonging to men."[48] If we teach women well, they will converse well, incorporating logic, analysis, and abstraction into their conversation, and they will find language other than ours to express themselves if they reject ours.[49] We overprivilege feminist theory and sentimentalize feminist practice if we restrict theory to the realm of academically constructed knowledge or assume that theory is what *we* do and *they* do not. Children, for example, relentlessly theorize (though the theories they construct are tacit), and students denied authority nevertheless are capable of theorizing themselves as agents and knowers. Among the tasks of academic feminists is to encourage students, women students in particular, to become self-reflective agents who both know and act.

But new plots require us to intervene for social as well as educational change. As long as we limit ourselves to educational institutions, even as we make feminist knowledge, we bind ourselves and other women to old plots. We can revise, emend, and even scrap the materials we have on hand, but only to emplot our telling stories in narratives whose conventions are always already there. New plots require us to rejoin feminist inquiry and social activism.

Notes

I want to thank Ellen Messer-Davidow and Larry T. Shillock for their helpful readings and acute responses to many drafts of this essay, and Patricia B. Craddock, Naomi Diamond, and Barbara Koenig Quart for their occasional readings.

1. James Boswell, *Life of Johnson*, ed. R.W. Chapman (London: Oxford University Press, 1953), 327.

2. Virginia Woolf, *A Room of One's Own* (1929; rptd. New York: Harcourt, Brace Jovanovich, Harvest/HBJ, 1957), 56.

3. Hayden White, "The Historical Text as Literary Artifact," in White, *Tropics of Discourse: Essays in Cultural Criticism* (Baltimore, Md.: Johns Hopkins University Press, 1978), 86. White developed his taxonomy of plots in *Metahistory: The Historical Imagination in Nineteenth-Century Europe* (Baltimore, Md.: Johns Hopkins University Press, 1973) to analyze four 19th-century historians: Michelet, Ranke, Tocqueville, and Burckhardt. He likens revising, emending, and scrapping the plots of histories to the reemplotment of life histories and the reinterpretation of traumatic events that occur in psychotherapy. See also Jerome Bruner, *Actual Minds, Possible Worlds* (Cambridge, Mass.: Harvard University Press, 1986), and Katherine Nelson, ed., *Narratives from the Crib* (Cambridge, Mass.: Harvard University Press, 1989).

4. Teresa de Lauretis tries, awkwardly and unsuccessfully, I think, to salvage both deconstruction and political action. She speaks of "a multiple, shifting, and often self-contradictory identity, a subject that is not divided in, but rather at odds with, language" and also political. Feminist politics, she specifies, is capable of redeeming "not merely a sexual politics but a politics of experience, of everyday life, which later then in turn enters the public sphere of expression and creative practice, displacing aesthetic hierarchies and generic categories, and which thus establishes the semiotic ground for a different production of reference and meaning" (de Lauretis, "Feminist Studies/Critical Studies: Issues, Terms, and Contexts," in *Feminist Studies/Critical Studies*, ed. Teresa de Lauretis [Bloomington: Indiana University Press, 1986], 9-10). In her politicized version of deconstruction, feminist politics terminate in the production of reference and meaning, not in social action. "New reference, new meaning" is not exactly a marching slogan. For a rehabilitation of the subject, as well as an account of its erasure, see Paul Smith, *Discerning the Subject* (Minneapolis: University of Minnesota Press, 1988); for a feminist rehabilitation, see Susan Bordo and Mario Moussa, "Rehabilitating the 'I,'" in *Questioning Foundations*, ed. Hugh Silverman (New York: Routledge, forthcoming 1991).

5. Agency "refers not to the intentions people have in doing things but to their capability of doing those things in the first place, which is why agency implies power" (Anthony Giddens, *The Constitution of Society: Outline of the Theory of Structuration* [Berkeley: University of California Press, 1984], 9-10).

6. Mary Field Belenky, Blythe McVicker Clinchy, Nancy Rule Goldberger, and Jill Mattuck Tarule, *Women's Ways of Knowing: The Development of Self, Voice, and Mind* (New York: Basic, 1986); Nadya Aisenberg and Mona Harrington, *Women of Academe: Outsiders in the Sacred Grove* (Amherst: University of Massachusetts Press, 1988).

7. Belenky et al., *Women's Ways*: "We wanted to hear what the women had to say in their own terms rather than test our own preconceived hypotheses" (11). Aisenberg and Harrington, *Women of Academe*: "We were determined to analyze it [the transcript] in its own terms, not to impose on it conceptions derived from the growing body of theory and observation concerning women's experience" (xi).

8. Aisenberg and Harrington, *Women of Academe*, located the "deflected" women through the Cambridge (Massachusetts) Alliance of Independent Scholars, founded in

1980; for demographic information about the 37 deflected and the 25 tenured women they interviewed, see their appendix (197–98). In 1983–84, when the interviews took place, all their subjects resided in the Boston area, though not all originated there; a preponderance held doctorates from Ivy League universities. They ranged in age from 34 to over 50.

9. "By the end of the 1970s, when women accounted for about 28 percent of the total Ph.D. recipients each year, they received 48 percent of the degrees in English, 63 percent in French, 40 percent in psychology, 40 percent in fine and applied arts, 29 percent in biology, and 27 percent in history—that is, in the 'soft' subjects, or subjects like history and biology containing 'soft' areas. To look at the 'hard' subjects in the same period, women received only 18 percent of the degrees awarded in political science, 13 percent in economics, 17 percent in math, 15 percent in chemistry, 10 percent in computer and informational sciences, 7 percent in physics, and 4 percent in engineering" (ibid., 87).

10. Adrienne Rich, "The Roofwalker," in Rich, *Snapshots of a Daughter-in-Law* (New York: Norton, 1967), 63, lines 22–23.

11. Aisenberg and Harrington (*Women of Academe*, 60) credit Carolyn Heilbrun with naming these plots. Her *Writing a Woman's Life* (New York: Norton, 1988) appeared after their *Women of Academe;* I assume they encountered her plots in a lecture.

12. I myself, of the generation of Aisenberg and Harrington's over 50, am struck by the professional savvy of younger women and by their mentoring, both by women now to be found as graduate professors and by some men.

13. Aisenberg and Harrington, "Epilogue: Four Lives," in *Women of Academe*, 157–95.

14. See Joan Cocks's review in *Academe* 74, no. 4 (July–Aug. 1988):38–40: "On the one hand, they [Aisenberg and Harrington] want to make a pitch for the professional rules of the academic game that women must learn to play. On the other hand, they are keen to show that women will transform the academy once they play those rules successfully, so that it becomes more of a place where the love of learning flourishes, less of a place where individuals battle it out to enhance their private occupational positions. Thus the book has a half-conventional 'how to succeed in academia' flavor and a half-critical 'how academia must be remade' one" (40).

15. Felice N. Schwartz suggested developing a slow or "mommy track" for corporate women (in "Management Women and the New Facts of Life," *Harvard Business Review* 67, no. 1 [Jan.–Feb. 1989]:65–76), a suggestion publicized in the *New York Times, USA Today,* and *Business Week,* and on talk shows. See Barbara Ehrenreich and Deirdre English's counterarguments for change in both family and corporate practices, in "Blowing the Whistle on the 'Mommy Track,'" *Ms.* 18, no. 1–2 (Aug. 1989):56–58.

16. Of their 135 subjects, 45 came from social agencies and 90 were students or recent graduates of Bard, Goddard, LaGuardia Community College of the City University of New York, and Wellesley, along with a few students at middle schools associated with Bard and LaGuardia (Belenky et al., *Women's Ways*, xi, 12).

17. Perry's undergraduates came from the Harvard and Radcliffe classes of 1958, 1962, and 1963, but chiefly from Harvard, and he draws his illustrations from the men. His collaborators dismissed differences between women and men as negligible. William G. Perry, Jr., *Forms of Intellectual and Ethical Development in the College Years* (New York: Holt, Rinehart and Winston, 1970), 7–8, 16.

18. Belenky et al., *Women's Ways*, call ways of knowing "epistemological perspectives"; I substitute "ways of knowing" to eliminate confusion between their use of "perspective" and ours. Perry calls ways of knowing "positions." Quotation, Belenky et al., *Women's Ways*, 15.

19. Belenky et al., *Women's Ways*, 15. The authors adapt the following positions of Perry: a *basic dualism* of right and wrong with great dependence on authorities; a recogni-

tion of *multiplicity* accompanied by a degree of confidence in personal authority; a *relativism subordinate*, in which "an analytical, evaluative approach to knowledge is consciously cultivated at least in the academic disciplines one is being tutored in, if not in the rest of one's life"; and a full *relativism*, in which meaning, in the world at large as well as in academic disciplines, is seen to depend "on the context in which that event occurs and on the framework that the knower uses to understand that event" (9–10).

20. Belenky et al., ibid., began to ask about sexual abuse halfway through their interviews, after women brought it up without prompting. From among 75 women (out of their total of 135), 38% of the group reached through colleges and 65% of the group reached through social agencies reported it. Childhood incest was particularly prevalent, at rates of 1 in 5 among college women and 1 in 2 among women reached through social agencies. Sexual abuse was not limited to particular classes, ages, ethnicities, or epistemological perspectives, "but the sense of outrage was most prominent among the subjectivists, who angrily recalled their past naiveté and silent submission" (58–59). Their anger contrasts with the irony exhibited by the women Aisenberg and Harrington interviewed.

21. The men Perry interviewed moved from *received* to *subjective knowledge* as adolescents, whereas the women Belenky et al. interviewed moved at various ages (Belenky et al., *Women's Ways*, 55), which suggests that male children are expected to acquire at least some authority before they attain their majority, whereas women are not and acquire it, if and when they do, fortuitously, often when male authority fails.

22. Ibid., 55. Although Western society emphasizes rationalism and scientific thought, there are still non-Western, nontechnological societies, Belenky et al. point out, that esteem subjectivity and intuition.

23. Ibid., 129. Or: "The voice diminishes in volume. It lacks authority" (94–95).

24. Behind the analysis of Fréchet stands Nancy Chodorow, *The Reproduction of Mothering: Psychoanalysis and the Sociology of Gender* (Berkeley: University of California Press, 1978); and Evelyn Fox Keller, *Reflections on Gender and Science* (New Haven, Conn.: Yale University Press, 1985), esp. 69–126.

25. Belenky et al., *Women's Ways*, 136.

26. Ibid., 121.

27. Francis Bacon, *The Advancement of Learning*, in *Essays, Advancement of Learning, New Atlantis, and Other Pieces*, ed. Richard Foster Jones (New York: Odyssey Press, 1937), 215. Bacon had a keen sense of how knowledge is imperiled by the egocentricity of knowers and their desire to show off their authority.

28. The women Aisenberg and Harrington interviewed mistrust the authoritative ("magistral and peremptory") voices of their (usually) male professors, which they remember as excluding them and denying their agency. *Women of Academe*, 79.

29. Paulo Freire, *The Pedagogy of the Oppressed* (1968), trans. Myra Bergman Ramos (New York: Herder and Herder, 1971).

30. "A progressive position requires democratic practice where authority never becomes authoritarianism, and where authority is never so reduced that it disappears in a climate of irresponsibility and license" (Paulo Freire, "Letter to North-American Teachers," trans. Carman Hunter, in *Freire for the Classroom: A Sourcebook for Liberatory Teaching*, ed. Ira Shor [Portsmouth, N.H.: Boynton/Cook and Heinemann, 1987], 212).

31. Kenneth Bruffee, "Collaborative Learning and the 'Conversation of Mankind,'" *College English* 46, no. 7 (Nov. 1984):637. Bruffee, looking to provide support for the production and reproduction of knowledge through the collaboration of peers, cites Stanley Fish, Clifford Geertz, Thomas Kuhn, Michael Oakeshott, Richard Rorty, and Lev Vygotsky (638–40); I should add Michel Foucault and Paulo Freire. See also Bruffee's "Liberal Education and the Justification of Belief," *Liberal Education* 68, no. 2 (Summer 1982):95–114,

and "Social Construction, Language, and the Authority of Knowledge: A Bibliographical Essay," *College English* 48, no. 8 (Dec. 1986):773–90.

32. Belenky et al., *Women's Ways*, 63–64.

33. Michael Oakeshott, "The Voice of Poetry in the Conversation of Mankind," in Oakeshott, *Rationalism in Politics and Other Essays* (London: Methuen, 1962), 197–247; Bruffee, "Collaborative Learning," 17. It is also used by Richard Rorty, *Philosophy and the Mirror of Nature* (Princeton, N.J.: Princeton University Press, 1979), 264, 389.

34. Fortune's analysis appears in Thomas J. Farrell's "The Female and Male Modes of Rhetoric," *College English* 40, no. 8 (Apr. 1979):909–21; Susan Osborn, "Revisioning the Argument: An Exploratory Study of Some of the Rhetorical Strategies of Women Student Writers," *Praxis* 12, no. 2 (Spring/Summer 1987):113–33.

35. M. Elizabeth Tidball, "Women's Colleges and Women Achievers Revisited," *Signs: Journal of Women, Culture, and Society* 5, no. 3 (Spring 1980):504–17; "Baccalaureate Origins of Entrants into American Medical Schools," *Journal of Higher Education* 56, no. 4 (July/Aug. 1985):386–402; and "Baccalaureate Origins of Recent Natural Science Doctorates," *Journal of Higher Education* 57, no. 6 (Nov./Dec. 1986):606–20.

36. "Benign authorities," Belenky et al. conjecture, "may be critical to the development of the voice of reason" in women (*Women's Ways*, 92).

37. A milestone achievement of the Second Women's Movement, for me, was the appointment of women to the presidencies of all the Seven Sisters colleges.

38. Sara Ruddick and Pamela Daniels, eds., *Working It Out: 23 Women Writers, Artists, Scientists, and Scholars Talk About Their Lives and Work* (New York: Pantheon, 1977).

39. Of the 18 institutions the contributors to *Working It Out* name, 13 are women's colleges. Ruddick and Daniels's selection of contributors may be skewed in favor of women's colleges because one of them was then teaching at Vassar, the other at Wellesley.

40. To honor them, I still list my degree, which I received in 1960, as being from Radcliffe. After 1963, when the Radcliffe Graduate School was abolished and Harvard began to award doctorates to women, previous recipients of Radcliffe doctorates were awarded Harvard doctorates retroactively and, as a token of Harvard's earnest acceptance of us, our dissertations were moved from Radcliffe to Harvard's Widener Library.

41. For such a division within a discipline, see Kathryn J. Gutzwiller and Ann Norris Michelini's essay in this volume, "Women and Other Strangers: Feminist Perspectives in Classical Literature."

42. See Marilyn Young, "Contradictions," 214–27; Pamela Daniels, "Birth of the Amateur," 55–70; Sara Ruddick, "A Work of One's Own," 129–46; Naomi Weisstein, "'How can a little girl like you teach a great big class of men?' the Chairman Said, and Other Adventures of a Woman in Science," 242–50; Evelyn Fox Keller, "The Anomaly of a Woman in Physics," 78–91. All in Ruddick and Daniels, *Working It Out.*

43. Aisenberg and Harrington describe the personal and social values of the women they interviewed as countervalues; they not only believe in and work for social change but also appear more active as agents of social than of academic change (*Women in Academe*, 136–56).

44. Alice Jardine and Paul Smith, eds., *Men in Feminism* (New York: Methuen, 1987), 34–35.

45. See Cary Nelson, "Men, Feminism: The Materiality of Discourse" (Jardine and Smith, *Men in Feminism*, 153–72). Smith, Nelson reports, characterized the sexuality of his language as "desperate irony." "Clearly he would have had a better chance of being understood," Nelson continues, "if he had reflected openly on this language while using it, perhaps talking about how men cannot for now altogether escape the air of sexual appropriation and possessiveness that surrounds their intellectual passions."

46. Ellen Messer-Davidow suggests a baseball metaphor: their theory is an inning in our ballgame, not ours an inning in theirs.

47. Aisenberg and Harrington, *Women in Academe*, 85.

48. Belenky et al., *Women's Ways*, 71.

49. According to de Lauretis: "These debates [between theory and practice] make us uncomfortable because they give incontrovertible evidence that sisterhood is powerful but difficult, and not achieved; that feminism itself, the most original of what we can call 'our own cultural creations,' is not a secure or stable ground but a highly permeable terrain infiltrated by subterranean waterways that cause it to shift under our feet and sometimes to turn into a swamp. The conflicting claims that are made for feminism, no less than the appropriation of feminist strategies and conceptual frames within 'legitimate' discourses or by other critical theories, make us uncomfortable because we know and fear what they signal to us beyond a doubt: the constant drive on the part of institutions (in which, like it or not, feminists are also engaged) to deflect radical resistance and to recuperate it as liberal opposition" (de Lauretis, "Feminist Studies," 7).

Part II

Perspectives

Part II

Perspectives

The meanings of *perspicere*—"to see through," "to see clearly," or "to examine"; and "to regard mentally" or "to ascertain"—suggest the discursive registers in which seeing and knowing historically have been played. Considered to be analogous processes by many classical thinkers, seeing and knowing became increasingly implicated in technology—the mathematical tradition in optics during the Middle Ages, early modern science during the Renaissance, and disciplinary technologies during the eighteenth century. The Italian Renaissance term, *prospettiva*, for instance, denoted particular techniques that were employed in painting not only to construct representations but also to position the artist, the viewers, and the painting according to spatial relations. In this kind of perspective, what is seen and known is produced by regulatory techniques.

Visually, *perspective* may be defined as the function of relatively positioning a person and a scene. The viewer's location and the configuration seen elicit the angle of vision, and conversely the viewer's location and angle of vision determine the configuration that is seen. Intellectually, *perspective* may be defined as the function of relatively positioning a knower and a subject of inquiry. The knower's perspective is determined by her values, ideas, and feelings, and these in turn are produced by her location in a society. What locates her in society are her cultural circumstances. Because the circumstances of knowers are diverse, their perspectives diverge. The circumstances that diversify the perspectives of knowers are: (1) their technical training, which differs not only across disciplines but also within a single discipline—the modes of analysis, the subjects of investigation, the assumptions that guide the inquiry; (2) their affiliations with a sex, race, class, affectional preference, and other cultural categories; (3) their personal histories; and (4) their critical reflection on the ways these circumstances organize intellectual endeavors.

Patricia Hill Collins's essay, "Learning from the Outsider Within: The Sociological Significance of Black Feminist Thought," shows how the social positioning of knowers compels them to produce certain kinds of knowledge. Sociological "thinking as usual" depends upon concepts, methods, and values developed by insiders who have "similar class, gender, and racial backgrounds." While the knowledge produced may seem perfectly adequate to insiders, it seems disorganized and contradictory to black feminist sociologists, who do not share their perspective. What black feminists see because of their paradoxical outsider-within status, whether as maids in white people's houses or as scholars in white men's disciplines, is what insiders fail to notice both about black women and about themselves. This knowledge, in turn, reveals the distortions of sociological knowledge. Perspective thus mediates so that in disciplines, as Hill Collins argues for sociology, we cannot separate "the structure and thematic content of thought . . . from the historical and material conditions shaping the lives of its producers."

In "Women and Other Strangers: Feminist Perspectives in Classical Literature," Kathryn J. Gutzwiller and Ann Norris Michelini observe that women are similarly positioned as outsiders within both classical civilizations and the discipline of classics. Enlightened by their estrangement, women scholars, like the strangers in Greece and Rome, are able to break the cultural codes of gender, sexuality, and alien status. By foregrounding the male sphere of activity and occluding the female, "the ancients themselves could not perceive or discuss the gendered structure of their culture; and most classical scholars, who have uncritically accepted the ancient perspective because it closely resembles their own, also have been blind to it." In "Seeing, Reading, Knowing: The Lesbian Appropriation of Literature," Bonnie Zimmerman asserts that lesbians, who see from the margins of heterosexist literary studies and culture, read "perversely." In a process which is the reverse of that executed by Gutzwiller and Michelini's classical scholars, lesbians foreground what traditionally is occluded, elaborating the background details of a story into an alternative woman-centered plot.

From the examples of perspectival seeing given in these essays, Sandra Harding develops a concept of "identity knowing" and analyzes it. Feminists have learned to embrace the identities they were taught to despise (female, black, lesbian, working-class) and have used them to learn what was never known. Yet how, she asks, can we use our traditionally privileged identities (male, white, heterosexual, bourgeois) to continue knowing and acting in feminist ways? Not wanting to limit feminist knowledge and action to those whom society has marginalized, Harding insists on "anti-racist behavior for whites" and "feminist behavior for men." She believes that "we can use our identities and the social locations that produce them — including the perverse ones — to generate new ways of seeing the world."

Most obviously, the essays in this section explore the cultural circumstances that diversify knowers' identities and their perspectives on knowledge. Perhaps less obviously, they reveal our disciplinary situatedness. First, they suggest that feminist knowledge is more readily accommodated in hermeneutic than positivist-empiricist disciplines. Lesbian-feminist readings can fit into disciplines that produce "interpretations" far more easily than feminist critiques of science can fit into disciplines that produce "truths." In this regard, sociology, classics, and philosophy are divided disciplines: sociology between empiricist and hermeneutic traditions, classics between British textual and

German interpretive traditions, philosophy between analytic and hermeneutic traditions. But in the United States, these disciplines have tended to be empiricist, textual, and analytic — in other words, positivist. Thus, Hill Collins's project of bringing black feminist thought into a predominantly empiricist sociology, Gutzwiller and Michelini's project of interpreting classical gender codes in a discipline that mainly emends texts, and Harding's project of theorizing identity knowing rather than doing analytic philosophy are similarly radical. Secondly, the essays suggest that any judgments of the radicality of feminist work in the disciplines must be contingent upon the particular formations and histories of those disciplines. Finally, the disciplinary range of the essays in this section provides an opportunity for us to reflect critically on feminist inquiry. If we view the essays comparatively, we can analyze the similarities and differences of feminist work in the disciplines. But if we take academic knowing itself as the object of analysis, then we must try to imagine postdisciplinary ways to organize and produce feminist knowledge.

Learning from the Outsider Within: The Sociological Significance of Black Feminist Thought

Patricia Hill Collins

African-American women long have been privy to some of the most intimate secrets of white society. Countless numbers of Black women have ridden buses to their white "families," where they not only cooked, cleaned, and executed other domestic duties, but also nurtured their "other" children, shrewdly offered guidance to their empoyers, and often became honorary members of their white "families." These women have seen white elites, both actual and aspiring, from perspectives largely denied to their Black spouses and these elite groups themselves.[1]

On one level, this "insider" relationship has been satisfying to all involved. The memoirs of affluent whites often mention their love for their Black "mothers," while accounts of Black domestic workers stress the sense of self-affirmation they experienced at seeing white power demystified, of knowing that it was not the intellect, talent, or humanity of their employers that supported their superior status, but the advantages of racism.[2] On another level, however, these same Black women knew they never could belong to their white "families." In spite of their involvement, they remained "outsiders."[3]

This "outsider within" status has provided for African-American women a special perspective on self, family, and society.[4] A careful review of emerging Black feminist literature reveals that many Black female intellectuals, especially those in touch with their marginality in academic settings, tap this perspective in producing distinctive analyses of race, class, and gender. For example, Zora Neal Hurston's 1937 novel, *Their Eyes Were Watching God*, most certainly reflects her skill at using the strengths and transcending the limitations both of her academic training and of her background in traditional African-American community life.[5] Black feminist historian E. Frances White suggests that Black women's ideas have been honed at the juncture of movements for racial and sexual equality, and she contends that African-American women have been pushed by "their marginalization in both arenas" to create Black feminism.[6] Black feminist critic bell hooks also captures the unique perspective that outsider-within status can generate. In describing her small-town, Kentucky childhood, she notes, "living as we did — on the edge — we developed a particular way of seeing reality. We looked both from the outside in and from the inside out . . . we understood both."[7]

In spite of the obstacles that can confront outsiders within, such individuals can benefit from this status. Simmel's essay on the sociological significance of what he called the "stranger" offers a helpful starting point for understanding the largely unexplored area of Black female outsider-within status and the usefulness of the perspective it can produce.[8] Some of the potential benefits of outsider-within status include (1) "objectivity," as Simmel defines it — namely, "a peculiar composition of nearness and remoteness, concern and indifference"; (2) the tendency for people to confide in strangers as they never would in those they know well; and (3) the ability of the "stranger" to see patterns that may elude those more immersed in a situation. Mannheim labels the "strangers" in academia "marginal intellectuals" and argues that the critical posture they bring to academic endeavors may be essential to the creative development of academic disciplines themselves.[9] Finally, in assessing the potentially positive qualities of social difference, specifically marginality, Lee notes, "for a time this marginality can be a most stimulating, albeit often a painful, experience. For some, it is debilitating . . . for others, it is an excitement to creativity."[10]

Sociologists might benefit greatly from serious consideration of the emerging cross-disciplinary literature I label Black feminist thought, precisely because "marginality" has been an excitement to creativity for many African-American women. As outsiders within, Black feminist scholars form one of several distinct groups of marginal intellectuals whose perspectives promise to enrich contemporary sociological discourse. Bringing this group, as well as others who share an outsider-within status vis-a-vis sociology, into the center of analysis may reveal views of reality obscured by more orthodox approaches. In this essay, I examine the sociological significance of Black feminist thought stimulated by Black women's outsider-within status. I begin by outlining three key themes that characterize the emerging cross-disciplinary literature I label Black feminist thought.[11] For each theme, I summarize its content, supply examples from Black feminist and other works, and discuss its importance. Next, I explain the significance these themes in Black feminist thought may have for sociologists, by describing why Black women's outsider-within status generates a distinctive perspective vis-a-vis existing sociological paradigms. Finally, I discuss one general implication of this essay for social scientists, namely, the potential usefulness of identifying and using one's own perspective in conducting research.

Three Key Themes in Black Feminist Thought

Black feminist thought consists of ideas created by Black women that clarify a perspective of and for Black women. Several assumptions underlie this working definition. First, the definition suggests that we cannot separate the structure and thematic content of thought from the historical and material conditions that shape the lives of its producers.[12] Therefore, while Black feminist thought may be recorded by others, it is produced by Black women. Second, the definition assumes that Black women possess a unique perspective on their experiences and share certain perceptions. Third, the definition permits different expressions of common themes as a result of the diversity of class, region, age, and sexual orientation that shape individual Black women's lives. Thus a Black women's perspective includes universal themes that, while defining African-American womanhood, are experienced and expressed differently by distinct groups of African-American women. Finally, the definition assumes that, while a Black women's perspective exists, its contours may not always be clear to Black women themselves. One role for Black female intellectuals, therefore, is to produce facts and theories about the Black female experience that will clarify a Black woman's perspective for Black women. In other words, Black feminist thought contains observations and interpretations of African-American womanhood that describe and explain different expressions of common themes.

No one Black feminist platform exists, nor should there be one, from which to measure the "correctness" of a particular thinker. Rather, a body of Black feminist thought long has used the above working definition. Much of the Black feminist platform has been oral and has been produced by Black women in their roles as mothers, teachers, musicians, and preachers.[13] Since the Civil Rights and women's movements, Black women's ideas increasingly have been documented and now are reaching wider audiences. The following discussion of three key themes in Black feminist thought is itself part of this emerging process of documentation and interpretation. The three themes I have chosen are not exhaustive but do represent much of the existing dialogue.

The Meaning of Self-Definition and Self-Valuation

An affirmation of the importance of Black women's self-definition and self-valuation is the first key theme that pervades historical and contemporary statements of Black feminist thought. Self-definition involves challenging the political knowledge-validation process that results in externally defined, stereotypical images of African-American womanhood. Self-valuation stresses the content of Black women's self-definitions and replaces externally derived images with authentic Black female images.

Both Mae King's and Cheryl Gilkes' analyses of stereotypes offer insights useful for grasping the importance of Black women's self-definition.[14] King suggests that stereotypes represent externally defined, controlling images of African-American womanhood that are central to the dehumanization of Black women and the exploitation of Black women's labor. Gilkes points out that Black women's assertiveness in resisting the multifaceted oppression they experience has been a consistent threat to the status quo. As punishment for their resistance, Black women have been assaulted with a variety of externally-defined negative images designed to control assertive Black female behavior.

The value of King's and Gilkes' analyses lies in their emphasis on the function of stereotypes in controlling dominated groups. Both point out that replacing negative stereotypes with ostensibly positive ones can be equally problematical if the function of stereotypes as controlling images remains unrecognized. John Gwaltney's interview with Nancy White, a seventy-three-year-old Black woman, suggests that Black women also are aware of these controlling images in their everyday lives. White assesses the differences between the controlling images applied to African-American and white women as being differences of degree, not of kind:

> My mother used to say that black woman is the white man's mule and the white woman is his dog. Now, she said that to say this: we do the heavy work and get beat whether we do it well or not. But the white woman is closer to the master and he pats them on the head and lets them sleep in the house, but he ain't gon' treat neither one like he was dealing with a person.[15]

This passage suggests that while both groups are stereotyped differently, the images function to dehumanize and control both groups similarly. Seen in this light, exchanging one set of controlling images for another makes little sense for Black women, even if, in the short run, positive stereotypes bring marginally better treatment.

Black female self-definition reframes the entire issue of definition: it moves the discussion from the technical accuracy of images to the power dynamics underlying the very process of definition itself. Black feminists have questioned not only what has been said about Black women, but the credibility and intentions of those with the power to define such women. When Black women define themselves, they clearly reject the assumption that those who have traditionally described and analyzed Black women's reality are entitled to do so. Regardless of the actual content of Black women's self-definitions, the act of insisting on Black female self-definition validates Black women's power as human subjects.

While Black female self-definition speaks to the power dynamics involved in the act of defining images of self and community, Black female self-valuation addresses the actual content of these definitions. Many Black female stereotypes are actually distorted renderings of aspects of Black female behavior seen as most threatening to white patriarchy.[16] For example, assertive African-American women are threatening because they challenge white patriarchal definitions of femininity. To ridicule assertive women by labeling them Sapphires reflects as well an effort to put all women in their place. As the figures who socialize the next generation of Black adults, strong mothers are similarly threatening, because they contradict patriarchal views of correct family power relations. To ridicule strong Black mothers by labeling them matriarchs reflects an effort to control another aspect of Black female behavior especially threatening to the status quo.[17]

When Black females choose to value those aspects of African-American womanhood that are stereotyped, ridiculed, and maligned in academic scholarship and the popular media, they act in defiance of their oppression. It is one thing to counsel African-American women to resist the Sapphire stereotype by altering their behavior to become meek, docile, and stereotypically "feminine"; it is quite another thing to advise Black women to embrace their assertiveness, to value their sassiness, and to use these qualities to survive in and transcend the harsh environments that circumscribe their lives. By defining and valuing assertiveness and other "unfeminine" qualities as necessary attributes of African-American womanhood, Black women's self-valuation challenges the content of externally defined, controlling images.

The Black feminist concern that Black women create their own standards for evaluating African-American womanhood pervades a wide range of literary and social-science works. For example, Alice Walker's 1982 novel, *The Color Purple*, and Ntozake Shange's 1978 choreopoem, *For Colored Girls Who Have Considered Suicide*, both are bold statements of the need for Black female self-definition and self-valuation. Lena Wright Myers' work, showing that Black women judge their behavior by comparing themselves to other Black women facing similar situations, demonstrates the presence of Black female definitions of African-American womanhood.[18] The recent spate of Black female historiography suggests that self-defined, self-valuing Black women long have populated the ranks of African-American female leaders.[19]

Black women's insistence on self-definition, self-valuation, and a Black, female-centered analysis is significant for two reasons. First, by defining and valuing one's own standpoint in the face of images based on a definition as the objectified "other," Black women resist the dehumanization and reductionism essential to systems of domination. The status of "other" implies being "other than" or different from the assumed norm of white male behavior. In this model, powerful white males define themselves as subjects, the true actors, and classify people of color and women relative to this white male center. Since Black women have been denied the authority to challenge their definitions, the white male model consists of images that define Black women as a negative "other," the virtual antithesis of positive male images. Moreover, as Brittan and Maynard point out, "domination always involves the objectification of the dominated; all forms of oppression imply the devaluation of the subjectivity of the oppressed."[20]

Judith Rollins provides an excellent example of this objectification process. As part of her fieldwork on Black domestics, Rollins worked as a domestic for six months. She describes several incidents in which her employers treated her as if she were not really present. On one occasion, while she sat in the kitchen having lunch, her employers had a conversation as if she were not there. Her "invisibility" became so great that she took out a pad of paper and began writing field notes. Even though Rollins wrote for ten minutes, finished lunch, and returned to work, her employers showed no evidence of having seen her at all. Rollins notes:

> It was this aspect of servitude I found to be one of the strongest affronts to my dignity as a human being. . . . These gestures of ignoring my presence were not, I think, intended as insults; they were expressions of the employers' ability to annihilate the humanness and even, at times, the very existence of me, a servant and a black woman.[21]

Racist and sexist ideologies treat dominated groups, the "others," as objects lacking full human subjectivity. Seeing Black women as obstinate mules and white women as obedient dogs objectifies both groups, but in different ways. Neither is seen as fully human, and both are forced to endure race/gender-specific modes of domination. But if Black women — the quintessential "other" in white, patriarchal society — refuse to accept their assigned status, then the entire rationale for such domination is challenged. Clearly, abusing a metaphorical mule or dog is easier than abusing a person who refuses to be objectified.

Black female self-definition and self-evaluation also enable African-American women to resist internalized psychological oppression.[22] The potential damage to African-American women's self-esteem can be great, even to the prepared. Enduring the frequent assaults of controlling images requires considerable inner strength. Nancy White points out how debilitating being treated as less than human can be if Black women are not self-defined: "Now, you know that no woman is a dog or a mule," she observes, "but if folks keep making you feel that way, if you don't have a mind of your own, you can start letting them tell you what you are."[23] Seen in this light, self-definition and self-valuation are not luxuries; they are necessary for Black female survival.

The Interactive Nature of Oppression

Attention to the interactive nature of race, gender, and class oppression is a second recurring theme in the works of Black feminists.[24] While different sociohistorical periods may have increased the saliency of one or another type of oppression, Black feminists long have argued that oppressions are linked. For instance, Ida Wells Barnett and Frances Ellen Watkins Harper, two prominent Black feminists of the late 1800s, both spoke out against the growing violence directed against Black men. They realized that civil rights held little meaning for Black men and women if the right to life itself went unprotected.[25] Black women's absence from organized feminist movements often has been mistakenly attributed to a lack of feminist consciousness. In actuality, Black feminists have had an ideological commitment to addressing interlocking oppressions, yet they have been excluded from arenas that would have allowed them actively to do so.[26]

As Barbara Smith points out, "The concept of the simultaneity of oppression is still the crux of a Black feminist understanding of political reality and . . . is one of the most significant ideological contributions of Black feminist thought."[27] This should come as no surprise, since Black women were among the first to realize that minimizing one form of oppression, while essential, still might leave them oppressed in other, equally dehumanizing ways. Sojourner Truth knew this when she stated, "There is a great stir about colored men getting their rights, and not colored women theirs, you see the colored men will be masters over the women, and it will be just as bad as before."[28] To use Nancy White's metaphors, the Black woman as "mule" knows that she is perceived to be an animal. In contrast, the white woman as "dog" may be similarly dehumanized and may think that she is an equal part of the family, when in actuality she is a well-cared-for pet. The significant factor shaping Truth's and White's clearer view of their own subordination — clearer, that is, than that of Black men or white women — is these two women's experience at the intersection of multiple structures of domination.[29] Both Truth and White are Black, female, and poor. They therefore view oppression more clearly than do other groups who occupy fewer contradictory positions vis-a-vis white male power. Unlike white women, these women have no illusions that their whiteness will negate female subordination; and, unlike Black men, they cannot use a questionable appeal to manhood to neutralize the stigma of being Black.

The Black feminist attention to the interactive nature of oppression is significant for two reasons. First, this perspective shifts the entire focus of investigation from one aimed at explicating elements of race, gender, or class oppression to one whose goal is to determine the links among these systems. The first approach typically prioritizes one form of oppression and then characterizes remaining oppressions as variables within the most important system — as, for example, do efforts to insert race and gender into Marxist theory. In contrast, the more holistic approach of Black feminist thought treats the interaction among multiple systems as the object of study. Rather than maintaining existing theories by inserting previously excluded variables, Black feminists aim to develop new theoretical interpretations of the interaction itself.

Black male scholars, white female scholars, and, more recently, Black feminists like bell hooks may have identified one critical link among interlocking systems of oppression. These groups have pointed out that certain basic ideas cut across multiple systems of domination. One such idea is dualistic thinking (either/or), which hooks claims is "the central ideological component of all systems of domination in Western society."[30]

While hooks' claim may be somewhat premature, there is growing scholarly support for her position.[31] Dualistic thinking, or what I will refer to as the construction of dichotomous difference, may well be a philosophical linchpin in systems of race, class, and gender oppression. One fundamental characteristic of this construction is the categorization of people, things, and ideas in terms of their difference from one another. For example, the terms in dichotomies such as black/white, male/female, reason/emotion, fact/opinion, and subject/object gain their meaning only in their difference from their oppositional counterparts. Another fundamental characteristic of this construct is that the difference is not complementary; the halves of the dichotomy do not enhance each other. Rather, the dichotomous halves are different and inherently opposed. A third and more important characteristic is that these oppositional relationships are intrinsically unstable. Since such dualities rarely represent different-but-equal relationships, the inherently unstable relationship is resolved by subordinating one half of each pair. Thus, whites rule Blacks, males dominate females, reason is touted as superior to emotion in ascertaining truth, facts supercede opinion in evaluating knowledge, and subjects rule objects. Dichotomous differences invariably imply relationships of superiority and inferiority, hierarchical relationships that mesh with political economies of domination and subordination.

The oppression experienced by most Black women is shaped by their subordinate status in an array of dualities. African-American women have been assigned the inferior half of several dualities, and this placement has been central to their continued domination. For example, the stereotypically "passionate" nature of African-American women long has been used as a rationale for their sexual exploitation. Similarly, denying Black women literacy and then claiming that they lack sound judgment is another instance of assigning a group inferior status and then using that inferior status as proof of the group's inferiority. Finally, denying Black women agency as subjects and treating them as objectified "others" represents yet another dimension of the power that dichotomous constructions have in maintaining systems of domination.

While African-American women have a vested interest in recognizing the dualities that oppress them, dualistic thinking is so pervasive as to suppress the alternatives. Dill points out that "the choice between identifying as black or female is a product of the patriarchal strategy of divide-and-conquer[,] and the continued importance of class, patriarchal, and racial divisions, perpetuate such choices both within our consciousness and within the concrete realities of our daily lives."[32] In spite of this difficulty, Black women experience oppression in a personal, holistic fashion, and their emerging Black feminist perspectives embrace an equally holistic analysis of oppression.

Black feminist attention to the interactive nature of oppression implies an alternative, humanist vision of societal organization. This alternative world view is expressed cogently in an 1893 speech by the Black feminist educator Anna Julia Cooper:

> We take our stand on the solidarity of humanity, the oneness of life, and the unnaturalness and injustice of all special favoritisms, whether of sex, race, country, or condition. . . . The colored woman feels that woman's cause is one and universal; and that . . . not till race, color, sex, and condition are seen as accidents, and not the substance of life; not till the universal title of humanity to life, liberty, and the pursuit of happiness is conceded to be inalienable to all; not till then is woman's lesson taught and woman's cause won — not the white woman's nor the black woman's, nor the red woman's, but the cause of every man and of every woman who has writhed silently under a mighty wrong.[33]

This passage represents one of the clearest statements of the humanist vision extant in Black feminist thought.[34] Black feminists who see the simultaneity of their oppression appear to be more sensitive to how these same oppressive systems affect African-American men, people of color, women, and the dominant group itself. Thus, while Black feminist activists may work on behalf of Black women, they rarely project separatist solutions to Black female oppression. Rather, their vision is one that, like Cooper's, takes its "stand on the solidarity of humanity."

The Importance of African-American Women's Culture

A third key theme that characterizes Black feminist thought involves efforts to redefine and explain the importance of Black women's culture. In doing so, Black feminists not only have uncovered previously unexplored areas of the Black female experience, but also have identified the social relations that allow African-American women to create and pass on the self-definitions and self-valuations essential to coping with the simultaneity of oppression they experience.

In contrast to views of culture stressing the unique, ahistorical values of a particular group, Black feminists have placed greater emphasis on the role of historically specific political economies in explaining the endurance of certain cultural themes. The following definition of culture typifies the approach taken by many Black feminists. According to Mullings, culture is composed of the

> symbols and values that create the ideological frame of reference through which people attempt to deal with the circumstances in which they find themselves. Culture . . . is not composed of static, discrete traits moved from one locale to another. It is constantly changing and transformed, as new forms are created out of old ones. Thus culture . . . does not arise out of nothing: it is created and modified by material conditions.[35]

Seen in this light, Black women's culture may help provide the ideological frame of reference, namely the symbols and values of self-definition and self-valuation that assist Black women in seeing the circumstances shaping race, class, and gender oppression. Mullings' definition of culture also suggests that the values accompanying self-definition and self-valuation have material expression and thus will be present in social institutions like the church and family; in the creative expressions of art, music, and dance; and in patterns of economic and political activity. Moreover, this conception of culture stresses its historically concrete nature. While common themes may link Black women's lives, these themes will be experienced differently by Black women of different classes, ages, regions, and sexual preferences, as well as by Black women in different historical settings. Thus there is no monolithic Black women's culture; rather, there are socially constructed Black women's cultures that collectively form Black women's culture.

The interest in redefining Black women's culture has directed attention to several unexplored areas of the Black female experience. One such area concerns interpersonal relationships among Black women. It appears that the notion of sisterhood, generally understood to mean a support, loyalty, and attachment to other women stemming from a shared feeling of oppression, has long been an important part of Black women's culture.[36] Two representative works in the emerging tradition of Black feminist research illustrate how this concept of sisterhood, while expressed differently in response to different material conditions, has been a significant feature of Black women's culture. Debra Gray White documents the ways that Black slave women assisted each other in childbirth, cared for each other's children, worked together in sex-segregated work units when pregnant or nursing, and depended on one another when married to men who were living on distant farms.[37] White paints a convincing portrait of Black slave communities where sisterhood was necessary and assumed. Similarly, Gilkes' work on Black women's traditions in the Sanctified Church suggests that the sisterhood Black women created had tangible psychological and political benefits.[38]

The attention to Black women's culture has stimulated interest in a second type of interpersonal relationship, that shared by Black women with their biological children, with the children in their extended families, and with the Black community's children. In reassessing African-American motherhood, Black feminist researchers have emphasized the connections between (1) choices available to Black mothers resulting from their placement in historically specific political economies, (2) Black mothers' perceptions of their children's choices as compared to what mothers thought those choices should be, and (3) actual strategies employed by Black mothers in raising their children and in dealing with institutions that affect their children's lives. For example, Janice Hale suggests that Black mothers are sophisticated mediators between the competing offerings of an oppressive dominant culture and a nurturing Black value structure.[39] Dill's study of the childrearing goals of Black domestics stresses the goals the women in her sample had for their children and the strategies they pursued to help their children go further than they themselves had gone.[40] Gilkes offers yet another perspective on the power of Black motherhood by observing that many of the Black political activists in her study became involved in community work through their role as mothers.[41] What typically began as work on behalf of their own children evolved into work on behalf of the community's children.

Another dimension of Black women's culture that has generated considerable interest among Black feminists is the role creative expression plays in shaping and sustaining Black women's self-definitions and self-valuations. In addition to documenting Black women's achievements as writers, dancers, musicians, artists, and actresses, the emerging literature also investigates why creative expression has been such an important element of Black women's culture.[42] Alice Walker's classic essay, "In Search of Our Mothers' Gardens," explains that Black women have used their creativity, even if in very limited spheres, to resist objectification and to assert their subjectivity as fully human beings.[43] Illustrating Walker's thesis, Willie Mae Ford Smith, a prominent gospel singer featured in the 1984 documentary, "Say Amen Somebody," describes what singing means to her: "It's just a feeling within. You can't help yourself . . . I feel like I can fly away. I forget I'm in the world sometimes. I just want to take off." For Mother Smith, creativity offers a sphere of freedom, one that helps her cope with and transcend daily life.

This third key theme in Black feminist thought — namely, the focus on Black women's culture — is significant for three reasons. First, the data from Black women's culture suggest that the relationship between oppressed people's consciousness of oppression and the actions they take in dealing with oppressive structures may be far more complex than is suggested by existing social theory. Conventional social science continues to assume a fit between consciousness and activity; hence, accurate measures of human behavior are thought to produce accurate portraits of human consciousness of self and social structure.[44] In contrast, Black women's experiences suggest that Black women may conform overtly to the social roles laid out for them, yet covertly oppose these roles in numerous spheres, an opposition shaped by their consciousness of being on the bottom. Black women's activities in families, churches, community institutions, and creative expression represent more than an effort to mitigate pressures stemming from oppression. The Black female ideological frame of reference that Black women acquire through sisterhood, motherhood, and creative expression also shapes a Black female consciousness about the workings of oppression. Moreover, this consciousness develops not only through abstract, rational reflection, but also through concrete, rational action. For example, while Black mothers may develop consciousness by talking with and listening to their children, they may also shape their own consciousness by taking actions on behalf of their children. That these activities have been obscured from traditional social scientists should come as no surprise. Oppressed peoples often hide their consciousness for purposes of self-protection.[45]

The focus on Black women's culture is significant also because it points to the problematical nature of existing conceptualizations of the term "activism." African-American women's experiences suggest that, while the interlocking structures of oppression limit Black women's lives, possibilities for activism exist even within these multiple structures of domination. Such activism takes several forms. For Black women under extremely harsh conditions, the decision to reject external definitions of African-American womanhood is itself a form of activism. When Black women find themselves in settings where total conformity is expected and where the traditional forms of activism, such as voting, participating in collective movements, and holding office, are impossible, then those women who choose to be self-defined and self-valuating are, in fact, activists. They are retaining a grip on their own definition as fully human subjects and rejecting definitions of themselves as objectified "others." For example, while Black slave women were forced to conform to the specific oppression facing them, they may have had very different assessments of themselves and slavery than did the slaveowners. In this sense, consciousness can be viewed as a potential sphere of freedom, one that may exist simultaneously with severe constraints on behavior.[46] As Black women simultaneously use all resources available to them — their roles as mothers, their participation in churches, their support of one another in Black female networks, their creative expression — to become self-defined and self-valuing and to encourage others to reject objectification, then Black women's everyday behavior itself will qualify as a form of activism. People who view themselves as fully human subjects become activists, no matter how limited the sphere of their activism may be. By returning subjectivity to Black women, Black feminists return activism as well.

A third reason that the focus on Black women's culture is significant is that an analytical model exploring the interrelation of oppression, consciousness, and activism is implicit in the way Black feminists have studied Black women's culture. With the exception of Dill, few scholars have set out deliberately to develop such a model.[47] However, the type of work done suggests that an implicit model paralleling that proposed by Mullings has influenced Black feminist research.[48]

Several features characterize these emerging Black feminist approaches. First, researchers stress the relationship between the oppression that has shaped Black women's choices and Black women's actions in response to this oppression. Black feminist researchers rarely describe Black women's behavior without attending to the opportunity structures shaping their subject's lives.[49] Second, the question of effect — whether the oppressive structures and limited choices evoke apathy and alienation or subjectivity and activism — is seen as ultimately dependent on Black women's perceptions of their choices. In other words, Black women's consciousness — their analytical, emotional, and ethical perspectives on themselves and their place in society — is critical in the workings of oppression and Black women's actions. Finally, this interrelation of oppression, consciousness, and action can be seen as a dialectical one. In this model, oppressive structures create patterns of choices, which are perceived in varying ways by Black women. Depending on their consciousness of themselves and their relationship to these choices, Black women may or may not develop spheres of influence where they validate what will be appropriate responses to oppression. Black women's activism in constructing Black female spheres of influence in turn may affect their perceptions of the political and economic choices offered to them by oppressive structures, influence the actions they take, and ultimately alter the nature of oppression.

The Sociological Significance of Black Feminist Thought

Taken together, the three key themes in Black feminist thought — namely, the meaning of self-definition and self-valuation, the interactive nature of oppression, and the importance of redefining culture — have made significant contributions to the task of clarifying a Black women's perspective on and for Black women. While this accomplishment is important in and of itself, Black feminist thought has potential contributions to make to the diverse disciplines housing its practitioners.

The sociological significance of Black feminist thought lies in two areas. First, the content of Black women's ideas has been influenced by and contributes to ongoing dialogues in a variety of sociological specialities. While this area merits attention, it is not the primary focus of my analysis. Instead, I investigate a second area of sociological significance, namely, the process by which these ideas were produced by this group of individuals. In other words, I examine the influence of Black women's outsider-within status in academia on the actual thought produced. Thus far, I have proceeded on the assumption that it is impossible to separate the structure and the thematic content of thought (in this case, the three key themes in Black feminist thought) from the historical and material conditions shaping the lives of its producers (in this specific case, Black women's outsider-within status in established academic disciplines). In this section, I spell out what form this relationship might take for Black women scholars generally, and for Black female sociologists especially.

First I specify the role sociological paradigms play in shaping the facts and theories used by sociologists. Next I explain how the outsider-within status might encourage Black women to have a distinctive perspective on sociology's paradigmatic facts and theories. I argue that the thematic content of Black feminist thought described above represents elements of just such a perspective, and I give examples of how the combination of sociology's paradigms and Black women's status as outsiders within sociology directed their attention to specific areas of sociological inquiry.

Two Elements of Sociological Paradigms

Kuhn defines a paradigm as the "entire constellation of beliefs, values, techniques, and so on shared by the members of a given community."[50] A paradigm consists of two fundamental elements — the thought itself and its producers and practitioners.[51] In this sense, the discipline of sociology is a paradigm (it consists of a system of knowledge shared by sociologists) and also a plurality of paradigms (e.g., functionalism, Marxist sociology, feminist sociology, existential sociology), each produced by its own practitioners.

Two dimensions of thought are of special interest here. First, systems of knowledge are never complete; they merely represent guidelines for "thinking as usual." Kuhn refers to these guidelines as "maps," while Schutz describes them as "recipes."[52] As Schutz points out, while "thinking as usual" is somewhat disorganized, unclear, and contradictory, to its practitioners it provides sufficient coherence, clarity, and consistency. Second, while thought contains diverse elements, I focus on the important fact/theory relationship. As Kuhn suggests, facts or observations become meaningful in the context of theories or interpretations of them. Conversely, theories "fit the facts" by transforming previously accessible observations into facts. Mulkay notes, "Observation is not separate from interpretation; rather these are two facets of a single process."[53]

The community formed by the practitioners of a sociological paradigm is of special interest to my discussion. First, group insiders have similar world views, acquired through similar educational and professional training, that separate them from everyone else. Insiders' world views may be especially alike if group insiders have similar class, gender, and racial backgrounds. Schutz describes the insider world view as the "cultural pattern of group life," meaning all the values and behaviors that characterize the social group at a given moment in its history. In brief, insiders have undergone similar experiences, possess a common history, and share the assumptions about knowledge that characterize "thinking as usual."

The process of becoming an insider is what produces the coincidence of insider world views and constitutes the community of practitioners. Merton suggests that socialization into the life of a group is a lengthy process of immersion, because only over time can "one understand the fine-grained meanings of behavior, feeling, and values . . . and decipher the unwritten grammar of conduct and nuances of cultural idiom."[54] The process is analogous to immersion in a foreign culture in order to learn its ways and its language. One becomes an insider by translating a world view into one's own language, until, one day, the individual has a conversion experience and begins to think and act according to that world view.

Finally, the process of remaining an insider maintains the community of practitioners. A sociologist typically remains an insider, furthering the discipline in ways described as appropriate by sociology generally and by areas of specialization particularly. Normal foci for scientific sociological investigation include (1) determining significant facts; (2) matching facts with existing theoretical interpretations to "test" the paradigm's ability to predict facts; and (3) resolving ambiguities in the paradigm itself by articulating and clarifying theory.[55]

Black Women and Outsider-Within Status

Black women may encounter much less of a fit between their personal and cultural experiences and the elements of sociological paradigms than other sociologists do. On the one hand, Black women who undergo sociology's lengthy socialization process, who immerse themselves in the cultural pattern of sociology's group life, certainly wish to acquire the insider skills of thinking and acting according to a sociological world view. But, on the other hand, Black women's experiences prior to contact and after initiation may provide them with "special perspectives and insights . . . available to that category of outsiders who have been systematically frustrated by the social system."[56] In brief, their outsider allegiances may militate against their choosing full insider status, and they may be more apt to remain outsiders within.[57]

In order to become sociological insiders, Black women must assimilate a perspective that differs from their own. White males long have been the dominant group in sociology, and the sociological world view understandably reflects their concerns. As Merton observes, "White male insiderism in American sociology during the past generations has largely been of the tacit or de facto . . . variety. It has simply taken the form of patterned expectations about the appropriate . . . problems for investigation."[58] In contrast, a good deal of the Black female experience has been spent coping with, avoiding, subverting, and challenging the workings of these same white males.

It should come as no surprise that Black women's efforts in dealing with the effects of interactive systems of oppression produce a perspective quite distinct from, and in many ways opposed to, that of white male insiders.

Seen from this perspective, Black women's socialization into sociology represents a more intense case of the normal challenges facing sociology graduate students and junior professionals in the discipline. Black women become, to use Simmel's and Schutz's terminology, penultimate "strangers":

> The stranger . . . does not share the basic assumptions of the group. He becomes essentially the man who has to place in question nearly everything that seems to be unquestionable to the members of the approached group. . . . To

him the cultural patterns of the approached group do not have the authority
of a tested system of recipes . . . because he does not partake in the vivid historical tradition by which it has been formed.[59]

Like everyone else, Black women may see sociological "thinking as usual"
as somewhat unorganized, unclear, and contradictory, and may question
these existing recipes. However, this questioning process may be more acute,
for the material that they encounter (namely white male insider-influenced
observations and interpretations of human society) places white male subjectivity at the center of analysis and assigns African-American womanhood
a position on the edges.

In spite of a lengthy socialization process, it also may be more difficult
for African-American women to undergo a conversion experience and begin
totally to think and act according to a sociological world view. Since past
generations of white male insiders have shaped a sociological world view
reflecting their concerns, it may be self-destructive for Black women to embrace that world view. For example, Black women would have to accept
such unquestioned assumptions as, first, that white males are more worthy
of study because they are more fully human than everyone else; and, second,
that dichotomous thinking is natural and normal. More important, Black
women would have to act in accord with their place in a white male world
view. They would have to accept their own subordination or regret the accident of not being born white and male. It may be extremely difficult, in
short, for Black women to subscribe to a world view predicated upon Black
female inferiority.

Remaining in sociology by doing normal scientific investigation also may
be less complicated for traditional sociologists than for African-American
women. Unlike Black women, learners from backgrounds where the insider
information and experiences of sociology are more familiar may be less likely
to see the unquestioned assumptions of sociology and may be more prone
to apply their creativity to "normal science." In other words, the transition
from being a student to being a practitioner engaged in finding the facts
that sociological paradigms deem important, matching these facts with existing theories, and furthering paradigmatic development may proceed more
smoothly for white middle-class males than for working-class Black females.
The latter are much more inclined to be struck by the mismatch of their own
experiences and the paradigms of sociology itself. Moreover, those Black
women with a strong foundation in Black women's culture (i.e., those who
recognize the value of self-definition and self-valuation, and who have a concrete understanding of sisterhood and motherhood) may be more apt to take
a critical posture toward the entire sociological enterprise. In brief, where
traditional sociologists may see sociology as "normal" and define their role

as furthering knowledge about a normal world, outsiders within are liable to see anomalies.

The types of anomalies typically seen by Black female academicians grow directly from Black women's outsider-within status and shape the direction of Black feminist thought. First, Black female sociologists typically report the omission of facts or observations about African-American women in the sociological paradigms they encounter. As Scott points out, "from reading the literature, one might easily develop the impression that Black women have never played any role in this society."[60] Where white males may see as "normal" studies about white males that generalize their findings to others, Black women are likely to see the situation studied as itself problematical. Similarly, when white feminists produce generalizations about "women," Black feminists routinely ask, "Which women do you mean?" In the same way that Rollins felt invisible in her employer's kitchen, African-American female scholars are repeatedly struck by their own invisibility, both as fully human subjects included in sociological facts and observations and as practitioners in the discipline itself. Much of Black feminist thought counters this invisibility by presenting sociological analyses of Black women as fully human subjects. For example, the growing research that describes Black women's historical and contemporary behavior as mothers, community workers, church leaders, teachers, and employed workers, as well as Black women's ideas about themselves and their opportunities, reflects an effort to respond to the dearth of facts about African-American women.

An anomaly often noted by Black female scholars concerns distortions of facts and observations about Black women. African-American women in academia are frequently struck by the difference between their own experiences and sociological descriptions of them. For example, while Black women have and are themselves mothers, they encounter distorted versions of their mothers and themselves under the mantle of the Black matriarchy thesis. For those Black women who confront racial and sexual discrimination and know that their mothers and grandmothers certainly did, explanations of Black women's poverty that stress low achievement motivation and the lack of Black female "human capital" also are less likely to ring true. Their response to these distortions has been to redefine the distorted images — that is, to debunk the Sapphire and Mammy myths.

Since facts or observations become meaningful in the context of a theory, this emphasis on producing accurate descriptions of Black women's lives has also refocused attention on major omissions and distortions in sociological theories themselves. Drawing on the strengths of sociology's many subdisciplines while taking a critical stance toward them, the work of Black feminist scholars poses fundamental questions facing all sociologists. One such question concerns the elements of society that should be studied. The response of Black feminist researchers has been to move Black women's voices to the center of analysis, to study people, and, by doing so, to reaffirm human subjectivity and intentionality. Black feminist researchers point to omissions and distortions that occur when sociological concepts are studied at the expense of human subjectivity. For example, a statistical analysis of African-American working women as a reconstituted amalgam of researcher-defined variables (e.g., race, sex, years of education, and father's occupation) differs from a study of Black women's self-definitions and self-valuations as workers in oppressive jobs. While both approaches can further sociological knowledge about work, the former runs the risk of objectifying Black women, of reproducing dualistic thinking, and of producing distorted findings about the nature of work itself.

Another question facing sociologists concerns the adequacy of current interpretations of key sociological concepts. Few sociologists would disagree that work and family are key concepts for sociology. However, bringing Black feminist thought into the analysis of these concepts raises questions about how comprehensive current sociological interpretations of these concepts really are. For example, labor theories that relegate African-American women's work to the fringe of analysis miss the critical theme of the interactive nature of Black women as female workers (e.g., Black women's unpaid domestic labor) and as racially oppressed workers (e.g., Black women's unpaid slave labor and exploited wage labor). Examining the extreme case offered by African-American women's unpaid and paid work raises questions about the adequacy of generalizations about work itself. For example, Black feminists' emphasis on the simultaneity of oppression redefines the economic system and renders its workings problematical. All generalizations about the normal workings of labor markets, organizational structures, occupational mobility, and income differences that do not explicitly see oppression as problematical become suspect. In short, Black feminists suggest that all generalizations about groups of employed and unemployed workers (e.g., managers, welfare mothers, union members, secretaries, Black teenagers) that do not account for group placement in an economy defined as interactively oppressive are simply less complete than those that do.

Similarly, sociological generalizations that do not account for Black women's experiences miss variations in household composition across social and class groupings, the integration of racial/ethnic family members into wage labor, and the alterations that families make to their household structure in response to changing political economies (e.g., adding more people and becoming extended, fragmenting and becoming female-headed, and migrating to better opportunities). Black women's family experiences represent a clear case of the workings of race, gender, and class oppression in shaping family life. Bringing undistorted observations of African-American women's family experiences into the center of analysis again raises the question of how other families are affected by these same forces.

While Black women who stand outside academia may be familiar with the omissions and distortions of Black female experience, as outsiders to sociology they lack the legitimated authority necessary to challenge sociological anomalies. Similarly, traditional sociological insiders, whether white males or their nonwhite and/or female disciples, certainly are in no position to notice the anomalies apparent to African-American women, because they are the sociological insiders who produce them. In contrast, those Black women who remain rooted in their own experiences as Black women and who master sociological paradigms while retaining a critical posture toward them are in a better position to bring a special perspective, not only to the study of Black women, but also to some of the fundamental issues facing sociology itself.

Toward Synthesis: Outsiders Within Sociology

Black women are not the only outsiders within sociology. As an extreme case of outsiders moving into a community that historically excluded them, Black women's experiences highlight the tension experienced by any group of less powerful outsiders encountering the paradigmatic thought of a more powerful insider community. In this sense, a variety of individuals can learn from Black women's experiences as outsiders-within — Black men, working-class individuals, white women, other people of color, religious and sexual minorities, and all individuals who, while from social strata that provided them with the benefits of white male insiderism, never have felt comfortable with its unquestioned assumptions.

Outsider-within status is bound to generate tension, for people who become outsiders within are forever changed by their new status. Learning the subject matter of sociology stimulates a re-examination of one's own personal and cultural experiences, yet these same experiences paradoxically help to illuminate sociology's anomalies. Outsiders within occupy a special place — they become different people, and their difference sensitizes them to patterns that may be more difficult for established sociological insiders to see. Some outsiders within try to resolve the tension generated by their new status by leaving sociology and remaining sociological outsiders. Others choose to suppress their difference by striving to become bonafide "thinking as usual" sociological insiders. Both choices rob sociology of diversity and ultimately weaken the discipline.

An alternative is to conserve the creative tension of outsider-within status by encouraging and institutionalizing outsider-within ways of seeing. This alternative has merit not only for actual outsiders within but also for all sociologists. The approach suggested by the experiences of outsiders within is one in which intellectuals learn to trust their own personal and cultural biographies as significant sources of knowledge. In contrast to approaches that require submerging these dimensions of self in the process of becoming an allegedly unbiased, objective social scientist, outsiders within bring ways of knowing into the research process. At its best, outsider-within status seems to offer its occupants a powerful balance between the strengths of their sociological training and the offerings of their personal and cultural experiences; neither is subordinated to the other. Rather, personal experience is used as a valid source of knowledge for criticizing sociological facts and theories, while sociological thought offers new ways of seeing that personal experience.

Many Black feminists are embracing the creative potential of their outsider-within status and using it wisely. In doing so, they move themselves and their disciplines closer to the humanist vision implicit in their work—that is, the freedom to be different and yet remain part of the solidarity of humanity.

Notes

1. In 1940, almost 60% of employed African-American women were domestics. The 1970 census was the first time this category of work did not contain the largest segment of the Black female labor force. See Judith Rollins, *Between Women: Domestics and Their Employers* (Philadelphia: Temple University Press, 1985) for a discussion of Black domestic work.

2. For example, in *Of Woman Born: Motherhood as Experience and Institution* (New York: Norton, 1976), Adrienne Rich reports fond memories of her Black "mother," a young, unstereotypically slim Black woman she loved. See Bonnie Thorton Dill, "'The Means to Put My Children Through': Child-Rearing Goals and Strategies Among Black Female Domestic Servants," in *The Black Woman*, ed. LaFrances Rodgers-Rose (Beverly Hills, Calif.: Sage, 1980), 107–23, for a study of Black domestic workers that reveals Black women's sense of affirmation in knowing that they were better mothers than their employers and in having to teach their employers the basics about children and interaction in general. Even though the Black domestic workers were officially subordinates, they gained a sense of self-worth in knowing that they were good at things that they felt mattered.

3. For example, in spite of Rich's warm memories of her Black "mother," she had all but forgotten her until beginning research for her book. Similarly, the Black domestic workers in both Dill, "The Means," and Rollins, *Between Women*, discussed the limitations that their subordinate roles placed on them.

4. For a discussion of the notion of a special standpoint or point of view of oppressed groups, see Nancy M. Hartsock, "The Feminist Standpoint: Developing the Ground for a Specifically Feminist Historical Materialism," in *Discovering Reality*, ed. Sandra Harding and Merrill Hintikka (Boston: Reidel, 1983), 283–310. See Robert K. Merton, "Insiders and Outsiders: A Chapter in the Sociology of Knowledge," *American Journal of Sociology* 78 (1972):9–47, for an analysis of the potential contributions of insider and outsider perspectives to sociology. For a related discussion of "outsider within" status, see Merton's section, "Insiders as 'Outsiders,'" 29–30.

5. Hurston has been widely discussed in Black feminist literary criticism. For example, see selected essays in Zora Neale Hurston, *I Love Myself When I Am Laughing . . . A Zora Neale Hurston Reader*, ed. Alice Walker (Old Westbury, N.Y.: Feminist Press, 1979).

6. E. Frances White, "Listening to the Voices of Black Feminism," *Radical America* 18, nos. 2–3(1984):7–25.

7. bell hooks, *From Margin to Center* (Boston: South End Press, 1984), vii.

8. Georg Simmel, "The Sociological Significance of the 'Stranger,'" in *Introduction to the Science of Sociology*, ed. Robert E. Park and Ernest W. Burgess (Chicago: University of Chicago Press, 1921), 322–27.

9. Karl Mannheim, *Ideology and Utopia: An Introduction to the Sociology of Knowledge* (New York: Harcourt, Brace, 1936; rptd. 1954).

10. Alfred McClung Lee, *Toward Humanist Sociology* (Englewood Cliffs, N.J.: Prentice-Hall, 1973), 64. By stressing the potentially positive features of outsider-within status, in no way do I want to deny the very real problems this social status has for large numbers of Black women. American sociology has long identified marginal status as problematical. However, my sense of the "problems" diverges from that espoused by traditional sociologists. For example, Robert Park states, "The marginal man . . . is one whom fate has condemned to live in two societies and in two, not merely different but antagonistic cultures" (Park, *Race and Culture* [Glencoe, Ill.: Free Press, 1950], 373). From Park's perspective, marginality and difference themselves were problems. This perspective quite rationally led to the social-policy solution of assimilation, a solution aimed at eliminating difference or, if that didn't work, pretending it was not important. In contrast, I argue that it is the meaning attached to difference that is the problem. See Audre Lorde, *Sister Outsider* (Trumansburg, N.Y.: Crossing Press, 1984), esp. 114–23, for a Black feminist perspective on difference.

11. In addition to familiarizing readers with the contours of Black feminist thought, I place Black women's ideas in the center of my analysis for another reason. Black women's ideas long have been viewed as peripheral to serious intellectual endeavors. By treating Black feminist thought as central, I hope to avoid the tendency to start with the body of thought needing the critique (in this case, sociology), fit in the dissenting ideas, and thereby reify the very system of thought one hopes to transform.

12. See Peter L. Berger and Thomas Luckmann, *The Social Construction of Reality* (New York: Doubleday, 1966), and Mannheim, *Ideology and Utopia*.

13. On this point, I diverge somewhat from Berger and Luckmann's definition of specialized thought. They suggest that only a limited group of individuals engages in theorizing and that "pure theory" emerges with the development of specialized legitimating theories and their administration by full-time legitimators. Using this approach, groups denied the material resources to support pure theorists cannot be capable of developing specialized theoretical knowledge. In contrast, I argue that "traditional wisdom" is a system of thought and that it reflects the material positions of its practitioners.

14. Mae King, "The Politics of Sexual Stereotypes," *Black Scholar* 4, nos. 6–7 (Mar.–Apr. 1973):12–23; and Cheryl Townsend Gilkes, "From Slavery to Social Welfare: Racism and the Control of Black Women," in *Class, Race, and Sex: The Dynamics of Control*, ed. Amy Swerdlow and Helen Lessinger (Boston: G.K. Hall, 1981), 288–300.

15. John Langston Gwaltney, *Drylongso: A Self-Portrait of Black America* (New York: Vintage, 1980), 148.

16. Gilke, "From Slavery to Social Welfare"; and Deborah Gray White, *Ar'n't I a Woman? Female Slaves in the Plantation South* (New York: Norton, 1985).

17. Elizabeth Higginbotham, "Two Representative Issues in Contemporary Sociological Work on Black Women," in *But Some of Us Are Brave*, ed. Gloria T. Hull, Patricia Bell Scott, and Barbara Smith (Old Westbury, N.Y.: Feminist Press, 1982), 93–98.

18. Lena Wright Myers, *Black Women: Do They Cope Better?* (Englewood Cliffs, N.J.: Prentice-Hall, 1980).

19. See Paula Giddings, *When and Where I Enter . . . The Impact of Black Women on Race and Sex in America* (New York: Morrow, 1984); and Bert James Loewenberg and Ruth Bogin, eds., *Black Women in Nineteenth-Century Life* (University Park: Pennsylvania State University Press, 1976).

20. Arthur Brittan and Mary Maynard, *Sexism, Racism and Oppression* (New York: Basil Blackwell, 1984), 199.

21. Rollins, *Between Women*, 209.

22. Joseph A. Baldwin, "The Psychology of Oppression," in *Contemporary Black Thought*, ed. Molefi Kete Asante and Abdulai S. Vandi (Beverly Hills, Calif.: Sage, 1980), 95–110.

23. Gwaltney, *Drylongso*, 152.

24. See Frances Beale, "Double Jeopardy: To Be Black and Female," in *The Black Woman*, ed. Toni Cade (New York: Signet, 1970), 90–110; Angela Davis, *Women, Race and Class* (New York: Random House, 1981); Bonnie Thorton Dill, "Race, Class, and Gender: Prospects for an All-Inclusive Sisterhood," *Feminist Studies* 9, no. 1 (Spring 1983):131–50; bell hooks, *Ain't I A Woman: Black Women and Feminism* (Boston: South End Press, 1981); Diane Lewis, "A Response to Inequality: Black Women, Racism and Sexism," *Signs* 3, no. 2 (Winter 1977):339–61; Pauli Murray, "The Liberation of Black Women," in *Voices of the New Feminism*, ed. Mary Lou Thompson (Boston: Beacon Press, 1970), 87–102; and Filomina Chioma Steady, "The Black Woman Cross-Culturally: An Overview," in *The Black Woman Cross-Culturally*, ed. Filomina Chioma Steady (Cambridge, Mass.: Schenkman, 1981), 7–42. Emerging Black feminist research is demonstrating a growing awareness of the importance of including the simultaneity of oppression in studies of Black women. For example, Paula Giddings' *When and Where I Enter* is a history of African-American women that emphasizes the role of class in shaping relations between African-American and white women and among Black women themselves. Elizabeth Higginbotham's "Race and Class Barriers to Black Women's College Attendence" (*Journal of Ethnic Studies* 13, no. 1 [Spring 1985]:89–107), is a study of Black college women that examines race and class barriers to Black women's college attendence. Especially noteworthy is the growing attention to Black women's labor market experiences. Studies that indicate a new sensitivity to the interactive nature of race, gender, and class include: Dill, "The Means"; Rollins, *Between Women*; Elizabeth Higginbotham, "Laid Bare by the System: Work and Survival for Black and Hispanic Women," in Swerdlow and Lessinger, *Class, Race, and Sex*, 200–15; and Leith Mullings, "Uneven Development: Class, Race and Gender in the United States Before 1900," in *Women's Work: Development and the Division of Labor by Gender*, ed. Eleanor Leacock and Helen Safa (South Hadley, Mass.: Bergin and Garvey), 41–57. By studying Black women, these scholars capture the interaction of race and gender. Moreover, by examining Black women's roles in capitalist development, they tap the key variable of class.

25. Loewenberg and Bogin, *Black Women*.

26. Davis, *Women, Race and Class*.

27. Barbara Smith, "Introduction," in *Home Girls—A Black Feminist Anthology*, ed. Barbara Smith (New York: Kitchen Table/Women of Color Press, 1983), xxxii.

28. Loewenberg and Bogin, *Black Women*, 238.

29. The thesis that those affected by multiple systems of domination will develop a sharper view of the interlocking nature of oppression is illustrated by the prominence of Black lesbian feminists among Black feminist thinkers. For more on this, see Barbara Smith, "Introduction"; Lorde, *Sister Outsider;* and E. Frances White, "Listening to the Voices," 22–24.

30. hooks, *Margin to Center*, 29.

31. For example, African and African-American scholars point to the role dualistic thinking has played in domestic racism. See Joseph Baldwin, "The Psychology of Oppression," 95–110; Dona Richards, "European Mythology: The Ideology of 'Progress,'" 59–79; and Molefi Kete Asante, "International/Intercultural Relations," 43–58; all in Asanti and Vandi, *Contempory Black Thought*.

Feminist scholars note the linkage of duality with conceptualizations of gender in Western cultures. See Michelle Z. Rosaldo, "Moral/Analytic Dilemmas Posed by the Intersection of Feminism and Social Science," in *Social Science as Moral Inquiry*, ed. Norma Hann, Robert N. Bellah, Paul Rabinow, and William Sullivan (New York: Columbia University Press, 1983), 76–96; Nancy Chodorow, *The Reproduction of Mothering* (Berkeley: University of California Press, 1978); and Evelyn Fox Keller, "Gender and Science," in Harding and Hintikka, *Discovering Reality*, 187–206. Recently Brittan and Maynard, two British scholars, in *Sexism, Racism, and Oppression*, have suggested that dualistic thinking plays a major role in linking systems of racial oppression with those of sexual oppression. They note:

> There is an implicit belief in the duality of culture and nature. Men are the creators and mediators of culture — women are the manifestations of nature. The implication is that men develop culture in order to understand and control the natural world, while women, being the embodiment of forces of nature, must be brought under the civilizing control of men. . . . This duality of culture and nature . . . is also used to distinguish between so-called higher nations or civilizations, and those deemed to be culturally backward. . . . Non-European peoples are conceived of as being nearer to nature than Europeans. Hence, the justification . . . for slavery and colonialism. (193–94)

32. Dill, "Race, Class and Gender," 136.

33. Anna Julia Cooper, quoted in Loewenberg and Bogin, *Black Women*, 330–31.

34. This humanist vision takes both religious and secular forms. For religious statements, see *Sisters of the Spirit*, ed. William L. Andrews (Bloomington: Indiana University Press, 1986), a collection of the autobiographies of three 19th-century Black female evangelical preachers. For a discussion of the humanist tradition in African-American religion that has contributed to this dimension of Black feminist thought, see Peter J. Paris, *The Social Teaching of the Black Churches* (Philadelphia: Fortress Press, 1985). Much of contemporary Black feminist writing draws on this religious tradition, but reframes the basic vision in secular terms.

35. Leith Mullings, "Anthropological Perspectives on the Afro-American Family," *American Journal of Social Psychiatry* 6, no. 1 (Winter 1986):13.

36. Dill, "Race, Class and Gender," 132.

37. Deborah G. White, *Ar'n't I a Woman?*

38. Cheryl Townsend Gilkes, "'Together and in Harness': Women's Traditions in the Sanctified Church," *Signs* 10, no. 4 (Summer 1985):678–99. During a period when Black women were widely devalued by the dominant culture, Sanctified Church members addressed each other as "Saints." During the early 1900s, when basic literacy was an elusive goal for many Blacks, Black women in the church not only stressed education as a key component of a sanctified life, but also supported each other's efforts at educational excellence. In addition to these psychological supports, the church provided African-American women

with genuine opportunities for influence, leadership, and political clout. The important thing to remember here is that the church was not an abstract, bureaucratic structure that ministered to Black women. Rather, the church was a predominantly female community of individuals in which women had prominent spheres of influence.

39. Janice Hale, "The Black Woman and Child Rearing," in Rodgers-Rose, *The Black Woman*, 79–88.

40. Dill, "The Means."

41. Cheryl Townsend Gilkes, "'Holding Back the Ocean with a Broom': Black Women and Community Work," in Rodgers-Rose, *The Black Woman*, 217–31.

42. Since much Black feminist thought is contained in the works of Black women writers, literary criticism by Black feminist critics provides an especially fertile source of Black women's ideas. See Claudia Tate, *Black Women Writers at Work* (New York: Continuum, 1983); and Barbara Christian, *Black Feminist Criticism: Perspectives on Black Women Writers* (New York: Pergamon Press, 1985).

43. Alice Walker, "In Search of Our Mothers' Gardens," in Walker, *In Search of Our Mothers' Gardens* (New York: Harcourt Brace Jovanovich, 1974), 231–43.

44. Marcia Westkott, "Feminist Criticism of the Social Sciences," *Harvard Educational Review* 49, no. 4 (Nov. 1979):422–30.

45. Lorde, in *Sister Outsider,* describes this conscious hiding of one's self: "For in order to survive, those of us for whom oppression is as American as apple pie have always had to be watchers, to become familiar with the language and manners of the oppressor, even sometimes adopting them for some illusion of protection" (114).

46. Westkott, "Feminist Criticism."

47. Dill, "Race, Class and Gender."

48. Mullings, "Anthropological Perspectives on the Afro-American Family."

49. See Higginbotham, "Race and Class Barriers"; Joyce Ladner, *Tomorrow's Tomorrow: The Black Woman* (Garden City, N.Y.: Anchor/Doubleday, 1971); and Myers, *Black Women.*

50. Thomas S. Kuhn, *The Structure of Scientific Revolutions,* 2nd ed. (Chicago: University of Chicago Press, 1962; rptd. 1970), 175.

51. In this sense, sociology is a special case of the more generalized process discussed by Mannheim, *Ideology and Utopia.* Also, see Morris Berman, *The Reenchantment of the World* (New York: Bantam, 1981), for a discussion of Western thought as a paradigm; Michael Mulkay, *Science and the Sociology of Knowledge* (Boston: George Allen and Unwin, 1979) for a sociology-of-knowledge analysis of the natural sciences; and Berger and Luckmann, *Social Construction of Reality,* for a generalized discussion of how everyday knowledge is socially constructed.

52. Kuhn, *Structure of Scientific Revolutions;* and Alfred Schutz, "The Stranger: An Essay in Social Psychology," *American Journal of Sociology* 49, no. 6 (May 1944):499–507.

53. Mulkay, *Science,* 49.

54. Merton, "Insiders and Outsiders," 15.

55. Kuhn, *Structure of Scientific Revolutions.*

56. Merton, "Insiders and Outsiders," 29.

57. Jacquelyn Jackson, "Black Female Sociologists," in *Black Sociologists,* ed. James E. Blackwell and Morris Janowitz (Chicago: University of Chicago Press, 1974):267–98, reports that 21 of the 145 Black sociologists receiving Ph.D's between 1945 and 1972 were women. Stephen Kulis, Karen A. Miller, Morris Axelrod, and Leonard Gordon, "Minority Representation of U.S. Departments," *ASA Footnotes* 14, no. 5 (1986):3, 6, report that Blacks comprised 5.7% of all sociology faculty in 1984. These data suggest that, histori-

cally, Black females have not been sociological insiders and that currently Black women as a group comprise a small portion of sociologists in the United States.

58. Merton, "Insiders and Outsiders," 12.

59. Schutz, "Stranger," 502.

60. Patricia Bell Scott, "Debunking Sapphire: Toward a Non-Racist and Non-Sexist Social Science," in Hull, Scott, and Smith, *But Some of Us Are Brave*, 85.

Women and Other Strangers: Feminist Perspectives in Classical Literature

Kathryn J. Gutzwiller and Ann Norris Michelini

Some classical scholars, many of them feminists, have begun a process of reevaluating the traditional emphases of their discipline by unearthing and then challenging the assumptions on which classical scholarship is based.[1] In this paper we argue that traditional approaches have an inherently masculinist bias and that feminist alternatives are needed not only to correct that bias but also to open large areas of potential investigation foreclosed by traditional methodologies. One of the most important of these areas is the gender system that structured the societies of the ancient Greeks and Romans.

In both classical culture and the modern Western cultures that derive from and model themselves on the classical world, a binary series of oppositions marks as appropriate to the male or female genders distinctive categories of behavior, language, physical appearance, and social and economic roles. A strong male dominance in ancient society created and perpetuated this gender system. It also acted to obscure the workings of gender by foregrounding only the male sphere of activity and by marking the female as negative or insignificant. As a consequence, the ancients themselves could not perceive or discuss the gendered structure of their culture; and most classical scholars, who have uncritically accepted the ancient perspective because it closely resembles their own, also have been blind to it. Scholars who in recent years have begun to investigate the lives of ancient women now have made it possible to see this gender division and to use it as a critical tool in the analysis of classical literature. While the purpose of this paper is a polemical comparison of traditional and feminist perspectives in classics, our study takes the evolution and permutation of the gender system from archaic and classical literature through Hellenistic poetry and down to the time when this system was adapted by Roman poets to a quite different form of discourse.

Modern study of classical texts began to emerge in the seventeenth century with such scholars as Richard Bentley, who proved that the letters attributed to the quasi-mythological dictator Phalaris were forgeries from a later period. Bentley's achievements suggested that close investigation of texts, with attention to grammar and vocabulary, could distinguish authentic from inauthentic work. In working with the texts of ancient poets, he displayed the utmost confidence that by eliminating erroneous or interpolated material he could restore ancient texts virtually as their authors had written them. Historians of classical scholarship remark on Bentley's confidence and certainty, his "belief that he knew what the poet ought to have written."[2]

In the nineteenth century, when classical scholarship began to flourish in Germany and England, much of the work preserved this tradition of minute attention to language, with the aim of determining which texts and which parts of texts were authentic. Sometimes even in the present day and very commonly until the second half of this century, articles published in the field consisted of nothing more than than a series of perhaps twenty or thirty suggestions ("conjectures") for the emendation of texts, for the deletion of passages judged spurious, or for the rearrangement of lines in a different sequence. Literary study was virtually nonexistent in mid-nineteenth-century classical scholarship, and the model of a rational and "scientific" study encouraged scholars to believe that they could accurately define and preserve the texts of literary works without becoming involved in the less exact procedures of literary analysis. Of course, in determining which lines to excise from their texts, these scholars used their intuitive sense of ancient style in conjunction with standards of taste, propriety, and relevance derived from contemporary culture. But they used and applied the latter relatively uncritically.

The German university system produced the most powerful and sophisticated classical scholarship; and German scholars by the end of the nineteenth century were creating a broader intelletual basis for the study of classical texts. But affinities of culture and language have made British classical studies a much stronger and more enduring model for Americans. In Britain, the norm of a scholarship purely devoted to the study of texts, textual transmission, and the minutiae of grammar and usage has survived and, though now embattled, continues to prevail.[3] The longevity of this norm is due partly to the persisting prestige of a conservative educational system in which upper-class males,[4] who may receive little training in modern languages or science, are taught Latin and Greek from an early age. Minutely careful study of texts is supplemented by writing exercises, culminating in the composition of Greek and Latin verses, which the best of the adepts can produce extemporaneously.[5]

Scholars with this background tend to unite a phenomenal level of language skill with a relatively uncritical view of classical culture, since the major literary works, presented without much analysis of perspective, have been the familiar material of their schoolroom exercises since early adolescence. In this elite world, women largely have been strangers, because the schools where children are drilled in Greek and Latin have not been open to them and most girls' schools have followed a different curriculum.[6] While this system of classical education produced a small number of classical scholars, it was also designed to serve more broadly educated members of the male elite; and the division between professionals and amateurs has remained somewhat flexible. Because the analysis of textual variants and the invention of conjectures are skills dependent on a narrow but deep literary background, the broad acquaintance with linguistics, anthropology, archaeology, or literary theory required of scholars who practice more complex and more modern approaches can still be treated as irrelevant to "true" scholarship. In at least one case, a posthumous collection of brilliant conjectures was the legacy of a working farmer whose leisure hours were devoted to classical study.[7] At the ideal level, gentleman and scholar could be one.

While American universities do not boast any measurable contingent of students who have studied classical languages since pre-adolescence, the model of British classical scholarship and the influence of British classical scholars remain very strong in this country.[8] The notion that "textual criticism" is the appropriate pursuit for any classicist of ability is still viable in some circles.[9] For many American classicists, the techniques of textual criticism and the art of conjecture making — on the face of it a form of speculation based on uncheckable intuition and guesses — continue to be the standard for rigorous, "objective," "hard" scholarship.

The problem of the textual critic's unanalyzed viewpoint still tends to be ignored or glossed over, and the magisterial confidence with which the traditional scholar approaches classical texts continues to lead him to overlook areas of incongruity that mark the divisions between ancient and modern cultural systems. For feminist scholars who are interested in the gender codes of ancient culture, this scholarly model can hold little attraction, since it accepts both ancient and modern cultural codes as natural and as identical. In the 1920s, a period already marked by feminist agitation in Britain, a prominent historian reassured classicists that Greek women were not treated very differently from women in modern civilized nations.[10] Gomme's complacent approval of the Greeks corresponds to an equal complacency toward contemporary attitudes and practices; indeed, the two are mutually supportive.

In recent years, however, better work on gender divisions and sexual mores in the ancient world has begun to appear. For the most part this work has come from the discipline of history, to which the study of culture generally has been consigned by traditional scholarship; and what these scholars have done is simply to shift attention from the masculine half of the gender code, which has privileged such masculine-gendered activities as warfare and political life, to the feminine half, which privileges sexuality, marriage customs, and family life.[11] Studies of the economic position of Greek women offered new explanations for strange customs, such as that which required an heiress to marry her nearest male relative, or for the institution of the dowry.[12] Another product of this trend is a number of books on Greek homosexuality. While the emphasis of these books is on male sexuality, the accession of such a topic to scholarly interest is based upon the shift toward the side of the gender paradigm that has been labeled female.[13]

An extension of the historical work are studies dealing with female figures in literature, female divinities, and related topics.[14] But, while all this work provides valuable and often exciting new material for the study of neglected areas of antiquity, it must be noted that it too observes the arrangement of gender categories set up in Hellenic society or in our own. Newer perspectives in the field began with studies by French scholars trained in structuralist techniques that made it easier to analyze the gender code as a whole and to place it in relation to other, better-known codes in ancient society.[15] The work of these French scholars in turn has enhanced the study of literary works in which gender codes are used.[16] Probably also reflective of this trend is the interesting recent book by Eva Keuls, who shows the interlocking systems of dominance that supported class and gender distinctions in Hellenic societies. Keuls's work provides a tonic antidote to the veiled apologetics of the first studies of "women," "the family," and "sexuality," indicating how a perspective that treats gender categories as cultural artifacts can cast new light on Greek culture as a whole.[17]

Some of the most interesting work in modern classical studies has aimed at defining the heroic value system embodied in the oldest and most paradigmatic work of Hellenic literature, the *Iliad* of Homer. A.D.H. Adkins has effectively revealed the alien quality of the ethic that underlies this epic and that projects itself, with certain modifications, into the classical period. This traditional value system is dominated by a concept of prowess or merit (*aretê*), based on the masculine ideal of the warrior.[18] By his deeds, the warrior may meet death; but, through the power of public memory preserved in heroic epic, he attains a kind of immortality, raising himself, through his death, to a status almost comparable to that of the gods themselves. War, the ultimate form of competition, is the model for other organized contests to determine prowess in physical (athletic) and mental (poetic) skills.[19] The losers in these contests are threatened with consignment to the inferior gender category.[20] Raised in such a culture, the Greek male had a strong motivation to win public rewards (*timê*) and avoid humiliation, and in order to achieve these ends he often might be tempted to engage in behavior considered illegal or immoral. To this system of values, Adkins sees opposed another system, subordinate and inferior to the first, based on what he calls the "quiet virtues." Ironically, these virtues are the social ones most obsessively praised in Greek poetry and philosophy: especially justice or fairness (*dikê*) and self-control or moderation (*sôphrosynê*). Adkins argues that these "weaker" virtues posed no real threat to the ethic of competition until the advent of new ethical systems proposed by the fourth-century philosophers Plato and Aristotle.[21]

Adkins has succeeded in isolating something fascinatingly alien about Hellenic culture and in the process has put his finger on a major cultural change that was effected by the revolution in thought in the Greek fifth century. But something is missing. How did the "quiet virtues," so defenseless and scorned, come to replace the "active" ones? And can it be possible that all the famous Hellenic preaching about justice and self-control is mere cant? Adkins provides a clue when he points out that, for women, the "weak" virtues were the dominant ones.[22] In the gender system of the heroic period, males were assigned the virtues of strength and intelligence associated with military and political efficacy; but these virtues had a strong antisocial component. The assignment of social virtues to the female side of the gender code only aggravated the paradox.

The *Iliad* itself can be seen as a working-out of this conundrum. Its hero Achilles, the embodiment of male prowess, who has explicitly chosen to die young rather than to live long without honor, is driven by his need for honor, first, to desert the ranks of his comrades and to sit out the war and, second, to revenge himself on an enemy in a brutal and inappropriate way. Yet, at the end of the poem, we witness a scene in which Achilles returns the body of his enemy and recognizes the senselessness of war. When Achilles and the aged king of Troy mourn together, Priam thinking of the death of his son Hector, Achilles of the sorrow of his own old father, each represents the same central paradox in the heroic ethic. In war, which is the most valued activity for males, the proper and natural order of life is reversed: the young die and the aged are left to mourn. An awareness of the Greek gender system makes it possible to see how a literary work that was paradigmatic of the heroic value system also incorporates a hidden code, operating parallel with, and in opposition to, the major one. The "weaker" virtues are required to resolve the intolerable paradoxes of the heroic view, yet they remain a kind of negative element in the system.[23]

This fruitful contradiction between two value systems ultimately produced a number of radical attempts at resolution, including the attempt by the Sophists to eliminate justice as a standard of conduct — or to redefine it in heroic terms as "the right of the stronger" — and the attempt by Plato to show that *all* virtues were comprehended under the rubric of "justice."[24] In the process, a new ethic was born, according to which the "weak" virtues, which the Sophists had shown were most desirable for weak people such as slaves and women, become dominant. This new ethic, the one still prevalent in the modern Western world, creates its own paradoxes: if the Greeks admired heroes, even when they were antisocial, moderns often have found it possible to admire or at least to sentimentalize figures such as women or children who have no real social power.

In the civic world of the Greek *polis*, where men took part in artistic, legal, military, intellectual, political, athletic, and social activities, women were peripheral figures, largely confined to the house, which itself was partitioned into carefully defined male and female areas.[25] The Greek city in which the new ethic was forged — Athens, the seat of the Greek enlightenment of the fifth century — was, if anything, more repressive of females than the world depicted in the Homeric poems. In a notoriously democratic and open society, women lived such private lives that their names could not be mentioned in public without the potential for disgrace.[26] Yet the literature of Athens is filled with female figures: how are we to explain this discrepancy?[27]

The answer must be that the alteration in the gender code began independently of any social reality. In Sophocles' great drama *Antigone*, a young girl defies an absolute ruler through her determination to uphold religiously enjoined burial customs, rituals traditionally carried out largely by women. Antigone displays the same lonely courage and the same assertive impatience with weakness as the heroes of epic and the protagonists of other Sophoclean plays.[28] Because she acts altruistically, in support of community values, Antigone uses behaviors and concerns appropriate to her female gender to define a new kind of heroism. This paradoxical figure, who is unlikely to represent anything familiar in Athenian life — where unmarried girls were subjected to a confinement little short of purdah and were married at fourteen or fifteen — represents the working-out of a cultural puzzle.[29]

The third of the great Athenian tragic playwrights, Euripides, brought stylistic changes into tragedy that have won him notoriety and admiration through the centuries. Where Sophocles creates in Antigone an unfamiliar but allusive figure who focuses central cultural concerns in a positive sense, Euripides presents us with women in more familiar situations who take unfamiliar approaches to their problems. *Medea* is the most striking and obvious example among the surviving plays. The protagonist is in a dilemma that must have been familiar in a society where males could contract any number of unofficial liaisons. She left her country and family out of love for Jason, who has betrayed her by forming a more prosperous marriage connection with the King of Corinth's daughter. Alone, without family or friends to help her, a woman like Medea usually had no resources and no choice except to acquiesce in her demotion to secondary status. But Medea is no ordinary woman. She will not tolerate this wound to her pride; and, explicitly expressing herself in terms of the masculine heroic ethic,[30] she formulates a revenge that will destroy what Jason most wants. Sons who will carry on the father's name are the most valuable thing that women give to men: therefore, when Medea kills Jason's new bride, his source of future sons, she must go on to kill her own sons as well. Far from being punished, this female rebel (who delivers a passionate indictment of the Hellenic marriage system in her first speech) triumphs, sailing off in a magic flying chariot and leaving Jason on the ground in helpless fury.

Rather than presenting us with a female hero who corrects the self-aggrandizing element in traditional *aretê*, Euripides gives us one who whole-heartedly accepts the masculine part of the gendered ethic and proceeds to put it into practice, asserting her honor at the expense of her enemy and achieving the kind of vengeance that a figure like Achilles would understand well. But the attempt to apply the competitive ethic in such a situation leads to radical questioning both of the gender system and of the gendered system of values that supports it. It is precisely because Greek males in the audience understood Medea's ethic too well that she disturbed them so profoundly.

Masculinist modern critics have usually seen Medea as a figure of typically female "passion." Unable to control her emotions and betrayed by her non-Greek heritage, Medea in this critical reading is a moving example of the dreadful results when women, savage and immoderate in their basic nature, break free of the controls of male-dominated "civilization."[31] As others have pointed out, however, the sympathy of the chorus of the play, which is made up of Greek women, is entirely with Medea. The great German scholar Wilamowitz observed that Medea is a new kind of heroic figure: "superhuman, not inhuman . . . in her greatness, [she represents] potentiated womanhood."[32]

Modern criticism of Euripides, especially that written from the traditional perspective sketched above, has offered many apologetic or scathing assessments of his artistic talent, the assumption being that the odd and awkward features of the plays are explicable as the mistakes of a playwright who lacked a sense of proportion or good taste.[33] In a book that remained influential for over a generation, a brilliant British textual critic attempted to excise large portions of the text of several plays on the grounds that these "melodramatic" passages were unworthy of a classical tragedian.[34] That Euripides spoiled the whole view of the fifth century for some nineteenth-century critics is indicated by Benjamin Jowett's dismissal of him as "no Greek in the better sense of the term."[35] Jowett, the famous translator of Plato, believed deeply that study of the classics provided the appropriate background for the British gentleman of his day. To him, the work "Greek" carried certain moral and ideological connotations; for those connotations to hold, artists such as Euripides had to be erased from the canon.

The poetry of the Hellenistic period marks another stage in the evolution of the gendering system informing Greek culture. The campaigns of Alexander and the resulting establishment of Hellenistic kingdoms in the Middle East and Egypt led to a breakdown in the insularity of the Greek world view. In this new cosmopolitan society, in which the Greeks were an elite minority in comparison with their barbarian subjects, the preservation of earlier Hellenic culture was a necessity. But a renewed viability could be given to that culture only by establishing distance from what had gone before. The phenomenon of Hellenistic literature, which sometimes has been compared to twentieth-century modernism, had at its core the imitation of inherited artistic forms, through opposition. Traditional scholars have identified the basic process by studying the minutiae of linguistic play.[36] But the broader and more interesting oppositions, those that reverse the values of the gender system, have not previously been discernible or analyzable.

All of the characteristic concerns of Hellenistic literature fall into the category that the Greeks labeled female, as interests not appropriate for the aristocratic males who dominated the culture. For the first time in Greek literature, romantic life becomes the dominant topic, even in epic.[37] Children, animals, rustics, the bourgeois — all act as central characters; heroes or gods, when present, are juxtaposed with the humble. The emphasis is on the particular, the delicate, the intricate, rather than the grand or weighty.[38] The audience reveled in this new subject matter precisely because it was the "other" of earlier Greek literature, the background brought to the foreground, the insignificant made significant. What was forbidden, peripheral, or shocking in Euripides was now the rule, expected as a challenge to an archaic code that seemed archaic and thus was preservable only by misuse.

It should not be surprising that traditional classicists have devalued the poetry of the Hellenistic age and assigned it a relatively low position in the canon of classical literature. Standard handbook assessments range from the openly hostile to the merely apologetic. The attack is two-pronged: the intimate qualities of the literature are dismissed as "sentimental," while its sophistication is denigrated as "erudite," the work of poets who took their scholarship too seriously. The preface to the translation of a respected German work on Hellenistic literature illustrates the point: "Professor Körte has skilfully [sic] brought out the rapidly increasing artificiality of emotion and sentiment in this Hellenistic-Alexandrian literature, the development of a 'learned' style in place of the genuine feeling of earlier writers."[39] Because of his own gendered (male) perspective, this scholar does not perceive the contradiction inherent in referring to emotion as artificial and dry. While he recognizes that the literature conveys feeling, he himself does not respond to it; so he blames the poetry itself, or its poet, for his own lack of response.

The groundwork has been laid for a feminist challenge to the traditional evaluation of Hellenistic literature by recent historical studies that point to increased literacy and power for women in the period following the death of Alexander.[40] Sarah Pomeroy has studied the influence of Ptolemaic queens, who, through ties of marriage and consanguinity, shared political, military, and economic power with the male rulers.[41] Both while living and after death as beneficent goddesses,[42] they provided models for the lives of other women, aristocrats and commoners alike. Pomeroy has pointed out as well that, by the fourth century, some women were engaged in professional pursuits — medicine, philosophy, science, the fine arts, and literature.[43] Female scholars also have studied with sensitivity the women poets of the Hellenistic period, such as Anyte, famous for her tender epitaphs on dead pets and her epigrams anticipating Theocritus' pastorals, and Erinna, whose lament for her girlhood friend Baucis made antiquity regret her early death at the age of nineteen.[44] These studies suggest that Hellenistic poetry, as the product of an age in which women acquired new intellectual freedom, may have been influenced by a female presence in the literary readership.[45]

While the historical influence of the female audience is now impossible to estimate, the recognition of its presence can encourage scholars to reevaluate, from a feminist perspective, important Hellenistic poetry that in the past has seemed recalcitrant to interpretation. By focusing on the gender code informing Greek literature, we are in a better position to appreciate Callimachus' depiction of female figures who derive their strength from traditionally female concerns. A feminist perspective on the *Hymns*, for instance, allows us to make sense of his powerful goddesses, who combine feminine traits with the ability to enforce their will.[46] In his sixth hymn, Demeter takes the form of a kindly priestess to dissuade an impulsive adolescent from destroying her sacred grove. Scorned, she provides the ironically feminine punishment of insatiable hunger, bringing social disgrace on his family. In the archaic period, the principal myth concerning Demeter emphasized her paralyzing grief over the loss of her daughter and her consequent withdrawal from divine society. Here, however, she proves that her motherly concern is not a sign of weakness but equates with the source of all nourishment and so demands proper respect. In the third hymn, Artemis matures from being a little girl, a "daddy's pet" who sits on Zeus' knee to beg for female playmates and mountains to roam, to being a vengeful huntress who devastates cities of wicked men. In earlier Greek culture, Artemis had been the perennial adolescent, displaying the spirited irresponsibility of the unmarried girl, but here her insistent determination is directed toward escaping from childhood dependency to adult automony.

As statements of religious belief, Callimachus' *Hymns*, have seemed either too playful or too unkind toward human error; and some scholars have suggested that they are instead highly ironic, perhaps even antireligious.[47] Associated with this line of thinking is the theory that the *Hymns* were intended only as comedy — as an amusing, if not openly hostile, parody of a by-gone literary form that had lost its utility as a mode of expressing belief.[48] But, if we take into account the potential female audience, our interpretation does not have to deprive the *Hymns* of all religious meaning,. From a feminist perspective, Callimachus seems concerned to revitalize the goddesses in a form that would appeal to contemporary interests. We should not fail to note the resemblance between his powerful goddesses and the Ptolemaic queens, who identified themselves not with the masculine Athena who protected the *polis*, but with the sexual and maternal pair of Aphrodite-Isis.[49]

Related to Callimachus' depiction of strong female characters are the personae that he as a male poet projects. He expresses his recognition of and opposition to archaic values by granting himself forms of maleness that are antithetical to the archetypal warrior figure. In a famous statement of intent, he vows that instead of writing thousands of lines on kings and heroes, he "rolls forth a short tale like a child, even though the decades of my years are not few" (prologue to the *Aetia*, fr. 1.5–6).[50] To celebrate Berenice's affection for her husband-brother, he speaks as a lock of her hair, which, shorn and metamorphosed into a constellation, laments extravagantly its separation from the queen (fr. 110). The charge of excessive objectivity that traditional scholars have frequently lodged against Callimachus arises from their belief that his personae are not merely ironic but even sterile and empty— posed for the sake of erudition alone, devoid of human emotion. But a feminist scholar may find less absolute the distance between the male poet and the various personae he projects. To see these personae as a means for a male poet to express concerns historically voiced only by women, and with sympathy rather than condescension, leads to more appreciative interpretations.

Just as traditional scholars failed to recognize the reversal of gender values in Hellenistic literature, they also have had difficulty explaining the great respect Latin writers, especially the poets of the Augustan age, had for this literature. In fact, the interest of these poets stems from the use they found for the Hellenistic code of values as a counterforce to the heavily moralistic patriarchal value system traditional in Roman society.[51] The traditional Roman value system was shaped by strict adherence to authority. Political leaders in the senate derived their own authority from their conformity to patterns of behavior set up by illustrious ancestors. Like their ancestors, these men had risen to positions of prominence by state service that in theory was unselfish, rewarded only by praise. But in the last decades of the Republic, a series of individuals succeeded in circumventing the authority of the senate through force of arms and so gained autocratic power for their own personal glory. In the collapse of societal values that both caused and accompanied these events, certain Romans looked to the Hellenistic world for a new code of behavior that might give meaning at least to their personal lives.

But the adoption of Hellenistic models involved more than a simple reversal in gender values, because the basic oppositional distinction shaping Roman culture was less directly attached to gender. In Rome, both men and women were expected to display similar virtues of courage, austerity, and personal reserve — a code of behavior tailored to men but adaptable to women.[52] The dichotomous "other" was provided by a complex of figures that included foreigners, slaves, pathic homosexuals, and sexually promiscuous women.[53] The bases for the division were sexuality and nationality, the "others" being those who could be dominated by Roman males. The link between the two categories is evident in the persistent Roman concern with the influence of Greek culture, which Romans perceived as dangerously seductive. Typically, the Romans thought that the Greeks lacked "manliness, alertness, and industry" and assigned them the converse traits of cowardice, deceit, and corruption through attachment to luxury and pleasure.[54] The "otherness" of the Greeks was both desired and feared, the focal point for conflict and rebellion.

Foremost among those who openly and rebelliously modeled themselves on Hellenistic precedent was the poet Catullus. Inspired by love for his mistress Lesbia, he adopts the posture of the Hellenistic poet before his queen: he declares himself poor, subservient, endowed with wit, irreverent toward orthodox values, interested like his lady in finer pleasures.[55] Pursuit of art and of passion are the goals of his life. In devotion to them, he has given up the political and military career that was the traditional and valued life of an upper-class Roman male. His love for Lesbia does not fit into the categories of erotic behavior that had previously been acceptable for Roman men — transitory passion for a courtesan or marital love aimed at procreation; rather, it rivals bonds found only in the male sphere, being like the love of a father for his sons and sons-in-law (72.3–4). Catullus even adapts the language of the political alliances that powered the inner workings of the senatorial system to describe his love for Lesbia: his relationship with her constitutes a "friendship," and their pledge of fidelity forms an almost sacred "pact" (87.3, 109.6).[56] The point of Catullus' misuse of social and political language is to show that the personal satisfaction he derives from his passion replaces the call to responsibility imposed by patriarchal authority. When he urges Lesbia to join him in a frenzy of kissing that will confound the jealous watching of "stern old men" (5.2), he wantonly defies the censorial system that demanded moderation in sensual pleasures as a mark of worthiness for office.

But despite the posture of subservience before his mistress, the lover's relationship with her was fundamentally different from that of subject to queen. Positions of power were not predetermined by political reality; and, by using the subversive strain of the Hellenistic to effect a covert reversion to the masculine ethos, Roman love poets found ways of reasserting traditional male dominance in matters of sex. Catullus' famous sparrow poem (2), for instance, seems at first glance to reproduce the tenderness of feeling for pets that characterized a long series of Hellenistic epigrams beginning with the gentle poetry of Anyte. But we soon realize that the charm of the sparrow's playfulness is not the main point of the poem, since Lesbia uses her fondness for the pet to avoid love-play with Catullus, who complains that he has no such solace for his ardor. The wit of Catullus here lies in preserving the Hellenistic ambiance of feminine sentiment, while showing us his own very different masculine perspective.[57] If a message to Lesbia is intended (and the poem becomes even wittier if we assume one), it consists of an attempt to win her sympathy and to alter her behavior for the satisfaction of the poet's passion. Such rhetorical manipulation of Hellenistic conventions for the purpose of persuading and controlling the mistress is typical not only of Catullus but also of the love elegists of the Augustan age, Propertius, Tibullus, and Ovid.

The politics of power and sexual dominance in Roman elegy have entirely escaped the notice of classicists working in the traditional mode. In the earlier decades of this century, scholars were concerned primarily with combing the poems for bits of information useful in reconstructing a "biography" of the love affair. The "hard facts" were important, not just as the common ground on which literary criticism and philology met, but also because love poetry was admired only insofar as it was perceived as "sincere," a "subjective" reflection of the poet's deepest emotions. The unrecognized assumption underlying this approach was an identification with the poet's presented view of the love affair: the terms of relationship between her lover and mistress were simply translated into forms acceptable to the scholar's own sexual ethos.[58] It is no wonder that "objective" Hellenistic poetry, which presented a feminine value system, was denigrated in comparison with "subjective" Latin poetry, written from a male point of view.

Although preoccupation with the historical reality behind the poetry has not disappeared from classical scholarship, many classicists now recognize that all literature is artificial and sincerity a matter of style.[59] Scholars of this persuasion have questioned the objective-subjective distinction and have argued that the persona of the lover is merely a convention, perhaps having little correspondence to reality. But even this more progressive group of scholars has been hampered in its analysis of the poet's rhetorical stance by an identification with the implied reader, who is almost certainly male. The classical scholar who is a feminist also has been trained to appreciate the readings most clearly suggested by the poetry itself. But her perspective, with its emphasis on gender and sexuality, grants her the means to escape the elegist's persuasion and to see more clearly his rhetorical techniques. She does this in part by imagining herself in the position of a historical reader who is female. This reader is not the implied reader, the one whose values the poet shares and projects, but she is often an implied recipient, that is, the object of the poet's persuasion. His manipulation of her, and his manipulation of the implied reader's view of her, are the means by which he uses his subservient pose to seek power and sexual control.

One final example serves to underscore the point. As a convention of the genre, the mistress will be unfaithful, and the poet will respond with poems of accusation and condemnation. In obscene terms, Catullus tells Lesbia to embrace her lovers three hundred at a time, while he compares his own fallen love to a flower crushed by a plow (11.17–24). Male-centered readers have admired these verses for the anguish they convey, the sense of beauty ruined, of purity defiled. But the feminist may note, in addition, the manipulation of the Hellenistic value system to reassert male dominance. By identifying himself with the usually feminine symbol of the flower, Catullus creates such a striking image, one so subversive to the traditional code of behavior for Roman males, that the reader tends to accept unquestioningly the accusations implicit in his exaggerated invective against Lesbia.[60] Only recently has a female scholar argued that the historical Clodia is not at all likely to have deserved the reputation established for her.[61] But whatever the historical realities, a feminist reader, in addition to appreciating the charm of Catullus' verse in traditionist terms, has the further capacity to analyze the artistry with which he manages to convey emotional sincerity.

The object of our study has been the gender dichotomies structuring the literary thought of three periods of ancient history: classical Greece, where women, absent from the public world, retained importance in a gender system that encoded the dilemmas of the heroic ethic; the Hellenistic period, in which the activities of women were valued positively as part of a general reversal of archaic thought; and Rome in the first century B.C., where the feminine-Greek counterforce was adopted as a mechanism for challenging the traditional patriarchal value system. We have shown that traditional scholars overlooked the gender system operating in each of these three periods, because they accepted without question the perspective of the males who controlled Greek and Roman society. Feminists, however, by focusing on ancient women, on what we know or can imagine them to have been, have brought into view a cultural substructure that previously was invisible. Feminist scholarship is not just an alternative or reverse image, then, but a way of completing our knowledge by taking account of gender polarity as a central aspect of human cultures.

Notes

1. The text of this article was put in final form in 1985, and it has since been overtaken by a considerable mass of classical scholarship dealing with gender, sexuality, and the like. We have added some of these items to the notes; but we have been unable to take account

of them adequately in the text itself. To do so would have involved major revisions that would have disrupted the plan of this volume.

2. Rudolf Pfeiffer, *History of Classical Scholarship from 1300 to 1850* (Oxford, England: Clarendon Press, 1976), 154. See also C.O. Brink, *English Classical Scholarship: Historical Reflections on Bentley, Porson and Housman* (New York: Oxford University Press, 1986); Brink's is an essentially hagiographical treatment, designed to define the role of each of these figures in the ideology of traditional British classical scholarship.

3. For at least two generations, almost everything written on the educational system described below has appeared as part of an account of the modernization of classics, the obsolescence and (eventual) disappearance of the old system being presumed. But repeated waves of "reform" only testify to the endurance of the system: see B.R. Rees' introduction to *Classics*, a series of essays describing fields of classical study in Britain for prospective college students (London: Routledge and Kegan Paul, 1970), 5. For a candid account of British classical instruction in the early part of the century, see Lord Greene's lecture *Classics and the Social Revolution of Our Time* (London: Oxford University Press, 1947), 20–21.

4. See R.W. Livingstone, "The Position and Function of Classical Studies in Modern English Education," in *England und die Antike*, ed. Fritz Saxt (Leipzig: Teubner, 1932), 255: "The line between those [in 19th century England] who received and those who did not receive a classical education is really one of class and sex." See also L.A. Moritz, "An Approach to Classical Literataure," in Rees, *Classics* 18–21.

5. For the place of Greek verse-writing in a "modernized" classical curriculum, see *The Teaching of Classics*, a publication of the Incorporated Association of Assistant Masters in Secondary Schools (Cambridge, England: The University Press, 1954), 107–9, and 174.

6. See Greene, *Classics and the Social Revolution*, 27.

7. See the introduction by Eduard Fraenkel to John Jackson's textual emendations, published in 1955 as *Marginalia Scaenica* (London: Oxford University Press).

8. For example, in 1987 the president as well as three of seven directors of the American Philological Association had received their higher education in Britain.

9. In Dec. 1985, at the annual meeting of the Amerian Philological Association, the moderator of a well-attended panel on textual criticism suggested that those who practice other forms of scholarship probably make a choice consonant with their lack of linguistic ability and training.

10. A.W. Gomme remarked, "I consider it very doubtful if Greek theory and practice [in the treatment of women] differed fundamentally from the average, say, prevailing in medieval and modern Europe" ("The Position of Women in Athens," 1925; cited in Gomme, *Essays in Greek History and Literature* [Oxford, England: Blackwell, 1937], 115). He pointed out that sexual modesty was esteemed in Englishwomen, too (99). Cf. H.D.F. Kitto, *The Greeks* (Harmondsworth, England: Penguin, 1951), 230.

More recently, Josine Blok, "Sexual Assymetry: A Historiographical Essay," in Josine Blok and Peter Mason, *Sexual Assymetry: Studies in Ancient Society* (Amsterdam: J.C. Gieben, 1987), 1–58, has divided classical approaches to women's history into "positivist" and "idealist" approaches (3), with Gomme and Kitto in the latter group (18–19). See also Roger Just, *Women in Athenian Law and Life* (London: Routledge, 1989), 1–12.

11. See Sarah Pomeroy, *Goddesses, Whores, Wives, and Slaves* (New York: Schocken, 1975); and, recently, Eva Cantarella, *Pandora's Daughters: The Role and Status of Women in Greek and Roman Antiquity*, trans. Maureen Fant (Baltimore, Md.: Johns Hopkins University Press, 1987).

See Blok, "Sexual Assymetry," on this tendency and its result, that womem are seen "as isolated from the general tendencies of history" (38, and see 33–41). For the application of new historical methodologies to the study of ancient women, see Phyllis Culham, "Ten

Years After Pomeroy," in *Rescuing Creusa: New Methodological Approaches to Women in Antiquity*, ed. Marilyn Skinner, special issue of *Helios* 13, no.2 (1987):9–30.

12. David Schaps, *The Economic Rights of Women in Ancient Greece* (Edinburgh: Edinburgh University Press, 1979). See also Pomeroy on social mechanisms for dealing with the problems created by dowries, "Charities for Greek Women," *Mnemosyne* ser. 4, vol. 35 (1982):115–35. See also Just, *Women in Athenian Law*, 95–104.

13. K.J. Dover, *Greek Homosexuality* (Cambridge, Mass.: Harvard University Press, 1978), was the first of these. For more recent work building on Dover, but with a greater emphasis on gender studies, see David M. Halperin, *One Hundred Years of Homosexuality and Other Essays on Greek Love* (New York: Routledge, 1990); and John J. Winkler, *The Constraints of Desire: The Anthropology of Sex and Gender in Ancient Greece* (New York: Routledge, 1990). See also David M. Halperin, John J. Winkler, and Froma I. Zeitlin, *Before Sexuality: The Construction of Erotic Experience in the Ancient Greek World* (Princeton, N.J.: Princeton University Press, 1990).

14. E.g., some essays in Helene P. Foley, ed., *Reflections of Women in Antiquity* (New York: Gordon and Breach, 1981), and in Averil Cameron and Amélie Kuhrt, eds., *Images of Women in Antiquity* (Detroit, Mich.: Wayne State University Press, 1983).

15. Jean Pierre Vernant, *Myth and Thought Among the Greeks* (first published in French, 1965; London: Routledge & Kegan Paul, 1983), demonstrates the gender-related significance of the goddess Hestia (pt. 3.5). M. Detienne, *The Gardens of Adonis*, trans. Janet Lloyd (Atlantic Highlands, N.J.: Humanities Press, 1977), illuminates the social and symbolic system in which outsider women (prostitutes and *hetairas*) and insider women (citizen wives) find their places. Nicole Loraux, *Les Enfants d'Athéna* (Paris: François Maspero, 1981), discusses the representation of the division of the sexes in Athenian myth. For influence, on gender's relation to other hierarchies, see Page Dubois, *Centaurs and Amazons: Women and the Prehistory of the Great Chain of Being* (Ann Arbor: University of Michigan Press, 1982), and Page Dubois, *Sowing the Body: Psychoanalysis and Ancient Representations of Woman* (Chicago: University of Chicago Press, 1988). See also Halperin, *One Hundred Years*, and Winkler, *Constraints of Desire*, who criticizes Detienne's "masculinist" opposition of concubines or prostitutes to legitimate wives (188–209).

16. See, e.g., Nicole Loraux, *Tragic Ways of Killing a Woman*, trans. Anthony Forster (Cambridge, Mass.: Harvard University Press, 1987); Ann L.T. Bergren, "*The Homeric Hymn to Aphrodite*: Tradition and Rhetoric, Praise and Blame," *Classical Antiquity* 8, no. 1 (Apr. 1989):1–41.

17. Eva Keuls, *The Reign of the Phallus* (New York: Harper and Row, 1985). Unfortunately, in Keuls' book documentation is minimal; although a bibliography accompanies each chapter, it is seldom possible to tell whether there is any outside support for some of her most interesting and controversial assertions. See also Winkler, *Constraints of Desire*, 17–44, on the power relations underlying ancient sexual categories; and the sophisticated discussion on the cultural orders encoding gender by H.S. Versnel, "Wife and Helpmate: Women of Ancient Athens in Anthropological Perspective," in Blok and Mason, *Sexual Assymetry*, 59–86.

18. A.D.H. Adkins, *Merit and Responsibility* (Oxford, England: Clarendon Press, 1960). See also Gregory Nagy, *The Best of the Achaeans* (Baltimore, Md.: Johns Hopkins University Press, 1978), for linguistic elements in this heroic code.

19. See the analysis of the Greek male obsession with contests by Alvin Gouldner, *Enter Plato: Classical Greece and the Origins of Social Theory* (New York: Basic, 1965).

20. See T.H. MacCary, *Childlike Achilles* (New York: Gordon and Breach, 1981), 152–62. See also Winkler, *Constraints of Desire*, 46–50.

21. See Adkins, *Merit and Responsibility*, 238–39.

22. Ibid., 36–37 and 161ff. See also the remarks on women's virtue attributed to two female Pythagorean philosophers, Phyntis and Perichthyone, in *The Pythagorean Writings: Hellenistic Texts from the 1st Century B.C.–3rd Century A.D.*, trans. Kenneth Guthrie and Thomas Taylor (Kew Gardens, N.Y.: Selene, 1986), 70–74.

23. See T.J. Reiss, *The Discourse of Modernism* (Ithaca, N.Y.: Cornell University Press, 1982), 96–97, on the existence of a hidden, negatively constituted alternative to the major cultural mode.

24. Both of these viewpoints are illustrated in the first and second books of Plato's *Republic*; the rhetorician and Sophist Thrasymachus presents a heroic definition of justice, which is then countered by Socrates. Note the opening of Book Two for a concise exposition of the moral dilemma.

25. The social mechanisms determining this are described by Just, *Women in Athenian Law*, who attempts to relate legal status to ideological codes defining gender. For a note of caution on women's status as "outsider," see Helene B. Foley, "The 'Female Intruder' Reconsidered: Women in Aristophanes' *Lysistrata* and *Ecclesiazusae*," *Classical Philology* 77, no. 1 (Jan. 1982):1–21.

26. See David Schaps, "The Woman Least Mentioned: Etiquette and Women's Names," *Classical Quarterly* 27, no. 2 (1977):323–30.

27. Note that Gomme, in "Position of Women," evidently confused by the split between literature and real life, believed that the female roles in Greek tragedy proved that women were not secluded and excluded from Athenian public life. For discussion of this problem, see Blok "Sexual Assymetry," and Just, *Women in Athenian Law*.

28. Cf. the contrast between Antigone and her "feminine" sister Ismene, who models a traditional Greek female role, reminding Antigone that they are only women and therefore weak. David Grene and Richmond Lattimore, *Complete Greek Tragedies, Sophocles I* (Chicago: University of Chicago Press, 1954), 157–62. For the personality traits of the Sophoclean hero, see Bernard M.W. Knox, *The Heroic Temper* (Cambridge, Mass.: Harvard University Press, 1964), 28–44.

29. Note that Jean Pierre Vernant, *Myth and Society in Ancient Greece*, trans. Janet Lloyd (Atlantic Highlands, N.J.: Humanities Press, 1980), in analyzing the traditional role of the goddess Athena, a female divinity who supervises male war making (23–24), has shown a similar paradox. Cf. also Halperin's analysis of the complex and even contradictory functions of Diotima's gender in Plato's *Symposium* (*One Hundred Years*, 113–51).

30. B.M.W. Knox, in "The *Medea* of Euripides," *Yale Classical Studies* 25 (1977):193–226, has pointed out Medea's affinities with the traditional heroic ethic that he had earlier defined for Sophocles in Knox, *Heroic Temper*.

31. See, e.g., Denys Page's edition (Oxford, England: Oxford University Press, 1938), where Medea's non-Greek background is stressed (xviii–xxi).

32. A translation from U. von Wilamowitz-Möllendorff's preface to his translation (Berlin: Weidmann, 1908), 31. Recent analyses of Medea's relation to gender codes include Helene B. Foley, "Medea's Divided Self," *Classical Antiquity* 8, no. 1 (Apr. 1989):61–85; Ann N. Michelini, "Neophron and Euripides' *Medea*, 1056–80," *Transactions of the American Philological Association* 119 (1989):130–35; and Emily C. McDermott, *Euripides' Medea: The Incarnation of Disorder* (University Park: Pennsylvania State University Press, 1988).

33. For an example of a very negative view on Euripides, cf. Gilbert Norwood, *Essays on Euripidean Drama* (Berkeley: University of California Press, 1954).

34. Denys Page, *Actors' Interpolations in Greek Tragedy* (Oxford, England: Clarendon Press, 1934); for his excisions in Euripides' *Iphigeneia at Aulis*, see 157, 158, 177, 186. See comment on the scholarly tradition on Euripides in Ann N. Michelini, *Euripides and the*

Tragic Tradition (Madison: University of Wisconsin Press, 1987), ch. 1; and "The Unclassical as Classical: The Modern Reception of Euripides," *Poetics Today* 9, no. 4 (1988):699–710.

35. Jowett was quoted by the poet Swinburne (who also despised Euripides as "the clumsiest of botchers") in Algernon C. Swinburne, "Recollections of Professor Jowett," in Swinburne, *Complete Works*, ed. E. Gosse and T.J. Wise (London: Heinemann, 1926), 5:252.

36. Foremost among this group is G. Giangrande, who has popularized the term *oppositio in imitando* (see his "'Arte allusiva' and Alexandrian Epic Poetry," *Classical Quarterly*, n.s. 17, no. 1 [1967]:85–97).

37. The story of Jason and Medea in Apollonius' epic poem the *Argonautica* is the obvious example. Because he lacks the traditional heroic qualities, Jason has been analyzed as a "love hero" by Charles Beye, *Epic and Romance in the "Argonautica" of Apollonius* (Carbondale: Southern Illinois University Press, 1982). Medea, though a direct descendant of Euripides' romantic heroines, is fascinating in her complexity: she progresses from a star-struck teenager to a threatening and ominous sorceress, when faced with possible abandonment by her lover.

38. Similar themes and interests appear in Hellenistic art. See Margarete Bieber, *The Sculpture of the Hellenistic Age*, rev. ed. (New York: Columbia University Press, 1961); Christine Havelock, *Hellenistic Art* (Greenwich, Conn.: New York Graphic Society, 1970); John Onions, *Art and Thought in the Hellenistic Period* (London: Thames and Hudson, 1979), 121–42; Barbara Fowler, *The Hellenistic Aesthetic* (Madison: University of Wisconsin Press, 1989).

39. Alfred Körte, *Hellenistic Poetry*, trans. J. Hammer and M. Hadas (New York: Columbia University Press, 1929), ix.

40. On the increased literacy of women during the 4th and 3rd centuries B.C., see Susan Cole, "Could Greek Women Read and Write?" in Foley, *Reflections on Women*, 229–33.

41. Sarah Pomeroy, *Women in Hellenistic Egypt: From Alexander to Cleopatra* (New York: Schocken, 1984), xvii–xviii. An older but still useful study is Grace H. McCurdy, *Hellenistic Queens: A Study of Woman-Power in Macedonia, Seleucid Syria, and Ptolemaic Egypt* (Baltimore, Md.: Johns Hopkins University Press, 1932).

42. On the ruler cults and their influence on society, see Dorothy Burr Thompson, *Ptolemaic Oinochoai and Portraits in Faience* (Oxford, England: Clarendon Press, 1973); and P.M. Fraser, *Ptolemaic Alexandria* (Oxford, England: Clarendon Press, 1972), vol. 1, ch. 5. Thompson makes the fascinating suggestion (68, 71, 118) that artistic contests may have been held at the celebration of the Arsinoeia, a festival in honor of the deified Arsinoe II.

43. Pomeroy, *Women in Egypt*, 59–72; additional information in her "*Technikai kai Mousikai*: The Education of Women in the Fourth Century and in the Hellenistic Period," *American Journal of Ancient History* 2, no. 1 (1977):51–68.

44. See Sarah Pomeroy, "Supplementary Notes on Erinna," *Zeitschrift für Papyrologie und Epigraphik* 32 (1978):17–21; Sylvia Barnard, "Hellenistic Women Poets," *Classical Journal* 73, no. 3 (Feb.–Mar. 1978):204–13; Marilyn B. Arthur, "The Tortoise and the Mirror: Erinna *PSI* 1090," *Classical World* 74, no. 2 (Oct. 1980):53–65; Marilyn B. Skinner, "Briseis, the Trojan Women, and Erinna," *Classical World* 75, no. 5 (1982):265–69; Marilyn B. Skinner, "Sapphic Nossis," *Arethusa* 22, no. 1 (Spring 1989):5–18; and Jane M. Snyder, *The Woman and the Lyre* (Carbondale: Southern Illinois University Press, 1989), ch. 3.

45. The Ptolemaic queens certainly had the power to reward and even make famous those poets who best reflected their feminine concerns. Theocritus' *Idyll* 15, in which two Alexandrian housewives attend a festival for Adonis, sumptuously provided by Arsinoe II, may be an example of a poem designed to please the female monarch.

46. The *Hymns* can be found in the Loeb Classical Library edition of *Callimachus*, ed.

A.W. Mair (Cambridge, Mass.: Harvard University Press, 1959); and *Callimachus: Hymns, Epigrams, Select Fragments*, trans. Stanley Lombardo and Diane Rayor (Baltimore, Md.: Johns Hopkins University Press, 1988).

47. See Anthony W. Bulloch, "The Future of a Hellenistic Illusion: Some Observations on Callimachus and Religion," *Museum Helveticum* 41, no. 4 (Oct. 1984):209–30, who concludes that "the religious sensibility itself . . . is fractured here" (230). It is instructive that he bases his argument on the "mimetic" hymns, which are in fact the ones about goddesses.

48. See the two studies by K.J. MacKay, *Erysichthon: A Callimachean Comedy* and *The Poet at Play: Kallimachos, The Bath of Pallas* (both, Leiden: E.J. Brill, 1962).

49. On the cult identification of the queens with these goddesses, see Fraser, *Ptolemaic Alexandria*, 1:213–46, and Pomeroy, *Women in Egypt*, 28–40.

50. The most important fragments of Callimachus are translated in the Loeb edition of C.A. Trypanis (Cambridge, Mass.: Harvard University Press, 1975).

51. Scholars are now beginning to adapt to the analysis of Roman society the methodology applied to Greek culture by Adkins, *Merit and Responsibility*. See, e.g., J.D. Minyard, *Lucretius and the Late Republic: An Essay in Roman Intellectual History* (Leiden: E.J. Brill, 1985).

52. While the relatively high status accorded women in Roman society has long been recognized, Judith Hallett, *Fathers and Daughters in Roman Society: Women and the Elite Family* (Princeton, N.J.: Princeton University Press, 1984), argues that its cause is the important position of the daughter in the family. See also Suzanne Dixon, *The Roman Mother* (Norman: University of Oklahoma Press, 1988), who argues that the salient role of the Roman mother was not that of a gentle nurturer, but, like the role of the father, that of a stern custodian of traditional morality.

53. See Amy Richlin, *The Garden of Priapus: Sexuality and Aggression in Roman Humor* (New Haven, Conn.: Yale University Press, 1983), esp. ch. 3.

54. The quotation is from the first *Letter to Caesar*, attributed to Sallust, 9.3. For additional information, see Nikolaos Petrocheilos, *Roman Attitudes to the Greeks* (Athens: Char. Kovanis, 1974); J.P.V.D. Balsdon, *Roman and Aliens* (Chapel Hill: University of North Carolina Press, 1979), 30–54; and Erich S. Gruen, *The Hellenistic World and the Coming of Rome* (Berkeley: University of California Press, 1984), 1:250–72.

55. On the uses of this "counter-culture" persona adopted by male elegists, see Judith P. Hallett, "The Role of Women in Roman Elegy," *Women in the Ancient World: The Arethusa Papers*, ed. John Peradotto and J.P. Sullivan (Albany: State University of New York Press, 1984), 241–62.

56. For details, see David O. Ross, Jr., *Backgrounds to Augustan Poetry* (Cambridge, England: Cambridge University Press, 1975), 9–15; and R.O.A.M. Lyne, *The Latin Love Poets: From Catullus to Horace* (Oxford, England: Clarendon Press, 1980), 24–41.

57. Even in antiquity (see Martial 11.6, 14–16) the poem was given an obscene interpretation, the sparrow being seen as a symbol for Catullus' penis. For modern interpretations of this sort, E.N. Genovese, "Symbolism in the *Passer* Poems," *Maia* 26, no. 1 (Jan.–Mar. 1974):121–25; Giuseppe Giangrande, "Catullus' Lyrics on the *Passer*," *Museum Philologicum Londinense* 1 (1975):137–46; Richard W. Hooper, "In Defence of Catullus' Dirty Sparrow," *Greece and Rome* 32, no. 2. (Oct. 1985) 162–78. H.D. Jocelyn, "On Some Unnecessarily Indecent Interpretations of Catullus 2 and 3," *Amerian Journal of Philology* 101 (1980):421–41, has argued against the interpretation. What is clear from the controversy is that some male readers factor out the feminine aspects of the poem and interpret it in terms of male sexuality.

58. See J.P. Sullivan, *Propertius: A Critical Introduction* (Cambridge, England: Cam-

bridge University Press, 1976), 91–101, who interprets Propertius' relationship with Cynthia in terms of one of Freud's character types, the man who loves only harlots. This interpretation assumes that social conventions in ancient and modern cultures are the same.

59. See the influential article by A.W. Allen, "Sunt Qui Propertium Malint," in *Critical Essays on Roman Literature*, ed. J.P. Sullivan (Cambridge, Mass.: Harvard University Press, 1962), 107–48.

60. On the feminine aspect of Catullus' pose as a lover, see Eve Adler, *Catullan Self-Revelation* (New York: Arno, 1981), esp. ch. 7.

61. Marilyn B. Skinner, "Clodia Metelli," *Transactions of the American Philological Association* 113 (1983):273–87.

Seeing, Reading, Knowing:
The Lesbian Appropriation of Literature

Bonnie Zimmerman

Feminist critics have demonstrated that literary texts and acts of reading are gendered, that it matters whether a writer, reader, or critic is male or female. The question addressed in this essay is, if a text has gender, does it also have sex? To put it more seriously, does the affectional preference, or sexual orientation, of a writer and more specifically of a reader or critic influence the ways in which she reads texts and criticizes them? How are "literary seeing and critical knowing"—to quote Joan Hartman and Ellen Messer-Davidow—"centered in a [lesbian] self?"[1] My assumption is that lesbianism, like heterosexuality, is a way of seeing and knowing the world. How we understand the self and the world that constitutes it — and that it constitutes — affects how we read and understand literature.

No one is born with a perspective; perspective is something we acquire as a result of living in the world. The kind of perspective we acquire is determined partly by the social meaning of certain conditions of birth, such as our gender or race. Gender, for instance, is supposed to be fixed at a very young age—perhaps as young as eighteen months. From that point on, family and society firmly impose a gendered perspective on the girl or boy, one that will mark the child's consciousness, her point of view, for her entire life, whether she accepts or rejects given gender constructs. Racial and ethnic perspectives, and possibly those of class as well (when not obscured by a social mythology of classlessness), may also be developed early in life. But the process of developing a lesbian or gay perspective is not so clear, partly because women become lesbians any time from puberty to old age. Furthermore, there is little agreement among lesbians as to whether or not one is born gay, as one is born female or black. Lesbian writers of retrospective narratives often claim to have felt themselves to *be* lesbian from birth, or age two, or certainly from puberty, and thus to have always had a lesbian perspective. Many claim that there is an "essential" lesbian vision, marked by strong attractions to another girl or woman, feelings of difference, or perhaps rejection of traditional female socialization.

But fictional and autobiographical accounts of lesbian identity formation are retrospective, products of the very perspective that they purport to explain. They tend to isolate factors that create a sense of continuity within the self, while ignoring factors that clash with current identity.[2] For example, a woman might focus on the fact that she was intimate friends with Sally at age six and fail to note that so were a dozen other girls, none of whom became lesbians. I would suggest that lesbianism is not an essential identity (whether biologically or developmentally produced) that somehow can be mined from the deep recesses of the self, but rather, a way of knowing and acting — a mode of communication between self and world. It may very well be that lesbian identity and perspectivity are fluid, overlapping with heterosexual female or gay male perspectives. Most lesbians see the world as a heterosexual for some period of their lives and develop a multiple perspectivity — a form of cultural "bilingualism" — that can reinforce the connections, rather than the oppositions, between lesbian and heterosexual feminist perspectives.

Nevertheless, at a certain point some women act upon their feelings, choose a different life path, and claim a personal and sometimes public self-definition as a lesbian. It seems to me, then, that *choice* is essential to our understanding of lesbian perspectivity, even if biological or developmental factors push some women toward making that choice. That choice may involve nothing more (nor less) than the gender of sexual partners, or it may involve a totally transformed political stance in the world. But, however it is understood by the individual, wherever she places herself on the "lesbian continuum," lesbian identity is established by seeing the world anew as a lesbian more than by a sexual act or by birthright.[3] Lesbianism is not something that happens to a woman, it is something she seeks and discovers, whether in the world or in herself. At some point a woman must "come out"— that is, adopt a lesbian identity or point of view. The more self-reflective and self-conscious one is — the more one is aware of one's agency — the more defined one's lesbian perspective will be. This is the position from which I will be developing my argument. As a self-conscious lesbian, I choose, I act, I claim responsibility for how I know the world. And I think this can serve as a useful model for how I choose to know the world (in my case) as a woman and a Jew. Our ubiquitous social mythology enforces a perspective that is white, male, Christian, straight; seeing from the position of the Other (to use Simone DeBeauvoir's existentialist terminology) forces me radically to restructure this pervasive ideology.

What then is a lesbian perspective? How do lesbians see, read, and know the world? Many lesbian critics and philosophers agree that lesbians see, not from the center of what Marilyn Frye names "phallocratic reality," but from its edge.[4] And because lesbians see "obliquely," as Monique Wittig puts it, we note different lights and shades, different presences and absences, different emphases and omissions.[5] Frye uses the metaphor of the theater to explain what lesbians see. Reality is organized by men as a stage on which they are the principal actors and women the stagehands and backdrop. To maintain the fiction of this reality, no one must attend to any other movements but those of the main actors, men. Reality relies on not seeing the background, women. But lesbians construct an alternative reality by attending to, or focusing on, that background. In Frye's words, lesbians "are in a position to see things that cannot be seen from within the system. What lesbians see is what makes them lesbians and their seeing is why they have to be excluded [from phallocratic reality]. Lesbians are woman-seers."[6]

How is lesbian seeing different from male or heterosexual female seeing? Traditionally, men see women in relation to themselves as sexual objects or as domestic servants. Throughout history, men also have seen women as exemplars or archetypes, both positive and negative: Eve or Mary, witch or saint, angel in the house or unsexed woman. Thus men see women either as appendages or as a class, but not as individual and independent persons with agencies and perspectives of their own. Heterosexual women see other women in more complex ways. Some state proudly that they do not see women at all ("I prefer talking with men"; "Sex has nothing to do with my work or life"), but this stance is ingenuous. In fact, these "queen bees" do see women in the background and are uncomfortable noticing what male-centered vision obscures. They may even more assiduously maintain the male illusion of female invisibility. Another way heterosexual women see other women, according to patriarchal mythology, is as rivals. This vision results when a woman watches the stage wearing the distorting lenses of androcentrism. She still sees men at the center, but takes note as well of any woman who inches closer to them than she is. Finally, a heterosexual woman may see other women within the roles and institutions established by a male-centered perspective: i.e., woman as wife, as mother, as seductress, as mistress, even as independent woman (since "independent" here actually functions as a synecdoche for "independent from men or marriage"). This was the approach taken by the earliest feminist critics in texts and courses generally titled "Images of Women" (an approach still used in classrooms) and is, to my mind, a basically heterosexual approach to literary criticism.

On the other hand, lesbian and heterosexual feminists see women similarly, in that their visions both include women relating to other women. To quote from an early lesbian-feminist polemic, "The Woman-Identified Woman": "It is the primacy of women relating to women, of women creating a new consciousness of and with each other which is at the heart of women's liberation, and the basis for the cultural revolution."[7] Lesbians brought female bonding to the center of feminist discourse, and now most feminists see women in relation to other women, often minimizing whatever male or heterosexual action is taking place on the world stage. Thus, one way I would restate Frye's definition is that lesbians are woman-relating-to-woman seers.

This places at the center of a lesbian perspective women-bonding and female friendship, as in Barbara Smith's interpretation of *Sula*, Blanche Wiesen
Cook's analysis of female support networks, and Lillian Faderman's study
of romantic friendship.[8] These critics and historians look obliquely at phal-
locentric reality, placing what had been central — men and women's dependence on men — off-center or indeed off-stage. Our perspective shifts to what
had been background, women's relationships with women, thus making reality gynocentric.

As I have stated, many if not all heterosexual feminists now see women
in this lesbian way. There is considerable overlap between a lesbian and
feminist vision. Patriarchs know this to be true. They insist that all feminists
are lesbians ("You're taking a women's studies course? But they're all dykes
over there!") and suspect that all lesbians are feminists. The key point made
by Adrienne Rich in "Compulsory Heterosexuality and Lesbian Existence"
is that no firm line can be drawn between lesbian experience and other female experience. But many lesbians know — or believe we know — that we
see women differently than do even the most feminist of heterosexual women.
What is the distinctiveness of, to paraphrase Djuna Barnes, this vision with
a difference?[9]

The most immediate and self-evident (to a lesbian) answer is that lesbians
include sexuality — desire and passion — as a possibility in women's relationships with each other. Lesbians not only *see* women, but desire and feel
passion for them. This is certainly one part of the discord that often exists between lesbians and heterosexual women, whether feminist or not. Heterosexual women may fear that lesbians will see them as sexual objects, as men
do. Indeed, many lesbians, particularly those who come out as a result of
feminist awakening, avoid the use of sexual imagery in their writing as a
reaction to patriarchal reification of both heterosexual women and lesbians.
But this is a futile avoidance. Lesbian being-in-the-world is sexual; it is
largely our sexuality that distinguishes us from other women. But not sex
alone — lesbians also feel romantic and passionate about women. Thus a
lesbian reader of literature will note women relating to each other, but see
and emphasize the sexual, romantic, and/or passionate elements of this relation. Furthermore, a lesbian perspective focuses on the primacy and dura-
tion of the female friendship. This is why *Sula* makes sense as a lesbian text,
despite its pervasive heterosexuality. The friendship between Sula and Nel
is primary; it is more important in their lives than any other connection,
and it endures beyond death.

Finally, lesbians look beyond individual relationships to female communities that do not need or want men. Although I wish to keep women center-
stage in my argument, I do need to point out that much lesbian reading and
writing quite explicitly excludes men (except, perhaps, as a symbol of danger)

from the newly designed theater. What lesbians see is what women may always have suspected: that men are not essential to women. Of course, in actual patriarchal societies men are represented as essential for survival, even for making the world meaningful. It is therefore simply impossible for women—even the purest lesbian separatist—to avoid seeing and interacting with men in some way. But in a literary text—the lesbian utopia—writers and readers imagine possibilities that do not actually exist. Thus Marilyn Frye's comment that lesbians are "woman-*seers*" is actually a pun. Lesbians "see" women, and also have a "prophetic" knowledge or idealized vision that women could live fully and contentedly without men. In a lesbian perspective, women are both necessary and sufficient.

The creation of new possibilities and the transformation of old realities by writers and readers is central to my theory of lesbian perspectivity. Because self-conscious lesbians see the world in a particular way, we also write and read literature from a unique vantage point. I want to explore here some ways in which lesbians read or "misread" texts. In *The Resisting Reader*, Judith Fetterley argued, "The first act of the feminist critic must be to become a resisting rather than an assenting reader and, by this refusal to assent, to begin the process of exorcising the male mind that has been implanted in us."[10] I would go even further and suggest that lesbian-feminist readers resist "heterotexts" by privately rewriting and thus appropriating them as lesbian texts. There is a certain point in a plot or character development— the "what if" moment—when a lesbian reader refuses to assent anymore to the heterosexual imperative, a point in the narrative labyrinth where she simply cuts a hole and follows her own path.

I am calling this reading strategy "perverse" to reclaim a word defined by the dictionary as "willfully determined not to do what is expected or desired."[11] The emphasis in this definition is on *will*, that is, again to turn to the dictionary, "the faculty of conscious and particularly of deliberate action; the power of control the mind has over its own actions." Thus a perverse reader is one highly conscious of her own agency, who takes an active role in shaping the text she reads in accordance with her perspective on the world.

Two parallel scenes from Jane Rule's story, "Inland Passage," demonstrate how a text can be interpreted according to the reader's perspective.[12] This is a simple story of two mature women falling in love as they cruise the inland passage to Alaska. Fidelity first presents herself to Troy as another heterosexual woman by interpreting a scene before them:

> "See those two over there?" Fidelity said, nodding to a nondescript pair of middle-aged women. "One's a lady cop. The other's her prisoner."
> "How did you figure that out?"
> "Saw the handcuffs. That's why they're sitting side by side."[13]

After Fidelity and Troy have fallen in love and come out to each other, they see the two women again. This time Fidelity explicates the scene differently:

> "I was wrong about those two over there," Fidelity said. "They sit side by side because they're lovers." "And you thought so in the first place," Troy said. Fidelity nodded.[14]

The text that Fidelity reads presents itself as a blank page: the two women are a "nondescript pair." It is Fidelity, the reader, the agent, who creates the story about them, derived not only from her point of view, but also from the point of view she wishes to make known to the world. In the first reading, Fidelity seems to read as a heterosexual; in the second, as a lesbian. But even the first time, she is reading not as a heterosexual but as a closeted lesbian. The clue is that the story she relates is one of imprisonment and bondage, an ironic reference to the heterosexual myth that lesbians capture and tie other women to them. The second reading deconstructs the first: imprisonment is revealed to be mutual love.

Fidelity is a very perceptive and creative misreader. She illustrates a feminist or lesbian-feminist reading strategy that Elaine Showalter and Sharon O'Brien describe as an oscillation between figure and ground.[15] Thus we might say that a lesbian has double vision, a self-reflective point of view that attends to the text as it has been constructed by hetero- or andro-centric readings (the traditional figure that becomes the ground) and as it is newly constructed by lesbian awareness (the traditional ground that is reconstituted as the figure). Further, a conscious lesbian reader—that is, a lesbian aware of her own agency, her role in constructing the meaning of a text— will attend to the way in which the figure is shaped by the ground, and the way the ground is changed by noticing the figure. If lesbians are women who attend to women attending to each other, then a lesbian will note the centrality of Sula and Nel's love and at the same time acknowledge that this love is powerfully muted by the heterosexual dynamics of the novel. A lesbian critic might point to the redemptive role of female friendship in George Eliot's novels and counterpoint the "homoerotic" climax of a novel (the meeting between Maggie and Lucy in *The Mill on the Floss,* or between Dorothea and Rosamond in *Middlemarch*) with its heterosexual climax (Maggie and Tom's death embrace, or Dorothea and Will's confession of love). A lesbian critic might attend to Lizzie's erotic plea to her sister Laura in Rossetti's "Goblin Market"—"Eat me, drink me, love me,/Laura, make much of me"— and "make much of" the poem as a parable of how pure love between women overcomes impure lust between women and men. In doing so, she would be able to explain why husbands are so conspicuously absent from the ostensibly heterosexual ending of the poem.

Another text that has drawn the attention of lesbian critics is Kate Chopin's *The Awakening*.[16] But, surprisingly, even they have failed to attend to the background of the novel where woman sees woman. Behind the romantic heterosexual plot that establishes the novel's foreground lies a shadowy lesbian story. Edna Pontellier has close friendships with two women, Adele Ratignolle and Mlle. Reisz. Each represents a road not taken by Edna: the path of the contented wife from which she strays and the path of the artist on which she stumbles and falls. These women are both monitory figures and real presences in the novel, with whom Edna forges "the subtle bond which we call sympathy, which we might as well call love."[17] Each suggests an alternative world for Edna, in which women might be primary for themselves and each other. With Adele Ratignolle, Edna shares one exquisite afternoon alone and unshackled on the beach, a moment in female space or what Elaine Showalter named the "wild zone."[18] Edna loosens her clothing (signifying both freedom and eroticism) as the hot sun, the novel's symbol of sexuality, pours over them. She recounts her adolescence, a time of possibility before marriage and motherhood tied her to her present life. The scene ends with the entrance of Robert, accompanied by the children the two women have momentarily forgotten. Robert is no liberatory figure here, but one more actor in the world of men, marriage, and motherhood that Edna is soon to flee.

The connection between Edna and Adele is exceedingly sensual; the one between Edna and Mlle. Reisz is spiritual and intellectual. Mlle. Reisz's self-definition, indifference to men and family life, and admiration for Edna can be read as subtle suggestions of the lesbian. After the Pontelliers return to New Orleans and Robert leaves for Mexico, Mlle. Reisz becomes Edna's mentor and confidante. But, as Robert's physical presence interrupts the communion between Edna and Adele on the beach, so his textual presence interrupts the communication between Edna and Mlle. Reisz. Their meetings revolve around his letters, and, while Mlle. Reisz soothes (and seduces) Edna with her music, Edna drifts back into fatal fantasies of heterosexual romance.

Such a lesbian reading of *The Awakening* has a number of consequences. One is simply that it makes the text more personally meaningful to lesbian readers. As one of my students responded when asked if she thought she read differently as a lesbian, "Of course. Rembember that scene in *The Awakening*? That's *my* scene!" Furthermore, by drawing attention to the lesbian figure in the ground, we are able to see new complexity in women's past and contemporary lives. Lesbian historians have established that many women did choose women over men in the late nineteenth century. What forces prevented Edna from doing so? How would her life have been different if she had? How would our lives be different were we able to wander or reside in the wild zone? And, finally, in a lesbian reading, *The Awakening* appears not so much as a pathetic or heroic tale, but rather as an ironic tragedy. Edna is a tragic heroine; her flaw is her inability to detach herself from men and male definitions of love and romance. Kate Chopin, however, distances herself from her heroine by portraying one way out of her muddle: the friendhsip and even the erotic companionship of other women.

Perverse reading reveals subtexts of female friendship previously unrevealed; it also leads to the rewriting of cultural stereotypes and literary conventions by reversing the values attached to the idea of lesbianism. In *Desert of the Heart*, for example, Jane Rule revised such negative conventions as the "mark of Cain," the "narcissistic mirror," and the "life against nature" that were used to establish a deviance model of lesbianism.[19] In this, Rule anticipated the lesbian feminist movement that emerged in the early 1970s and revised the old text that society had written for lesbians. That text was so riddled with errors that is was not even fit for editing, so lesbian readers, of life and literature, claimed the right to have a literature infused with positive symbolism. Our authors, many of them writing for the first time, provided positive, validating images steeped in the emerging mythology of lesbian-feminism. Molly Bolt replaced Stephen Gordon as the quintessential lesbian hero; Patience and Sarah idylled in the green world undisturbed by any intrusive corn god; the hill women of the Wanderground infused the old Amazonian myth with new power and sensuality.[20]

Furthermore, lesbian readers approach the old destructive stereotypes obliquely, with contemporary lesbian and feminist consciousnesses, exposing the partiarchal and heterosexual bias behind them, stripping them of their negativity, and sometimes transforming them into images of power and promise. The lesbian vampire becomes a Lilith figure who is our ancestral sister. The man-hating dyke arrogantly states her reasons for coming to such a position. The mark of Cain is worn proudly as a talisman against patriarchal evil. The existence that patriarchy labels as a sin or perversion, the lesbian, from her vantage point, sees as a logical strategy for survival.

What is also necessary for the survival of the lesbian resisting reader is an imaginative mind that can invent lesbian plots even if they are not exactly there. My theory of perverse reading was developed from just such a spinning of a new plot from an author's actual text. Let me give one example of this reading strategy taken from popular culture. During the 1984 television season, the writers of *Dallas* introduced a new character, Jamie Ewing, who first appeared as a tough, no-nonsense tomboy. A strong friendship developed between her and Suellen Ewing, herself rebelling against the infidelity of her notorious husband, J.R. As a lesbian reader/viewer, I immediately noticed that the scenes between Jamie and Suellen almost always took place in the bedroom, suggesting both lesbian eroticism and that female space in which Edna and Adele idylled in *The Awakening*. The triangle created by the three characters finally was sundered in a remarkable confrontation, during which Jamie challenged J.R.'s control of Suellen. The powerful iconography of the scene contrasted an isolated J.R. with the two closely bonded women.

At that moment, the lesbian viewer could move in two directions. She could follow the writer's lead toward the conventional heterosexual (and sexist) resolution: J.R. breaks up the two women, precipitating Suellen's decline into alcohol dependency (for the second or third time in the series' history), and Jamie's transformation into a spiteful, clinging feminine stereotype. Or the lesbian viewer could write her own plot — the one that is never seen on prime-time television — in which Suellen and Jamie thumb their noses at J.R. and the entire Ewing clan, and walk off the set together. Like Carolyn in Lisa Alther's *Other Women*, I put myself and my point of view in the text:

> As she sipped her coffee, she watched a movie about two career girls on the make in New York City. She realized she'd seen it before. The good-looking one got Jimmy Stewart and the other one got promoted to editor. If only once the girls would get each other. But probably that was asking too much of Twentieth Century Fox.[21]

That may be too much to ask, but lesbians must ask just the same. As one of my students put it, we're constantly frustrated at what's not there (as well as at what is *endlessly* there). The world lesbians live in consists of women with short hair and jeans, or long hair and pearls, who are lesbians. Daughters come out and do or do not break their mothers' hearts. Married women get fed up with men or simply fall in love with their next-door neighbors. Some women who get breast cancer, or write Gothic novels, or go underground, or get tenured are lesbians. But, except for the submerged genre of lesbian fiction that seldom can be found outside feminist bookstores, our literature and mass media rarely express a lesbian point of view. Even in mainstream feminist literature, life is unremittingly and often uncritically heterosexual. When it is not, as in a novel like Doris Grumbach's *Chamber Music*, the lesbian reader experiences a moment of almost sublime surprise and satisfaction. More often, however, we feel betrayed. To continue reading at all, we must somehow see and know literature differently, imagining possibilities otherwise ignored and suppressed. In this way we appropriate it for our own needs and incorporate it into our own world view.

In short, lesbians come to literature with different emotions and experiences. For us, the feminist ideal is not necessarily an equal partnership between a previously domineering husband and a dominated wife — the staple feminist plot. Adolescent crushes on best friends or older women are not phases to outgrow. Two adult women falling in love is not another obligatory lesbian interlude. A lesbian character getting her head sliced off is neither amusing nor ironic. We have a different perspective, certainly on everything involving sexuality, gender identity, and human relations. One woman's happy ending may be another's disappointment. And one woman's embarrassment may be another's reward.

Let me emphasize that the lesbian resisting reader, reading perversely, is not merely demanding a plot or character study that the writer has not chosen to create. She is picking up on hints and possibilities that the author, consciously or not, has strewn in the text. A text that manifests certain symbolic elements—perhaps the absence of men, of women's attention to men, or of marked femininity; perhaps the presence of female bonding, or of strong and independent female characters—may trigger the act of lesbian reading. The reader is simply bringing to the text an understanding of the world as *she* has learned to read and thus to know it.

Lesbians (like most members of stigmatized groups) learn very quickly to "read" life. The very nature of lesbianism—a minority status that can be identified by few if any visible signs—requires that lesbians become skilled readers of external appearance and behavior. Judy Grahn's short story, "Boys at a Rodeo," is an excellent illustration of this ability.[22] As the narrator watches the competition for rodeo queen, she notices that the "last loser sits well on a scrubby little pony and lives with her aunt and uncle. I pick her for the dyke even though it is speculation without clues. I can't help it, it's a pleasant habit."[23] Later she observes other participants in the rodeo: "One small girl is not disheartened by the years of bad training, the ridiculous cross-field run, the laughing superior man on his horse, or the shape shifting goat. She downs it in a beautiful flying tackle. This makes me whisper, as usual, 'that's the dyke.'"[24] As Grahn's phrase, "speculation without clues," suggests, lesbians are like cryptographers or detectives—or literary critics—for all life presents itself to lesbians as a coded text in need of deciphering and explication.

But there is a significant difference between such active explication as a "common reader" (to use Virginia Woolf's term) and traditional literary criticism. That difference provides insight into the impact of professional training on literary reading and into the way in which academics construct knowledge. In my explication of Jane Rule's story, for example, I functioned as a trained literary critic bringing her personal perspective to an interpretation of an unambiguously lesbian text. But this training more often causes conflicts as I read "perversely" texts that are ostensibly heterosexual or ambiguously sexual. I have been taught to have such respect for, or fear of, the written text, that when I compensate for the paucity of lesbian literature—for the false world projected by our culture—by spinning a different story out of the author's material, I consider such behavior to be irresponsible.

I suspect myself of indulging in wish fulfillment. In other words, my literary training eliminates my individuality, my perspective, from my reading. As a common reader of life and literature, I feel responsible to myself and to a community of lesbian readers. But as a trained critic, I am uncomfortably aware of my membership in a literary community that finds my perspective "narrow" or "distorting." Like Grahn's narrator, I worry that I am speculating without clues, that, "as usual," I am seeing what is not there. The very social context (heterosexism) that my reading intends to challenge becomes a constraint upon the possibility of such a reading.

The only way out of this circular prison, I believe, is to un-train the critical self, not by abandoning the techniques of criticism, but by abandoning the impersonal attitude that critical training cultivates. This means reading audaciously and often "naively"—i.e., as one reads privately but fears to do publicly. By doing so, lesbian critics have provided fresh and radical interpretations of literary texts, traditions, and even values. As Melanie Kaye puts it, "What does it mean when people can envision only two possible ends to any story [i.e., marriage or death]?"[25] The self-conscious lesbian reader sees or imagines other possible endings that expand opportunities not only for writers of texts but also for women actively creating their lives. Thus, lesbian critical readings are not only possible but necessary to revitalize the conventions we find stale and meaningless.

This discussion of how a lesbian perspective shapes reading and knowing leads me to thoughts about a feminist theory of perspectivity. White heterosexual men define their perspective on the world as objective truth and thus discount women, people of color, and homosexuals as deviant perceivers. Feminists, as well as other theorists, have insisted, with modest success, that "truth" be redefined to account for the values and visions of those considered "other" in the Western world view. Who will determine the values assigned to competing perspectives? To adapt questions raised by Jane Tompkins concerning the relationship between discourse and power: "What makes one set of perceptual strategies or literary conventions win out over another? If the world is the product of interpretation, then who or what determines which interpretive system will prevail?"[26] I guess that the determiners of truth will be those with the power of definition. Currently, in the academy, this power lies in the hands of those who edit texts and journals, hire and fire junior faculty, approve or reject dissertation topics, disperse grants, and so on. These hands still belong, for the most part, to the very white men who have established their perspective as objective truth.

But women's studies have had an impact on the academy. Increasingly women are being absorbed into the decision-making body, and some of them articulate a feminist notion of literary value and meaning. Given the fact that people with power will prefer to incorporate newcomers as similar to themselves as possible, it is hardly to be expected that, now or in the long run, these new powermongers will be lesbians, women of color, or women outside academia. It is therefore possible that feminist inquiry itself will maintain the competitive marketplace of ideas. We have often battled between a radical feminist perspective and a socialist feminist perspective, or between separatist and integrationist strategies. Of particular relevance to my argument are the struggles between lesbians and heterosexuals. Lesbians insist that heterosexuality is the result of brainwashing and not at all a feminist option. Heterosexuals devoutly wish lesbians would stop making trouble and return to the bedroom where they belong. The history of the Women's Movement suggests that feminists are vulnerable to the same tendency that we urge the academy to abandon—the tendency to impose a dominant perspective.

Nevertheless, many feminists have proven to be sensitive to the moral persuasion of people who articulate perspectives different from those of individuals in the mainstream (or the feminist tributary) of literary criticism. Feminist critics understand that criticism must incorporate actively the visions and insights of lesbians, women of color, and working-class women. And lesbians (for example) need to encourage replacing the competitive model of academic inquiry with a communicative model based on empathic understanding and respect for diversity.

The model of inquiry proposed by this essay could be one alternative to the quasi-military model alluded to in Tompkins' question quoted above. Ours is a model that should appeal to literary critics who understand that no single interpretation of a text is complete without reference to many others. Conflicts and differences will always occur among varying interpretations. Far from agonizing over these differences, literary critics revel in them (albeit quite nastily at times). In fact, our careers depend upon our ability to come up with new interpretations of old texts. Literature can best be understood and appreciated through interactions among differing interpretations. Perhaps this is why lesbians and other "deviant" perceivers have had an increasing influence on literary study.

Does this mean that all perspectives are equally tolerable, valid, and valuable? Certainly not. All perspectives result from the same set of factors, primarily a person's social and cultural situation (her sex, race, class, sexuality, and so on) and personal history. What distinguishes the validity of one perspective from another is how self-reflective it is and how open it is to admitting the validity of other perspectives. There is nothing wrong with seeing and knowing the world as a heterosexual, but there is a good deal wrong with seeing and knowing it as a heterosexist. The heterosexual perceiver would be aware of how her perspective is shaped by her particular situation, and she would seek out and welcome lesbian perspectives that resonate with her own. The heterosexist perceiver, on the other hand, might not even be aware of other agents or her own agency, and thus would posit her perspective as the natural or universal vision of the world. Furthermore, once aware of lesbian perspectives, she might cling to her culturally dominant and privileged position and dismiss them as irrelevant.

I believe that feminist inquiry must continue to trust that such narrow-mindedness is the product of ignorance, not malice, and that, as lesbian scholars articulate both a lesbian perspective and a critique of the heterosexist perspective, most unreflective thinkers will change and adjust their own vision of the world. The only perspective that has no place in feminist inquiry is the one born of prejudice and maintained in anger or fear. Furthermore, perspective or point of view is only part of the project feminist scholars are undertaking. I cannot agree that "the world is the product of interpretation" alone; the world is also the product of human activity. *Point of view* — how we as concrete historical agents understand the world — must become *standpoint* — the position from which we try to change the world. At this time, the similarities among various feminist perspectives — radical, socialist, lesbian, heterosexual, black, white — may be more crucial than their differences. When it comes to acting in the world, even when the world is nothing more than the academy, it is often to our advantage, indeed our survival, to act from one standpoint.

I have been searching for a concluding metaphor to express my vision of feminist inquiry. Perhaps this inquiry is like a mosaic of contrasting yet harmonizing viewpoints, or a kaleidoscope continually transforming patterns as it is twirled. But the metaphor I like best is one that I often use in literature classes. The encyclopedia my family owned when I was a child had a marvelous section on human anatomy. Each system of the body was drawn on transparencies laid one on top of the next. Each system could be viewed separately with complete attention to its use and meaning in the human body. But viewed together, one through the other, a three-dimensional image of the body as a whole was obtained. Our perspectives — of class, race, sexuality, political persuasion — are not discrete entities that, to use yet another metaphor, can be mixed and matched like Villager separates. Perspectivity, rather, involves the continual layering and deepening of visions in communication, not in competition, with each other.

Notes

1. Joan Hartman and Ellen Messer-Davidow, "Learning to See: Feminist Perspectives in Literary Study," paper presented in the session on "Critical Issues in Feminist Inquiry: Agency and Perspective," National Women's Studies Association Convention, New Brunswick, N.J., June 1984.

2. See Bonnie Zimmerman, "The Politics of Transliteration: Lesbian Personal Narratives," *Signs* 9, no. 4. (Summer 1984):667–68; and Marilyn Frye, review of *The Coming Out Stories*, ed. Julia Penelope Stanley and Susan J. Wolfe, in *Sinister Wisdom* 14 (Summer 1980):97–98.

3. The phrase "lesbian continuum" was coined by Adrienne Rich in "Compulsory Heterosexuality and Lesbian Existence," *Signs* 5, no. 4 (Summer 1980):631–60. Rich uses it to indicate the congruence between female friendship and lesbian love. I am using it to suggest the variety of self-concepts among lesbians.

4. Marilyn Frye, *The Politics of Reality: Essays in Feminist Theory* (Trumansburg, N.Y.: Crossing Press, 1983), 162.

5. Monique Wittig, "The Point of View: Universal or Particular?", *Feminist Issues* 3, no. 2 (Fall 1983):65.

6. Frye, *Politics of Reality*, 173.

7. Radicalesbians, "The Woman-Identified Woman," rptd. in *Liberation Now!*, ed. Deborah Babcox and Madeline Belkin (New York: Dell, 1971), 292.

8. Barbara Smith, "Toward a Black Feminist Criticism," *Conditions Two* (Oct. 1977):25–44; Blanche Wiesen Cook, "Female Support Networks in the Nineteenth Century," *Chrysalis* 3 (Autumn 1977):43–61; Lillian Faderman, *Surpassing the Love of Men* (New York: William Morrow, 1981).

9. Djuna Barnes, *Ladies Almanack* (New York: Harper and Row, 1972), 26. What follows is a discussion of one way of thinking about lesbian seeing. There are many other ways. Monique Wittig, for example, suggests that a lesbian point of view requires the "suppression" of gender ("The Point of View," 64). For Bertha Harris, lesbian existence and vision are those of the "unassimilable" and the "outrageous"; Harris, "*What we mean to say*: Notes Toward Defining the Nature of Lesbian Literature," *Heresies* 3 (Fall 1977):6.

10. Judith Fetterley, *The Resisting Reader* (Bloomington: Indiana University Press, 1978), xxii.

11. All dictionary definitions are taken from *The Random House College Dictionary* (1975).

12. Jane Rule, "Inland Passage," in Rule, *Inland Passage* (Tallahassee, Fla,: Naiad Press, 1985), 211–36.

13. Ibid., 221.

14. Ibid., 235.

15. Elaine Showalter, "Feminist Criticism in the Wilderness," *Critical Inquiry* 8, no. 2 (Winter 1981):204; Sharon O'Brien, "'The Thing Not Named': Willa Cather as a Lesbian Writer," *Signs* 9, no. 4 (Summer 1984):597.

16. See Adrienne Rich on Chopin, *The Awakening*, in Rich, "Compulsory Heterosexuality," 657. Also Kathryn Pyne Addelson, "'On Compulsory Heterosexuality and Lesbian Existence': Defining the Issues," *Signs* 7, no. 1 (Autumn 1981):195–97.

17. Kate Chopin, *The Awakening* (New York: Avon, 1972), 26.

18. Showalter, "Feminist Criticism," 200–1.

19. See Marilyn R. Schuster, "Strategies for Survival: The Subtle Subversion of Jane Rule," *Feminist Studies* 7, no. 3 (Fall 1981):431–50.

20. See Rita Mae Brown, *Rubyfruit Jungle* (New York: Bantam, 1977); Isabel Miller, *Patience and Sarah* (New York: Fawcett Crest, 1973); Sally Miller Gearhart, *The Wanderground* (Watertown, Mass.: Persephone Press, 1979).

21. Lisa Alther, *Other Women* (New York: Knopf, 1984), 19.

22. Judy Grahn, "Boys at the Rodeo," *Lesbian Fiction*, ed. Elly Bulkin (Watertown, Mass.: Persephone Press, 1981), 11–16.

23. Ibid., 12.

24. Ibid., 13.

25. Melanie Kaye, "Culture Making: Lesbian Classics," *Sinister Wisdom* 13 (Spring 1980):25.

26. Jane P. Tompkins, "The Reader in History: The Changing Shape of Literary Response," in *Reader-Response Criticism: From Formalism to Post-Structuralism*, ed. Jane P. Tompkins (Baltimore, Md.: Johns Hopkins University Press, 1980), 226.

Who Knows?
Identities and Feminist Epistemology

Sandra Harding

As outsiders within, Black feminist scholars form one of several distinct groups
of marginal intellectuals whose perspectives promise to enrich contemporary
sociological discourse. Bringing this group, as well as others who share an
outsider-within status vis-a-vis sociology, into the center of analysis may reveal
views of reality obscured by more orthodox approaches.

> — Patricia Hill Collins, "Learning from the Outsider Within:
> The Sociological Significance of Black Feminist Thought"

. . . traditional scholars overlooked the gender system operating in each of these
three periods, because they accepted without question the perspective of the
males who controlled Greek and Roman society. Feminists, however, by focusing on ancient women, on what we know or can imagine them to have been,
have brought into view a cultural substructure that previously was invisible.

> — Kathryn J. Gutzwiller and Ann Norris Michelini,
> "Women and Other Strangers: Feminist Perspectives in Classical Literature"

. . . lesbians see, not from the center of what Marilyn Frye names "phallocratic
reality," but from its edge. And because lesbians see "obliquely," as Monique
Wittig puts it, we note different lights and shades, different presences and absences, different emphases and omissions. . . . In Frye's words, lesbians "are in a
position to see things that cannot be seen from within the system."

> — Bonnie Zimmerman, "Seeing, Reading, Knowing:
> The Lesbian Appropriation of Literature"

Claiming Identities We Were Taught to Despise[1]

It has been a struggle for feminists to learn precisely how to claim, on behalf
of our research and scholarship, the perspectives that arise from our identities as women, as Black women, as Third World women, as lesbians, as
working-class women. We have claimed the historical realities of our lives
as the places from which our thought and politics not only *do* begin, but
also *should* begin. It has also taken courage to claim these identities for such
purposes when the fathers of our intellectual traditions have insisted for centuries that we are exactly *not* the kinds of persons whose beliefs can ever

be expected to achieve the status of knowledge. They still claim that only the impersonal, disinterested, socially anonymous representatives of human reason — a description that refers to themselves, of course — are capable of producing knowledge. Mere opinion is all that folks like us can hope to produce. (*We* reply that "human reason," reason that claims to be race-free, gender-free, free of sexual identity, and class-free, *is* in fact unselfconsciously racist, sexist, heterosexist, and bourgeois reason.) So it is an extraordinary achievement of feminist thought to have shown, as the essays in this section do, that the perspectives provided by our devalued identities are epistemologically powerful and that the unselfconscious perspective that claims universality is in fact not only partial but also distorting in ways that go beyond its partiality.

The political companion to this kind of feminist epistemological claim has been called "identity politics"; it involves working to emancipate ourselves instead of "humanity." As the Combahee River Collective explains, "Focusing upon our own oppression is embodied in the concept of identity politics. We believe that the most profound and potentially the most radical politics come directly out of our own identity, as opposed to working to end somebody else's oppression."[2] We could think of this politics as "situated politics," and of its epistemological companion as "situated knowledge."[3] In these projects, feminists develop the view that explicitly originates in our own socially devalued activities, instead of the view from a purportedly anonymous perspective or from somebody else's life.

Here I want to add another kind of identity knower to those feminists have developed — one that is derived from the primary identities responsible for feminist ways of knowing, one that must become a widespread and powerful generator of additional feminist insights. In order to prepare the way for presenting this contributor to feminist understandings, I begin by focusing on the ways in which the authors in this section conceptualize identity knowing and on questions their discussions raise for me.

Patricia Hill Collins points out that it is only Black feminists, who have had Black women's experience, who can articulate Black feminist thought, although that thought makes important contributions to the discipline of sociology and so to everyone's knowledge. While the consequences of racism generate common themes in this thought, the diversity of Black women's experiences in different classes and cultures produces different expressions of these themes. Collins develops the notion of a Black feminist standpoint that directs research projects to start off from the understandings available to "outsiders within," such as Black women in disciplines traditionally dominated by elite white men. She argues that we can encourage and institutionalize these "outsider-within" ways of seeing for those who do not have such identities. I do not have an identity as a Black, for I am white. I can use

Black feminist ways of seeing. But can I simultaneously use my own racial identity — my racial situation — as a resource in producing feminist analyses? Or must I suppress my identity as a white in order to do research and scholarship that have antiracist feminist goals? What would it mean to *activate* my identity as a white in seeking antiracist feminist understandings?

Bonnie Zimmerman makes the point that lesbian seeing contributed to heterosexual feminist analyses the ability to see female bonding. Today most feminists, not just lesbians, can see women in relation to other women, and not just to men, in both life and literature. Nevertheless, most lesbians think that in some ways they still do see the world differently not only from sexists, but also from heterosexual feminists. She proposes three such still-distinctive foci of lesbian seeing: women's sexual, romantic, and passionate feelings for other women; the centrality of women's relations with other women; and the possibility that men are not essential to women. Zimmerman also draws attention to the wonderful phenomenon of "perverse readings" in lesbian approaches to heterosexual texts. These readings are perverse in the sense that lesbians are willfully determined not to do what is expected or desired of the reader. Was the ability to see female bonding perverse before heterosexual feminists began to adopt it? Will the presently perverse readings come to be produced also by heterosexual feminists if "feminist policy" expects and desires them to provide such readings? Will these readings be produced by heterosexual male feminists? (Can there be such persons? Are there any?)

Kathryn J. Gutzwiller and Ann Norris Michelini show how it is only feminist analysis, with its concern for women as historical agents in both literature and social life, that has enabled us to see the gender code that structured ancient Greek and Roman poetry and drama. This code was invisible to the traditional upper-class and male classics scholars who identified only with the male heroes and presumed male audiences for these genres. I think it does not distort Gutzwiller and Michelini's intent to interpret them as seeing valuable new feminist analyses as emerging from certain kinds of "relations between women"— a kind of "female bonding," if you will — between the contemporary feminist women scholars and both the women who are characters in classical dramas and poetry and those who are and were in the audiences for these writings. As I read their essay, I found myself identifying with, and vicariously experiencing the situations of, heroic Antigone, Medea the foreigner, and Lesbia the unfaithful mistress who is the target of abuse. (Don't we experience such situations in our institutions every week?!) I think this kind of "female bonding" is central to feminist analyses in every discipline.[4] But how can our male students and colleagues who intend to be antisexist — to be feminist?— activate their identities to generate analyses about gender codes? We certainly don't want them pretending to "read as women" when they cannot have the lives or the experiences that would enable them to do so. How can they use their different identities to generate their own distinctive (feminist?) analyses? Moreover, what are the feminist assumptions that permit contemporary women to identify with other women across two millennia, across the vast cultural differences between Antigone's culture and ours, across the class, race, and sexual identity differences between contemporary female feminist readers and the imagined female audiences for these literatures but that make the possibility of male feminists so problematical?

I raise these questions not as criticisms of these authors or of the knowledge strategies they so brilliantly articulate, but because I think that I glimpse additional forms of situated knowing through the logic of their analyses. I can imagine other feminist identities, secondary ones, standing in the shadows directly behind the ones on which they focus, identities also struggling to emerge as legitimate producers of feminist knowledge. I want to add them to the powerful cast of agents of knowledge they have assembled for us. To do so will not be easy, of course, for these identities that must be activated as generators of knowledge, as historical agents of feminist knowledge, appear to be contradictory or close to it. A male feminist appears to be one such additional socially situated and contradictory knower. Should women spend our time legitimating male feminists? If not, then how can white feminists legitimately generate antiracist knowledge, economically privileged feminists learn to see the world in ways informed by working-class women, heterosexual feminists to think in ways that have been originated by lesbians? I begin by reflecting on the resources that multiple and self-contradictory identities and social locations have provided for the ways of knowing that feminisms have tended to favor.

Contradictory Identities and Social Locations: Resources for Female Feminist Thought

One could reasonably think that all feminists have identities that are multiple and even contradictory, and that learning to function effectively out of that multiplicity and contradiction is an important part of becoming a feminist. A woman scientist is a contradiction in terms, as the feminist critics of science point out; but in trying to specify why, women scientists have generated some of the most startling new understandings of science in the twentieth century. While bearing an identity that is perceived as a contradiction in terms is a serious disadvantage within the political structure, it becomes an advantage epistemologically. In activating our identities as women scientists, Black women sociologists, lesbian literary critics, feminist classicists, women philosophers, we exploit the friction, the gap, the dissonance between these multiple identities. Our identities appear to defy logic, for "who we are" is in at least two places at once—outside and within, margin and center, to use Collins' terms. Moreover, these two or more identities are not just different from each other, they are oppositionally related, in that they define each other as polarities. At the center one cannot speak at all, we are told, as a woman, let alone as a Black woman, a lesbian, or as feminists; one can speak, uncomfortably, only as a scientist, sociologist, literary critic, classicist, philosopher. A woman scientist is a misfit because a man scientist is an all-too-perfect fit. The group of feminist epistemologists who have come to be called the Standpoint Theorists—Dorothy Smith,[5] Nancy Hartsock,[6] and Hilary Rose,[7]especially—discuss in different ways the scientific and epistemological importance of this gap between the understanding of the world available if we start from women's activities and the understanding provided by the dominant conceptual schemes. (I capitalize "Standpoint" to distinguish this use of the term to mean an understanding achieved only through science and politics—a use that originates in Hegel, Marx, and Lukacs' "standpoint of the proletariat"—from the increasingly everyday use of it in feminist discourses as interchangeable with the immediate views or "perspectives" that express our unmediated experiences. Standpoints are mediated, while views, perspectives, and experiences are unmediated; the two sets are contrasted, not interchangeable, in the Standpoint theories.)

The Standpoint Theorists do not intend the understandings generated by these approaches to research to be available only to members of the group whose social situation some particular Standpoint analysis privileges. For example, Collins insists that people who do not have the marginal identities can learn from and learn to use the knowledge generated from the perspective of the outsiders within. Collins' contribution is to sociology and to Black women, not only to marginal intellectuals. Now we all can see aspects of race and gender relations that Black feminists first saw. For instance, since Black and white define each other—or, rather, white racism constructs what it is to be white, as a mirror image of the Black identity it tries to define and control—I have also learned certain things about white experience and white privilege that I took for granted as simply human experience or my particular experience. But note that *activity* is required in this kind of use of another's insights. I cannot just endlessly repeat what Black feminists say and never take responsibility for generating my own analyses of my situation as a white woman. If I did so, I would be thought stupid or insidious—one who undermines the legitimacy of the Black feminist analysis. So I must learn actively to see the world differently, with the help of their insights.

I find it paradoxical—and, frankly, suspicious—that most white feminists I know who admire, learn from, and use the understandings of feminists of color believe: (a) that white feminists are perfectly capable of generating anti-racist analyses (recollect, they would say, the important contributions made by Adrienne Rich,[8] Minnie Bruce Pratt,[9] Marilyn Frye,[10] Bettina Aptheker,[11] Elizabeth V. Spelman,[12] Phyllis Palmer,[13] and many others), but that (b) men cannot be feminists (forget, they imply, Mill,[14] Marx and Engels,[15] Eli Zaretsky,[16] William Chafe,[17] and others). A kind of monster lurks in the logic of white feminist discourses: he is a white, economically privileged, Western, heterosexual man — and he is a feminist, too! Does this "monster" discourage white women and heterosexual women from imagining that they/we should *generate* antiracist and antihomophobic analyses, and ones that have different projects, at least in part, from the analyses of women of color and lesbians? Does he haunt other feminist discourses, too?

Some feminist epistemological positions have appeared to claim that only people who have women's experiences can generate feminist insights; that only those who have Black or lesbian or working-class or Third-World experiences can originate antiracist or antihomophobic or antibourgeois or antiimperialist insights. Such claims sometimes have been made on behalf of "gynocentrism" and various sexual, racial, and cultural separatisms. Is it true that only the oppressed can generate knowledge? That one can contribute to the growth of knowledge only out of one's own *oppression*?

Perhaps critics of the idea of feminist men are thinking that they don't agree with everything Mill, Marx, Engels, and such other men have said. But where is the feminist book or essay with which any feminist totally agrees? Perhaps they are thinking that they want to maintain a distinction between an antisexist and a feminist, such that men can be antisexists but not feminists. However, feminists are made, not born. Biology isn't enough to make Marabel Morgan or Margaret Thatcher feminists. In other eras — the nineteenth century, for example — distinctions between female and feminine, between feminine and feminist may have been virtually nonexistent, but only the ignorant confuse these terms today. (Of course we analyze such phenomena as the way patriarchal culture constructs biology and permeates even feminist analyses, but that is different from thinking it appropriate to use "female," "feminine," and "feminist" interchangeably.) Why, then, do critics of the idea of feminist men reserve the label "feminist" for women with so many different political agendas — liberal feminism, Marxist feminism, radical feminism, socialist feminism, Black and Third-World feminisms, lesbian feminism — but refuse to bestow it on any men, no matter what their political agendas or accomplishments?

Most likely the problem is far simpler. Men love appropriating, directing, judging, and managing everything that they can get their hands on — especially women — and the most arrogant have tried to do so in the name of feminism, thereby inadvertently revealing that they have not grasped even the most basic of feminist principles.[18] While elite white men generally tend to be the most domineering in these ways, no doubt similar criticisms can be made about the rest of white people (including feminists) by Blacks, about heterosexuals (including feminists) by lesbians and gays, and about bourgeois people (including feminists) by working-class people. In view of these histories, how could it be other than reasonable for each oppressed group to insist that the theoretical and political direction of more adequate research and scholarship must originate in the first-hand experience of the oppressed? We have heard entirely too much from men about women and gender, from whites about Blacks and race, from heterosexuals about lesbians, gays, and sexual preference, and from economically powerful people about workers and why the poor are poor. Claiming to be able to adopt the critical persona of the Other in the name of her emancipation is unlikely to earn one the applause of the Other. As Elaine Showalter pointed out, men who try to "read as women" have tended to come off only as "Tootsies"— as men who think they know more about women than women know, and who refuse the difficult and painful work it takes to enter feminist discourse specifically as a man.[19]

The feminist Standpoint Theorists may appear to be ambiguous on the issue of whether, for instance, only women can achieve a feminist standpoint, but their argument, if carefully followed, suggests that oppression does not provide all of the identities that can ground emancipatory knowledge.[20] On the one hand, they assert the importance of starting analysis from women's experiences of our own activities, instead of from men's experiences of either their own or women's activities. And they point to the importance of women's "bifurcated consciousness" for generating both the politics of the Women's Movement and the most important feminist analyses. This consciousness arises, for example, in a female graduate student in sociology who finds that the way the dominant conceptual schemes of sociology lead her to think about women's activities conflicts with the way she experiences her own life.[21] On the other hand, these theorists insist that our *experiences* of our activities often lead to distorted perspectives and claims, because a male-dominant social order *arranges our activities* in ways that hide their real natures and functions. We experience only the injustice of our own master and cannot see the system that insures that every other one will be just as bad. Consequently, they argue that the politics of the Women's Movement are needed to bring women together as a group "for itself," and feminist analysis is needed to provide the tools to articulate our collective situation that is occluded by the isolated experience each one of us has.

But if analysis and politics clarify Black women's lives for Black women, as the Combahee River Collective claims, doesn't that very same analysis, when conjoined with a white antiracist politics, also clarify white peoples' lives for them? And can't feminist analysis and feminist politics clarify men's lives for men? I mean to point out the distinction between "reading as a (feminist) woman" and "reading as a feminist man"; seeing the world as a feminist woman does, and as a feminist man can. Whether or not to bestow the term "feminist" on men is only part of the problem. The main part is to specify in a positive way what the differences are between a feminist woman and a feminist man. It seems to me not a luxury but a necessity for feminism that I start from my white experience and, using Black feminist analysis, actively seek to explain that (thereotically unmediated) white experience—how that white experience is created by social factors outside my immediate experience. Is it not also a necessity that we encourage men to start from their male experience and, using feminist analysis, actively to explain that male experience? Or should I put the point the other way around? Men should start from feminist analyses, and then think from their lives, with the help of those analyses, about their experiences and their lives.[22]

One more consideration. The Combahee River Collective authors say that they "find it difficult to separate race from class from sex oppression because in our lives they are most often experienced simultaneously."[23] But I am white and economically privileged; not only do I experience sexism in those least- though still-exploitative forms, but also I experience race and class relations as white and economically privileged. If it is a virtue for the Combahee River Collective not to separate the dimensions of socially constructed experience within which they apprehend the world, why is it not also for me? How can I learn and generate knowledge out of an identity (mine) that is half-repressed? If I take the stance that I can separate these dimensions of my experience, how am I different from men who claim that they, too, can separate the authority of their knowledge claims from their social identities as men? But if we white women can become feminist knowers in this way, so can the Monster. If he can't, then neither can we. Is not his destiny linked to ours?

Perverse Identities: More Resources?

As I indicated earlier, exactly these kinds of "perverse" identities already figure in a few striking feminist analyses. I borrow Bonnie Zimmerman's phrase to refer to these identities as perverse because they choose to become marginal (in Collins' sense) by willfully refusing to do what the culture of the center expects them to do. I am thinking here of the white and antiracist identities that are the topics of analyses by feminists such as Adrienne Rich and Minnie Bruce Pratt, among others.[24] Rich vividly describes the disloyalty to the principles of racism that white feminists must practice if we are to avoid constructing an unselfconsciously racist feminism. Of course she speaks not as a Black woman, but as a white woman reflecting on her experience as a white woman who grew up in the South. Pratt, too, activates her white identity in the service of antiracism. She reenvisions the southern town in which she grew up, contrasting the partial and distorted vision of it her father tried to give her with what she knows of it from learning southern history from the standpoint of Blacks. She struggles to fit together both her identity as a white southerner and her hatred of what the South means to southerners.[25] While these feminists speak out of their social locations, they focus not upon their own oppression, as the Combahee River Collective did, but critically on their own white consciousness and world — or, at least, the kind of consciousness and world characteristic of oppressors who, like them, are white. They know, first-hand, what that world is and how one sees it through an unreflectively white consciousness. Their contributions to how *we* see the world are distinctive, exactly because of the ways they have found to activate their identities as whites in the project.

A similar kind of contradictory identity is the protagonist — or at least, a desired protagonist — for some of the authors, male and female, in *Men in Feminism*:[26]

> You have everything to tell us about your sexuality,[27] your relations to your mother, to your fathers,[28] to death, scopophilia, fetishism . . . , the penis and balls, erection, ejaculation (not to mention the phallus), madness, paranoia, homosexuality, blood, tactile pleasure, pleasure in general, desire . . . , voyeurism, etc. Now this *would* be talking your body, not talking *about* it.[29]

> We should probably start by trying to grasp *who we are as men*, asking that from feminism rather than wondering what "they" want from an assumed male us.[30]

These men do not speak as the "critical cross-dressers" that Showalter criticized, who know better than women do what is and isn't "really feminist," or who try to "read as a woman," or who tell female feminists how to think, or who commit the multitude of other sins that men have exhibited in the name of their purported feminism as they failed to distinguish what is in the power of women and men in feminism to do. (But my point is that we female feminists have not been all that clear, either.) Instead, they speak specifically as men, of themselves, of their bodies and lives, and of texts, using feminist insights to see the world as men who are as knowledgeable about female-generated feminist analyses as female feminists are expected to be.

Of course, generating new insights through research and scholarship originating in perverse identities certainly is not the only or perhaps the most important task that people who choose perverse identities can undertake. Men who want to be "in feminism" can advance the understandings produced by women feminists. They can teach and write about women's thought, writings, accomplishments. They can acknowledge their debts to feminisim. They can sponsor women students and feminist projects for men students. They can criticize their male colleagues. They can move material resources to women and to feminists. In short, they can be politically active as feminists. After all, as men they have access to economic, political, social, and psychological resources that often are not available to women. They can show that they really are "in feminism" and not just advancing their careers by using it. As feminists know, political struggle is a precondition for knowledge: men *will* discover what patriarchal power is really about as they criticize their male colleagues' sexism.[31] However, we feminists (women and men) must engage in these same struggles as white antiracists, heterosexual antihomophobics, economically privileged anticapitalists, Western anti-imperialists. Let us reread this paragraph, making the substitutions that will construct the most important parts of "perverse" political agendas for each of these struggles.

My intention here is to make it both harder and easier to *become* a perverse identity. It will be harder, because I must undertake difficult tasks all by myself in order effectively to generate antiracist insights. I cannot just repeat what women of color have said. I have to educate myself about people of color, their struggles and their cultures. I have to study my own ignorance as well — the culturally rewarded white ignorance Marilyn Frye discusses.[32] I have to study white exploitation, domination, oppression, and privilege. I have to generate the kinds of explanations of these conditions that I expect men, for example, to generate of theirs. If the process is not painful, I probably am not doing it right. Achieving a perverse identity or Standpoint requires me to perform difficult and painful tasks. Thus I am developing the arguments for a *demand* for antiracist behavior for whites, feminist behavior for men, etc. — not for a *gift* of such identities. However, some people enjoy the challenge of such tasks; and articulating the requirements for achieving these perverse identity Standpoints — what must be done — provides concrete agendas for people who desire these perverse identities. The mixed message to whites from people of color, to men from women, the "do as I do" but "do not dare to do as I do," has the effect of immobilizing and pacifying some of the people who do want to develop disloyalties to civilization. Specifying agendas for achieving these perverse identity Standpoints makes it easier to achieve them. We have no more excuses for complaining that we're wrong if we don't and wrong if we do.

There are a few more good reasons for developing traitorous identities beyond those I have discussed. I mention them briefly. If I cannot learn to think critically out of these identities, my ways of seeing race and class will tend to gravitate toward focusing on the oppression of others rather than on my own situation and the perspective available from within it. It is my kind of race and class persons, after all, who perpetrate racism and class exploitation. If I fail to legitimately activate my experience of my race and class, then implicitly I encourage the kind of "studying down" that feminists have criticized in sexists. Furthermore, in learning about my race only from racists or people of color, I deprive myself of *my* perspective on myself. I fail to take an active role in defining what my racial identity *can* be. I accept the passive, nonresistant, noncreative role assigned to me in these discourses by others. There always have been people of European descent who struggled publicly and in their personal lives to undermine racism and imperialism, to use their white privilege to undermine the institutionalization of privilege. They have used the view from Black lives (generated originally by Blacks) to gain a less partial and distorted grasp of their own situation. This, too, is what "being white" can mean to whites. Finally, many of us want to recruit women and men to feminism and other liberatory studies and politics. But people are not enthusiastic about participating in efforts where they are constantly told that they are the wrong kind of people and that their learning can only be passive—thinking what others have thought up for them to think. In order to invite people into our women's studies classes, as well as into our politics and scholarship, we need to devise liberatory agendas for all of the social identities our potential recruits carry. If women, Blacks, and lesbians can create counter-"centric" agendas for ourselves, then so can men, whites, and heterosexuals. This decentering of central identities appears contradictory; but in this world, what choices lack contradiction?

Biddy Martin and Chandra Talpade Mohanty argue that only by questioning "the all-too-common conflation of experience, identity, and political perspective" can we begin to unsettle our belief in "discrete, coherent, and absolutely separate identities . . . based on absolute divisions between various sexual, racial or ethnic identities." The reason to unsettle this idea, they say, is that "the reproduction of such polarities only serves to concede 'feminism' to the 'West' all over again."[33] I agree with them; but I have been arguing that identity knowing doesn't necessarily have to concede "human knowledge" all over again to the "center." Valuing perverse identities, ones that are disloyal to civilization, that willfully refuse to do what the center expects them to do, can be a means to attract center identities to the opportunities for liberatory knowedge and politics originally generated on the margin.

Against Relativism and Pluralism

The authors in this section discuss the contributions to knowledge made by the different ways of seeing the world that can arise from the activities of groups that are devalued and oppressed by the "center." I have been arguing that some identities normally used to define the privilege of oppressors — white, heterosexual, male, Western — can be used perversely in the service of the very same emancipatory projects. The logic of the identity Standpoint arguments requires us to learn to use these other identities perversely, I have argued. But am I (are we?) arguing for relativism or pluralism?

Many of our liberal institutions are busy these days trying to deal with demands for the legitimation of new political and intellectual voices by institutionalizing what they refer to as "diversity" and "multiculturalism." These new curriculum requirements, course foci, conference topics, committees, and the like are justified by arguments for relativism, pluralism, and toleration of difference. (The salient context for these arguments is that the group that has controlled social systems and definitions of reality — white, straight males — rapidly is being swamped demographically in the United States, including in its educational institutions, and delegitimated politically by rainbow coalitions.) Contrary to the opinion of some radical critics, I think these moves toward "diversity" and "multiculturalism" are well worth making; I have struggled in various contexts to put them in place. However, I do not think that, by themselves, they assure us of radical results, and the arguments for pluralism and tolerance of difference that we usually make to get them institutionalized are, in my opinion, politically regressive. They certainly are not the reasons I think these "different voices" should be heard. Nevertheless, as those of us who have been engaged in institutional struggles know well, even weak nods to the legitimacy of the perspectives of Others are regarded as far too radical by many of our traditional colleagues and students. It would take us too far afield to review the strengths and weaknesses of these efforts. Instead, I want to differentiate this advocacy of diversity and multiculturalism from the identity knowing and perverse identity knowing that I have been discussing.

Of course, I cannot speak from a mythical "universal feminist" position; these issues are reasonably approached in different ways, depending upon the goal of one's feminist project. In addition, trying to reach understandings across different disciplinary backgrounds is always a somewhat precarious undertaking. My own thinking always returns to a central set of problems for feminist social and natural scientists and for the public-policy agendas of our feminisms: what are the causal accounts of social relations that will best enable women — all women — to gain greater control of our lives? This project may seem quaint to literary or cultural critics immersed in anti-Enlightenment, postmodernist projects, but it remains mine.[34]

In this context, I remain unconvinced that appeals to diversity, multiculturalism, relativism, pluralism, and tolerance of difference serve women well — no matter what their race, sexual identity, class, or culture. This claim deserves an extended argument, but let me at least indicate how I think we should argue *against* the idea that one story of the world is true but *for* the idea that some stories of the world are definitely less false than others. In this context, I think it is appropriate to assume that there are "ways the world is" and to use such terms as "false beliefs." How do these positions fit together?

We have criticized the "center"'s claim that it alone can provide the one true story of the world. Even the central tendency in mainstream thought about science undermines such an idea. Scientific work — at least twentieth-century scientific work — never claims to produce true statements, but only statements that are less likely to be false than the alternatives that have been considered.[35] The very idea of empirical *truths* is foreign to scientists, with their commitment (theoretically, at least) to revising their beliefs in light of the inevitable appearance of subsequent evidence. But we need not be equally skeptical of the idea that some beliefs are less false, better supported by the existing evidence, than others.

However they function in logic texts, appeals to truth and falsity do not function symmetrically in scientific activity. Nor do they function symmetrically in feminist epistemologies developed to account for the flowering of research in the natural and social sciences that starts off from the lives of women instead of only from the lives of men in the dominant groups. In particular, sexist and feminist claims never are said by feminists to be acceptably diverse or equally false. It is false that my womb will wander around in my body if I take a math course, contrary to the claims of eminent nineteenth-century physicians. In fact, appeals to diversity, relativism, pluralism, and multiculturalism frequently serve exploitative interests in androcentrism, racism, compulsory heterosexuality, and bourgeois hegemony. Tolerance of diversity at the margins of power is a typical ploy of the powerful that enables them to think that they are being fair to others without having to give up any of their ability to control others' destinies. Historically, relativism appears as an intellectual possibility and as a "problem," *from the perspective of the dominating groups*, only at the point when the hegemony of their views begins to be challenged. As a modern intellectual position, it emerged in the recognition by nineteenth-century Europeans that the apparently bizarre beliefs and behaviors of non-Europeans had rationalities of their own. Perhaps, these Europeans realized, the preferred Western beliefs might not be the only reasonable ones. Thus relativism is not a problem originating in, or justifiable in terms of, the experiences or agendas of the oppressed. It is fundamentally a response by the powerful that attempts to preserve the legitimacy of their claims in the face of contrary evidence: "You have your views, I have mine. Who is to claim value-free grounds upon which to say that one is better than another?" The Standpoint Theorists have an answer to this kind of liberal argument, because it takes that kind of theory, one that places analyses of power relations at the center of its epistemology, to answer it.[36]

In my view, absolutism and relativism are complementary — not contradictory — moral and epistemological positions in any culture still stratified by gender, race, compulsory heterosexuality, and class. We should perceive the choice between them to be one defined and insisted on by the absolutists. It leaves them in power. We need not accept it. And "after the revolutions?" Well, then we will have to rethink this matter.

In the meantime, feminists need, and can have, justifiable grounds for our claims to tell less false stories about women and men, gender and social relations, nature and "reality." The theorization of how we can use our identities and the social locations that produce them — including the perverse ones — to generate new ways of seeing the world makes a necessary contribution to such an epistemology.

Notes

A different version of this essay appears as "Reinventing Ourselves as Other: More New Agents of History and Knowledge," in *Whose Science? Whose Knowledge? Thinking from Women's Lives*, ed. Sandra Harding (Ithaca, N.Y.: Cornell University Press, 1991), ch. 11.

1. Apologies to Michelle Cliff, *Claiming an Identity They Taught Me to Despise* (Watertown, Mass.: Persephone Press, 1980).

2. Combahee River Collective, "A Black Feminist Statement," in *This Bridge Called My Back: Writings by Radical Women of Color*, ed. Cherríe Moraga and Gloria Anzaldua (Watertown, Mass.: Persephone Press, 1981), 212.

3. "Situated knowledge" is Donna Haraway's phrase; see her "Situated Knowledges: *The Science Question in Feminism* and the Privilege of Partial Perspective," *Feminist Studies* 14, no. 3 (Fall 1988): 575–600.

4. See Sara Ruddick, Carol Ascher, and Louise DeSalvo, eds., *Between Women: Biographers, Novelists, Critics, Teachers and Artists Write about Their Work on Women* (Boston: Beacon Press, 1984).

5. Dorothy Smith, *The Everday World as Problematic: A Feminist Sociology* (Boston: Northeastern University Press, 1987).

6. Nancy Hartsock, "The Feminist Standpoint: Developing the Ground for a Specifically Feminist Historical Materialism," in *Discovering Reality: Feminist Perspectives on Epistemology, Metaphysics, Methodology and Philosophy of Science*, ed. Sandra Harding and Merrill B. Hintikka (Dordrecht, Netherlands: Reidel, 1983).

7. Hilary Rose, "Hand, Brain and Heart: A Feminist Epistemology for the Natural Sciences," *Signs* 9, no. 1 (Autumn 1983): 73–90.

8. Adrienne Rich, "Disloyal to Civilization: Feminism, Racism, Gynophobia," in Rich, *On Lies, Secrets and Silence: Selected Prose, 1966–1978* (New York: Norton, 1979).

9. Minnie Bruce Pratt, "Identity: Skin Blood Heart," in *Yours in Struggle*, ed. Elly Bulkin, Minnie Bruce Pratt, and Barbara Smith (Brooklyn, N.Y.: Long Haul Press, 1984), 9–63.

10. Marilyn Frye, "On Being White: Toward a Feminist Understanding of Race and Race Supremacy," in Frye, *The Politics of Reality: Essays in Feminist Theory* (Trumansburg, N.Y.: Crossing Press, 1983).

11. Bettina Aptheker, *Woman's Legacy: Essays on Race, Sex, and Class in American History* (Amherst: University of Massachusetts Press, 1982).

12. Elizabeth V. Spelman, *Inessential Woman: Problems of Exclusion in Feminist Thought* (Boston: Beacon Press, 1988).

13. Phyllis Palmer, "White Women/Black Women: The Dualism of Female Identity and Experience in the United States," *Feminist Studies* 9, no. 1 (Spring 1983): 151–70.

14. John Stuart Mill, "On The Subjection of Women," in *John Stuart Mill and Harriet Taylor Mill: Essays on Sex Equality*, ed. Alice S. Rossi (Chicago: University of Chicago Press, 1970).

15. Frederick Engels, *The Origin of the Family, Private Property and the State* (New York: International Publishers, 1972).

16. Eli Zaretsky, *Capitalism, the Family and Personal Life* (New York: Harper and Row, 1976).

17. William Chafe, *Women and Equality: Changing Patterns in American Culture* (New York: Oxford University Press, 1977).

18. See, e.g., Scarlet Friedman and Elizabeth Sarah, eds. *On the Problem of Men* (London: Women's Press, 1982); and Alice Jardine and Paul Smith, eds., *Men in Feminism* (New York: Methuen, 1987).

19. Elaine Showalter, "Critical Cross-Dressing: Male Feminists and the Woman of the Year," in Jardine and Smith, *Men in Feminism*, 116–32.

20. In addition to the work of the theorists cited earlier, see the discussion of this work in Sandra Harding, *The Science Question in Feminism* (Ithaca, N.Y.: Cornell University Press, 1986), ch. 6.

21. Dorothy Smith's example in *Everyday World*, 62, 68.

22. See a number of the essayists in Jardine and Smith, *Men in Feminism*, and the white feminist antiracist writings cited earlier.

23. Combahee, "Black Feminist," 213.

24. Rich, "Disloyal"; Pratt, "Identity."

25. See also discussions of Pratt's work in Biddy Martin and Chandra Talpade Mohanty, "Feminist Politics: What's Home Got to Do with It?", in *Feminist Studies/Critical Studies*, ed. Teresa de Lauretis (Bloomington: Indiana University Press, 1986). Caren Kaplan, "Deterritorializations: The Rewriting of Home and Exile in Western Feminist Discourse," *Cultural Critique* 6 (1987):187–98.

26. Jardine and Smith, *Men in Feminism*.

27. Attributed to Hélène Cixous by Alice Jardine, "Men in Feminism: Odor di Uomo Or Compagnons de Route?," in Jardine and Smith, *Men in Feminism*, 60.

28. Jardine, "Men in Feminism," 60.

29. Ibid.

30. Stephen Heath, "Men in Feminism: Men and Feminist Theory," in Jardine and Smith, *Men in Feminism* 33–40.

31. See Jardine, "Men in Feminism," 60. In addition to the sources cited, see Susan

Hardy Aiken et al., "Trying Transformations: Curriculum Integration and the Problem of Resistance," *Signs* 12, no. 2 (Winter 1987):255–75, to find projects for men.

32. Marilyn Frye, "On Being White."

33. Martin and Mohanty, "Feminist Politics," 192.

34. See, e.g., Sandra Harding, "Feminism, Science and the Anti-Enlightenment Critiques," in *Feminism/Postmodernism*, ed. Linda Nicholson (New York: Methuen/Routledge and Kegan Paul, 1989).

35. See Sandra Harding, ed., *Can Theories Be Refuted?* (Dordrecht, Netherlands: Reidel, 1976).

36. I have discussed this issue in a number of places. See, e.g., chs. 5, 6, and 7 of Harding, *Whose Science?*

Part III

Value Judgments

Part III

Value Judgments

Also, she told him that she knew nothing about music really, but that she knew what she liked. As she passed with him up the aisle, she said this again. People who say it are never tired of saying it.
— Max Beerbohm, *Zuleika Dobson*

Beerbohm's irony cuts at least two ways. On the one hand, he registers the irritation of educated men who express their preferences in discourse about enduring values; on the other, he registers the dazzling security of Zuleika, an entertainer celebrated more for her beauty than for her conjuring tricks, who expresses hers as exclusively personal. Although she is not self-reflective in the senses approved by the contributors to *(En)Gendering Knowledge*, she knows the power of her beauty and, even if she were familiar with the discourse of value employed by the Oxford men among whom she finds herself, would see no reason to deploy it in support of what she likes and dislikes.

Values are located neither in an extratemporal realm that transcends persons, as educated men would have it, nor in the persons who evaluate, as Zuleika would have it. Radically contingent, they emerge from a network of transactions among those who evaluate and what they evaluate in a variety of social contexts. Traditional academic ideology, however, maintains that we can and should separate our professional from our personal selves, our objective performances from our subjective states. Our education teaches us to conduct our inquiries apart from personal concerns, to exclude our beliefs, values, feelings, political intentions, aesthetic preferences, and other "subjective" states. Feminist knowers subvert this ideology. We have values and articulate them; we attribute them to our personal histories, our cultural circumstances, our socialization into disciplines, and our professional status.

In "Whose Research Is This?: Values and Biology," Ruth G. Doell recommends participation. She analyzes the blurred divisions between constitutive and contextual values in genetic engineering and *in vitro* fertilization. The intersection of these fields of research is a site of competition among pure research and its therapeutic applications, commercial interests and their social consequences, and the ideologies of scientific inquiry, pronatalism, and feminism. Although scientists see laypersons' values as constraining the practice of science, laypersons, she argues, need structures like oversight committees that will allow them to review and reconstruct the values guiding scientific research and its applications.

In "Contingencies of Value in Feminist Anthropology," Micaela di Leonardo highlights differences in the values of knowers and those of the subjects they study. Ethnographic writing, she notes, "often has functioned as disguised social commentary." It is the discourse of a discipline that has been both imperialist and oppositional, sometimes legitimating the oppression of non-Western peoples by devaluing their cultures in relation to Western culture and sometimes criticizing ours by valuing theirs as superior. Problematizing ethnographic interactions between Western feminists and the women they study, she warns feminist anthropologists to pay close attention to differentials of power and shifting frames of value.

In "Black Woman Scholar, Critic, and Teacher: The Inextricable Relationship Among Race, Sex, and Class," Joyce A. Joyce shows the play of conflicting values not only in her discipline but also through her person. Speaking as one doubly disadvantaged — by gender as well as by race — she struggles to maintain alliances with Black male critics whose values are not hers. They have, from her perspective, adopted the fashionable modes of analysis valued by white male theoreticians and secured their professional status by proving that they can speak the masters' language. African-American literature, she argues, both reflects and saves the lives of Black people; she objects, consequently, to its deconstruction.

Doell, di Leonardo, and Joyce all see the possession of knowledge as conferring power and, reciprocally, the possession of power as legitimating the right to pose the questions that get answered. In "Who Wants To Know?: The Epistemological Value of Values," Naomi Scheman affirms two points reiterated in this section — the contingency of values and their importance to academic inquiry — and moves on to practical matters. She looks at and across divisions among people of all colors, gendered female and male, powerless and privileged, lay and academic. She asks how all their values can be inserted in the realm of epistemology, especially the values of those whose questions do not get asked and answered, and she tries to imagine a representative democracy of knowers in which, by analogy with a representative democracy of citizens, multiple and conflicting values would be brought into play. As feminists we want our values inserted, even as we subscribe to an analysis of values that stresses their contingency.

Whose Research Is This?
Values and Biology[1]

Ruth G. Doell

Until quite recently, feminist critics have not seen the restructuring of the natural sciences as their major concern. Because they are more centered in the humanities and social sciences, they quite naturally have developed feminist theory from literary, social, and historical perspectives. Now, however, recognizing the central role that biology plays in maintaining the gendered organization of society, they have begun to envision a changed science, a nonsexist and nonhierarchical science compatible with the egalitarian goals of feminism.[2] Although the new feminist criticism of science and technology bears on both the natural and the social sciences, it is more vocal with respect to the latter and also to biology, where it owes much to the pioneering criticism of reproductive technology. Reclaiming for themselves their bodies and their reproductive lives, women have begun constructing a new vision of science.[3]

Biology has always been central to women's oppression. Through centuries of writing about women, male scientists have claimed that "anatomy is destiny." No sooner was one biological determinist position questioned and refuted than another arose to take its place. For instance, when brain size failed to account for the supposedly inferior intelligence of women, neurobiologists turned to differential lateralization in their search for an "explanation." Biological determinists attributed women's less aggressive behavior to their hormonal status, ignoring the social pressures that women experience.[4] But in recent years, feminist critics have wrought significant changes in some areas — for instance, in sociobiology, primatology, and evolutionary biology. The "man the hunter" hypothesis of human evolution has given way to an equally speculative but woman-centered hypothesis, "woman the gatherer."[5] Building upon these broadened interpretations of the scientific record, Charlene Siegfried has provided new insight into what a feminist biology could be like: a "cooperation with rather than opposition to nature."[6] Her view is akin to the one attributed to Barbara McClintock in Evelyn Fox Keller's recent biography, that science requires a "special kind of sympathetic understanding" of nature.[7]

Doing science within a different and broader theoretical framework, McClintock saw interaction between organism and environment, where previously her male colleagues had seen only a linear relation, the gene in control of the organism. Keller argues persuasively that the masculinist values of domination and control associated with science are acquired partly through the developmental processes.[8] Whether or not one accepts the psychoanalytic theory that informs Keller's work, the effectiveness of these processes in creating strong gender roles for men and women in our society seems both plausible and evident. Like Carol Gilligan,[9] who studied women's developmental experiences in order to understand differences in moral reasoning between men and women, Keller sees that men are encouraged to be autonomous and competitive, whereas women are led to value relationships and responsibility.

These differences in the socialization of men and women, along with the resulting dominant positions of men, have led to a devaluing of those emotional and empathic aspects of human intelligence most often associated with women. These aspects therefore have been largely absent from the (mostly male) reasoning about science.[10] Feminist scientists emphasize the linkage of emotion and cognition in all human thought and see that the repression of empathy leads to a distorted view of human nature as well as a distorted practice of science.[11] By including emotion and empathy in their perspective, scientists can address directly their reasons for doing science and bring their own values into the open.

A feminist science can be envisaged only vaguely as yet, but it will be one in which, contrary to the traditional view, values are explicitly addressed at every level of the scientific process.[12] Traditionally, scientists have claimed a value-free status for their discipline. As has been pointed out by philosophers and historians of science, however, science is clearly influenced by values.[13] What scientists mean by "value-free" is that personal desires must not influence the reasoning about and interpreting of observations. Nevertheless, discernible sets of values operate at different levels within science. First, constitutive values — e.g., truth, accuracy, explanatory power — define the goal of science, which is the acquisition of "true" knowledge about the natural world. Second, contextual values arise from the fact that science is a social activity performed by socialized and gendered beings. These values affect the scientific enterprise at the practical level of choosing and promoting particular projects[14] and may also enter, unbeknownst to the researcher, into reasoning about and interpreting of data in the form of unquestioned and unproven assumptions.

Another distinction within science is that between basic and applied research. Scientists who seek new knowledge, which they take to be good in and of itself, usually refer to their work as basic research, while those who use the new knowledge to solve problems, presumably for the benefit of individuals and society, refer to theirs as applied research. These distinctions, however, become blurred in the actual doing of science. Biologists, for example, justify basic research on cell physiology by arguing that we need to understand what is normal in order to understand the abnormal cell processes that lead to cancer. They also justify basic research by citing the value that applications might have for society. The acquisition of new knowledge, while important in itself, is further bolstered by its contextual value in the competition for research funds.

As with so many dichotomous schema, these two — constitutive versus contextual values and basic versus applied research — are in fact interactive. Although we can conceptually distinguish constitutive from contextual values, in practice they interact in the reasoning and emotions of the scientist or administrator who is deciding upon the merits of a particular project. We find, too, that the distinction between basic and applied research is frequently blurred by the speed with which the findings of basic research are applied to solve problems, particularly in clinical settings. For instance, during the period when virologists and immunologists were seeking to discover and characterize antibodies against the antigens of the AIDS virus in order to develop a screening test for blood to be used for transfusion, one would have been hard put to say whether the research was basic or applied. It was both. Indeed, whether research is basic or applied sometimes depends upon the perspective of the researcher. In feminist science, the perspective of the scientist would be recognized as an inescapable aspect of doing science. Later I will argue that the perspectives of those for whom science is ostensibly done also must enter into the structuring of scientific projects.

But, when the histories and values of the participants are included, what then protects science from becoming merely opinion? First, I would argue that scientists never have been uninfluenced by values; they have been unaware of them. Only by reflecting upon the influence of values on their thinking can scientists attain any degree of "objectivity" in science. Unfortunately, self-reflection is not encouraged in the atmosphere of domination and control characteristic of traditional science. Second, at the level of data collection in individual scientific projects, the accepted methodologies tend to impose standards of verifiability and disconfirmation compatible with what is understood to be scientific "objectivity." Beyond this methodological level, however, scientists sometimes are prone to speculation, which may be fraught with the biases of social and scientific ideology. When their research excites the interest of their colleagues and the public, they may be blind to the possible negative consequences or overly optimistic about the possible applications. Journalists find utopian views of the future newsworthy, and nonspecialists are eager to embrace them. The appeal of utopianism makes it difficult to criticize scientific research; after all, who wants to discourage our hope for a more perfect future?

One of the fields within biology where such speculation is currently rampant and controversial is genetic engineering.[15] Using recombinant DNA technology, gene engineers have made such rapid advances in techniques for gene manipulation that the science has become commercialized into one of the fastest-growing segments of the economy.[16] The threat to fundamental scientific values -- free communication of information and freedom of inquiry — that this commercialization represents is widely recognized,[17] but the lure of wealth and prestige has proved more than adequate to attract biologists into business.

Thus far, the major applications of gene engineering have occurred in the pharmaceutical industry and in agriculture, creating controversy, discussion, and litigation. The manipulation of genes in people has begun with an experiment on terminally ill cancer patients, and a first attempt to treat a genetic disease (one of the immune deficiencies is a prime candidate) is likely within the year.[18]

In this essay I want to focus on how social values affect the promotion of two particular projects in biology that could directly impinge upon women's reproductive lives. It is an accident of history that, at this particular time, one kind of gene engineering in humans, the engineering of future generations, appears to depend for its advancement upon the availability of human embryos for research. About the only way in which these embryos can be ethically obtained is through the techniques of *in vitro* fertilization (IVF).[19] This particular conjunction, IVF with research on human gene engineering, seems to me to offer an interesting opportunity to explore the interaction of values in the practice of biology.

The dominant gender ideology within which biologists in the field of reproductive technology perform their research and apply their findings holds that women are primarily reproductive beings. In our gendered society, they are granted second-class citizenship, typically justified on the basis of their biological function as reproducers. Women are expected to gain their identity and self-esteem mainly from child-bearing, mothering, and nurturing occupations. Judith Blake was one of the first to write about the constraining of women's choices by societally imposed pronatalist prejudice.[20] The influence of pronatalism on women's and men's lives by now has received considerable attention,[21] but its influence upon biology is, I think, less well understood. Its restrictiveness is evident today for women at all stages of the reproductive cycle, from the high school dropout who chooses motherhood over abortion to the woman in her early forties who is listening to the ticking of the biological clock. Pronatalism is not the only influence pressing upon these women, but it is a powerful and often subliminal one. It influences those women who cannot conceive because of fallopian tube blockage to seek help from manipulative technological procedures like IVF. Nowhere is the interaction between the biological and the social more apparent than in the realm of infertility. Inherently a biological state, sterility becomes a social and personal problem when women are defined by their biological capacity for reproduction. If women's only means to satisfaction is through mothering, then the lack of alternative roles will lead them to almost any extreme to "fix" their infertility. Feminists insist that society recognize women not only as reproductive beings, but also as agents who make their own lives and who might make them differently if they had more choices and fewer restraints than they have now.

Another factor that influences biologists, although it is seldom addressed by them, is self-interest. Biologists gain satisfaction from making new discoveries and being useful to society.[22] But with maturity and achievement come recognition and perhaps a personal stake in their own success. The prizes, the chairs of prestigious departments, and the media attention that follow upon noteworthy discovery may be irresistible. In addition to personal interests, disciplinary interests are an important consideration. Those who believe that "what's good for science is good for society,"[23] may use scientific societies to lobby Congress for favorable budget decisions or may promote the interests of science more subtly. In the promotion of a particular scientific study, however, the status of science is itself an issue often hidden in the rhetoric. This is what I think is happening in promoting the use of human embryos for research. The issues are charged with strongly held religious and philosophical beliefs. Under these conditions, proponents of the research might appeal to societal values in order to promote their research when perhaps that research is not in the best interest of those it is proposed to help.

Both gene engineering and IVF are in the forefront of biological research. The publicity accompanying their development during the 1970s directed public attention to the ways in which biological research impinges upon social affairs and social affairs upon biological research. A small group of biologists triggered the famous recombinant DNA debate when they recognized the possibility that an engineered organism might escape into the environment with perhaps disastrous consequences for public health.[24] The resulting widespread public concern subsided as the research progressed under new guidelines and within containment systems that seemed to work well. Interestingly, some of the scientists soon regretted having "gone public" with their concerns. They saw the public fear and the resulting oversight committee (Recombinant DNA Advisory Committee [RAC]), which eventually produced the guidelines administered by the National Institutes of Health, as unnecessarily restricting their freedom to do research.[25] For these biologists, the value of freedom of inquiry within science seemed to outweigh that of public safety—a judgment that violates the norm that freedom is always limited by responsibility.[26]

Safety was not the only topic to receive public attention as a result of the recombinant DNA debate. The controversy soon extended to other topics, including the possible alteration of the botanical and microbial environments by such "new" organisms as weeds that contain nitrogen-fixing genes and bacteria that can feed on unusual substrates. Finally, biologists and laypersons alike began to speculate about alterations to the human gene pool that might have unknown, longterm effects on the evolution of our species. These concerns eventually led scientists and laypersons to realize that oversight committees were needed to make policy, to establish guidelines for proposed research, and to regulate the diverse applications.

Although recombinant DNA technology provided the basic methods, gene engineering could not be pursued until the safety of its techniques was ensured. Moreover, one type of human genetic engineering, that which involves the manipulation of future generations, also could not be pursued without the use of human embryos for basic research. This research is needed to ensure that what works in mouse embryos, where the techniques are developed, also works in human embryos, where genetic regulatory elements and gene orders may well be different. At present, human embryos can be obtained only by the procedure of IVF. Because this procedure usually produces more embryos than are implanted in the uterus of the patient who provides the eggs, it makes "extra" embryos available for gene engineering and other kinds of research. Hence the fortuitous conjunction between these two areas of biology. Research on human embryos is not openly under way in this country because of the controversy surrounding their use at the present time. (I shall return to this point after discussing the IVF procedure.)

IVF is the procedure whereby an egg is fertilized outside the body and cultured in a plastic petri dish until it reaches the stage at which it can be implanted into the uterus of the egg donor or of a surrogate mother. Since 1978, when Louise Brown, the first infant whose conception was known to have occurred outside her mother's body, was born, IVF has enabled a woman with blocked fallopian tubes to become pregnant. The procedure may not be entirely innocuous for the infant: a recent analysis of the incidence of congenital abnormalities seems to show an increase of conditions such as spina bifida.[27] The number of infants born with defects is still too small for reliable incidences to be determined.

For the women undergoing the procedure, the outcome is often less than satisfactory. The physician frequently uses powerful hormone treatment to increase the number of eggs produced by the patient. A few days later, her abdomen is entered and the ovaries manipulated to recover the eggs. These manipulations can change ovarian functioning as well as damage the ovaries. Tubal pregnancy is also a possible outcome of the procedure and can result in serious complications. These undesirable outcomes are infrequent, however, and are not the major concern of the women who undergo the procedure; nevertheless, they should not be dismissed as inconsequential. The major concerns of these patients are the psychological stress associated with the manipulations required over a considerable time period and the disappointingly low success rate. Even after several attempts at obtaining eggs, fertilizing them, and implanting the embryos, most women will not become pregnant. The success rate is at best about 20 percent; that is, a pregnancy is achieved in only one out of five attempts to obtain eggs.[28] Moreover, those women who do become pregnant seem to suffer a higher than normal rate of miscarriage,[29] an experience that can be devastating for a woman who has undergone the manipulations of IVF.[30] A more realistic estimate, counting as successes only those attempts at egg retrieval that result in a live infant, would bring the success rate to about 9 to 10 percent.[31]

Knowing the psychological and physical traumas associated with IVF, to say nothing of the expense, we are faced with the obvious question of why women elect to undergo it at all. Is it the best solution to infertility, or are there alternatives? To begin to answer this question, we must consider those social values that influence women's choosing to bear children. For many women, motherhood is simply a given; it is what women do. For others, it is a decision reached after careful consideration of their own desires and of alternative lifestyles. Writing about the role of mothering in women's lives, feminists emphasize its prescriptive nature.[32] Women in Western cultures are sometimes seen by themselves and others to have failed to become fully human if they do not attain the state of motherhood. This culturally derived psychological pressure to reproduce has resulted in the notion that women, all women, have a "right" to bear children, instead of the more realistic assessment that most women have the capacity to do so. The technique of IVF seems to restore to women with blocked fallopian tubes the "right" to bear children—a "right" whose restoration, however, is limited in our society to married and economically well-off women. Moreover, pressure is subtly tuned toward having one's own child. For some women who are sterile, adoption is a less satisfactory alternative than IVF. Does this preference result from the cultural importance of the birthing process, an emphasis on the body, left over from the determinism that defines women by their biology? Or is it influenced by the need for continuity and for identification of paternity, so much a part of our male-dominant culture? The pronatalist view is criticized by some feminist writers as being too deterministic and somewhat simplistic, since it figures women as "dupes" of their social conditioning.[33] While it is probably true that some women accept motherhood as their chief role and satisfaction in life without much thought, that can hardly be said for the women undergoing IVF. These women have considered their situation carefully and often have undergone much clinical investigation and treatment in the hope of conceiving. It is to be expected that they are aware of their options. Feminists have responded to this expectation by insisting that the choice to bear a child is less free than it should be in a society where educational opportunities and career choices are limited for women and where the ideology of motherhood prevails. This particular lack of freedom underscores the fact that choices are always constrained by social, cultural, and biological circumstances.[34]

Our growing awareness of how the unfair limitations on women's choices in the economic sphere affect their reproductive decisions reminds us that we must increase opportunities and choices for women. In addition, it suggests that women must develop a "reproductive consciousness" so that they can see themselves as self-conscious agents in the decision to reproduce or not.[35] Women need to think through what are appropriate reasons for having or not having children. Such a "reproductive consciousness" would allow a woman to judge less prejudicially whether adoption offered her a means to the satisfactions of mothering. It would also allow sterility to be perceived as a positive alternative rather than as a failure of identity and role. While IVF offers some women the only opportunity for pregnancy, an overemphasis on it as *the* solution to infertility leads those who practice and fund science to neglect scientific education and research that could be more fruitful in the long run. For instance, the public needs to be more aware of the direct relationship between chlamydia-caused sterility in women and the use of the pill.[36] Thus the emphasis on "curing" sterility in women has tended to diminish the efforts to prevent sterility.

We have seen that a social value, that of bearing one's own child, has justified the development and use of the IVF procedure, and also that this procedure offers an opportunity for research on human embryos that could lead to the kind of human genetic engineering that can alter indiviudals and their descendents. To what extent, then, might the procedure of IVF be promoted for the biologist's own interest in research rather than for the benefit of sterile women? It is difficult for biologists to turn away from an opportunity to do fascinating work that also enhances their careers. So long as no obvious harm is associated with IVF (in a society where motherhood is almost compulsory, the potential benefits will be more easily anticipated by prospective patients than the possible risks), biologists can be expected to encourage IVF in order to undertake "cutting-edge" research on human embryos that could lead to human gene engineering.[37]

Genetic engineers utilize the techniques of recombinant DNA to manipulate genes. They snip them out of their normal sites in the DNA molecules, perhaps recombine them in a different order or add extraneous bits, and then insert them into a particular (or random) position in the genome of a suitable cell. This part of the work is well advanced in bacterial systems, much less so in a few mammalian organisms (the mouse is the favorite species), and as yet not really begun in humans, although the genes inserted into human cells in the laboratory have been shown to function in them.[38] Here we need to distinguish between the two kinds of genetic engineering that could be undertaken in humans. In many clinical situations, the desired alteration of the genome *must* take place within certain somatic cells of the individual—for example, replacing a faulty gene for hemoglobin in the bone-marrow cells with a functional one. Bone-marrow cells can be removed from a patient, the gene inserted, and the cells later reinjected into the patient. Only the cells involved in the disease process need to be manipulated. This treatment is termed somatic-cell gene therapy. But more ambitiously and more controversially, the goal may be to alter faulty genes in individuals and their descendents. For this kind of manipulation the gene must be altered in all the cells of the organism. At present, the technique of IVF offers the only feasible route to what is called germ-line gene therapy, since only by manipulation at the earliest stages of development can it be accomplished. Not only is IVF the technical means to the genetic manipulation of future generations, but also it is, as I mentioned earlier, the single source of human embryos for the basic research that could lead to this kind of gene engineering in humans. Although biologists speculate that, within the foreseeable future, human embryos may be made available for this kind of experimentation by growing ovarian tissue in culture to the stage where it can produce mature eggs, the techniques for doing so have not yet been developed.[39] IVF with its "extra" embryos is the only procedure that now offers this material to researchers, since using women only to obtain eggs for research would be considered unethical. Even so, one group of biologists[40] recently has made a plea for permitting the extraction of eggs for research purposes from women undergoing tubal ligation.

In either kind of genetic engineering, in somatic cells of individuals or in embryos that develop to maturity, safety is of great concern to the experimenters and to the public. This concern cannot be as easily assuaged as it was with respect to the early recombinant DNA work, where safety was ensured by developing containment systems as well as organisms that would self-destruct, so to speak, if they did escape from their laboratory environment. While the containment of organisms was a relatively straightforward task, the insertion of genes into a recipient's cells is a much more problematical one. The most promising agent of insertion is a retrovirus that has the desirable property of self-inserting its genetic information, along with any genes added to it by the experimenter, into the genomes of animal cells, including those of humans. Great caution has to be used, however, in inserting genes this way, because some retroviruses are carcinogenic; they carry oncogenes, which help to turn on the cancerous process in the cell. Moreover, sometimes, in the process of insertion, rearrangements occur that permit the eventual development of malignancy in the cell. Other precautions will have to be observed in using these viruses, but their carcinogenicity is a major problem that has motivated longterm studies in mice and nonhuman primates to ensure safety prior to any experimental manipulation in patients.[41] In addition to the problem of carcinogenicity, researchers have major difficulties in regulating and maintaining the expression of transferred genes.[42]

Nevertheless, this work is progressing rapidly in experimental animals, and several laboratories have readied proposals for human applications to correct defects in somatic cells as soon as the preliminary tests are completed. Now that guidelines for somatic-cell gene therapy have been developed and approved by the RAC, it appears that this work will be able to proceed.[43] Indeed, it may proceed more rapidly than anyone foresaw a year or two ago, since the RAC recently modified its earlier cautious stance with resepct to longterm animal experiments.[44] The RAC rationale is that the patients who volunteer for the first of these experiments will be desperately ill, with no alternative treatment available. Under these circumstances, the possibly life-saving nature of the treatment outweighs even the potentially grave risks associated with it.

The guidelines for somatic-cell gene therapy have been developed after years of discussion among scientists, ethicists, politicians, and laypersons about what kind of regulation is needed to control the diverse applications of genetic engineering techniques, including those proposed for humans. During this period, pressures have mounted to undertake a whole variety of gene engineering experiments and applications. Afflicted individuals and their families want to proceed as rapidly as possible with the research that could lead to a cure for genetic disorders. Commercial firms, which comprise the new biotechnology establishment, are rushing to develop lucrative pharmaceutical and agricultural applications of gene engineering techniques. Researchers are drawn to do this work by the prestige and competitiveness attached to it. University professors develop courses in order to teach students the techniques and to provide research opportunities for them; and, conversely, they cite job opportunities in newly organized companies to justify program development, while neglecting to address the ethical complexities of this work in their teaching.[45] Within each of these interacting but still separate levels of the biology establishment, the values of science — knowledge and progress — as well as commercial interests drive the process onward. Is it reasonable to expect, then, that when proposed projects are evaluated, the values and interests of these diverse constituencies will be distinguished to the extent that it is possible to do so? Instead of self-consciously analyzing these values and interests, many biologists have conflated them: they assume that the interests of the scientific establishment and the interests of society are the same.

The recommendations of Clifford Grobstein and Michael Flower, two biologists who have been deeply involved in basic embryological research and policy making for genetic engineering, exemplify the commingling of values. Discussing the type of oversight mechanism needed to evaluate issues and promulgate guidelines for the conduct of human genetic engineering, they suggest four principles.[46] Three of these principles, designed to protect human individuals and the gene pool, call for a review of proposed interventions to mitigate not only technical risks but also "political, social and moral impacts as well." These principles can be seen as arising from the desire of biologists to be useful, not harmful, to society. However, the fourth principle affirms the "primacy of the free conduct of research, unless it endangers fundamental human rights." Their concern about technical risks is well taken, but their emphasis on the free conduct of research raises questions about who is to decide what research will be undertaken and what is a fundamental human right. In the area of reproduction and human genetic engineering, where the consequences of research directly affect the lives of people, especially women, such decisions should not be left to biologists alone. Decisions about research should not be made without considering the values and interests of those for whose benefit the research is to be undertaken.

Grobstein and Flower's appeal for the primacy of freedom of inquiry implies that what is good for science is necessarily good for society and that only scientists should make decisions about scientific research. But what is good for science — more technology, for example — often conflicts with what is good for society. While it is true that completely unforeseen applications of great benefit to society sometimes emerge from basic research, usually the applications are obvious when the research is undertaken. Whether or not the applications can be anticipated, the decisions about which projects to undertake ought to be made not by scientists alone but by the broadest possible representation of the society that may benefit from and does pay for the research and its applications (e.g., health insurance premiums in the case of medical technology). I am not by any means suggesting that scientists abandon research for its own sake. Most human beings have a curiosity about the natural world, and satisfying that curiosity brings pleasure to all of us. I do believe, however, that a thoughtful examination of the purposes for which research is intended, along with forthright statements of these purposes, could make the entire research establishment more responsible and more beneficent. It is the "unexamined exercise of cognitive authority" that needs to be avoided.[47]

Grobstein and Flower recommend that an advisory committee be formed that resembles the broadly based President's Commission for the Study of Ethical Problems in Medicine and Biomedical and Behavioral Research, which was established in 1979 to open up public discussion in a number of controversial areas. In its report on human gene engineering,[48] this commission did much of the groundwork for the previously mentioned guidelines developed by the RAC to regulate somatic-cell gene therapy. The report also discussed various forms that future oversight committees for gene engineering research might take. Grobstein and Flower's proposed committee would, however, be composed of a majority of experts, contrary to the recommendation of the President's Commission, which specifically stated that such a body should not be "dominated by geneticists or other scientists."[49] In England, where a broadly based licensing body has been proposed[50] to oversee IVF and research on human embryos, the proposal is viewed by some scientists as not safeguarding their interests.[51] These questions — of broad versus narrow representation and expert versus nonexpert majority — lie at the heart of the debate about oversight committees. Biologists who want their work to proceed rapidly are more likely to proceed rapidly if they constitute a majority of the oversight committee. The RAC, originally a narrowly specialist organization, later was broadened by the addition of a number of representatives from outside the sciences. It remains dominated by experts, however, and whether it would be competent to deal with the knotty issues raised by germ-line gene therapy and human embryo research is difficult to say. My own feeling is that a very broadly based commission would best serve this function. Now that the RAC, after much controversy over its appropriate role in overseeing biotechnology, has been limited to reviewing proposed biomedical research,[52] and now that somatic-cell therapy will proceed as rapidly as possible under its new guidelines, speculation about the more controversial germ-line gene therapy can be expected to increase.

Germ-line gene therapy was mentioned specifically in the report of the President's Commission as contraindicated because of "technical uncertainties, ethical implications, and the low probability of actually treating an affected person."[53] A background paper from the Office of Technology Assessment, a scientific fact-finding and advisory body for the United States Congress, similarly concluded that at present gene therapy in humans should be limited to somatic cells.[54] The RAC now declines to accept proposals for germ-line gene therapy, in the belief that there has not been sufficient public discussion of its implications and that somatic-cell therapy needs to progress before the more controversial germ-line work is attempted. This delay provides us with a welcome breathing space in which to look ahead before proceeding with human embryo research or germ-line gene therapy. But the opportunity to discuss the kind of future we should like to see may not last long. The technical advances are here, and one way or another they are likely to alter the future. If feminists want to influence that future, they must know how the new technology may be applied for their ends and must enter forcefully into these discussions.

Given the restrictions for the immediate future on any germ-line gene therapy in humans, why are biologists so eager to go ahead with research on human embryos? This research, they reply, may yield knowledge (e.g., about the effects of drugs and other chemicals on early development) that helps pregnant women. It may also provide information about the physiology and molecular biology of early human development and, of course, may improve the technique of IVF.[55] So biologists justify research on human embryos (when germ-line gene therapy is not an option) primarily in terms of its usefulness to human reproduction. In other words, the values of pronatalism are used to bolster the biologists' interests in pursuing this research.

What would happen if scientists mentioned the value of research to women contemplating IVF? Would the less-than-free choice of reproduction become even more coercive if these women were told that their "extra" embryos would contribute to scientific research? It seems plausible that some women would be more inclined to undergo IVF if they knew they would be contributing to research and doing something for others as well as for themselves. My point is not that research on embryos is morally wrong (although people from some religious constituencies believe it is), but that, in an ideological environment where real choice is denied to women, any increase in coercive influences is morally wrong.[56] When the value of scientific progress is added to the value of pronatalism, then women's "right" *not* to reproduce is further constrained. The constraint in this light becomes synonymous with doing harm. If pronatalism were attenuated, researchers could no longer justify their interest in genetic engineering by recourse to reproductive therapies. This coercive influence is, no doubt, subtle: to researchers, it is probably insignificant; to women, it should be a signal of the pervasive erosion of their self-determination by a masculinist and manipulative social system.

If pronatalism were attenuated, we can predict a similar diminution of interest in germ-line gene therapy, were it to become acceptable. Future parents-to-be, who contemplate gene therapy to counteract genetic disease,[57] might not seek such therapy if adoption and childlessness were considered satisfactory alternatives. If we as a society considered them satisfactory, these alternatives would be real choices without the connotation of failure that is attached to them now. Already, women who do not reproduce are finding satisfying opportunities for nurturing that are more compatible with their career goals.[58] If demand for therapy were attenuated, then the provision of human embryos for research on reproductive processes might be unnecessary. Since biologists can use mouse embryos as the material to investigate other research questions (e.g., how genes can be transferred, bad ones "fixed," and embryonic development regulated), they would not be able to continue rationalizing their research on human embryos.

In the meantime, despite the *de facto* ban on germ-line gene therapy and human embryo research, public discussion of the pros and cons of the research continues, including discussion of the personhood of the early human embryo. Because the status of the human embryo is controversial, embryo research is a dubious procedure.[59] In Great Britain, research is permitted for a period of only two weeks after fertilization (two weeks marks the beginning of development of the primitive nervous system and the possibility of sentience in the embryo).[60] In the United States, even limited work on human embryos has been blocked by lack of public agreement on the status of the embryo and by political wrangling over funding priorities. Some of the participants in the debate believe that it will be difficult to prevent either human-embryo research or germ-line gene therapy indefinitely. One participant, Jonathan Moreno, believes that the procedures are so widely desired that regulation will not be enforced over the long run. "Human egg cells," he says, "are not the sort of commodity that is easily restricted and experimentation in this country and abroad would be immensely difficult to police."[61] Grobstein appears to share his view of the inevitability of this work. According to Moreno, he has testified before a congressional committee that "a new age of genetic and developmental intervention clearly lies ahead."

Whatever organization eventually houses the oversight committee that looks into human embryo research and germ-line gene therapy, its composition will be critical. Biologists generally call for a committee with a majority of scientific experts, whereas public advocates recommend a majority of nonscientists. To address questions that are so diverse, the committee will need nonbiologists who can bring to bear the necessary expertise in the humanities and social sciences. Questions about the propriety of manipulating human embryos, about equal availability of the procedures to all who might benefit from them, about alternative solutions to the underlying problems (e.g., prevention as opposed to cure), and about costs and cost distribution will have to be addressed by the broadest possible representation of professionals and laypersons. Were such a body to be composed of a majority of scientists, they could override the nonscientists in their eagerness to get on with the work, since scientists are unlikely to regard conflicting values among nonscientists as sufficiently important to warrant delaying their research.

We have had considerable experience in attempting to deal with questions as complex as these in the recent past, when controversy erupted over such issues as resuscitation of very premature newborns, organ transplantation, abortion, and the treatment of terminally ill patients. The accumulated experience of committees that have overseen these procedures will be invaluable to those who are to wrestle with the issues I have been discussing. This experience may help them avoid the danger of relying on absolute principles in seeking solutions, a danger most obvious when scientists consider the preservation of a life in any condition more important than the ability of a family to cope with these circumstances. We should not forget that, for many reproductive technologists as well as for everyday people, motherhood has the status of an absolute value.

A further consideration in regard to the composition of such a committee is that it should be made up of approximately equal numbers of women and men. Only by this means will women's perspectives be given the serious consideration they deserve, since surely the advent of germ-line gene therapy will, like all procedures involving reproduction, impinge more heavily upon the lives of women than upon those of men. What women can better articulate is the interaction between the appropriate roles for women prescribed by society and the particular kinds of research promoted by biologists. It would be reprehensible to allow the research on human embryos necessary for germ-line gene therapy to proceed without considering fully that it might lead to the encouragement of IVF in order to obtain those embryos. The practice of IVF adds pressure to define women by their reproductive role, and the publicity surrounding the procedure increases the demand for it. As long as women see themselves as gaining their self-fulfillment from reproduction, they will be more likely to undergo IVF and to make more embryos available for research. The promotion of IVF reinforces a conventional view of women that is stultifying for those women who desire a genuine range of opportunities besides motherhood. But even for those women who do desire motherhood, the current restriction of IVF to married couples reinforces other aspects of the conventional view of women, such as heterosexuality and married status. An oversight committee ideally would address issues of social equity as well as issues of scientific feasibility and public safety. For IVF to be performed equitably in an egalitarian society—that is, to satisfy the self-conscious need of some women to bear their own children—it would have to be available to all women regardless of sexual orientation, marital status, race, or economic class.

The oversight committee that is entrusted with developing recommendations about the difficult questions of germ-line gene therapy and human embryo research will have its hands full. Its members must not be reluctant to slow the pace of research in order to ensure the free and open discussion of all the values that underlie its doing. The oversight committee should actively seek "ways of negotiating the distance between knowlege and its uses . . . between expert and nonexpert."[62] Ideally, it will help scientists to see the wisdom of "using knowledge as a tool of liberation rather than one of domination." In the meantime, we surely can rely upon them to provide expert technical information and to promote the well-being of their scientific enterprise. But it is not their role solely to determine what directions the research should take or which applications of science are in the best interests of society.

Notes

1. I wish to thank Helen Longino and the editors of this volume, Joan E. Hartman and Ellen Messer-Davidow, for their very helpful criticisms during the preparation of this essay.

2. See Sandra Harding and Merrill B. Hintikka, eds., *Discovering Reality* (Dordrecht, Netherlands: Reidel, 1983); Marian Lowe and Ruth Hubbard, eds., *Woman's Nature* (New York: Pergamon Press, 1983); Ruth Bleier, *Science and Gender* (New York: Pergamon Press, 1984); Evelyn Fox Keller, *Reflections on Gender and Science* (New Haven, Conn.: Yale University Press, 1985); Charlene Haddock Siegfried, "Second Sex: Second Thoughts," *Women's Studies International Forum* 8, no. 3 (1985):219–29; Elizabeth Fee, "Critiques of Modern Science: The Relationship of Feminism to Other Radical Epistemologies," in *Feminist Approaches to Science*, ed. Ruth Bleier (New York: Pergamon Press, 1986), 42–56; and Hilary Rose, "Beyond Masculinist Realities: A Feminist Epistemology for the Sciences," in Bleier, *Feminist Approaches to Science*, 57–76.

3. See the Boston Women's Health Book Collective, *Our Bodies, Our Selves* (New York: Simon and Schuster, 1971); Linda Gordon, *Woman's Body, Woman's Right* (New York: Penguin, 1977); Ruth Hubbard, Mary Sue Henefin, and Barbara Fried, eds., *Women Look at Biology Looking at Women* (Cambridge, Mass.: Schenkman, 1979); and Jalna Hanmer, "Reproductive Technology: The Future for Women?", in *Machina Ex Dea*, ed. Joan Rothschild (New York: Pergamon Press, 1983), 183–97.

4. Anne Fausto-Sterling, *Myths of Gender* (New York: Basic, 1985).

5. See Frances Dahlberg, ed., *Woman the Gatherer* (New Haven, Conn.: Yale University Press, 1981); Sarah Blaffer Hrdy, *The Woman That Never Evolved* (Cambridge, Mass.: Harvard University Press, 1981); and Nancy Makepeace Tanner, *On Becoming Human* (Cambridge, England: Cambridge University Press, 1981).

6. Siegfried, "Second Sex."

7. Evelyn Fox Keller, *A Feeling for the Organism* (San Francisco: W.H. Freeman, 1983).

8. Keller, *Reflections on Gender and Science*. Of course, underlying the developmental process is the ideology of "rational man," which has had a long history in Western culture. See Genevieve Lloyd, *The Man of Reason: "Male" and "Female" in Western Philosophy* (Minneapolis: University of Minnesota Press, 1984).

9. Carol Gilligan, *In a Different Voice* (Cambridge, Mass.: Harvard University Press, 1982).

10. Lloyd, *Man of Reason*, provides an elegant description of how reason and emotion became separated in the thinking of philosophers and scientists.

11. Bleier, *Science and Gender*, ch. 3.

12. For recent discussion of the forms a feminist science might take, see the articles in two issues of *Hypatia* devoted to feminism and science: 2, no. 3 (Fall 1987); and 3, no. 1 (Spring 1988). See also Helen Longino, *Science as Social Knowledge* (Princeton, N.J.: Princeton University Press, 1990), 187–94.

13. Loren Graham, *Between Science and Values* (New York: Columbia University Press,

1981); and Gerald Holton and Robert S. Morrison, eds., *Limits of Scientific Inquiry* (New York: Norton, 1979).

14. Helen E. Longino, "Beyond 'Bad Science': Skeptical Reflections on the Value-Freedom of Scientific Inquiry," *Science, Technology and Human Values* 8, no. 1 (Winter 1983):7–17. Longino notes that the distinction between these sets of values collapses in the actual practice of science.

15. See Liebe F. Cavalieri, *The Double-Edged Helix* (New York: Columbia University Press, 1981), ch. 3; Theodore Friedman, *Gene Therapy: Fact and Fiction* (Cold Spring Harbour, N.Y.: Cold Spring Harbour Laboratory, 1983); and Jeremy Rifkin, *Algeny* (New York: Penguin, 1983).

16. For a comprehensive view of the commercialization of genetic engineering techniques, see Edward Yoxen, *The Gene Business: Who Should Control Biotechnology?* (New York: Oxford University Press, 1983).

17. David Blumenthal, Michael Gluck, Karen Seashore Louis, Michael A. Stoto, and David Wise, "University-Industry Research Relationships in Biotechnology: Implications for the University," *Science* 232 (13 June 1986): 1361–66.

18. Barbara J. Culliton, "ADA Deficiency: A Prime Candidate," *Science* 246 (10 Nov. 1989):751.

19. Early experimentation on IVF techniques utilized eggs obtained from women without their knowing the experimental nature of the procedure. The dubious practices of egg donation for experimental procedures are described in Gena Corea, *The Mother Machine: Reproductive Technologies from Artificial Insemination to Artificial Wombs* (New York: Harper and Row, 1985). On the other hand, Braude et al. argue that women should donate eggs for research purposes; see Peter R. Braude, Martin H. Johnson, and Hester P. M. Pratt, "Should Medical Research Be Made a Criminal Act?", *Bioessays* 1, no. 5 (May 1984):232–37.

20. Judith Blake, "Coercive Pronatalism and American Population Policy," in *Pronatalism: The Myth of Mom and Apple Pie*, ed. Ellen Peck and Judith Senderowitz (New York: Crowell, 1974), 29–67.

21. See Mary O'Brien, *The Politics of Reproduction* (Boston: Routledge & Kegan Paul, 1981), and Martha E. Gimenez, "Feminism, Pronatalism, and Motherhood," in *Mothering: Essays in Feminist Theory*, ed. Joyce Trebilcot (Totowa, N.J.: Rowman and Allenheld, 1984), 287–314.

22. Edward S. Golub, "Paradigms Regained," *Immunology Today* 3, no. 3 (Mar. 1982): 59–61.

23. The question of the appropriate relation between modern biology and society is addressed directly by, among others, Cavalieri, *Double-Edged Helix*; and Yoxen, *Gene Business*.

24. June Goodfield, *Playing God* (New York: Harper and Row, 1979). See also the articles in *Environment* 24, no. 6 (July/Aug. 1982), devoted to the subject of rDNA and biotechnology; Leonard A. Cole, *Politics and the Restraint of Science* (Totowa, N.J.: Rowman and Allenheld, 1983), 136–38; and the review of Cole's book by Sheldon Krimsky, *Hastings Center Report* 13, no. 6 (Dec. 1983):42–43.

25. C. Keith Boone, "When Scientists Go Public with their Doubts," *Hastings Center Report* 12, no. 6 (Dec. 1982):12–17.

26. Cavalieri, *Double-Edged Helix*, 132.

27. Gena Corea and Cynthia de Wit, "Current Developments and Issues: A Summary," *Reproductive and Genetic Engineering* 1, no. 3 (1988):287–307.

28. Clifford Grobstein, Michael Flower, and John Mendeloff, "External Human Fertilization: An Evaluation of Policy," *Science* 222 (14 Oct. 1983):127–33.

29. Gena Corea and Susan Ince, "Report of a Survey of IVF Clinics in the U.S.," *Made*

to Order: The Myth of Reproductive and Genetic Progress, ed. Patricia Spallone and Deborah Lynn Steinberg (New York: Pergamon Press, 1987), 133–45.

30. IVF sometimes is used to circumvent male infertility due to low sperm production, since relatively few sperm are needed for *in vitro* fertilization, compared to *in vivo* fertilization. The procedure is then even more manipulative of the woman. For a description of this variation on IVF, see Jacques Cohen, Carole B. Fehilly, Simon B. Fishel, Robert G. Edwards, Jonathan Hewitt, George F. Rowland, Patrick C. Steptoe, and John Webster, "Male Infertility Successfully Treated by *In Vitro* Fertilization," *Lancet* i, no. 8388 (2 June 1984):1239–40.

31. Gena Corea and Cynthia de Wit, "Current Developments and Issues: A Summary," *Reproductive and Genetic Engineering* 2, no. 3 (1989):253.

32. Blake, "Coercive Pronatalism," 29–67; O'Brien, *Politics of Reproduction*; Gimenez, "Feminism, Pronatalism," 287–314.

33. See, e.g., comments by Kathryn Pyne Addelson in her review of Rosalind Petchesky's *Abortion and Woman's Choice* in *Women's Review of Books* 1, no. 8 (May 1984):11–12.

34. Barbara Katz Rothman, "The Meaning of Choice in Reproductive Technology," in *Test Tube Women: What Future for Motherhood,* ed. Rita Arditti, Renate Duelli Klein, and Shelley Minden (Boston: Pandora Press, 1984), 23–33.

35. Janice Raymond calls for women to recognize the male-directed manipulation of women involved in reproductive technology and to develop an "ecological vision" of the possible future for women freed of compulsory reproduction. Raymond, "Feminist Ethics, Ecology and Vision," in Arditti, Klein, and Minden, *Test Tube Women,* 427–37.

36. A.E. Washington, S. Gove, J. Schachter, and R.L. Sweet, "Oral Contraceptives, *Chlamydia trachomatis* Infection and Pelvic Inflammatory Disease," *Journal of the American Medical Association* 253, no. 15 (10 Apr. 1985):2246–50.

37. Robyn Rowland makes this same point. Rowland, "Reproductive Technologies: The Final Solution to the Woman Question," in Arditti, Klein, and Minden, *Test Tube Women,* 356–70.

38. Harry E. Gruber, Kim D. Finley, Robert J. Harshberg, Scott S. Katzman, Paul K. Laikind, J. Edwin Seegmiller, Theodore Friedmann, Jung-Kuan Yee, and Douglas J. Jolly, "Retroviral Vector Mediated Gene Transfer into Human Hematopoietic Progenitor Cells," *Science* 230 (29 Nov. 1985):1057–61.

39. Ditta Bartels, "Built-In Obsolescence: Women, Embryo Production and Genetic Engineering," *Reproductive and Genetic Engineering* 1, no. 2 (1988):141–52.

40. Braude, Johnson, and Pratt, "Should Medical Research Be Made a Criminal Act?"

41. W. French Anderson, "Prospects for Human Gene Therapy," *Science* 226 (26 Oct. 1984):401–9.

42. Jean Marx, "Gene Therapy—So Near and Yet So Far Away," *Science* 232 (16 May 1986):824–25.

43. Marjorie Sun, "Gene Guidelines Therapy Approved," *Science* 230 (18 Oct. 1985):302; *Federal Register,* 19 Aug. 1985.

44. Barbara J. Culliton, "Gene Therapy Guidelines Revised," *Science* 228 (3 May 1985): 561–62.

45. In my own department, the ethics section of the current gene engineering course stresses problems of safety and problems associated with the regulation of research. Less emphasis is placed on the complex issues of economic cost to society, actual need for the product manufactured, and so forth.

46. Clifford Grobstein and Michael Flower, "Gene Therapy: Proceed with Caution," *Hastings Center Report* 14, no. 2 (Apr. 1984):13–17.

47. Kathryn Pyne Addelson, "The Man of Professional Wisdom," in Harding and Hintikka, *Discovering Reality*, 182.

48. U.S. President's Commission for the Study of Ethical Problems in Medicine and Biomedical and Behavioral Research, *Splicing Life* (Washington, D.C.: U.S. Government Printing Office, 1983), 44.

49. Ibid., 4.

50. *Report of the Committee of Inquiry into Human in vitro Fertilization and Embryology* (London: H.M. Stationery Office, 1984). Hereafter cited as Warnock Report.

51. Braude, Johnson, and Pratt, "Should Medical Research Be Made a Criminal Act?"

52. Marjorie Sun, "White House to Release Biotechnology Guidelines," *Science* 232 (6 June 1986):1189.

53. President's Commission, *Splicing Life*, 48.

54. U.S. Office of Technology Assessment, *Human Gene Therapy: Background Paper* (Washington, D.C.: Office of Technology Assessment, 1984).

55. Robert G. Edwards, "The Case for Studying Human Embryos and Their Constituent Tissues *in vitro*," *Human Conception in vitro*, ed. R.G. Edwards and Jean M. Purdy (New York: Academic, 1982), 371–88; and Susan Abramowitz, "A Statement on Test-Tube Baby Research," *Hastings Center Report* 14, no. 1 (Feb. 1984):5–9.

56. Janice Raymond discusses this point in "At Issue: Of Eggs, Embryos and Altruism," *Reproductive and Genetic Engineering* 1, no. 3 (1988):281–85.

57. The curing of genetic disease is the only foreseeable use of this kind of human gene engineering. Manipulation of embryos to alter personality and intelligence is impossible at present, given the current state of our ignorance about the genetics of such characteristics.

58. Margaret A. Simons, "Motherhood, Feminism and Identity," *Women's Studies International Forum* 7, no. 5 (1984):349–59.

59. Leon R. Kass, "'Making Babies' Revisited," presents a thoughtful examination of the values involved in considering research on human embryos from the conventional point of view of marriage and the family, in *Public Interest* 54 (Winter 1979):32–60.

60. Warnock Report.

61. Jonathan D. Moreno, "Private Genes and Public Ethics," *Hastings Center Report* 13, no. 5 (Oct. 1983):5–6.

62. Fee, "Critiques of Modern Science," 47.

Contingencies of Value in Feminist Anthropology

Micaela di Leonardo

Anthropology, like so many other disciplines, has been both of interest to and transformed by the feminism of the past fifteen years. Issues of agency and value judgment have been central to this process of transformation. In order to understand their centrality, however, we need to consider the broader canvas of feminist anthropology.

Anthropology drew the interest of second-wave (1960s and 1970s) feminists first as a source of hypotheses concerning the possible origins of women's secondary status, and later as a disciplinary center for documenting the varieties of women's perceptions and experiences — a way to overcome the ethnocentrism of our emphasis on Western women's lives in thinking about sources of, and remedies for, women's oppression. Interest in the former topic has now declined, and the latter has broadened to include work by sociologists, economists, political scientists, and literary critics; but anthropology remains an important locus of feminist theorizing.

While anthropology shares much of its history with other social sciences, it also has certain unique features: particular intellectual traditions and a particular historical location. First, anthropology's holistic "four fields" coverage (physical anthropology, archeology, social-cultural anthropology, linguistic anthropology) ensures that the discipline as a whole crosses the boundaries of the humanities, social sciences, and natural sciences. Thus, anthropological consideration of "the female" includes female protohumans, prehistoric women, and female nonhuman primates. Second, anthropology was first defined as a discipline and flourished in late Victorian Britain and the United States. Early fieldworkers often were missionaries or colonial administrators, and nineteenth-century anthropological concepts reflected both imperialist and oppositional ideologies. Some anthropologists combined Victorian Social Darwinian notions with new information on "savage" lifeways to legitimate the oppression and exploitation of what would come to be called the Third World. Others labored long to establish the complexity of "primitive" religion, kinship, politics, and, particularly, languages. In Max Weber's term, they strove to experience *einfuhlung*, or the intimate sense of others' consciousness. These anthropologists demanded acceptance of the equal humanity of the different peoples among whom they had lived and of their ability to govern themselves.[1] (Of course, such is the complexity of human consciousness that at times the "good" and "bad" anthropologists were the same people.)

Third, but less well remarked upon, is the centrality of sexual politics to late Victorian anthropological debates. Using reports of the varieties of "primitive" kinship and studies of classic and prehistoric civilizations, theorists constructed differing models of "Ur," or primeval, kinship and sexual relations. Fierce debates among the propounders of prior patriarchy, matriarchy, and equality took on color and impact from the contemporary political agitations of first-wave British and American feminists. If prehistoric societies were characterized by male rule, as McLennan argued, then one could use this past to legitimate the present and to argue against feminist reform. Or, equally, if one argued, as Engels did, that women and men had been equal until the rise of private property, then women's new equality would come with the downfall of capitalism.[2]

For these historical reasons, issues of agency and value take particular forms in feminist anthropological discourse, and we can group the questions that tend to arise under two headings. First, anthropology's legacy of evolutionary and other kinship theory, its tradition of participant-observation fieldwork (ethnography), and its documentation of "exotic" lifeways mean that women seldom have been entirely ignored as members of particular societies—as, for example, they have been in many historical studies. The questions that arise instead are: Has the agency of women been adequately studied? Do ethnographers also note the constraints, both material and cultural, on women's agency?

Second, the traditional subjects of anthropological study—whether colonized tribal groups, Third-World or European peasantry, or the urban poor everywhere—are by definition less powerful than the ethnographers who study them. Even Western middle-class informants lack some power in ethnographic interaction, by virtue of its one-way character. When these objects of study are also female, the potential for uneven power dynamics is heightened. Does the ethnographer recognize this effect of *her* agency on that of others? Does she attempt to understand how these circumstances affect the responses she receives and her interpretation of them? Finally, is she self-conscious in considering how these power dynamics affect her judgments of her informants and the cultural and social environments in which they live?

Here is the link in anthropology between agency and value judgments. Just as "primitives" long have represented projections of desirable and undesirable characteristics in the Western mind, so ethnographic writing often has functioned as disguised social commentary. As I have noted, it is not only that anthropologists have interpreted non-Western lives; they have interpreted them *with reference to* evaluations of contemporary Western societies. Margaret Mead's *Coming of Age in Samoa*, which criticizes the anxiety-creating institution of American adolescence by lauding the gentle age transition on a South Seas island, is only one of the better-known examples of ethnographic social commentary.[3] Of course, such projections are not limited to those espousing the "noble savage" interpretation. Anthropologists have also described "nasty, brutish, and short" primitive lives, thus implicitly underlining the superiority of their own societies or decrying the possibility of social reform because of the limits of human nature.

The irony here is that all of the societies studied by anthropologists have been profoundly altered by the agency of the observers themselves — as I noted above — and by that agency writ large — that is, by the forces of Western contact, colonialism and imperialism. Thus the issue of value judgments I have phrased in terms of social projection becomes more complex. Anthropologists not only judge other societies with reference to their perceptions of their home societies; they also implicitly or explicitly evaluate the character of the historical interaction between their home and their field societies. Feminist anthropologists have inherited this conundrum, with consequences that I explore below.

In what follows, I discuss these two sets of questions as I have formulated them, highlighting the issue of agency and incorporating the issue of value judgments as they are logically entailed by the discussion. Because there is no single tradition of anthropology, but rather congeries of competing and of mostly androcentric schools, I tread heavily in those paths already frequented by feminist anthropologists. For this reason and because I am a cultural anthropologist, I only touch on work in physical anthropology and archeology and focus primarily in this essay on feminist revisions of the study of living humans.

For more than a decade now, feminist anthropologists have considered female agency. As Michelle Rosaldo asserts in her influential introduction to *Women, Culture and Society*, we must see women as "social actors working in structured ways to achieve desired ends."[4] Women's agency, though, has not necessarily been ignored by earlier (often male) ethnographers. For example, in 1969, Robert Netting and Walter Sangree, who worked, respectively, with the Kofyar and Irigwe of Nigeria, wrote about the kinship and marital lives of these women with considerable attention to their gender-based interests and actions:

> Kofyar women . . . feel in no sense bound to stay married. . . . To leave her husband, a woman merely goes out to collect firewood or attend market and never returns home.
> [Irigwe] women depend heavily on co-wives . . . when planning and carry-

ing out secondary alliances. . . . A woman's prior marriages are never formally terminated by her switching residence to another spouse; she may return to any of her spouses at any time and usually finds herself welcomed back.[5]

In fact, some male anthropologists have even criticized other men for flagrant disregard of women's agency. Marvin Harris, for example, takes Ward Goodenough to task for ignoring women's perspectives in analyzing a Trukese father's beating of his married daughter as "just what she deserved": "Do the injured ladies agree with the anthropologist that a good hard jolt is just what they need?"[6]

Attending to women's agency in a complex field situation, however, is difficult even for women ethnographers. Janet Siskind's *To Hunt in the Morning*, an ethnography of the Sharanahua Indians of Peru, is a *tour de force* that merges a political-economic analysis of the encroachment of capitalism and Peruvian cultural imperialism on Indian life with a poetic evocation of this group's tropical forest environment and well-adapted lifeways.[7] Siskind's daily companions and major informants were Sharanahua women, and her affection for them is clear. But women's work and perceptions play little role in Siskind's analysis of Sharanahua life. Each year, I regularly ask my anthropology-of-gender students to assess Siskind's analytic attention to Sharanahua women's agency, and they as regularly turn in ferocious essays that document her neglect of women's sexual, kinship, productive, and economic choices, and her lopsided focus on male agency. For example, Siskind justifies her focus on (male) hunting and neglect of (female) agriculture with reference to the Sharanahua obsession with meat. But she fails here to study the complexity of women's role as meat *distributors*. By Siskind's own evidence, women use meat distribution choices politically to cement or to break alliances. But Siskind sees only the men as important social actors.

Siskind wrote in the early 1970s, when second-wave feminist anthropologists were just beginning to publish. We now have not only revisions of old ethnography and theory, but a rich literature of new feminist ethnography—including linguistic studies—that considers women's agency and the constraints within which women must operate in a wide variety of cultural and economic contexts. From work with highly diverse groups—impoverished Black American women; elite Brahmin Indian women; young village women on the Austro-Hungarian border who refuse to speak Hungarian or marry peasant men (choosing instead to speak German and to identify themselves as "urban" and "Austrian"); Malaysian peasant women working in new factories, who become "possessed by demons" in order to cope with work speedups—feminist anthropologists document the varieties of female experience and action.[8]

Physical anthropology and archeology too have witnessed a wave of critical feminist rethinking over the past fifteen years, a wave most memorably represented in the "woman the gatherer" model devised to counter the hegemonic "man the hunter" theory of human evolution. Among modern foraging groups, women's gathering activities supply the bulk of food, so, even if we wish to infer a similar hunting/gathering sexual division of labor in the protohuman and early hominid past (a doubtful logical connection, since types of economies do not determine specific types of gender relations), envisioning men as the primary economic actors is an error. Feminists have elaborated alternative models of human evolution and have restudied living nonhuman primates with particular attention to female and juvenile behavior.[9] But the most important effect of feminist correctives has been a shift in the presumptions and inferences of physical anthropologists in general — the changes in "normal science." Scientists who are uninterested in claiming the label "feminist" nevertheless now consider gender an important category and assume equal possibilities for "agency" in fossil Australopithecines and langur monkeys, male and female.[10] Even within sociobiology, long considered a sphere of antifeminist reaction, self-identified feminists such as Sarah Hrdy assume female monkeys' conscious and separate reproductive strategies.[11]

Feminist critiques of archeological models of the human past have been neither as many nor as influential as those in physical anthropology. Nevertheless, archeologists nowadays more rarely "map" assumed (often sexist) sex-role behavior onto constructions of prehistoric social life.[12] And feminist ethnohistorical literature, particularly that focusing on the Americas, is growing rapidly. Irene Silverblatt's work on Andean women's responses to Inca and Spanish colonialism, for example, creatively uses available documents to discern women's opposition to new oppressions.[13]

Thus far I have discussed attention to female agency in anthropology in a relatively simple fashion, leaving the category "woman" undifferentiated. Even in looking at the most egalitarian small-scale societies, however, we need to specify *which* women's agency we are acknowledging. Women do not always group together or perceive their material interests in terms of the single criterion of gender. They may divide themselves on the basis of generation, status, or kinship — and they may, of course, ally most closely not with women at all, but with particular men or with men as a group. Louise Lamphere and Jane Collier have written insightful theoretical essays examining the necessarily multiple readings of female agency and constraint in a variety of kinship contexts.[14] The classic oppressive relationship between mother-in-law and daughter-in-law in prerevolutionary China illustrates the ironic feminist insight that some women's agency may be constrained by that of other women.

The numerous types of female actors one must consider multiply further in contexts of class and caste stratification. Since relatively classless small-scale societies represent an insignificant proportion of the world's population, feminist anthropologists ordinarily must deal with field situations in which some women have much greater access to material resources than others—where, in fact, some women are the agents who maintain unequal resource allocations. Analyses of such situations inevitably involve both judgments of and reflections on our own roles as relatively privileged women in our native societies. I recently observed a lively illustration of this point in an anthropology-of-gender seminar at Yale. Late in the semester, after considering and accepting radical analyses of the experiences of Third-World women impoverished by colonialism, imperialism, and native class formations, as well as by gender ideologies, the students read two articles on the perceptions and behavior of elite Brahmin women in India and a privileged ethnic group in Sierra Leone.[15] To my surprise, a significant number of students protested the ethnographic descriptions of these women's efforts to ensure their families' continued status and their discrimination against women of other, lower-status groups. They maintained that the anthropologists were "unfair and unsympathetic" to these women. My students' response reflected our general feminist reluctance to acknowledge stratification among women and the ruthlessness that privileged women, no less than men, may display. It also revealed the students' genuine capacity for anthropological imagination: despite great cultural differences, they identified these elite Third-World women with their own mothers and defended them accordingly. The same questions arise when we consider the differences of race, nationality, and sexual identity among women: To which women do we attend when we attend to women's agency? And how do we evaluate situations where agency and domination converge?

Widespread female marriage resistance in Kwangtung, China, during the late nineteenth and early twentieth centuries provides an interesting illustration of the complex role of female agency in male-dominated, stratified, state societies. As described by Margery Topley, marriage resistance was a widespread cross-class phenomenon enabled by the separate residence of girls and unmarried women, by unmarried women's key productive roles in the region's silk industry, and by the ideology of the local syncretic cult, the "Great Way of Former Heaven."[16] This millenarian religion (with many female leaders) deemed heterosexual contact and childbirth polluting to women and urged them to avoid marriage and biological motherhood. Many women could and did resist their arranged marriages, either by gaining their parents' permission to avoid marriage, live with sister initiates, and help to support their parents; or by refusing to consummate arranged marriages, returning home to live with sister silkworkers, and purchasing concubines for the legal husbands (children borne by a concubine legally belonged to the resisting wife). Lesbian expression, unlike heterosexual contact, was culturally coded as pure, and Topley finds evidence of its practice.

Marriage resistance represents an extraordinary conjunction of women's extra-household capitalist market production, female emotional and sexual solidarity, male and maternal acquiescence in women's resistance, and legitimizing ideologies. It also represents (at least for some women) a culturally-defined escape from spiritual pollution and an achievement of lesbian expression for one class of women on the backs of their less fortunate sisters. Thus, the agency of one group of women is not the agency of all.

We need, then, to try to understand how divisions among women operate within overall male-dominated systems. Historians of American women have been laboring over the past decade to correct a tendency to reproduce the feminist metonymic fallacy: to portray white, middle-class women's experiences as the whole of American women's history. Much recent work not only documents the very different lives of women excluded from the mainstream by virtue of race, ethnicity, or class, but also explores relations among women across these fundamental social divisions. Jacqueline Dowd Hall and Barbara Omolade, for example, discuss the personal meaning to both Black and white southern women of the dichotomous construction prescribing white women's helplessness, gentility, and sexless purity and Black women's presumed hardiness and libidinousness.[17] Other historians are working on the complexity of mistress-servant relations in the late nineteenth and early twentieth centuries. Phyllis Palmer, in her excavation of a 1920s YWCA campaign for employer-employee contracts, demonstrates how white middle-class women's refusal to label housework and childcare as skilled labor worthy of specific hours and adequate remuneration was connected to a larger denigration of themselves as women.[18]

The ways in which women are divided, the ways in which they exercise agency against one another — and against themselves — are clearly important features of women's historical and present realities. *Women United, Women Divided*, an ethnographic collection edited by Patricia Caplan and Janet Bujra, focuses on the varieties of material and cultural circumstances that enable or prevent women's alliances across divisions of kinship, class, and culture.[19] This critical perspective is often lacking, however, in recent American feminist scholarship from a variety of disciplines, scholarship that assumes women's innate solidarity with one another on the basis of their maternal roles. This essentialist strand in feminist scholarship, from literary criticism to political theory to psychology, derives from Western cultural constructions of womanhood developed during the nineteenth century and often defines women as biologically and/or morally superior to men, partaking automatically in an egalitarian and nurturant "women's culture." This perspective has been attacked from within disciplines. For example, Nancy

Hewitt criticizes the historians' "women's culture" concept as inapplicable to Black American women's experiences.[20] (Of course, women have created and do create localized women's cultures. What Hewitt and I dispute is the presumption that such cultural worlds exist across space and time and are everywhere alike.) A crosscultural and historical perspective that stresses divisions among women on the basis of class, color, era, and culture is the best corrective to this ubiquitous tendency to assume one homogeneous form of female agency and, *a priori*, female moral superiority.

Attending to class and color differences and avoiding the presumption of women's moral superiority, however, does not exhaust the problematics of conceptualizing women's agency. There is the further issue of gender division itself. Over the past decade, feminist anthropologists have debated and refined their perspectives on the cultural constructions of gender. In the mid-1970s, Michelle Rosaldo posited a universal dichotomy between public/male and private/female domains, and Sherry Ortner hypothesized a universal cognitive association, nature is to female as culture is to male.[21] Both claims have had wide influence on feminist scholarship, and both have been criticized by other anthropologists and ultimately by their authors.[22] Particular cultures may not dichotomize public and private at all, or may do so in ways whose social meaning is profoundly at variance with our Western associations with these terms. Similarly, MacCormack and Strathern's *Nature, Culture and Gender* points out that other cultures do not necessarily conceptualize nature and culture dichotomously; even where some division of the world is associated with the two sexes, the larger cultural context, including notions of the supernatural, may make such a division fundamentally noncomparable to Ortner's Western-based examples.[23] And even in the West, women have been as associated with culture (the angel in the house, the schoolmarm) as with nature; it is not the referent, but the dichotomizing process and its use in stigmatizing one pole that are important. In fact, Ortner and Whitehead, in the more recent *Sexual Meanings*, focus on differential evaluation alone as the new universal. They claim that cultural constructions of gender and of prestige spheres are simultaneous.[24]

The whole question of gender-based prestige or status has been a thorny one for feminist anthropologists. In the first place, as Naomi Quinn has pointed out, "women's status" has been used very loosely to refer to a wide variety of variables, such as women's relative role in production, the presence or absence of female supernatural beings, or the frequency of rape.[25] But, putting the definitional issue aside, those who have accepted some notion of women's universal lower status, in native and in anthropological perceptions, have tended to seek explanations for its reproduction either in structural or symbolic analyses, as do Rosaldo and Ortner, or in a range of Marxist perspectives emphasizing women's roles in production, reproduction, and distribution, as do most contributors to *Towards an Anthropology of Women*.[26] Some feminist anthropologists, however, claim that women's lives in their separate spheres (assuming, of course, that these exist) are as prestigious in native eyes as are men's. Annette Weiner revises Malinowski's ethnography of the Trobriand Islanders to claim such a separate sphere and source of prestige in women's symbolic exchanges and in their symbolic status as vehicles of cultural continuity. She chides Marilyn Strathern for not considering the symbolic value of women's exchange in the culturally connected Mount Hagen group of Papua, New Guinea. Strathern, however, points out that, among the New Guinea group she studied, women's exchange has no such meaning.[27] Taking the "women's perspective" for one society, as Weiner says she does, does not guarantee that one grasps it for any other. Most important, perceiving women's agency in any society does not translate to proving their equal status in native or anthropological eyes. Modern histories of American slave cultures demonstrate this point for the analogous sphere of race. Some feminist anthropologists consider these insights so central that they deny the validity of any crosscultural statements about women's status or women's experience.[28]

This recurrent attempt at, and the difficulties of, cultural translation bring us to the second set of questions concerning agency and value judgments in feminist anthropology. Does an ethnographer recognize her own agency and its effects in the field? Can we claim a distinctly feminist research methodology that reflects a sensitivity both to observed power dynamics and to the freighted interactional processes through which "data" are gathered? Given the complexities of Western and professional privilege, and their effects on our own interpretations of other women's lives, how do we judge gender arrangements in our own and other societies?

Ethnographers traditionally have offered unsystematic but often insightful or revealing accounts of their roles in particular field situations. E.E. Evans-Pritchard, for example, paints a portrait of himself among the transhumant Nuer of then Anglo-Egyptian Sudan as a helpless hanger-on, begrudgingly endured by his interlocutees for the sake of offerings of tobacco. In a footnote, he claims with bumptious humor to have developed "Nuerosis." Laura Bohannon, an American, in her fictionalized account of fieldwork among the Tiv of Nigeria, both unselfconsciously identifies with former colonial administrators and portrays herself in Tiv eyes as an ignorant and backward child.[29]

The systematic attempt to understand the effect of interactional situations on knowledge gathered as a result of these interactions derives not from feminism but from a variety of trends in 1960s social science that originate ultimately in the phenomenological school of philosophy. Whether called ethnomethodology, symbolic interactionism, frame analysis (all schools of thought in sociology), or interpretation (a pan–social science trend focused on anthropology), these approaches all attend to interaction itself and problematize both the "taken for granted" encounters of everyday life and the artificially "natural" interactions through which social scientists gather information.[30]

Becoming sensitive to interaction does not necessarily entail sensitivity to power differentials in interaction. Alvin Gouldner, in *The Coming Crisis of Western Sociology*, criticizes ethnomethodology and symbolic interactionism for precisely this reason, and, closer to home, Nancy Henley criticizes recent "body language" research for insensitivity to male/female power issues.[31] What is particularly interesting is the way in which ethnographers may have a keen awareness of some layers of power and not of others. For example, Paul Rabinow, the editor of *The Foucault Reader* and an important figure in interpretive anthropology, in 1977 published a poetically self-reflexive memoir, *Reflections on Fieldwork in Morocco*. A major point of the book is the necessity of understanding "facts" as products of the interpretation of interactions, interactions that may be fraught with power differences. Rabinow is extremely sensitive to the psychological heritage of colonialism and the extraordinary difficulties of crosscultural translation—until he comes to the issue of gender. In a passage almost laughable in its naiveté, Rabinow describes a sexually adventurous trip into the Berber countryside with his male, urban, "demimondaine" friends: "[I]t was the best single day I was to spend in Morocco." Surrounding this description are a series of statements implying that prostitutes' lives are pleasant, filled with "expensive clothes and jewelry which they longed for in their mountain villages," and often end in conventional marriage: "Men said that they made good wives, because they had sown their wild oats early [and] become dependable later." With the entry of women actors, the self-reflexive interpretive social scientist withdraws, to be replaced by the self-justifying john who wants to believe that buying sex involves no power dynamic, that the whore desires the encounter as much as he, and that she is not harmed by her status and his use of her.[32]

Other examples of selfconscious ethnography are sensitive to gender and power and document the changes wrought by observed on observers. In *Guests of the Sheik*, Elizabeth Fernea describes her involuntary seclusion in the Muslim women's world of an Iraqi village as a result of her arrival with her ethnographer husband. At first intensely resentful of her exclusion from the male world, Fernea comes to appreciate the relative freedom and intimacy of the women's society, its power in the male public world through monopoly over certain kinds of knowledge, and its space for the development of female medical and religious professionals. Carol Stack and Nancie Gonzalez, in fieldwork among impoverished Black American and Guatemalan

Indian women, respectively, are prodded by their female informants to question their white middle-class American assumptions concerning the necessity of nuclear families headed by men. Gaining strength from their field experience, both choose to head their own households and to care for their children without male protection. Finally, my own field research among California Italian-Americans focused on the middle-aged women with whom I had greatest rapport. As a younger woman and a feminist, I had tended to elevate women's labor market activities and to slight women's work in the home. I learned from these women a deeper respect for the labor of housework and child care and discovered, in the course of fieldwork, that these women (and all American women) also undertook the "work of kinship"—the labor of creating and maintaining cross-household kin and quasi-kin alliances.[33]

It is obviously terribly difficult to achieve rigorous self-reflection. If we are privileged enough to join an intellectual discipline, to do research and writing, we are likely to wish to defend these privileges because of material interests and *esprit de corps*. Self-reflective interpretive analysis, involving both shifting understandings of our social positions vis-à-vis those of others and a partial denial of disciplinary authority, can only be a constantly renewed process.

Misjudgments or ignorance of power, however, may run in the opposite direction as well. Sensitive interpretation of the lives of those the ethnographer perceives as relatively powerless can become special pleading. Over-advocacy may induce the suppression of the less attractive behaviors of one's informants. Marxists sometimes have erred in portraying the moral superiority of all oppressed workers, peasants, or members of racial groups; feminists, as I have noted, have made similar errors in ascribing to all women traits of automatic pan-gender solidarity and unselfish maternal nurturance. Suffering, alas, does not necessarily ennoble. It does not even necessarily enlighten. A fine line must be drawn between contextualizing and condoning particular perceptions and behaviors.

How then do we evaluate the gendered worlds of others? Does a feminist perspective, if not a distinctly feminist methodology, provide the answers? What about particular conditions of multiple agencies and complex constraints among those we study?

Evaluation can only be a constant process of renewed self-reflexivity. While we may obey a checklist of errors to avoid in judging others (check for homophobia, check for racism), we inevitably represent a perspective, a historical era, a part of the globe in our constructions of value. Recognizing that value is radically contingent (cf. Herrnstein Smith[34]) does not absolve us from participating in its construction, but it notifies us of the continuous necessity of reconstruction.

But what framework do we use in the evaluation process? My own choice is a Marxism radically transformed by feminism. The Marxist tradition provides attention to and explanations of the movements of material life. It is explicitly historical and internationalist. Marxism's historical emphasis on the self-knowledge and activity of oppressed masses is a foundation for feminism's more recent broadening of the definition of the oppressed to include all women and all those with unconventional sexual preferences. I believe that any attention to agency demands a critical perspective on stratification processes, a perspective that contains within it a value judgment against those processes and a commitment to work to overcome them. Feminism thus heightens the democratic impulses of Marxist thought.[35]

What does such an analytic frame look like when applied to particular gendered phenomena? What do we learn from this process about agency and value judgments in feminist theory? In the last section of this essay, I adduce two examples of Marxist-feminist analyses of situations involving multiple agencies and constraints.

Ritual operations — the deliberate, institutionalized, and permanent alteration of or addition to the body to mark status and/or enhance attractiveness — are ubiquitous human phenomena. Many examples of ritual operation are bisexual, such as much African tribal scarification; or solely male, such as Jewish circumcision and Australian aboriginal subincision. Western feminists, however, have focused attention on operations performed solely on women that seem obviously harmful and degrading, such as historic Chinese footbinding and contemporary North African clitoridectomy and vaginal infibulation. Feminists often have associated past or present Western practices — Victorian "therapeutic clitoridectomy," say, or the wearing of stiletto high heels — with these non-Western phenomena.[36]

The cultural meanings of similar processes, though, may vary greatly, and it ill behooves Western feminists to condemn particular practices in the absence of a genuine attempt to understand their interpretation in their own cultural contexts. A recent introductory women's studies text, for example, captions an illustration of a scarified Nigerian tribal woman thus: "The scarification across her chest and the ivory pick hanging from her lower lip are examples (like traditional Chinese footbinding) of the ways in which cultures require women to submit to physical discomfort as a badge of gender."[37] No other information is offered. Consider that a number of the young readers of this text may have multiply pierced earlobes. The authors demonstrate to us no significant difference between the viewers and the viewed. If their judgment is not based on the presumption of Western women's superior status and civilization, should they not equally condemn the bodily mutilation of multiple ear piercing, currently fashionable among lesbian feminists — to say nothing of young women in general — and increasingly so among young men?

How then *should* Western feminists evaluate non-Western female ritual operations? A stance of cultural relativism, while preferable to ignorant condemnation, is in the end actually a refusal to evaluate. Let us consider the most extreme case of a contemporary non-Western ritual operation, the North and East African practice of female circumcision. This operation may include the removal of the clitoris and the external labia, as well as possibly the suturing (in order to narrow) of the vaginal/urethral opening. How and why does such an extreme operation take place? How do we as Western feminists evaluate its meaning?

First, we need to recognize that depersonalized language (as in "cultures require" in the above quotation) often masks women's agency with regard to such operations. That is, it is often women who demand them for their young female relatives and who carry them out. A Malian feminist activist, Assitan Diallo, points this out by noting that she alone cannot prevent her daughters' circumcision. Her mother and other female relatives also have rights in her daughters and might carry out out the operation in her absence.[38]

Attending to Third-World women's agency helps us to overcome our tendency to see practices such as female circumcision as occurring in a historical and economic vacuum. For example, Stella Efua Graham discovered that clitoridectomy in Ghana had been part of a complex women's initiation ceremony that included education in sexuality and reproduction, but that the British discouraged this education as "un-Christian."[39] Thus we must consider our own agency as Western observers of and commentators on Third-World practices we find oppressive to women. We need to understand that we cannot approach such phenomena "purely." That is, we are not simply women who identify with other women as an oppressed group, but part of a historical line of powerful, usually exploitative Westerners who presume the right to force change in Third-World cultures.

Given this context, one might still wish that the physical operation itself be abandoned or modified. How does a Western feminist proceed? Carol Vance, an American anthropologist who specializes in the study of sexuality, is involved in ongoing research on circumcision in the Middle East and Africa. Vance decided that the first order of business was to examine native opposition to the operation. She determined that the rhetoric of elite African women, focusing on the Western feminist language of women's sexual autonomy, was less successful than that of African health workers who phrased their objections in terms of maternal and child health rather than in terms of male assaults on women's sexuality.[40] Vance's work is salutary in that she attempts to discern both multiple constraints and agencies. She does not assume that her own native cultural assessment of the operation is the final word; but neither does she retreat from evaluating its effect on women's lives. She respects Africans enough to study their own movements opposing clitoridectomy and to assess their effects.

The second example of a complex gendered phenomenon is less specifically regional. The creation of new industrial factories by transnational corporations is now widespread throughout the Third World. These factories, whether in Mexico or Malaysia, the Philippines or Thailand, whether producing jeans or microchips, tend to rely on a native, young, female labor force. Western and Third-World analysts have exposed the meager pay, stressful working conditions, and constraints against worker organizing that characterize most of these settings. Commentators also have pointed out that often such factories are "runaway shops"; they are relocated from the West to escape unionized wage rates, health and safety regulations, and worker militance. Western feminists criticize not only transnational companies but also Third-World "platform" (host) states: "Crudely put, the relationship between many Third-World governments and multinational corporations is like that of a pimp and his customers. The governments advertise their women, sell them and keep them in line for the multinational 'john.'"[41] Often the young women, who are sent by their impoverished agrarian families to work in these world-market factories, gain reputations for sexual looseness and become unmarriageable. In some cases, firms fire women after ruining their health and leave them with no recourse but prostitution.

We might be tempted to infer from these facts that we should campaign to shut down these factories and return their female workforce to agrarian life. And there would be a selfish Western protectionist payoff: jobs that did not "run away" to the Third World would remain open to Western women workers. A historical Marxist-feminist analysis, however, provides a more complex view, with some surprising Western/Third-World analogies.

First, the establishment of world-market factories is part of the larger process of the internationalization of capital and labor. Firms increasingly employ their capital in global rather than in national or hemispheric markets and make use of labor pools in all countries. This process is an extension of the original European and American industrial revolution that has drawn Western women into the capitalist labor market. While women workers have been exploited by this process (and, specifically, exploited more than male workers), their entry into the capitalist labor force over the nineteenth and twentieth centuries undeniably has advanced their potential for independence. Employment has given women access to cash in societies in which, increasingly, only money has had social value. Employment, moreover, has brought large numbers of women together, making it possible for them to envision and organize themselves as a group with common interests.

What we can call for is, again, the analogue to progressive movements

in the West: Third-World women workers autonomously organizing themselves against exploitation by their firms, their governments, and at times
their own male kin and co-nationals. Diane Elson and Ruth Pearson argue that

> such organizations do not require (Western) policy advisors to tell them what
> to do, supervise them and monitor them; they require access to resources, and
> protection from the almost inevitable onslaughts of those who have a vested
> interest in maintaining both the exploitation of women as workers, and the
> subordination of women as a gender.[42]

Second, we must note that "world-market factories" exist at home as well,
in sweatshops and illegal home work and in many firms' threats to move
abroad if employees do not end demands for better pay and working conditions. Western feminists' best protection of their own jobs lies in a dual
struggle. The economic fates of Western and Third-World women are bound
up together. Both Western scholarship and organizing efforts must be informed
by knowledge of Third-World women's working situations and activism.[43]
Finally, we must recognize the work of Third-World women researchers and
activists in these areas. Too often, in our ignorance, we assume that Third-
World women remain quiescent under oppression until Western women
discover and name that oppression for them.[44]

A feminist anthropological perspective on agency and value judgments,
then, is first of all not a fixed set of givens, but rather a constantly renewed
process involving the dialectical engagement of *einfuhlung* and self-reflection, the back-and-forth attention to and absorption in others' mental and
material worlds — and our own. The participant-observation method, con-
founding observer and observed, aids in this process and has been adopted
by feminists outside anthropology — for example, by Janice Radway in her
study of American women readers of romance novels.[45]
Second, feminist anthropologists have in general abandoned attempts to
find an "easy fix," a single evolutionary explanation for women's lower status.
They have turned instead to historically informed research on gender arrangements among particular groups. This research often includes assessments of Western anthropological agency — both that of individuals and
that of the West or native elites in general. Finally, for many feminist anthropologists, evaluations of our own and others' lifeways are tied to the
recognition of the web of multiple agencies and values that characterize our
situations in studying others. We cannot eschew judgment; we must understand that it is always contingent not only on the changing lives of those we
study but also on our own.

Notes

1. See Talal Asad, ed., *Anthropology and the Colonial Encounter* (New York: Humanities Press, 1973); J.W. Burrow, ed., *Evolution and Society* (Cambridge, England: Cambridge University Press, 1966); Dell Hymes, ed., *Reinventing Anthropology* (New York: Random House, 1974).

2. See Elizabeth Fee, "The Sexual Politics of Victorian Social Anthropology," in *Clio's Consciousness Raised*, ed. Mary Hartman and Lois Banner (New York: Harper and Row, 1974), 86–102; Frederick Engels, *The Origin of the Family, Private Property and the State* (1884; rptd. New York: International Publishers, 1972).

3. Margaret Mead, *Coming of Age in Samoa* (1928; rptd. New York: American Museum of Natural History, 1973).

4. Michelle Zimbalist Rosaldo, "Introduction," in *Women, Culture and Society*, ed. Michelle Zimbalist Rosaldo and Louise Lamphere (Stanford, Calif.: Stanford University Press, 1974), 1–15, esp. 9.

5. Robert Netting, "Women's Weapons: The Politics of Domesticity Among the Kofyar," *American Anthropologist* 71, no. 3 (Nov. 1969):1087–96, esp. 1093; Walter H. Sangree, "Going Home to Mother: Traditional Marriage Among the Irigwe of Benue-Plateau State, Nigeria," *American Anthropologist* 71, no. 3 (Nov. 1969):1046–57, esp. 1052. See also Micaela di Leonardo, "Methodology and the Misinterpretation of Women's Status in Kinship Studies: A Case Study of Goodenough and the Definition of Marriage," *American Ethnologist* 6, no. 4 (Nov. 1979):627–37.

6. Marvin Harris, *The Rise of Anthropological Theory: A History of the Theories of Culture* (New York: Crowell, 1968), 590–91.

7. Janet Siskind, *To Hunt in the Morning* (New York: Oxford University Press, 1973).

8. Carol Stack, *All Our Kin: Strategies for Survival in a Black Community* (New York: Harper and Row, 1984); Patricia Caplan, "Women's Organizations in Madras City, India," in *Women United, Women Divided*, ed. Patricia Caplan and Janet M. Bujra (Bloomington: Indiana University Press, 1982), 99–128; Susan Gal, "Peasant Men Can't Get Wives: Language Change and Sex Roles in a Bilingual Community," *Language in Society* 7 (Apr. 1978):1–16; Aihwa Ong, "Global Industries and Malay Peasants in Peninsular Malaysia," in *Women, Men and the International Division of Labor*, ed. June Nash and Maria Patricia Fernandez-Kelly (Albany: State University of New York Press, 1983), 426–39.

9. See Sally Slocum, "Woman the Gatherer: Male Bias in Anthropology," 36–50, and Leila Leibowitz, "Perspectives on the Evolution of Sex Differences," 20–35, both in *Toward an Anthropology of Women*, ed. Rayna Rapp Reiter (New York: Monthly Review Press, 1975); Jane Lancaster, *Primate Behavior and the Emergence of Human Culture* (New York: Holt, Rinehart and Winston, 1975); Nancy Tanner, "Women in Evolution, Part One: Innovation and Selection in Human Origins," *Signs* 3, no. 3 (Spring 1978):585–608; Adrienne Zihlman, "Women in Evolution, Part Two: Subsistence and Social Organization Among Early Hominids," *Signs* 4, no. 1 (Autumn 1978):4–20.

10. Alison Richard, *Primates in Nature* (New York: W.H. Freeman, 1985).

11. Sarah Blaffer Hrdy, *The Woman that Never Evolved* (Cambridge, Mass.: Harvard University Press, 1983).

12. Andrew Moore, Department of Anthropology, Yale University, personal communication.

13. Irene Silverblatt, "Andean Women Under Spanish Rule," in *Women and Colonization: Anthropological Perspectives*, ed. Mona Etienne and Eleanor Leacock (New York: Praeger, 1980), 149–85.

14. Louise Lamphere, "Strategies, Conflict and Cooperation Among Women in Do-

mestic Groups," 97–112, and Jane Fishburne Collier, "Women in Politics," 89–96, both in Rosaldo and Lamphere, *Women, Culture and Society*.

15. Caplan, "Women's Organizations"; Gaynor Cohen, "Women's Solidarity and the Preservation of Privilege," in Caplan and Bujra, *Women United*, 129–56.

16. Margery Topley, "Marriage Resistance in Rural Kwangtung," in *Women in Chinese Society*, ed. Margery Wolf and Roxanne Witke (Stanford, Calif.: Stanford University Press, 1975), 67–88. See also my analysis of this phenomenon and others in Micaela di Leonardo, "Warrior Virgins and Boston Marriages: Spinsterhood in History and Culture," *Feminist Issues* 5, no. 2 (Fall 1985):47–68.

17. Jacqueline Dowd Hall, "The Mind that Burns in Each Body: Women, Rape and Racial Violence," 328–49, and Barbara Omolade, "Hearts of Darkness," 350–67, both in *Powers of Desire: The Politics of Sexuality*, ed. Ann Snitow, Christine Stansell, and Sharon Thompson (New York: Monthly Review Press, 1983).

18. Phyllis Palmer, "Housewife and Household Worker: Employer-Employee Relations in the Home, 1928–1941," in *To Toil the Livelong Day: America's Women at Work, 1780–1980*, ed. Carol Groneman and Mary Beth Norton (Ithaca, N.Y.: Cornell University Press, 1987).

19. Caplan and Bujra, *Women United*.

20. Nancy Hewitt, "Beyond the Search for Sisterhood: American Women's History in the 1980s," *Social History* 10, no. 3 (Oct. 1985):299–321. See also Micaela di Leonardo, "Morals, Mothers and Militarism: Antimilitarism and Feminist Theory," *Feminist Studies* 11, no. 3 (Fall 1985):599–618.

21. Michelle Zimbalist Rosaldo, "Women, Culture and Society: A Theoretical Overview," 17–42, esp. 23ff., and Sherry Ortner, "Is Female to Male as Nature Is to Culture?," 67–88, both in Rosaldo and Lamphere, *Women, Culture and Society*.

22. See Michelle Zimbalist Rosaldo, "The Uses and Abuses of Anthropology: Reflections on Feminism and Cross-Cultural Understanding," *Signs* 5, no. 3 (Spring 1980):389–417; Sherry Ortner and Harriet Whitehead, "Introduction: Accounting for Sexual Meanings," in *Sexual Meanings: The Cultural Construction of Gender and Sexuality*, ed. Sherry Ortner and Harriet Whitehead (Cambridge, England: Cambridge University Press, 1981), 1–28.

23. Carol MacCormack and Marilyn Strathern, eds., *Nature, Culture and Gender* (Cambridge, England: Cambridge University Press, 1980).

24. Ortner and Whitehead, *Sexual Meanings*.

25. Naomi Quinn, "Anthropological Studies of Women's Status," *Annual Review of Anthropology* 6 (1977):181–225.

26. Reiter, *Toward an Anthropology of Women*.

27. Annette Weiner, *Women of Value, Men of Renown* (Austin: University of Texas Press, 1976); Marilyn Strathern, "Culture in a Netbag," *Man* 16, no. 4 (Dec. 1981):665–88.

28. See, e.g., Penelope Brown, "Universals and Particulars in the Position of Women," in *Women in Society*, ed. Cambridge Women's Studies Group (London: Virago Press, 1981), 242–56.

29. E.E. Evans-Pritchard, *The Nuer* (Oxford, England: Oxford University Press, 1940); Elenore Smith Bowen (Laura Bohannon), *Return to Laughter: An Anthropological Novel* (New York: Harper and Brothers, 1954).

30. I can only refer here to some basic texts in these fields. See Harold Garfinkel, *Studies in Ethnomethodology* (New York: Prentice-Hall, 1967); Herbert Blumer, *Symbolic Interactionism: Perspective and Method* (New York: Prentice-Hall, 1969); Erving Goffman, *Frame Analysis: An Essay on the Organization of Experience* (Cambridge, Mass.: Harvard Uni-

versity Press, 1974); Paul Rabinow and William M. Sullivan, eds., *Interpretive Social Science: A Second Look* (Berkeley: University of California Press, 1987). For feminist efforts to integrate and transform these perspectives (although some authors do not acknowledge their theoretical predecessors), see Helen Roberts, ed., *Doing Feminist Research* (London: Routledge and Kegan Paul, 1981).

31. Alvin Gouldner, *The Coming Crisis of Western Sociology* (New York: Avon Press, 1971); Nancy Henley, "Power, Sex and Nonverbal Communication," in *Language and Sex*, ed. Barrie Thorne and Nancy Henley (Rowley, Mass.: Newberry House, 1975).

32. Paul Rabinow, ed., *The Foucault Reader* (New York: Pantheon, 1984); Paul Rabinow, *Reflections on Fieldwork in Morocco* (Berkeley: University of California Press, 1977), 60–61.

33. Elizabeth Fernea, *Guests of the Sheik: An Ethnology of an Iraqi Village* (New York: Doubleday, 1969); Stack, *All Our Kin*; Nancie Gonzalez, "The Anthropologist as Female Head of Household," *Feminist Studies* 10, no. 1 (Spring 1984):97–114; and Micaela di Leonardo, *The Varieties of Ethnic Experience: Kinship, Class and Gender among California Italian-Americans* (Ithaca, N.Y.: Cornell University Press, 1984), and "The Female World of Cards and Holidays: Women, Families and the Work of Kinship," *Signs* 12, no. 3 (Spring 1987):440–53.

34. Barbara Herrnstein Smith, "Contingencies of Value," *Critical Inquiry* 10, no. 1 (Sept. 1983):1–35.

35. I cannot do justice to the corpus of late-twentieth-century Marxist-feminist literature in one footnote. Some now-classic works in the United States and Britain are Lydia Sargent, ed., *Women and Revolution: A Discussion of the Unhappy Marriage of Marxism and Feminism* (Boston: South End Press, 1981); Zillah Eisenstein, ed., *Capitalist Patriarchy and the Case for Socialist Feminism* (New York: Monthly Review Press, 1979); Annette Kuhn and Ann Marie Wolpe, eds., *Feminism and Materialism: Women and Modes of Production* (London: Routledge and Kegan Paul, 1978); Sheila Rowbotham, Lynne Segal, and Hilary Wainwright, eds., *Beyond the Fragments: Feminism and the Making of Socialism* (Boston: Alyson Publications, 1981). A specifically anthropological Marxist-feminist collection is Kate Young, Carol Wolkowitz, and Roslyn McCullagh, eds., *Of Marriage and the Market: Women's Subordination Internationally and Its Lessons*, 2nd ed. (London: Routledge and Kegan Paul, 1984). All of these works tend to focus on gender, economies, and politial activism. I am interested in integrating a more sophisticated theory of culture and consciousness into Marxist-feminist perspectives.

36. See, e.g., Adrienne Rich, "Compulsory Heterosexuality and Lesbian Existence," in *The Signs Reader*, ed. Elizabeth Abel and Emily K. Abel (Chicago: University of Chicago Press, 1980), 139–68, esp. 146–47.

37. Hunter College Women's Studies Collective, *Women's Realities, Women's Choices: An Introduction to Women's Studies* (New York: Oxford University Press, 1983), 35.

38. Assitan Diallo, "Tackling Tradition," interview with Adi Gevins, *Connexions: An International Women's Quarterly* 17–18 (Summer/Fall 1985):45–46. See also Scilla McLean and Stella Efua Graham, eds., "Female Circumcision, Excision and Infibulation," Report no. 47 (London: Minority Rights Group, 1985).

39. Stella Efua Graham, "Tackling Tradition," interview with Adi Gevins, *Connexions: An International Women's Quarterly* 17–18 (Summer/Fall 1985):46–47.

40. Carol Vance, "The Female Body and Social Construction Theory," lecture, Yale University, 14 Oct. 1985.

41. Annette Fuentes and Barbara Ehrenreich, *Women in the Global Factory* (Boston: South End Press, 1983), 36–37.

42. Diane Elson and Ruth Pearson, "Women in World Market Factories," in Young, Wolkowitz, and McCullagh, *Of Marriage and the Market*, 18–40, esp. 40.

43. Nash and Fernandez-Kelly, *Women, Men and the International Division of Labor*, bring together articles on United States and Third-World economies and working women.

44. An excellent example of collaboration between First- and Third-World feminist scholars working on gender and transnationals is Wendy Chapkis and Cynthia Enloe, eds., *Of Common Cloth: Women in the Global Textile Industry* (Washington, D.C.: Transnational Institute, 1983).

45. Janice Radway, *Reading the Romance: Women, Patriarchy and Popular Literature* (Chapel Hill: University of North Carolina Press, 1984).

Black Woman Scholar, Critic, and Teacher: The Inextricable Relationship Among Race, Sex, and Class

Joyce A. Joyce

WORTH HIS WEIGHT IN GOLD (RALLY ROUND)

Chorus
Rally round the flag
Rally round the red
Gold black and green

Marcus say sir Marcus say
Red for the blood
That flowed like the river
Marcus say sir Marcus say
Green for the land Africa
Marcus say
Yellow for the gold
That they stole
Marcus say
Black for the people
It was looted from. . . .
          —Sung by Steel Pulse on *True Democracy*

The reggae song "Worth His Weight in Gold," written by David Hinds, functions as the epigraph to this essay and as a model for my values as a scholar, critic, and teacher. It summons us to rally around the red, gold, black, and green Rastafarian flag that represents the red blood of Africans killed by white men, the yellow gold stolen by them, the Black people both oppressed and murdered by them, and the green land appropriated by them. Rastafarians believe they are Nazarites, descendents of the tribe of Judah, the first of the twelve tribes of Israel. They view Haile Selassie I, the first crowned king of an ancient African country, Ethiopia, as a direct descendent of King David, son of Solomon, and thus the rightful heir to all Africa, and they refer to him as the Lion of Judah. Yet their long dreadlocks signify more than the boldness and courage of the lion. Rastafarians separate themselves from the established order of evil and corruption; in Hebrew, *Nazarite* means *to separate.* Their hair symbolizes their spirituality and discipline. Numbers 6:5 — "All the days of the vow of his separation there shall no razor come upon his head: until the days be fulfilled, in which he separateth himself unto the Lord, he shall be holy, and shall let the locks of the hair of his head grow"— explains the relationship between the Rastafarians' practice of letting their hair grow and their spirituality and separation from worldly endeavors.[1]

Marcus Garvey, a Jamaican immigrant to the United States, advocated the liberation of Blacks from white oppression, physically and economically, through a return to Africa. Garvey has become a symbol of repatriation to the Rastafarians. Reggae music, originating in Jamaica, popularized by Rastafarians like Bob Marley and Peter Tosh, and now played all over the world, disseminates the Rastafarians' message. Like the Old Testament Jews exiled from their homeland in Egypt, Rastafarians, mindful of their displacement, attempt in their music to keep their traditions alive, to educate, and spiritually to strengthen those of us who feel their rhythms and understand the need for Black people to unite in their struggle to destroy racial oppression. Thus my epigraph is an invitation to rally around the Rastafarian flag, to come together for a common purpose, and to recover our past, Africa.

As a Black woman scholar, teacher, and critic, I regard my tasks to be arousing the feelings of my students and readers, provoking them into questioning the relationship between the works they read and the world around them, and preventing neutral responses. I invite students and readers candidly to discuss the racism, sexism, and classism that dominate Black literary criticism and theory. I also ask them to clarify the values that make it difficult for Black women critics either, on the one hand, to devise the sort of systematic feminist ideologies devised by white women critics or, on the other hand, to share the status of Black male critics.

As a Black woman in predominantly white institutions, I am doubly isolated and triply in jeopardy: from white females by race, from Black males by gender, and from white males by race and gender both. However, though some of my white male students and my female students, Black and white, have been angry about receiving grades other than the ones they thought they deserved, none has exhibited the hostility shown me by some Black male students. At the University of Maryland, College Park, I had to tell three of them that I would call the university police if they continued to threaten me and refused to leave my office. Another followed me from office to classroom hurling insults at me and later wrote a letter to my department chair, falsely accusing me of calling his house and attempting to disrupt his parents' marriage by inviting his father to lunch. I also was sexually harassed, once, by a white male administrator. When I went to his office to express my interest in a position under his jurisdiction, he told me that, as a junior professor, I did not qualify. The next day, however, he telephoned to say that he would like to talk to me at my home about several issues that had come to mind about the job; once at my apartment, he said that what he really wanted was to have sex with me.

In describing these incidents, I do not aim to exacerbate the divisions between Black men and Black women already exacerbated by Michelle Wallace's *Black Macho and the Myth of the Superwoman* and Alice Walker's *The Color Purple*. Rather I aim to ground my analysis of values in the experience that underlies my intellectual activity and to debunk the notion that the university is a protected and privileged environment. For I see an inextricable relationship between my experiences as a Black woman and my experiences as a Black scholar, teacher, and critic—experiences that have their roots in the historical oppression of Black women. The hostile behavior of some of my Black male students and my sexual harassment by a white male administrator illustrate the points that Angela Davis and Paula Giddings, tracing the history of Black women in America, make: Black women have always been victims of the double discrimination of racism and sexism, and consequently have not enjoyed economic, political, social, and educational gains to the same degree as white women, Black men, and, of course, white men.[2] However, because we are Black and share the racial oppression of Black men, we have bonded with them rather than with white women who are victims of sexism. As examples of the racism that historically has alienated Black women from white women, Davis and Giddings cite the refusal of Susan B. Anthony and other suffragettes to support Black women's efforts to form a separate suffrage association, because Anthony and her colleagues did not want to antagonize southern white women suffragettes; Anthony's request to Frederick Douglass, one of the founding members of the American Equal Rights Association, that he not speak at a southern meeting, again because she did not want to antagonize white southern women; and, perhaps more striking, Elizabeth Cady Stanton's efforts to prevent Black men from receiving the vote before white women.[3]

Therefore, despite the sexist oppression that characterizes the lives of Black and white women, Black women recognize the patronizing, condescending, paternalistic attitudes of white women, who habitually view them as inferior. In feminist discourse, Black women have been quite exact in expressing their differences from white feminists. Alice Walker describes herself as a womanist. Black feminist critic Nellie McKay responded cautiously to Ellen Messer-Davidow's essay, "The Philosophical Bases of Feminist Literary Criticisms," by pointing out that Black and Third World women have perspectives different from those of white feminists because of experiences peculiar to them. She underscored connections between racism and sexism already addressed by Angela Davis, Paula Giddings, bell hooks, and Audre Lorde, among others. McKay writes:

> Black feminists especially, the largest minority in the Third World group, constantly remind us of the marginality of black and Third World women on the basis of their race and sex. As a result of their position, it remains critical for black and Third World feminist literary critics, dancing through the "minefield" of white and black patriarchal dominance and white female racism, to seek areas of cooperation with white feminist critics and still find a separate autonomy. They must remain alert when they subscribe to conclusions on the philosophical bases of white feminist literary criticism, and criticism of men of color.[4]

McKay's response opens a Pandora's box filled with differences between the inquiries of Black and white women literary critics, especially the issues of how Black women *choose* to deal with the Black patriarchal dominance of literature.

Black women literary critics must still confront the sexist behavior and reproaches of their Black male colleagues as they struggle to combat racial oppression, much as Sojourner Truth, Frances Harper, Ida B. Wells, Mary Church Terrell, Anna Julia Cooper, and Shirley Chisholm confronted them. Sexism among Black men still prevails in academic institutions. In 1897, when the American Negro Academy was organized to promote scholarly work, establish an archive, and bring together leading Black intellectuals like Alexander Crummell, W.E.B. DuBois, and Francis Grimké (graduates respectively of Cambridge, Harvard, and Princeton universities), its by-laws stipulated that only men of African descent could participate. To Crummell's patronizing description of Black women as tender, modest, sweet, humble mothers with superior aboriginal qualities, Anna Julia Cooper responded: "While our men seem thoroughly abreast of the times in every other subject, when they strike the woman question, they drop back into a sixteenth-century logic."[5] Today Black women academics may echo her sentiments. Yet African-American history demands that we remain ever mindful of the racial bond we share with Black men.

While the economic, political, and educational aspects of racism unite Black men and women, they also create psychological wounds that impede harmonious relationships between them in both their personal and their professional lives. In point of fact, the personal and the professional interrelate and impact upon each other. Because I believe it is my responsibility to address issues that bear upon the lives of my students, I speak candidly in my African-American literature classes about the historical dilemma that confronts Black women and men, and I encourage my students to discuss the problems we face in relating to each other, particularly in predominantly white environments. While these discussions begin with some character or scene in the literature we read, I allow a fair amount of freedom before bringing them back to it. The three hostile young Black men I mentioned earlier responded to these discussions either by sitting silent and uneasy, as if they wanted to speak but were afraid to, or by attempting to dominate the class.

My response to them reflects my sense of myself as a teacher and a literary critic. I pointed out that they would regard me with more respect were I a white man, a white woman, or a Black man. Instead of dismissing them as irrevocably sexist, I attempted to address the paradoxical anger and intimidation I had excited in them, and the legacy of racism that perennially disrupts and distorts the ways Black men and Black women relate to each other. Black women critics cannot ignore or dismiss dominant male aesthetic standards, as Elaine Showalter proposes for white feminists. Because the well-being of the Black family depends on understanding between Black men and Black women, and because racism has caused their misunderstandings, we must challenge, correct, modify, revise, and humanize critical theories that deemphasize, and perhaps even deny the significance of, racism in African-American literary history. If we understand our peculiar relationship to the hegemony and to Black men, we are in a unique position not only to empower ourselves but also to create new visions and values that can make an impact upon the entire literary-critical community. In his discussion of oppressed people's reaction to their dehumanization, Paulo Freire sums up what I see as valuable tasks for Black women critics. He says:

> This, then, is the great humanistic and historical task of the oppressed: to liberate themselves and their oppressors as well. The oppressors, who oppress, exploit, and rape by virtue of their power, cannot find in this power the strength to liberate either the oppressed or themselves. Only power that springs from the weakness of the oppressed will be sufficiently strong to free both.[6]

Recently my friend Dr. Ruth Muschel, an assistant professor of pathology and laboratory medicine at the University of Pennsylvania School of Medicine, and I discussed sexism in our respective departments: the lack of a tenured Black woman full professor in the English Department at the University of Maryland (where I then was) and the lack of a tenured female doctor of any race in her department. Our discussion then turned to poststructuralist literary theories. The most recent formulations of African-American literary theory, I explained — those by Houston A. Baker, Jr., and Henry Louis Gates, Jr. — treat Black literature as if it were exclusively a sys-

tem of linguistic signs divorced from feeling, meaning, and social and political relevance.[7] Dr. Muschel replied that the practices of Gates, Baker, and
Euro-American poststructuralists were in keeping with major twentieth-
century scientific and mathematical discoveries that changed the way we
view our place in the universe. Heisenberg's uncertainty principle, for example, articulates limits to what can be known about the phenomenal world:
all properties of an object cannot be known simultaneously, and the observer
watching it in motion significantly "distorts" it; Godel's proof and the Tur-
ing machine demonstrate that not all propositions can be decided. Consequently, according to Dr. Muschel — and according to poststructuralists,
with such notable exceptions as Michel Foucault and Edward Said — scientistic man cannot be certain of the meaning of anything in or about our
world.

My sensibility is that of a humanist, not a scientist, and my intellectual,
analytic, emotional, intuitive, and pedagogical values arise from my concern for the welfare of human beings. I do not imply that Dr. Muschel (and
other scientists) are indifferent to the welfare of humanity; their work dis-
proves this far-too-simple idea. Yet our disparate views of our own agency
have been molded by our respective training and its applications. It is ironic
that, while Dr. Muschel holds that we cannot be absolutely certain about
anything, including the nature of our existence, she works indefatigably to
discover a cure for cancer. It is ironic, too, that I, a Black woman — a representative of a group that always has been relegated to the margins of American society — struggle to challenge Black male sexism, white racism, and
epistemological elitism in predominantly white educational institutions.

Skill in using standard English, I point out to students, has less to do with
innate intelligence than with circumstances of class, home environment,
and educational opportunities. No example demonstrates my point better
than Charles Chesnutts's *Conjure Woman* tales (1899), in which the northern
farmer, a pretentious, educated white liberal, is convinced of his superiority
to Uncle Julius, an ex-slave. The northern farmer is pedantically skillful in
his use of English but lacks the wisdom, intelligence, and imaginative power
that underlie Uncle Julius's Black dialect. Ironically, the farmer's ignorance
empowers the ex-slave, who represents intuition and passion (as opposed to
the farmer's reason) and uses language as a means to survive in an environment that not only sees him as less than human but also equates objectivity
and inactivity with language. Understanding his environment and his relationship to it, Uncle Julius survives by using language — his Black dialect —
to camouflage his keen intelligence and his self-assured awareness of his
humanity.

Black artists, like Uncle Julius, are positioned as outsiders; they are, among
other things, able to stand apart from Western divorce of art from life, This

ability emerges as a salient aspect not only of Black literature but also of Black criticism, from their beginnings to the initial deployment of post-structuralist theories. James T. Stewart summarizes the predominant view of white aesthetics in the Black community in the late 1960s: "The artist is a man in society, and his social attitudes are just as relevant to his art as his aesthetic position. However, white western aesthetics is predicated on the idea of separating one from the other — a man's art from his actions. It is this duality that is the most distinguishable feature of western values."[8] However, in 1979, the essays in *Afro-American Literature: The Reconstruction of Instruction* revealed Black male literary critics, academic critics, subscribing to the duality of Western aesthetic values.[9]

The Euro-American literary establishment privileges the separation of art and social circumstances and judges literary works with overt moral values and didactic subjects inferior to those whose covert meanings are expressed in figurative and obscure language. Black critics who follow this establishment adopt its elitist values. Two well-known essays by Darwin T. Turner and Houston A. Baker, Jr., provide overviews of African-American literary criticism.[10] Both make it clear that, before 1970, the most prominent critics of African-American literature were creative writers themselves; however, in the 1970s, African-American criticism began to be dominated by academics, and by academics whose vanguard is exclusively male. Despite the pioneering work of Black women critics like Barbara Christian, Gloria Hull, and Mary Helen Washington, Black male critics consistently have determined the values, issues, and trends in Black American criticism. Moreover, the best-known Black women critics — Daryl Dance, Thadious Davis, Frances Foster, Joanne Gabbin, Sandra Govin, Trudier Harris, Carol Herron, Jennifer Jordan, Deborah McDowell, Nellie McKay, Marilyn Mobley, Margaret Reid, Valerie Smith, Hortense Spillers, Claudia Tate, and Eleanor Traylor, in addition to the three named above — so far have produced work that resists allegiance to deconstruction, though Spillers' criticism sometimes suggests a poststructuralist sensibility. This resistance on the part of Black women critics attests not only to their differing values but also to their differing notions about the function of criticism. Making common cause with Black women critics and creative artists like Amiri Baraka, Mari Evans, Sarah Fabio, Haki Madhubuti, and Carolyn Rogers (who also write criticism) are Stephen Henderson and Addison Gayle, Black male academic critics who differ from their male peers (those who champion poststructuralist play with language) by continuing to write critical analyses that call attention to, and attempt to transform, social values.

Adopting poststructuralist ideology requires Black critics both to renounce the history of African-American literature and criticism and to estrange themselves from the *political* implications of their *black* skin. Therefore Gates (and other Black deconstructionists) attempt to invalidate the ideas of Henderson and Gayle, the most prominent advocates of Black Aesthetics, who assert that Black literature must challenge the aesthetic, economic, educational, political, and spiritual deprivations of racism. Consequently, in "Literary Theory and the Black Tradition," Gates remonstrates against the ideas of Henderson and Gayle while meticulously surveying the ideas of Euro-American philosophers, politicians, men of letters, and aestheticians (Bacon, Hume, Jefferson, Kant, Hegel, and Max Eastman, I.A. Richards, and Allen Tate, for example) who publicly express their belief in the innate inferiority of the Black race.[11]

According to Gates, "nearly the whole of Afro-American writing," beginning with *A Narrative of the Uncommon Sufferings and Surprising Deliverance of Briton Hammon, a Negro Man* (published in 1760), has focused on "the idea of a determining formal relationship between literature and social institutions," an idea that "has often encouraged a posture that belabors the social and documentary status of black art."[12] This focus (or "posture"), he claims, is a reaction to the white man's notion of the Black man's inferiority. Black intellectuals like W.E.B. DuBois, J.A. Rogers, and Carter G. Woodson have been cognizant of racism as an intellectual insult. But they — like Frederick Douglass, Frances Harper, Langston Hughes, Margaret Walker, Richard Wright, Toni Morrison, Stephen Henderson, and Addison Gayle — do not react to the "*idea* of a determining formal relationship between literature and social institutions" (emphasis mine), anymore than they accept the white establishment's definition of literary values. In other words, Black American literature (and criticism) is not a reaction to an *idea*. It is a means of survival, a record of Black lives lost in the Middle Passage, in the cottonfields, on plantations, in swamps, in back alleys, and on city streets, and a means of spiritually empowering those of us who understand the need to rally around the goal of transforming society.

Black American literature (and criticism) has functioned, historically, not as a response to the white establishment's devaluing of it, but as a response to the complex network of environmental conditions designed to stifle the productivity of Blacks in all their endeavors. Hence African-American critics, from W.E.B. DuBois to Stephen Henderson and Addison Gayle, held unflinchingly to the idea that literature, especially African-American literature, should be used to reinforce values. Poet, novelist, and critic Lance Jeffers, in a keynote address delivered to the Fifth National Congress of Afro-American Writers, boldly expresses his commitment to the active role of literature in society. He says:

> This is the role of any literature that is worth reading or listening to: to make men change themselves, to make women grow, to make men rip up the roots

of society and create a new humanity! Any literature that does not — directly or indirectly, subtly or overtly — any literature that does not seek to create a new humanity is worthless, and worse than worthless, destructive![13]

Jeffers' values demand that literature be active rather than passive and that artists be involved in improving the quality of their peoples' lives.

Gates proposes to alter the historical role of African-American criticism by renouncing the racial subject matter that informs what he calls "race and superstructure criticism." He argues, first, that Henderson, Gayle, and other proponents of a Black Aesthetic value content over form, and second, that race is a trope, a figure of absence for Black people's humanity and intelligence. His scientistic contentions that races (or racial differences among people) do not exist and that the white Western world has used race as a trope to deny Black people's humanity enable him to ignore millions of Black lives subject to poverty and other oppressions because of the color of their skin. He holds that Black Aesthetic criticism has been "locked in a relation of thesis to antithesis in a racist discourse embedded in Western philosophy" because the white world has refused to accept Black humanity.[14] Ironically, he seems unaware of his own internalization of that discourse. Black poets and aestheticians in the 1960s, refining the ideological accomplishments and correcting the practical weaknesses of the Harlem Renaissance, not only raised questions about the content and form of Black literature but also rejected the definitions and values imposed upon it by Euro-American aesthetics. Gates, unlike Langston Hughes, Sterling Brown, Lance Jeffers, Julian Mayfield, Stephen Henderson, Addison Gayle, Chinua Achebe, Ngugi wa Thiong'o, and other Black writers (and critics), evidences no concern about his relationship to the Euro-American aesthetic tradition, nor about the role he plays in its propagation. Rejecting the concept of race — Blackness is a trope of absence — he both dismisses the political and cultural oppression imposed as a result of that concept, and ignores the political implications of his theory.

Whether or not we accept Gates's notion that Black literature and criticism function as the antithesis to "racist discourse embedded in Western philosophy," we see him ironically caught in the same historical trap that he sees Henderson and Gayle caught in. Gates's theory — his adopting the white Western literary establishment's definition and deconstruction of art — brings Black American letters full circle. For if once, as Gates suggests, Briton Hammon, Phillis Wheatley, Ignatius Sancho, Frederick Douglass, and W.E.B. DuBois struggled to prove their humanity to whites by mastering their language, so do Black male academic critics now. Prior to the 1960s, the strength of Black American writers came from their vantage point outside the system of corrupt Western values. However, after the political accomplishments of the 1960s, Blacks began to merge with mainstream culture, especially in the academy. Carter G. Woodson (in *The Mis-education of the Negro*), and Frantz Fanon (in *Black Skins, White Masks* and *The Wretched of the Earth*), and Paulo Freire (in *The Pedagogy of the Oppressed*) all warn that educated Blacks, suffering internalized inferiority and alienation from the roots of their culture, evince their vulnerability by absorbing the ideas and values of the powerful who oppress them.[15]

This process of stripping oppressed Blacks of their identity in order to inculcate them with values necessary for them in turn to oppress other Blacks is a salient characteristic of all societies in which one group oppresses another. Fanon, discussing the "Negro of the Antilles," who believed himself to be a human being in proportion to the lightness of his skin and his mastery of the French language, describes a situation analogous to that of Gates, Baker, and other Black males who adopt poststructuralist methods. Fanon writes:

> Every colonized people . . . every people in whose soul an inferiority complex has been created by the death and burial of its local cultural originality — finds itself face to face with the language of the civilizing nation; that is, with the culture of the mother country. The colonized is elevated above his jungle status in proportion to his adoption of the mother country's cultural standards. He becomes whiter as he renounces his blackness, his jungle.[16]

Gates, having fully accepted the white establishment's values for literature and criticism, appears unaware of the political realities underlying all notions of what are and are not the proper subjects and forms of literature. Jane Tompkins, inquiring "But Is It Any Good?", surveys introductions to anthologies of American literature to show that our notions of "good" and "bad" literature "emerge from within a dynamic system of values [our tastes, emphases, preferences, and priorities], which determine what, at a given moment, will be considered best."[17] She shows how neither meaning nor values have remained constant throughout the history of American literature and that judgments about major and minor writers, rather than being self-evident, are instead "constantly being produced and maintained by cultural activity: by literary anthologies, by course syllabi, book reviews, magazine articles, book club selections, radio and television programs." Like Tompkins and other feminists, scholars in various fields of literary study are addressing the elitism and myopia that underlie critical definitions and privilege one kind of literature over another. Lee Patterson, a medievalist, provides a Marxist analysis of political and social issues affecting the definitions, boundaries, and purposes of historical criticism. Echoing Tompkins, he writes:

There is no inherent, ahistorical essence that marks one written document as literary and another as nonliterary: literariness, as a special quality possessed by a certain category of writing, is a self-justifying idea generated by a criticism that seeks to mystify its own grounding within social institutions that carry an undeniably political valence. The refusal of criticism to acknowledge this fact, and its counterclaim that it is called into being by an object that exists wholly apart from itself, is simply an effect of its reluctance to reflect upon the political nature of its authority.[18]

African-American critics, because of perspectives acquired as a result of their location on the margins of American society, traditionally have directed their attention to the hegemonic political forces that aim to control their lives and their art. Among their concerns — but scarcely their exclusive concern — is the inclusion of African-American literature in the canon of American literature. African-American critics associated with the Black Aesthetic understand that there are no sacrosanct definitions of literature, criticism, or theory, and consequently that the hegemony constructs values and determines rules for inclusion and exclusion, good and bad, major and minor, according to its social, economic, and political needs.

Amiri Baraka expresses ideas similar to Frantz Fanon's and Paulo Freire's. Oppressors, he explains, select individuals from the ranks of the oppressed to serve as overseers and to inculcate the oppressed with the values of the hegemony. Gates (as well as Baker), in condemning the issue of race as it pervades Black American literary criticism, reenacts the roles of James Baldwin and Ralph Ellison in the dispute over the protest literature associated with Richard Wright. According to Baraka, Baldwin and Ellison, in disapproving of the content of protest fiction, acted out their roles as overseers appointed to subvert the issue of race in African-American literature.[19] Although Baldwin later retracted, Ellison — and Gates — continue to dismiss the relationship between the forces of oppression and the aesthetic rules set up by the hegemony. Baraka, providing an example of this relationship, suggests that the New Criticism, with its emphasis on literature as a "self-contained artifact removed from real life," was a reaction to the McCarthyism and conservatism of the 1950s.[20] Thus the white power structure privileges *how* a literary work is made over *what* is said, because it is not politically advantageous for the hegemony to provide disturbing accounts of oppression that in turn would provoke the oppressed into thinking about and acting to secure their liberation.

I choose neither silence nor neutrality in teaching and in writing about the two issues I regard as critical to African-American literature and literary criticism: whether form is more important than content, and whether race is a subject appropriate to literary analyses. I am influenced by creative artists and by critics like Stephen Henderson and Addison Gayle; by critics of African literature like Chinweizu Oyekan Dwomoyela and Onwuchekwa Jemie; and by African writers like Chinua Achebe, Ayi Kwei Armah, Alex La Guma, Bessie Head, and Ngugi wa Thiong'o. The titles alone of Ngugi's collections of essays — *Homecoming: Essays on African and Caribbean Literature, Culture and Politics*; *Barrel of a Pen: Resistance to Repression in Neo-Colonial Kenya*; *Decolonizing the Mind: The Politics of Language in African Literature*; and *Writers in Politics* — attest to what he sees as the function of African literature. I agree with him when he says that our pens should give voice to silence and should "be used to increase the anxieties of all oppressive regimes."[21] As a critic and teacher, I am also responsible for locating points of merger between political commitment in African-American literature and in aesthetics.

Authentic political commitment can come only from African-American critics who are undeniably Black. Journalist Jack White unequivocally asserts his Blackness as the main source of his empowerment:

> You will note that I don't say, as many blacks do, journalists and creative artists who "happen" to be black. My color is more a part of me than my arm — if you cut that off, I'm still black. And that changes everything about the way I go about my work and live my life. I simply do not approach my work in the same way a white person who is otherwise much like me approaches his/her work. As a black journalist, my duty, and it is nothing less than that, is to be more complete than my white counterparts might be, particularly when I am writing about black subjects. That obligation to tell all I know arises because, as a black American, I see the world, including the white world, from a different angle than my white counterparts. My duty — as a journalist — is to present the facts as well as I can, particularly those which are most likely to be overlooked. Obviously my color influences the way I unearth them.[22]

Black critics, like Jack White, ought not hesitate either to affirm that they write from the perspective of African-Americans or to challenge mainstream society.

There is no sacrosanct rule that form in literature is more valuable than content. To champion form over content and to condemn racism as a subject, as I have suggested, are political contrivances masked as "universal" aesthetic principles. When African-American critics understand the relationship between their perspectives and the creative process, they will accept the ineradicable relationship between form and content in all literature. Perhaps no other work in the African-American literary canon more appropriately demonstrates the integration of literary art and political commitment than Richard Wright's *Native Son*, which is also the most controversial novel in the canon. Because Wright addresses the psychological, political, and economic issues of racism unflinchingly, and because *Native Son* is so powerful, it has had an ambivalent reception. In *Richard Wright's Art of Tragedy*, I have shown how aspects of language — structure, characterization, setting, imagery, symbolism, and point of view — "form an intricate net of skillfully woven linguistic threads that become manifestations of Bigger Thomas's consciousness."[23] Although my approach may appear New Critical, I deploy it to reflect and demonstrate the merger between Euro-American aesthetic principles and African-American political commitment. The power of *Native Son* lies in the intimate relationship between Wright's perception of racial realities and his adroit shaping of his vision.

It is true that in African-American criticism formal achievement has been overlooked or subordinated to sociological and biographical issues. But it is an oversimplification to assert, as Gates does, that Black writers, especially those of the Black Aesthetic, held that "content is primary over form and indeed is either divorced completely from form, in terms of genesis and normative value, or else is merely facilitated by form as a means to an end."[24] Perhaps the most important essay in *The Black Aesthetic*, Addison Gayle's undervalued collection, is James A. Emanuel's "Blackness Can: A Quest for Aesthetics." Emanuel, using a series of essays by creative writers that appeared in the *Negro Digest* from September 1968 through November 1969, provides a comprehensive analysis of the ideology and stylistic innovations of writers associated with the Black Aesthetic.[25] Emanuel, like Baraka,[26] substantiates the complex and profound relationship between political commitment and form in Black American literature. Black American artists and critics have consciously attempted to shape their plots and characters in order to provide society, as Jane Tompkins puts it, with "a means of thinking about itself" and "defining certain aspects of social reality."[27] The issues I see as critical to African-American literature and criticism involve the hegemony's elitist requirement that all literature adhere to the same unquestioned criteria of value, the propensity of some Black male critics to defend this position, and the doctrine that racial issues are parochial rather than "universal." Any critic, Black or white, who holds that racial issues are not universal denies both the omnipresence of racism and the role of the hegemony in racism's origin and promulgation. In other words, racism, rather than being parochial, instead is among the most universal of topics writers can address. It denotes relationships between oppressor and oppressed, or white and nonwhite, relationships that include all the peoples in the universe, which is the noun form of the adjective *universal*.

The condemnation of "propaganda" and "protest" in literature manifests the values of an elite that determines the production and promulgation of what counts as literature. Critics, perhaps more than artists, play a significant role in establishing standards. This elite — which includes publishers,

editors, reviewers, and critics as well as scholars and academic critics—
functions, according to Lawrence Hogue,

> as a kind of conduit for many of the established cultural, ideological, and in-
> tellectual preferences. They are instrumental in keeping certain ideas, social
> habits, myths, moral conventions, and stereotypes alive in the public's mind.
> . . . These editors and critics seek their own definitions of the literary experi-
> ence in texts that come to their attention. . . . They exclude those texts that
> do not conform in subject or perspective, on the grounds that they are inferior
> aesthetically—thereby effecting certain silences in the discourse of literature.[28]

In an essay published in *New Literary History*, "The Black Canon: Recon-
structing Afro-American Literary Criticism," I apparently broke another
silence in the discourse of literature—in academic discourse concerning
African-American literature—by attempting to reclaim an older and currently unfashionable generation of Black critics.[29] The editor invited both
Houston Baker and Henry Louis Gates to respond to me. In their responses—
Baker's "In Dubious Battle" and Gates's "What's Love Got To Do With It?:
Critical Theory, Integrity, and the Black Idiom"—I discern the same dis-
respect, contempt, and hostility exhibited by the Black male students I described earlier. Our discussion, in which they rebuke, censure, and attempt
to silence me, illuminates the extent to which, among Black males in academe, elitism and sexism are wedded.

An issue of *Critical Inquiry*, edited by Gates and entitled "'Race,' Writing, and Difference," suggests that Black male critics view literary theory
as a sophisticated and rigorously intellectual activity suitable for men, both
Black and white, and perhaps a few white women: of its thirteen essays, four
are by women, only one of them Black.[30] While Baker venomously describes
my essay in *New Literary History* as a work of "minstrel simplicity" that is
"dreadfully flawed by factual mistakes" and accuses the editors of racism for
publishing it, in a later issue of *Critical Inquiry*, he adopts the donnish
humor more characteristic of his prose. A few sentences from his response
to Anthony Appiah, a Black male, evince the diplomacy he uses when disagreeing with Black males, white males, and white females. Appiah denies
racial differences. Baker writes: "Clearly, Appiah is one who has journeyed
among mirrors and captured the language of the overseers. For one is po-
tently aware on reading this essay that one is in the presence of eloquence—
an elegant mind analyzing. . . . In short, Appiah's eloquent shift to the
common ground of subtle academic discourse is instructive but, ultimately,
unhelpful."[31] His tactful collegiality is quite different from his truculence in
"In Dubious Battle."

Similarly, when Gates disagrees with Tzvetan Todorov, a white male, the best invective he can summon is to accuse him of "shallow thinking."[32] To-dorov believes that racism is a type of behavior; Gates, that it is a "transcen-dent 'metaphysical' *character.*" Nevertheless, Gates does not state what he implies, that Todorov's notions of racism are naive, nor does he call him, as he called me, "silly." When, in another essay, he disagrees with Greg Tate, a Black writer for the *Village Voice,* he exercises equal diplomacy. Respond-ing to Tate, who challenges Blacks to develop a criticism commensurate with the complexities of Black culture and who criticizes contemporary African-American criticism for its propensity to "fun and games," Gates deemphasizes those points of Tate with which he disagrees and amplifies those with which he agrees. Rather than castigating Tate, Gates empowers and is empowered by him. He writes: "Only by reshaping the critical canon with our own voices in our own images can we meet Tate's challenge head on. . . . Tate's challenge is a serious one because neither ideology nor criti-cism nor blackness can exist as an entity of itself, outside its forms or its text."[33] Thus, in response to Black and white males who disagree with them, Baker and Gates display the camaraderie appropriate to meaningful profes-sional dialogue. But Black women, as their replies to my essay indicate, are not yet integrated into the African-American professional — that is, the African-American *theoretical* — scene.

The sexist, elitist treatment of Black women academics substantiates bell hooks's analysis of the connection between racism and sexism. "Black men may be victimized by racism," she writes,

> but sexism allows them to act as exploiters and oppressors of women. . . . Black male sexism has undermined struggles to eradicate racism just as white female racism undermines feminist struggle. As long as these two groups or any group define liberation as gaining social equality with ruling class white men, they have a vested interest in the continued exploitation and oppression of others.[34]

Baker and Gates, viewing themselves as the leading spokespersons for African-American literary criticism, attempt to wield the same power over the African-American literary community as the hegemony does over the underclass. In "In Dubious Battle" and "What's Love Got To Do With It?", they solidify their power by setting up a call-and-response pattern by which they buttress and propagate each other's ideas both in these essays and, even more gratu-itously, in the prefaces and endnotes of Baker's *Modernism and the Harlem Renaissance* (1987) and Gates's *The Signifying Monkey: A Theory of Afro-American Literary Criticism* (1988).

The power of the Black male literary establishment extends beyond the prefaces, body, and endnotes of their work. As with Booker T. Washington and other Blacks who were recognized by the hegemony as spokespersons for their race, Baker and Gates judge the works of other scholars of African-American literature, serve on the editorial boards of journals that influence the reception of literary works, and determine the criticism that is published. For example, Baker, after serving on the executive council of the Modern Language Association (the major professional organization of professors of English literature), is the first Black elected to the succession of vice-president and president; he also serves as an associate editor of *Black American Literature Forum* (BALF). Gates is a member of the editorial collective of *Cultural Critique*, is book review editor of BALF, and has served on the editorial board of *Publications of the Modern Language Association* (PMLA).

Hence it is not coincidental that my exchange with Baker and Gates in *New Literary History* reverberates elsewhere. Michael Awkward, a former graduate student of Baker and now an assistant professor at the University of Michigan, vindicates Baker against me in an essay in BALF. R. Baxter Miller, in another essay in BALF, refers in an endnote to "the rancorous tone of the recent debate which appeared on the pages of *New Literary History* between Houston Baker and Henry Louis Gates on the one hand and the ridiculed Joyce Joyce [*sic*] on the other."[35] His insulting use of the word "ridiculed" and, more important, his perception of me as having been made to look absurd, is both sexist and elitist. His comment reveals the same view — that Baker and Gates are superior and I inferior — as colleagues of mine did when they asked if I were "set up" by Ralph Cohen, the editor of *New Literary History*. To suggest that I was set up or made to look ridiculous is to imply that I lack the intellect and training necessary to challenge the Black male hierarchy. The double discrimination of racism and sexism means that no one asks whether Baker and Gates were "set up" or whether Cohen published my essay because he appreciated my ideas and my presentation.

In spite of racist, sexist, and elitist obstacles, Black women critics have produced impressive works; among them are Toni Cade Bambara, *The Black Woman: An Anthology* (1970); Mary Helen Washington, *Black-Eyed Susans* (1975), *Midnight Birds* (1980), and *Invented Lives* (1987); Roseann P. Bell, Bettye J. Parker, and Beverly Guy-Sheftall, *Sturdy Black Bridges* (1979); Barbara Christian, *Black Women Novelists* (1980) and *Black Feminist Criticism* (1985); Trudier Harris, *From Mammies to Militants* (1982) and *Exorcising Blackness: Historical and Literary Lynching and Burning Rituals* (1984); Gloria Hull, Patricia B. Scott, and Barbara Smith, *But Some of Us Are Brave: Black Women's Studies* (1982); Mari Evans, *Black Women Writers (1950–1980): A Critical Evaluation* (1983); Barbara Smith, *Home Girls: A Black Feminist Anthology* (1983); Claudia Tate, *Black Women Writers at Work* (1983); Gloria Hull, *Give Us This Day: The Diary of Alice Dunbar-Nelson* (1984) and *Color, Sex, & Poetry: Three Women Writers of the Har-*

lem Renaissance (1987); Gloria Wade-Gayles, *No Crystal Stair: Visions of Race and Sex in Black Women's Fiction* (1984); Marjorie Pryse and Hortense Spillers, *Conjuring: Black Women, Fiction, and Literary Tradition* (1985); Nellie McKay, *Critical Essays on Toni Morrison* (1988); Cheryl Wall, *Changing Our Own Words: Essays on Criticism, Theory, and Writing by Black Women* (1989); Joanne Braxton and Andrée McLaughlin, *Wild Women in the Whirlwind: Afra-American Culture and the Contemporary Literary Renaissance* (1990); and essays far too numerous to list by scholars such as Thadious Davis, Deborah McDowell, Frances Foster, Carol Herron, Marilyn Mobley, Priscilla Ramsey, Valerie Smith, and others.

Despite this impressive production, the works of Black women critics are viewed through even more discriminatory lenses than Black studies courses in general. While a few predominantly white institutions such as Harvard, Temple, Cornell, and the University of Iowa have reputable African-American studies departments, most white institutions relegate courses in African-American studies to the inferior status of programs offering certificates rather than degrees. African-American studies are conceived of as marginal, divorced from issues central to those who make up the larger society. African-American women's studies are doubly marginal, central neither to the larger society nor to African-American studies. Ironically, however, the criticism of African-American women scholars offers a means of undermining the impersonal, pedantic, and oppressive standards that characterize literary study and of facilitating humanistic understanding among individuals both inside and outside the academy. All the works of the Black women scholars cited above address social and political issues that affect the values held by both Black men and Black women. Although Black women critics like Carol Herron, Deborah McDowell, and Nellie MacKay have bonded with white feminists, they persist in their fidelity to historical definitions of African-American literature and its moral values — values paradoxically instilled in Black Americans as a result of their peculiar inferior status in American society.

Unlike Black male critics, Black women critics are not held hostage to the myth of white intellectual superiority. They continue to challenge the mainstream and to emphasize differences in their cultural and literary heritage. Black women critics' persistent concentration on meaning in literature and Black male critics' Euro-American propensity to escape meaning by viewing language as a playful system of signs involve yet another level of irony. For, in classroom discussions about the relationship between Black women and Black men, I encourage female students to remember how Black men live in a hostile environment, their physical and emotional well-being threatened by the judicial apparatus and codes of manhood laid down by a white establishment, while, in the academy, Black male critics demonstrate their intellectual prowess by adopting these very white establishment codes.

I do not want to repudiate racism as a subject nor devalue it in African-American literature and African-American criticism. Instead of accepting Euro-American notions of New Criticism, poststructuralism, or any other *ism*, I question their value for African-American history and literature. I conclude that, if literary theory parallels other texts, as Gates contends it does, there is no inherent value in writing that does not enliven my sensibilities, warm my spirit, and make me feel that I am experiencing, as I read or write, another text with equal or even deeper meaning than the original. Gates's *The Signifying Monkey: A Theory of Afro-American Literary Criticism*, despite its author's indefatigable energy and prodigious research, does not bring us any closer to understanding people and their cultural circumstances or to breaking down the racist, sexist, elitist barriers that divide women from men, fathers from sons, mothers from daughters, rich from poor, intelligent from unintelligent, beautiful from ugly, Blacks from whites. As a Black woman scholar, critic, and teacher who is aware of such needs, I want to achieve a pivotal balance between a subjective and an objective tone, using both first and third persons to integrate history, politics, culture, and aesthetics as they bear on African-American literature.

For, like computers and literary theories, words were invented to serve us. None of them has power without women and men. I believe that Black feminist critics can ignore neither Black men's attitudes toward us nor their critical theories when they oppress us. Black women and Black men, as well as other critics of African-American literature, must rally around candid, intellectually challenging — but not vicious — discussion, first to disclose the issues that estrange us and then to work our way through them "by whatever means necessary," to use Malcolm's words. Only then will African-American literary criticism attain the sophistication a dignified people deserve. In the words of Sonia Sanchez:

> who's gonna make all
> that beautiful blk/rhetoric
> mean something.
> . . . .
> like. this. is an S.O.S.
> me. Calling. . . .
>   Calling. . . .
>   Some/one.

pleasereplysoon.[36]

Notes

1. Stephen Davis and Peter Simon, *Reggae International* (New York: Knopf, 1982), 63.

2. Angela Davis, *Race, Sex and Class* (New York: Random House, 1981); Paula Giddings, *When and Where I Enter: The Impact of Black Women on Race and Sex in America* (New York: Bantam, 1984).

3. Davis, *Race, Sex and Class*, 111–13; Giddings, *When and Where I Enter*, 63–74.

4. Nellie McKay, "Response to 'The Philosophical Bases of Feminist Literary Criticism,'" *New Literary History* 19, no. 1 (Autumn 1987):164.

5. Giddings, *When and Where I Enter*, 115–16.

6. Paulo Freire, *The Pedagogy of the Oppressed*, trans. Myra Bergman Ramos (New York: Seabury, 1970), 28.

7. Houston A. Baker, Jr., *Modernism and the Harlem Renaissance* (Chicago: University of Chicago Press, 1987); Henry Louis Gates, Jr., *Figures in Black: Words, Signs, and the "Racial" Self* (New York: Oxford University Press, 1987) and *The Signifying Monkey: A Theory of Afro-American Literary Criticism* (New York: Oxford University Press, 1988).

8. James T. Stewart, "The Development of the Black Revolutionary Artist," in *Black Fire: An Anthology of Afro-American Writing*, ed. Leroi Jones [Amiri Baraka] and Larry Neal (New York: William Morrow, 1968), 9.

9. Dexter Fisher and Robert B. Stepto, eds., *Afro-American Literature: The Reconstruction of Instruction* (New York: Modern Language Association, 1979).

10. Darwin T. Turner, "Afro-American Literary Critics: An Introduction," in *The Black Aesthetic*, ed. Addison Gayle (Garden City, N.Y.: Doubleday, 1971), 59–77; Houston A. Baker, Jr., "Generational Shifts and the Recent Criticism of Afro-American Literature," *BALF* 15, no. 1 (Spring 1981):3–21.

11. Gates, *Figures in Black*, 3–58; also Henry Louis Gates, Jr., "Preface to Blackness: Text and Pretext," in Fisher and Stepto, *Afro-American Literature*, 44–69, and "Criticism in the Jungle," in *Black Literature and Literary Theory*, ed. Henry Louis Gates, Jr. (New York: Methuen, 1984), 1–24.

12. Gates, *Figures in Black*, 3.

13. Lance Jeffers, "To Sharpen the Sword of Our Struggle," *Sagala* 4 (1984):6.

14. Gates, *Figures in Black*, 14.

15. Carter G. Woodson, *The Mis-education of the Negro* (1933; rptd. New York: AMS Press, 1977); Frantz Fanon, *Black Skin, White Masks*, trans. Charles Lam Markmann (New York: Grove Press, 1967); Frantz Fanon, *The Wretched of the Earth*, trans. Constance Farrington (New York: Grove Press, 1968); Freire, *Pedagogy of the Oppressed*.

16. Fanon, *Black Skin, White Masks*, 18.

17. Jane Tompkins, *Sensational Designs: The Cultural Work of American Fiction, 1790–1860* (New York: Oxford University Press, 1985), 193–94.

18. Lee Patterson, *Negotiating the Past* (Madison: University of Wisconsin Press, 1987), 41–42.

19. Amiri Baraka, "The Revolutionary Tradition in Afro-American Literature," in Baraka, *Daggers and Javelins: Essays, 1974–1979* (New York: Quill, 1984), 146.

20. Amiri Baraka, "Afro-American Literature and Class Struggle," in Baraka, *Daggers and Javelins*, 312.

21. Ngugiwa Thiong'o, "Freedom of the Artist: People's Artists Versus People's Rulers," *Barrel of a Pen* (Trenton, N.J.: Africa World Press, 1983), 69.

22. Jack White, "The Black Person in Art: How Should S/he Be Portrayed? (Part I)," ed. Henry Louis Gates, Jr., *BALF* 21, nos. 1–2 (Spring–Summer 1987):20.

23. Joyce A. Joyce, *Richard Wright's Art of Tragedy* (Iowa City: University of Iowa Press, 1986), 26.

24. Gates, *Figures in Black*, 39.

25. James A. Emanuel, "Blackness Can: A Quest for Aesthetics," in Gayle, *The Black Aesthetic*, 192–223.

26. Baraka, "Afro-American Literature and Class Struggle," 310–34.

27. Tompkins' description of works whose value is discounted by F.L. Matthiessen (Tompkins, *Sensational Designs*, 200).

28. W. Lawrence Hogue, *Discourse and the Other: The Production of Afro-American Texts* (Durham, N.C.: Duke University Press, 1986), 3.

29. Joyce A. Joyce, "The Black Canon," *New Literary History* 18, no. 2 (Winter 1987): 335–45 and, in the same issue, Houston A. Baker, Jr., "In Dubious Battle," 363–69; Henry Louis Gates, Jr., "What's Love Got To Do With It?", 345–63; and Joyce A. Joyce, "Who the Cap Fit: Unconsciousness and Unconscionableness in the Criticism of Houston A. Baker, Jr., and Henry Louis Gates, Jr.," 371–81.

30. *Critical Inquiry* 12, no. 1 (Autumn 1985); the four women are Hazel Carby, Barbara Johnson, Mary Louise Pratt, and Gayatri Spivak.

31. Houston A. Baker, Jr., "Caliban's Triple Play," *Critical Inquiry* 13, no. 1 (Autumn 1986):185–86.

32. Henry Louis Gates, Jr., "Talkin' That Talk," *Critical Inquiry* 13, no. 1 (Autumn 1986):205.

33. Henry Louis Gates, Jr., "Authority, (White) Power, and the (Black) Critic: It's All Greek to Me," *Cultural Critique* 3, no. 1 (Fall 1987):35.

34. bell hooks, *Feminist Theory: From Margin to Center* (Boston: South End Press, 1984), 15.

35. Michael Awkward, "Race, Gender and the Politics of Reading," BALF 22, no. 1 (Spring 1988):5–27; R. Baxter Miller, "Baptized Infidel: Play and Critical Legacy," BALF 21, no. 4 (Winter 1987):410. He does, however, acknowledge: "Several scholars appreciated something of the truth and value in both positions: Joyce Joyce, R. Victoria Arana, George Hutchinson, Jerry W. Ward, Jr., and innumerable other colleagues at MLA and throughout the United States."

36. Sonia Sanchez, "blk/rhetoric," in *We A BaddDDD People* (Detroit: Broadside Press, 1970), 15–16.

Who Wants To Know?
The Epistemological Value of Values

Naomi Scheman

The question "Who wants to know?" is a gangster movie staple: it signifies the value of knowledge, the ways in which having or withholding it are forms of power, and the dangers of its falling into the wrong hands. The question to which it is a response is often straightforward enough ("What is your name?" or "Where is Lefty?"), as is the true answer, no matter how unlikely it is that the questioner will ever receive it. The answer, the knowledge in question, is taken to be a quite definite thing, a fact or a set of facts: one either has it or one doesn't. Viewed this way, "knowledge is power" means that facts are useful things. You can do things with them, especially if you have some that other people don't.

The essays in this section, in a number of related ways, problematize all these assumptions. They lead us to see that "Who wants to know?" may challenge more than someone's right to obtain possession of a preexisting commodity. In the cases that concern the authors of these essays, if we don't know who wants to know — and why — we won't know how to understand, let alone to answer, the question posed, whether that question concerns the technical feasibility of forms of reproductive technology, crosscultural commonalities of gender, or the interpretation and evaluation of African-American literature and criticism.

More deeply still, reflection on these essays reveals that the values that constitute communities of knowers and motivate the pursuit of knowledge shape that knowledge, which is consequently never value-free: the request for "just the facts, ma'am," meaning the bare truth, unadorned by interpretation, is ultimately incoherent. Without interpretation and value-laden human social activity, there are no facts. On this view, "knowledge is power" means that knowledge is socially constructed in accordance with norms of authoritativeness and thus both embodies and furthers the values and interests of the powerful; or, alternatively, knowledge is constructed as subversive challenges to those norms, values, interests, and power. On such a view, truth is not straightforward, value-neutral conformity with the world, and the notion that it *is* is an ideological fiction that renders invisible the workings of the dominant norms of authoritativeness.

Think of the question "How long is the eastern coastline of the U.S.?" To get an idea of the problems in answering it, take a piece of curly-leafed lettuce and tear a strip about an inch from the curly edge. Hold the strip taut along a ruler and note the length. Then tear that strip again, this time one-half inch from the edge, and measure it again: depending on how curly the lettuce is, the difference in length will be anywhere from significant to astounding. Obviously, if you keep on tearing, the length will keep on getting longer: how long the edge is depends on how close to the edge you're measuring. It won't work to say that the true answer is the one that measures right at the edge: you *might* be able to do it for the lettuce leaf (try it sometime), but it doesn't even make sense for the coastline. Which of the irregularities of the coastline count? Depending on which we conform to and which we skim over, we'll come up with radically different answers. It's not a matter of more or less accurate figures; answers will differ by orders of magnitude. We get stable answers by having an idea of why we want to know. Do we want to drive the distance? On interstates or back roads? If we want to sail, will we be hugging the shoreline, or will we be at sea? Or do we plan to fly? Until we know who wants to know, and why, the question about the length of the coastline is unanswerable.

Even so apparently simple and objective a question as length depends on the purposes for which we are measuring, and those purposes reflect the values of those who are asking the question, even if only such values as a preference for coastal sailing over plying the open sea. Even if we grant the realist's contention that the true answer is the one that conforms to the world, we need to have some idea of how closely we are to conform, which of the irregularities of whatever we are examining are of significance, and which are to be smoothed out in our representation.

If truth is to conform to the world, however closely, it would seem that we need, in our pursuit of it, varying degrees of pliancy and flexibility. According to the *Oxford English Dictionary*, a "lesbian rule" is "a mason's rule made of lead, which could be bent to fit the curves of a molding" (the reference is to Aristotle's *Nicomachean Ethics* V.x.7). Such flexible rules would seem to be called for if knowing the world requires conforming to its curves. But the figurative meaning of "lesbian rule" is, presumably, less favorable: it means "a pliant principle of judgment." Principles, in the world of orthodox epistemology, cannot be pliant, ought not to bend to fit the circumstances. Their rigidity is what restores the knower's virility, which was challenged by the requirement that his knowledge pliantly conform to a world independent of his will. The pursuit, at least, can be in his control; he can and should go straight. As necessary as it would seem to be that knowledge conform to the world, on the level of methodology, of rules, we are taught to be suspicious of those that bend, to reject the pliant for the upstanding. Knowledge, of course, does not remain unaffected by the rules governing its pursuit: if nature, with its slippery curves, cannot be captured, we can wait until it dies, or kill it: rigor will set in and the straight rule will work.

There is another sense in which the rule determines the measurement of the world. Thinking of the literal lesbian rule, the flexible mason's tool for measuring moldings, we can see that length will depend in part on exactly how flexible the rule is: moldings, like lettuce leaves and coastlines, will be of very different lengths depending on how closely the rule measuring them hugs their perimeters. (Were we to go down to the molecular level, the molding around my study, for example, would be measured in miles.) The choice of the rule will be dictated by interests and values. Contemporary philosophers of science will, for the most part, acknowledge the sort of relevance of purpose represented by the coastline example. They will acknowledge, that is, that values and interests influence what questions people care to ask—or to fund, hire, or tenure others for asking. But they will also maintain that, once the question is specified precisely enough (once we know how we want to travel down the coast), it will have one answer, and all competent researchers will arrive at it.

To ensure this interchangeability of authorized knowers, the rules they use should not be differently flexible in different hands: once the rule is formulated, it should be pliant neither to the values and interests of those who are using it nor to the filigreed complexities of the world they are studying. Values, interests, and other ways in which people differ from each other can and must be segregated so as not to contaminate the process of finding the one true answer. Authorized knowers cannot have, as individuals or groups, distinctive epistemic styles, or their results will not be replicable and will not count as knowledge. Authority consists in being trusted to use the straight rules that guarantee uniformity. The rules determine one's epistemic orientation, and, in this domain as in the sexual one, straightness, not deviance, is normative.

As Evelyn Fox Keller has argued in *Reflections on Gender and Science*,[1] the epistemology of modern science developed around interrelated conceptions of knowing subjects and their methods, both of them fully constituted prior to the act of knowing and untransformed by it. The object of knowledge, by contrast, is inert; it does not tell us how it wants to be known (it does not shape the rule), nor does it know us in return. In her accounts of the geneticist Barbara McClintock,[2] Keller explores the workings of a different epistemic orientation, one in which knowledge emerges dialogically from the evolving relationship between the knower and the known, a relationship that changes them both, one whose terms are not laid down in advance.

When we turn from the acquisition of knowledge to its transmission, we need to consider other perspectives and other ways of posing the question of who wants to know. In addition to the knower and the known, there are those with interests in learning what the knowers know, as well as those who will be affected, whether they like it or not, by what comes to be taken as knowledge. From the perspective of traditional epistemology, they don't make a difference, any more than it makes a difference to what my name *really* is or to where Lefty *really* is whether it's the boss or the cops that want to know. Knowledge — so the story goes — consists in facts, and facts are facts, no matter who has them or wants them or why. People who are rich or powerful are more likely to get their questions answered (especially questions that directly concern the acquisition and maintenance of wealth and power), but their money and their power, if the rules are working properly, are supposed to have no influence on what those answers are. Our culture's separation of production from consumption is apparent here: consumer demand sets the whole apparatus in motion, but consumers are external to the processes of production and passive with respect to it. Still less do those who are "passive consumers," affected by knowledge created in the interests of others, have any say, any more than do those who live downstream from a toxic chemical plant.

It needn't be like that. Imagine breaking down the distinction between the producers and the consumers of knowledge: we all come to learn what we all need to know. Clearly such an ideal is unworkable in those terms as soon as we need to know more than the barest basics about ourselves and the world: it is impossible that we could all come to learn for ourselves what we would have to know for our cars to run, our bread to be baked, our illnesses to be cured, our roofs to keep the rain out, our currency to be stable, and our airplanes to fly. But when we face analogous problems of scale in the political realm — when we recognize that the town-meeting won't work for polities larger than towns — we abandon direct democracy, not for autocracy, but for representative democracy. (That is, we do so in theory; the reality of our political process is quite different.) Why, in the realm of epistemology, do we make the opposite choice? We don't (in theory, anyway) divide the political realm into the governors and the governed, those who produce government and those who consume it; why do we do that in the epistemic realm?

Ideally, at least, in a representative democracy those who govern do so in the name of the others, who are the final authorities. Their values and interests are meant to inform the processes of government at every level: elected officials are their surrogates, even if in the name of doing that job well, they have to become more expert about features of the political world than any of their constituents. Epistemologically, by contrast, experts are accountable to each other and to no one else (professionalism and academic freedom are meant to insure this). Certainly (again, in theory), academic experts of various sorts are supposed to be discovering truths because it will be good for all of us to have those truths: in that sense, they, like elected officials, are supposed to be doing what they do on our behalf. But, unlike the constituencies of elected officials, we are not supposed (even in theory) to have anything at all to say about whether academic experts are doing their job well. When a purported discovery is presented, the jury of peers called upon to judge it is drawn very narrowly from among those whose disciplinary mastery authorizes their opinions. The rest of us are presumed incompetent even to have an opinion, let alone to have one that carries any weight.

It is hard to imagine how it might be different. Certainly, once academic experts are inside a research program, taking for granted what questions to ask, what research methods to use, what background knowledge to draw upon, which experts to consult, and which educational methods to rely on for the training and certifying of new researchers (within, that is, a paradigm, in Kuhn's sense[3]), most questions *will* have determinate and uncontroversial answers. Producing such agreement is precisely one of the functions of paradigms: within them, experts can make progress, as those working in the field build on each other's previous successes. But such progress leaves as an open question whether the paradigm provides effective strategies for acquiring what everyone should take to be truths about the world, or whether it just ensures that its initiates — the experts — will share a common set of delusions. That is, what reasons do *we*, the nonexperts, have for believing what the experts believe, beyond the fact that they are socially authorized to produce what is supposed to count as knowledge? Why should we be any more respectful of that authority than our founding political documents tell us to be of *political* authority in which we have no ultimate say?

Scientific realists (those who argue that science does, by and large, lead to truths about the world)[4] will often refer at this point to the successes of scientific methods (the flight of airplanes, the moon landing, the eradication of or cures for diseases, the stability of bridges, the explosion of bombs) as providing grounds for believing that such methods produce not delusions, but truth, since they are effective in predicting and controlling nature within certain temporal and spatial bounds. The evidence for such effectiveness is, even from our lay perspective, quite good: that is, science does what it was designed to do. But what we are increasingly discovering is that science as we know it is not very good at understanding the interconnectedness of diverse phenomena beyond those spatial and temporal bounds. As we are learning, mostly to our terror, phenomena interconnect far beyond the bounds of our investigations — that is, beyond the bounds of our prediction and control — and something that was done there and then is coming back to haunt us here and now. Even (especially?) scientists are unprepared for these discoveries, in part because drawing spatial and temporal bounds, defining a problem, and specifying the parameters of investigation are integral to scientific method. But if, for example, the eradication of the smallpox bacillus counts as reason to believe that scientific method is reliably truth-producing, why don't the longterm, unforeseen complexities of atmospheric changes count as reason to believe that it might not be?

Scientific knowledge also categorizes. It is general, not specific: it is knowledge of the type and not the individual. To know scientifically, we look for similarities, particularly those that bring diverse phenomena under the same law. Their obedience to that law is what they have in common, and it is the most important thing about them: it is how we understand them. The diversity — say, between the tides, the orbits of planets, and the behavior of dropped objects — is demonstrated to be merely apparent. They all exemplify the law of gravity, and it is their falling under the same law, this way in which they are tokens of the same type of phenomenon, that, scientifically, allows us to understand them, in abstraction from the specificities of water, heavenly body, and homely object.

These two features of scientific knowledge, the attempt to delimit interconnectedness and the reduction of diversity to underlying similarity, are repudiated in current feminist theorizing. Feminists working in a wide range of fields[5] have argued that women tend to see the world and themselves in it in terms of a web of interconnectedness, rather than as isolated atoms or as links in linear causal chains — and that to do so is an ability worth cultivating, not just a product of women's oppression (though it is, problematically, that as well[6]). Many have focused on the related idea of responsibility as a relationship to people and events that is not defined by the scope of one's power and control.[7] Work in feminist ethics also has stressed the need to attend to the particularities of persons and of situations, rather than, as traditional moral theorists would have us do, identifying "morally relevant features" in order to treat all like situations alike.[8] And attention to diversity (most centrally in the work of women who saw their lives and perspectives ignored or misrepresented in the work of women of privilege) has shifted the attention of many feminist theorists away from the attempt to describe and explain what all women have in common.[9]

The two ideas — of interconnectedness and particularity — are related. If we are attempting to make sense of the world, whether through science, literature, or common sense, we need to find patterns, ways things hang together. One way to do that is both to sharply narrow and define the scope of our inquiries and to look for similarities that allow a reduction in the number of laws that govern phenomena. (The search for a Unified Field Theory is the ultimate goal of this line of thought: it would epitomize the ideal of elegance by subsuming all physical phenomena under one overarching set of laws.) If we resist doing this, by insisting both on the importance of following the web out beyond the limits of our own agency and on the irreducible particularity of individuals and the value of differences, we will need a new epistemology, one which takes as central not similarities, but connections. It is no accident that the new politics forged by feminists and others in liberation movements has led to the same conclusion: not what we have in common, but how our lives and choices affect each other, is what ties us together and makes coalitions possible. We need, epistemologically as well as politically, the ground for trust, and we need to acknowledge that such ground needs to be literal, lived, and struggled for, not the imagined result of the application of abstracting rules.

Attention to interconnectedness can also make possible an epistemology that doesn't start by positing a separation between the knower and the known, and then enforcing that separation in the name of maintaining objectivity. Such an epistemology would also acknowledge the irreducible particularity not only of the objects of knowledge, but of knowers, as well as the ways in which both are shaped by the forces around them, including, for knowers, the forces of race, class, gender, and other systems of domination and privilege. Knowledge would always be seen as especially problematical when it was constructed only by those in positions of privilege that afforded them only distorted views of the world. When experts were trusted to discover for us things too obscure to be generally evident, we would always want to know as much as we could about how they went about finding them out, and part of our trust would be grounded in our knowing that the values that structured their investigations were ones we shared. The experts, that is, would be our representatives in the laboratory or the archives or the field, as the members of Congress are supposed to be our representatives in Washington.

Ruth G. Doell's recommendations for the composition of an oversight commission on germ-line therapy and human embryo research (more than half nonscientists, equal numbers of women and men) reflect these concerns and could, if implemented, have more than a braking effect. It isn't just that some research is potentially too dangerous or too ethically questionable to be undertaken. The politics around AIDS research is a clear example of how attitudes of privilege (heterosexism and homophobia in the early days, now also racism, classism, and sexism) can prevent or stall research that is urgently needed. What Doell's essay points toward is precisely a representative democratic model of science, where the orientation of research is set dialogically by all those who have an interest in it, rather than monologically by those who are encouraged to think they own it.

Oversight groups also are potentially sites for the forging of coalitions, as people from diverse social positions discover common interests and confront the issues that divide them. Knowledge is supposed, abstractly, to belong to everyone, but such abstract universality masks the exclusivity of privilege.

We would go further in reaching universality by working to make knowledge concretely shared among individuals and groups that seem initially to see the world in very different ways but who have a real interest in finding an account of things complex enough to do them all justice. Thus, for example, groups overseeing reproductive research would need to include people with interests in overcoming infertility, as well as those with interests in the possible use of fetal tissue to counter the effects of Parkinson's disease, as well as those with interests in not defining the female body primarily in terms of an ability to produce babies *or* fetal tissue.

Not all research ought to be guided by specific practical agendas. What many scientists report as a spirit of play — curiosity given free rein — is undoubtedly valuable, and not only because we cannot predict in advance which hunches will pay off. But what is usually taken to follow from that observation — that scientists should be left alone to follow their muse — is false to actual scientific practice (which is always deeply influenced by what others than scientists find it important to look at), while it obscures attempts to examine just why the spirit of play, of supposedly unconstrained curiosity, leads in some directions and not in others, or how differently socialized and rewarded scientists might hear a different muse, beckoning them in different directions.

An interest in unconstrained pure science, to the extent that there is such a thing, is not the only interest we have, and it needs to be balanced with others, ranging from the immediate and practical (a cure for AIDS) to the concretely political (genuine, noncoerced reproductive choice for all women) to the foundationally political (the effective empowerment of people who now correctly perceive themselves as impotent with respect to the creation and use of the knowledge that structures their lives). Professionalism and academic freedom, at their best protectors of heterodoxy, have become guardians of unexamined privilege, in part because of the enormous amounts of money involved in research (especially in the sciences), but equally because of the ways in which academics of all sorts are selected and socialized: a large part of graduate education, for example, consists in learning which people, groups, ideas, and approaches are to be scorned.

Democratization, rather than stifling creativity, could open up a world that is becoming progressively more closed, not only to outside, nonscientific influence (except, of course, for the military, governmental, and corporate funding of whatever issues are currently important to them), but to potentially revolutionary work within science. As Kuhn has argued,[10] major scientific breakthroughs typically come from people outside the field, people whose view of things is not shaped by the paradigm their theory challenges. If only recognized experts are allowed to have any say, such breakthroughs will be harder to effect. Similarly, research agendas are unreflectively shaped by the interests of those with economic and political power, with little or no influence from those without the clout to make their interests heard. Democratization would serve both to make evident the influence of nonscientists and to diversify that influence. Without such democratization, what we have is an ideology of unfettered research conducted by independent scientists and a reality of skewed research controlled by those with economic and political power. That essentially the same groups of people effectively control the nominally democratic processes of government points to the need for democracy to be substantively guaranteed, not just formally decreed.[11]

Micaela di Leonardo argues for a radically dialogical epistemic democracy in the crosscultural anthropological situation, especially when, as is nearly always the case, the ethnographic subjects are, in a variety of ways, less powerful than their ethnographers. If the meanings of facts, and even the facts themselves, are the products of culturally embedded interpretive practices, then Western feminist anthropologists need not only to understand the complexity of those practices in the societies they study but also reflectively to examine their own practices and the relationships of power between them. Di Leonardo cautions us against a too-facile perception of similarity and urges that we bridge crosscultural gaps, not by aiming to discern commonality beneath the differences but by attending closely to the interconnections between the lives of others and our own. Not only do we need to attend, for example, to the ways in which our standard of living as affluent Americans depends on the exploited labor of Third-World women (and men), but we need to learn about the webs that constitute the meaningfulness both of their lives and of our own.

Both Doell's and di Leonardo's essays make clear that, whatever knowledge may ostensibly be about (the efficacy of a technique for *in vitro* fertilization or an ethnographic account of a community), it is always in part about the relationships between the knowers and what they know. The acquisition of that knowledge always further shapes those relationships and others as well, including relationships between the original knowers and those who, actively or passively, consume that knowledge, and between those consumers and what has now come to be known, which may be a part of their own lives. The values that inform those relationships always are implicated in the acquisition of knowledge, in ways that typically are neither democratic nor equitable.

Doell and di Leonardo help us see how knowledge could be constructed differently, informed dialogically by the values and perspectives of all those who are implicated in it. Part of the difference of such knowledge would be its explicit inclusion of reflectiveness about those relationships, about how they were constituted and about how they have been changed — for example, how the experience of pregnancy and parenthood is changed by reproduc-

tive technology,[12] or how relationships between communities are changed
when members of one do an ethnographic study of the other. We need, as
di Leonardo stresses, to come to these understandings in the context of forming alliances: questions of who wants to know and why need to be answered
not in terms of pursuing pure research for its own sake, but in terms of developing a common vocabulary for social and political action.

The need to develop such a vocabulary is at the heart of a debate now
going on in feminist inquiry. One central question concerns the usefulness
of attempting to find and to articulate commonalities among all women:
is it necessary to do so in order to have a theory and a politics that will be
genuinely about and for (all) women? Or is the very attempt necessarily
either falsely essentializing or spuriously universalizing, trapping women in
a limiting and unchangeable definition, or applying to all women features
of the lives of some, usually those with the privilege to have their accounts
recognized by those even more privileged than they? Are there really two
jointly exhaustive and mutually exclusive categories — men and women —
with crossculturally applicable necessary and sufficient conditions? Or is the
dichotomizing of gender, perhaps even of sex, itself a cultural artifact? If
so, to what extent do we need to use it (at least to describe the cultures in
which it applies), and to what extent do we, in using it, reify it?

To avoid gender essentialism, some feminists assert that it is a social rather
than an essential taxonomy, while arguing that without some unified account of gender, without some universal claims about what it is and how
it operates as a social taxonomy, we will lose the political point of doing this
work; our theories will fail to be usable.[13] Certainly, much of the deconstructive challenge to a unified theory of gender is, explicitly or implicitly,
antipolitical (although it needn't be: Teresa de Lauretis, for example, is explicit about the importance of the political usefulness of theory[14]). But worries about universally applicable definitions of gender need not come from
deconstructionists.

Such a worry can, for example, be raised about the assertion that gender,
as a taxonomy, is defined by the power of men over women, yielding an oppression distinctive of women as a class. One problem with this assertion is
that, stated universally, it isn't true. We need to ask: power of *which* men
over *which* women? As Elizabeth V. Spelman has argued in *Inessential
Woman*,[15] we need to be very careful about statements about "women" and
"men" and the relationships between them, given the ways in which gender
is constructed always in relation to race and class. Spelman points out, for
example, that, in the U.S. during slavery and its aftermath, gender has not
been about the power of *Black* men over *white* women: they have had no
such power. Spelman's book makes clear that universal statements about
"women" have been challenged most tellingly not by deconstructionists (whom

she never mentions) but by women of color and others who found themselves misrepresented—or failed to find themselves at all—in the histories and theories of white middle-class academic feminists. That is, the critique is a deeply political one, aimed not at depoliticizing gender theory but at making that theory responsive to the demands of a more inclusive politics.

Gender *is* about power, but so are race, class, and other institutionalized systems of inequality, and the ways in which they interact render suspect any simple statement of who, with respect to any one of them, has power over whom. Gender and race in the U.S., for example, have been in part about the power of white men over white women, who are infantilized; over Black men, who are terrorized, in alleged response to what Angela Davis has named the Myth of the Black Rapist[16]; and over Black women, whose rape and exploitation are supposed to reflect, not their abusers' bestial nature, but their own. To speak simply of men's power over women reinforces the racist assumption that Black men, because they are men, do have some sort of power over white women, even in circumstances where a Black boy can be lynched for daring to whistle at a white woman.

What is true is that dominant models of masculinity in the U.S. normatively include power over women, so that men who in any real sense lack this power often experience that lack as emasculating. They may also respond to their emasculation with violence against women, but when that violence (if the woman is white) evokes, not the trivializing indifference of society to rapes committed by privileged men, but cries for the death penalty, it can hardly be considered an expression of *power*, however horrible it may be for the woman who suffers it. We need to be clear about these matters, not out of a desire for theoretical sophistication but out of the need to overcome the white solipsism that has blocked alliances between white women and women of color.

Such alliances—and theories of gender that facilitate them—needn't be grounded in similarities, whether an unchanging essence of womanhood or the features of socially constructed genders. Rather, they can be grounded in our interconnectedness, in how our very different ways of being constructed as women have implicated each other, how we have been used against each other, threatened by each other, and learned to see each other as an enemy, a rival, or a dreaded alter ego. To look for commonalities necessarily simplifies all our lives; when we look instead at webs of interconnection, we can do justice to the complexities of those lives.

Certainly any culture that constructs gender dichotomously will make categorical *normative* claims about all and only women in the culture (that's just what it means to construct gender dichotomously). But in any real woman's experience, those claims will be mediated by other features of her life, including whether or not those like her are meant to be fully included in the normative construction of womanhood. The normative claim about women in contemporary American culture, for example, that domesticity is the central arena for self-definition, is experienced differently by the upper-class, nonemployed, suburban wife and mother; by the undocumented immigrant woman who tends that woman's children, hoping to earn enough to bring her own children from Mexico; by the single mother who works outside the home; and by the career woman who has resisted family pressures to marry and have children. For some of these women, the normative claim is simply false (though they are not unaffected by its normativity); for others it is true, but in very different ways. As a statement of something they are meant to have in common, it is unilluminating. As a way of organizing how their lives interact, it can be helpful.

Classification can be illuminating, but we need to attend to our own agency in constructing any classificatory scheme, whether it be of elementary particles or of people, and not mistake it for how the world itself divides up. The warnings of the deconstructionists about dichotomization are apt here: Western thought has been so structured around binary oppositions that we fall into them "naturally" and find them satisfyingly explanatory, when what we are doing is finding in them not an illumination of the subject matter but a reflection of our own need to divide the world in two. Such dichotomies serve to blur the complexities that the real world has a nasty habit of multiplying. Thus, much recent feminist theory has attempted to repudiate unified models of gender oppression, emphasizing instead the irreducible — albeit socially constructed — differences among people, along lines of gender, race, class, sexual identity, etc., and arguing for a politics of equality not based on the denial of diversity.

We block the development of such a politics by posing questions about gender fairness that assume that the only alternatives are equality-as-sameness (which holds everyone to the identical set of standards, usually framed around the experiences and needs of privileged men), or gender essentialism (which tailors standards to the supposedly fundamentally different experiences and needs of women). We need to know what "fundamentally different" can mean, if we reject essentialism; certainly all people are fundamentally different from each other, and those differences are partly a matter of their membership in various groups that are constructed and maintained hierarchically. But how can we speak of *two* fundamentally different *kinds* of human beings without either essentializing gender or glossing over the roles of race, class, sexual identity, and so on in people's lives?

In our society gender *is* constructed as a binary opposition. Not all cultures have two, but ours does so with a vengeance, surgically or hormonally "correcting" those whose bodies fail to put them securely in one box or the other. But we need to be careful not to reify gender, even as a pair of *social* categories, not to give it more reality than it has. One way to see this point is to think about race. Race, on the face of it, is not a matter of binary opposition, but of complex amalgams of genetic and cultural differences. Whatever else we can say about race, we can safely say that there are more than two of them; race is not dichotomous. Or so one would think, were it not for the workings of racism, which precisely dichotomizes the world's peoples into white and nonwhite (or people of color or Third-World people: it is hard to find a respectful term for a category the existence of which is an artifact of racism). Nonwhite people, after all, have no more in common with each other than any one group of them has with white people, except within the grammar of racism, in which what matters above all else is whether one is white or problematically other.

One point of calling race or gender a "discourse" is to argue that these categories have a logic, a grammar—that is, a structure that works in some ways like the structures of a language—and that we can learn something about how they work by looking at language and people's use of language—how race and gender are talked about, how they are used as metaphors to explain other things. To note what I have noted about the logic of racism (not just the social-constructedness, but also the instability and illogicality of the categories) ought not to undermine the possibility of an antiracist politics.[17] Joan Scott, for example, argues well for the value of discourse-based theorizing, within a context that is explicitly and always political.[18] But the problems many feminists and others find with academic poststructuralism are nonetheless real, and painfully evident in Joyce A. Joyce's essay. These problems bring us back to the fundamental questions about who wants to know and why: research questions and methods do not exist in a vacuum; they are developed and used by people situated in various ways in various institutions, with various loyalties, values, responsibilities, privileges, and identifications.

Joyce is clear about her responsibilities as a Black woman critic and English professor. Central among them are bringing out the potential of works of literature to empower those who can challenge the oppressions of race and gender. It is to such people, groups, and movements that Joyce holds herself accountable and to whom she is loyal. Academic professionalism, by contrast, has won for those it authorizes and protects the right to be subject only to the opinions and the demands of those who are similarly authorized (one's "peers"—most of whom, of course, are privileged by race, class, gender, and so on). A professional's loyalty is supposed to be given, concretely, to those "peers" and to the academic institutions they inhabit and, abstractly, to the subject matter, the discipline itself, and the supposedly disinterested pursuit of knowlege. Joyce's loyalties are, from this perspective, subversive. It is clear to her that the academy could accept her fully only if she appeared both in white-face and in drag: the "protection" that academic freedom offers from the opinions and demands of those outside the charmed circle fails to protect the integrity of those whose identities, let alone words, challenge its authorizing practices.

It is precisely those outsiders who rightly claim Joyce's loyalty, as they ought to claim the loyalty of all of us who write and teach as feminists or as African-Americanists, even as we work in colleges and universities, publish in academic journals, and train and accredit others as we were trained and accredited. It is no mean feat. Especially for those who are in some way privileged (notably, by being white or male), the academy is seducing: it more and more frequently acts as though it can accept us for who it thinks we really are, rewarding our loyalty to it and punishing us if our loyalties are perceived to lie elsewhere. Crucially, many of the tools we use for whatever we do were forged in the academy by others whose loyalty to it was far less ambivalent. What are we, any of us subversives, doing?

In an essay critical of what she calls the "race for theory," Barbara Christian concludes that her major objection to the hegemony of theory over literature "really hinges on the question, 'for whom are we doing what we are doing when we do literary criticism?'" Her answer is that she writes what and how she does in order, literally, to save her own life. Literature for her is a confirmation that her perceptions are not hallucinations and that "sensuality is intelligence, that sensual language is language that makes sense." She writes as a response to the writers she reads (notably Toni Morrison) and to their other readers, out of the knowledge that the academy has an interest in their voices' being lost (since they speak from points of view that the academy presumes not to exist, and certainly not to carry authority) and that "writing disappears unless there is a response to it."[19]

As someone who does read Toni Morrison, I am among those to whom Barbara Christian writes, although, as a white woman, my relationship both to Morrison's novels and to Christian's criticism is necessarily different from that of a Black woman or another woman of color (as either's will, of course, be different from the other's). If Morrison's and Christian's writing — and my own — are to save my life, the ways and means need to be different: I need, for example, to discover that some of what I have been taking for clear-eyed perception *is* a hallucination of sorts. One role of privilege in my life (beyond that of race, there are those of class and sexual identity) has been to make me feel thoroughly at home in the world of academic philosophy and to make it difficult for me to see through the eyes in my own mortal, embodied, female head, rather than through the lenses of disembodied Reason. One way I can come, literally, to my senses is by listening to the voices of those who have come, through however different a journey, to theirs. More particularly, the writings of women of color can help replace the hallucinated version of the world privilege provides with the complexity of reality, whose hallmark is that it looks different depending on where you're seeing it from.

The academy thrives on theories and rewards those who produce them, but a major problem with theories is that they flatten reality's complexity. However much diversity went into their construction, they are ultimately monologic. In order to construct one, you may need to listen to a lot of people, but then you retire to a quiet place and put it all together, in one maximally anonymous voice. Christian's preference for the verb ("theorizing") reflects in part the concern that the conversation not stop, that one voice not presume to speak for all the others. In the multivocality of theorizing, we are both discovering the complexity of reality and, simultaneously, constructing ourselves and each other as creatures and creators of that reality and as speakers and listeners in the conversation about it.

I've written something here about my sense of myself in these conversations, in part because I want to discuss a particular unease I feel reading the essays in *New Literary History* that form part of the background to Joyce's discussion in this volume.[20] The exchange there began with an essay of Joyce's sharply critical of the use of deconstruction and other currently fashionable literary theories to discuss African-American literature. Her essay was followed in the same issue by responses from a number of the theorists she criticized, notably Henry Louis Gates and Houston Baker, whose replies to Joyce I find painfully cruel. It is hard to focus on what they are saying about their own practices as "critics of Afro-American literature" (significantly, a designation Gates prefers because it is "less ethnocentric" than "the Black Critic"[21]); it is hard not to get stuck in the pain, hard not to wonder what they are really arguing about (if arguing is an appropriate term for what they are doing). And, for a white reader, it's hard not to feel embarrassed, as though I were eavesdropping on a painful, intimate family scene. I feel awkward and confused in part because it's not that I have stumbled in where, as a white person, I wasn't wanted or expected: these essays appear, after all, in *New Literary History.*

Beyond the pain in these particular essays is a question that currently haunts theoretical and academic work that would claim solidarity with liberatory movements. Some of the theoretical tools that seem most powerfully subversive in our hands have met with acclaim from the very disciplines and institutions we aim to subvert. And those who most skillfully wield those tools have been rewarded in ways that it is hard not to see as attempts at cooptation. However committed such individuals are to resisting what amounts to a bribe, divisiveness inheres in the singling out of a few for acclaim by a system that still disdains and disparages—if it notices at all—the work of the many others who sustain the conversation that gives sense and importance to the voices being isolated from it. Individuals can, of course, use their positions and influence for collective empowerment, and we need to honor those who use their power in this way, but that doesn't change the uneasy fact that institutions of privilege decide who is to have such power and what achievements are to be rewarded.

Thus, it is hard not at least to suspect that those Joyce is critical of are academically rewarded less for the work they have done preserving and presenting the writings of African-American women and men than for the theoretical discourses they have mastered and helped to shape. My suspicion here comes from my own experience as a feminist theorist, noting that the deployment of sophisticated maneuvers against the tradition, however radical in content, is more acceptable than is opening up the conversation to academically untrained voices. It can seem sometimes that almost anything one says is acceptable so long as only the initiated can understand it — something that ought not to surprise us, since the exclusionary effect of incomprehensibility serves in fact to protect the structures of privilege we take ourselves to be so brilliantly skewering.

We need as individual theorists to grapple with these issues, but we need also to recognize that we come to them differently because of how we are placed in the world. So, for example, as the academy and much of the rest of American society stand today, it is easier for me to act in perceived solidarity with Baker and Gates than with Joyce, much as I would like to think I would choose otherwise. As argued by bell hooks,[22] the liberation of Black women challenges the structures of domination in a fundamental way; it is inconceivable on any merely reformist agenda. Black men and white women in the academy, by contrast, share the experience of divided identities, mixtures of privilege and oppression. (Maleness may be problematically a privilege for inner-city Black men living in poverty; it is clearly a privilege for Black male academics.) Racism and sexism function as, among other things, backups for each other. Those who are oppressed by one can — and often do — take refuge in the other. That is, they do if they can: if they are white or male. It is on this most uncomfortable of grounds, linked to Black men by our guilty participation in conflicting privileges, that I find myself, as a reader of the *New Literary History* essays and of Joyce's essay in this volume.

It is not where I want to be. Joyce is right to see the issues as those of responsibility (as she says in the essay in this volume), as well as of identity, "perspective, commitment, involvement, and love-bonding" (as she says in her reply to Baker and Gates).[23] The Black teacher/critic needs, she argues, to "merge the roles of critic and political activist."[24] Analogous arguments have been made about the role of the feminist teacher/critic (or teacher/theorist), and feminist journals and anthologies these days are full of debates about the relationship of feminism as a political movement to academic theory, especially to poststructuralism and deconstruction.[25] If those debates are marked by less intimate rancor than this one, it is in large measure because the participants, being for the most part white academic women, are divided only by theoretical affiliations and are joined by the ambivalence of their positions in the academy.[26]

Baker argues that the theories he and others use and develop "bring their work into harmony not with a *mainstream*, nor with an academic *majority* (both of which remain wedded to an old literary history), but with an avant garde in contemporary world literary study."[27] Within this avant garde, the nature of the literary canon is being profoundly challenged, as is the nature of literature itself, in order to provide a comparativist, non-Eurocentric theoretical framework for studying the literatures of the world. This is an aim I find hard to fault, as I find it hard to disagree with deconstructive moves against European and Euro-American theoretical hegemonies, whether in literature or elsewhere. (Most of my own work, in fact, consists in performing such moves against the philosophical tradition.) But Baker's words, and the attitudes expressed in his and Gates's essays, make me very uneasy.

It's the avant garde that has me worried. The current situation is reminiscent of that of the avant garde in the arts in the early part of this century. What started out as a profoundly political challenge to the repressive structures of the art world, as they were embedded in and abetted other structures of domination, became the accepted, prestigious, expensive art of the Establishment. Duchamp's urinal was, in the end, far less potent than the gallery wall on which it was hung. At the heart of the canonization — and taming — of the avant garde was the undermining of its democratic impulses: when humble objects became art, it was because those the powerful recognized as artists elevated them. Only Andy Warhol could make a Campbell's soup can into art: in the hands of a woman painter, it would have remained full of soup, a dismissible emblem of women's preoccupation with the domestic.

Things are now at a similarly critical point. The underlying impetus for postmodernity is the struggle of peoples of color and of women against the terms on which white men might be persuaded to offer equality to a token few of us — namely, our ability successfully to impersonate them. That struggle takes the form of a fundamental challenge to the norms of selfhood that white men have formulated for themselves, using tropes of darkness and effeminacy as standards against which to define themselves. Deconstruction can be a powerful tool to expose the logic of domination, as it lurks in the egalitarian rhetoric of the Enlightenment; it has a place in a revolutionary's toolbox.

But deconstruction is as undiscriminating a tool as were the shock tactics of the artistic avant garde. Its appeal is that it *can* dismantle the master's house.[28] But it dismantles *our* houses just as effectively, and, unlike the master, we are unlikely to have multiple residences. So the master faces us scornfully, after we've collaborated in the playful tearing down of our houses, and we are left homeless, as he moves on to his ten-room *pied-à-terre* overlooking Central Park or his Tuscany villa or his Vail condominium. Privilege, as Elizabeth Spelman demonstrates in *Inessential Woman*, has many hiding places, and one of them is nihilism: if the world can't be adequately known from where I stand, it can't be known at all.[29] Such nihilism will appeal primarily to those who know deep down that, however many houses are torn down, they will not be on the streets.

We do need to tear down the master's house, along with the badly built ugly houses many of the rest of us have been told were the best that could be done by way of affordable housing. But we need, with equal urgency, to build new, sturdy, beautiful houses, and for that task the master's tools are worse than useless. That's where the writing—of Toni Morrison and others—that saves Barbara Christian's life and inspires Joyce A. Joyce's passion as a teacher/critic comes in, and that's where questions of loyalty, responsibility, identity, commitment, involvement, and love-bonding have their greatest force. Some of us—in particular, white women and Black men—are cooptable by the masters, who are showing an increasing willingness to indulge us in our housewrecking. It's a heady and empowering activity, but we need to listen to the Black women and others who warn us about what we are to likely to end up having done.

We need, those of us who aspire to be feminist academics, to take seriously the contradictions in that aspiration. Both feminists and academics are concerned with coming to know aspects of the world and with sharing that knowledge with others. But each of these roles (not to mention all the others we play, as the actual people we are) carries with it values that shape what counts as knowledge and how it is reliably obtained. We have, to use Sandra Harding's term from this volume, "perverse identities," and we need to learn to live them responsibly—responsible, that is, to the values we affirm and to the communities with which we identify, as well as those with which we wish to ally. As academics we need to question the loyalty expected of us to the structuring norms of disciplinarity and exclusive "peer" accountability. We need to think concretely about the colleges and universities where we work, about all the people who constitute them and whose lives are affected by them; our loyalty should be that of the loyal opposition, committed to challenge and transformation.

Those with perverse identities (perhaps everyone, but certainly every feminist and other radical academic) can have no easy answers to what counts as acting responsibly; we have no straight paths to follow. The perversity we have chosen means that we cannot walk directly from where we are to where we need to be, since we have chosen to walk on the grounds of institutions that have laid out their paths according to plans we do not fully share, to lead to places we do not choose to go. If we have reasons for staying (and we need to be clear about what they are), then we need to get good at taking detours. To change the metaphor, we need, in Emily Dickinson's words, to "tell all the truth but tell it slant."[30]

The slant will come in part from our using tools that were developed by others who do not share our interests, tools that were designed to construct knowledge by and for those who benefit from structures of domination and privilege. But the maintenance of domination is not the whole story of the social construction of knowledge, even at the privileged sites for that construction; if it were, universities would be no place for any of us. Just as the egalitarian language of the founding documents of the United States has been usable in generations of liberatory struggles, despite those documents' having been drafted by and for propertied male slave-owning Europeans, so can the epistemology of liberalism provide points of entry for radical critique, despite having primarily served to empower straight white middle- and upper-class males and those who can impersonate them. Conceptual tools are not neutral, but neither are they untransformable in the hands of those who never were meant to touch them.

Sheer numbers are of great importance: it is far easier to "pass"— that is, to agree to the tacit bargain to bracket your nonprivileged identity as the price of being taken seriously — when there's no one else like you around. It becomes a lot harder to pretend that *everyone's* a middle-class straight white man if most of the people in the room aren't. When people are empowered to speak in their own voices, out of their own bodies, lives, and communities, and not as impersonators of the privileged, the tools of thought are transformed. Truth becomes a goal of ever-broader coalitions, the hallmark of knowledge shareable by more and different particular others, for more and different particular ends. Who those others and those ends are become explicitly political questions, revealed behind the liberal façade of supposedly anonymous, value-neutral universality.

Thus, it is especially important to write and teach in ways that include in the conversation those whose liberation we say we champion. Hegemonic theorists often have said that they had the best interests of the disadvantaged at heart and that they knew better than those unfortunate others what those best interests were. Feminist and other radical academic theorists risk perpetuating that arrogance. Bringing about revolutionary change is conceptually, as well as practically, difficult; it is not meant to be easy to see through the obfuscations of privilege and to reveal the deep structure of domination. Academically sophisticated conceptual tools can be of use in this labor. But such sophistication itself is an expression of privilege and, like all privileges, needs to be acknowledged as such and used responsibly. Romantic downward mobility is no more an adequate response to the privilege of academic training than it is to the privilege of class. (Only those whose family backgrounds have allowed them to take decades of formal education for granted are likely to toss it away frivolously.) The harder, more honest course consists in acknowledging privilege, its limitations *and* its advantages, and putting those advantages to use, in alliance with others who do not share them. The success of such a course depends in part on our reliability as allies, which in turn depends in part on whether we use the sophisticated languages we have learned as shareable tools or as marks of exclusivity. We need to ask ourselves, as we embark on a piece of research, who wants or needs to know what we are trying to find out — and why. And we need to be open to the ways in which the answers to that question subtly shape the work we do.[31]

Notes

1. Evelyn Fox Keller, *Reflections on Gender and Science* (New Haven, Conn.: Yale University Press, 1985).

2. Evelyn Fox Keller, *A Feeling for the Organism: The Life and Work of Barbara McClintock* (New York: Freeman, 1983).

3. Thomas Kuhn, *The Structure of Scientific Revolutions*, 2nd ed. (Chicago: University of Chicago Press, 1970).

4. See Jarrett Leplin, ed., *Scientific Realism* (Berkeley: University of California Press, 1984), esp. Richard N. Boyd's essay in that volume, "The Current Status of Scientific Realism," 41–82.

5. Caroline Whitbeck, "A Different Reality: Feminist Ontology," in *Beyond Domination: New Perspectives on Women and Philosophy*, ed. Carol Gould (Totowa, N.J.: Rowman and Allanheld, 1984), 64–88; and Carol Gilligan, "In a Different Voice: Women's Conceptions of Self and Morality," *Harvard Educational Review* 47, no. 4 (Nov. 1977):481–517.

6. For a discussion of the problems of valorizing features of women's characters under patriarchy, see Joan C. Tronto, "Beyond Gender Difference to a Theory of Care," *Signs* 12, no. 4 (Summer 1987):644–63.

7. On an ethic of responsibility, see the essays in Eva Feder Kittay and Diana T. Meyers, eds., *Women and Moral Theory* (Totowa, N.J.: Rowman and Littlefield, 1987). Issues of responsibility are central to Sarah Lucia Hoagland's *Lesbian Ethics: Toward New Value* (Palo Alto, Calif.: Institute of Lesbian Studies, 1988). Claudia Card is working on a comprehensive study of the nature of responsibility and its place in feminist moral theory.

8. On the ways in which particularity enters into moral thinking, see Kittay and Meyers, *Women and Moral Theory*; Lawrence A. Blum, *Friendship, Altruism, and Morality* (London: Routledge and Kegan Paul, 1980); and Sara Ruddick, "Maternal Thinking," *Feminist Studies* 6, no. 2 (Summer 1980):342–67.

9. On the need to attend to the diversity in women's experiences and perspectives, see bell hooks, *Feminist Theory: From Margin to Center* (Boston: South End Press, 1984); María C. Lugones and Elizabeth V. Spelman, "Have We Got a Theory for You! Feminist Theory, Cultural Imperialism, and the Demand for 'The Woman's Voice,'" *Women's Studies International Forum* 6, no. 6 (1983):573–81; and Elizabeth V. Spelman, *Inessential Woman: Problems of Exclusion in Feminist Thought* (Boston: Beacon Press, 1988).

10. Kuhn, *Structure of Scientific Revolutions*.

11. I keep waiting for a Soviet or Chinese or Eastern European reformist to respond to the questioning of American reporters about what they think of democracy in the U.S. with a paraphrase of Gandhi on Western civilization: "It would be a wonderful idea."

12. For a discussion of such changes and a challenge to the ideology that knowledge is always a good thing, see Barbara Katz Rothman, *The Tentative Pregnancy: Prenatal Diagnosis and the Future of Motherhood* (New York: Viking Penguin, 1986).

13. For feminist accounts of gender as a culturally variable social taxonomy, in conjunction with attempts to provide crosscultural generalizations to ground a global feminist politics, see the essays in Michelle Zimbalist Rosaldo and Louise Lamphere, eds., *Women, Culture, and Society* (Stanford, Calif.: Stanford University Press, 1974). Denise Riley addresses the question of what happens to feminist politics when we fully acknowledge the social-constructedness of the category "woman" in *Am I That Name? Feminism and the Category of 'Women' in History* (Minneapolis: University of Minnesota Press, 1988). See also Sandra Harding, "The Instability of the Analytical Categories of Feminist Theory," *Signs* 11, no. 4 (Summer 1986):645–64, and the references in n. 24.

14. See de Lauretis's introductory essay in Teresa de Lauretis, ed., *Feminist Studies/ Critical Studies* (Bloomington: Indiana University Press, 1986). De Lauretis, *Alice Doesn't: Feminism, Semiotics, Cinema* (Bloomington: Indiana University Press, 1984), approvingly quotes Julia Kristeva: "Believing oneself 'a woman' is almost as absurd and obscurantist as believing oneself 'a man.' I say almost because there are still things to be got for women: freedom of abortion and contraception, childcare facilities, recognition of work, etc. Therefore, 'we are women' should still be kept as a slogan, for demands and publicity" (95).

15. Spelman, *Inessential Woman*.

16. Angela Davis, *Women, Race and Class* (New York: Random House, 1981).

17. Whether or not a discourse-based analysis *does* undermine antiracist politics is part of what is at stake in the disputes discussed in Joyce A. Joyce's essay. For examples of such analyses, by people who for the most part at least *intend* their work to be politically usable, see *"Race," Writing, and Difference*, a special issue of *Critical Inquiry* 12, no. 1 (Autumn 1985); and *The Nature and Context of Minority Discourse*, two special issues of *Cultural Critique*, nos. 6 and 7 (Spring and Fall 1987).

18. Joan Scott, *Gender and the Politics of History* (New York: Columbia University Press, 1988).

19. Barbara Christian, "The Race for Theory," *Cultural Critique* 6 (Spring 1987):51–63; quotation, 61.

20. *New Literary History* 18, no. 2 (Winter 1987). The essays under discussion are: Joyce Ann Joyce, "Reconstructing Black American Literary Criticism" (335–45) and "Who the Cap Fit: Unconsciousness and Unconscionableness in the Criticism of Houston A. Baker, Jr., and Henry Louis Gates, Jr." (371–81); Henry Louis Gates, Jr., "What's Love Got to Do With It: Critical Theory, Integrity, and the Black Idiom" (345–63); and Houston A. Baker, Jr., "In Dubious Battle" (363–69).

21. Gates, "What's Love Got to Do With It?", 349.

22. hooks, *Feminist Theory*.

23. Joyce, "Who the Cap Fit," 381.

24. Ibid., 377.

25. See, for example, Jane Flax, "Postmodernism and Gender Relations in Feminist Theory," *Signs* 12, no. 4 (Summer 1987):621–43, along with Daryl McGowan Tress's "Commentary," *Signs* 14, no. 1 (Autumn 1988):196–200, and Flax's "Reply" in same issue, 201–3; Linda Alcoff, "Cultural Feminism versus Poststructuralism: The Identity Crisis in Feminist Theory," *Signs* 13, no. 3 (Spring 1988):405–36; Nancy Fraser and Linda Nicholson, "Social Criticism without Philosophy: An Encounter between Feminism and Postmodernism," *Theory, Culture, and Society* 5, nos. 2–3 (June 1988):373–94; Donna Haraway, "Situated Knowledges: The Science Question in Feminism and the Privilege of Partial Perspective," *Feminist Studies* 14, no. 3 (Fall 1988):575–600; Susan Bordo, "Feminist Scepticism and

the 'Maleness' of Philosophy," and Naomi Scheman, "Further Thoughts on 'Theories of Heterogeneity'" (abstract), both in *Journal of Philosophy* 85, no. 11 (Nov. 1988):619–29, 630–31; and Frances E. Mascia-Lees, Patricia Sharpe, and Colleen Ballerino Cohen, "The Postmodernist Turn in Anthropology: Cautions from a Feminist Perspective," *Signs* 15, no. 1 (Autumn 1989):7–33.

26. There *are* deep and painful divisions around "the theory question" among feminist academics, though not usually in print, and these do, I think, have a lot to do with differences in how (many) older and younger women have experienced the academy and themselves as women or as feminists in it—that is, with at least perceived differences of privilege. See Annette Kolodny, "Dancing between Left and Right: Feminism and the Academic Minefield in the 1980s," *Feminist Studies* 14, no. 3 (Fall 1988):453–66.

27. Baker, "In Dubious Battle," 366.

28. Audre Lorde, "The Master's Tools Will Never Dismantle the Master's House," in Lorde, *Sister Outsider* (Trumansburg, N.Y.: Crossing Press, 1984), 110–13.

29. Spelman, *Inessential Woman*, 183ff.

30. Emily Dickinson, *Complete Poems*, ed. Thomas H. Johnson (Boston: Little, Brown, 1960), poem no. 1129, pp. 506-7.

31. As this paper went through successive drafts, Joan E. Hartman and Ellen Messer-Davidow were of enormous help in clarifying both the issues (which in the process became more complex) and my expression of them (which I hope became simpler).

Part IV

Disciplinary Selections

Part IV

Disciplinary Selections

M aking selections at the Saturday farmers' market, as Angelika Bammer describes it, is "deciding what we need at a given time, knowing what is available, and taking what is useful." In a farmers' market, the produce is on display and so are the shoppers' on-the-spot choices and rejections. In the physical sciences, art history, and literary studies, the disciplines represented here, selections are less visible. Nevertheless, disciplines are constituted by knowers who have selected and continue to select what they need from among what they know to be available. Their selections, regularized and institutionalized, constitute disciplinary canons and paradigms. These constructs, while not immutable, are resistant to change because they are used to train future disciplinary practitioners and thereby to reproduce the disciplines.

The culture of the physical sciences is more hegemonic and their boundaries more tightly drawn than those of the humanities. In "Toward a Post-Phallic Science," Denise Fréchet traces the paternity of the physical sciences to Baconian empiricism and Cartesian rationalism. She links their conceptual and practical formations with masculinity as constructed by the gendered dynamics of the family; both are characterized by detachment, control, and renunciation of the libido. While Fréchet privileges psychohistorical analysis and Angelika Bammer sociohistorical analysis, Nanette Salomon moves between them.

Although physical scientists concern themselves with a limited number of paradigmatic problems, the nature they investigate is present as "a big blooming buzzing confusion" (to quote William James). Disciplinary selections, influencing what they see, do not keep them from reenvisioning it or looking elsewhere. Humanists are more constrained by the selections of their predecessors, because artifacts that do not receive canonical attention vanish, often without a trace. We can view or read, restore or edit, and interpret only those preserved. These activities we braid into narratives of art and literary history, from which in turn we draw the standards of excellence that solidify artistic and literary canons.

In "The Art Historical Canon: Sins of Omission," Salomon analyzes the narrative that extends from Georgio Vasari's *Lives* to H.W. Janson's *The History of Art* (1962), a narrative that features the individual (male) genius, explicates his achievements through biography, and determines their value by assessing his innovation and influence. The authors of this narrative legislate taste; they determine what gets made, bought, displayed in museums, and reproduced for wider consumption. The insertion of women artists into the narrative reveals how selections are made and the power relations they reproduce; the insertion of women critics reveals the extent to which the narrative makes men the measure of both significance and pleasure.

In "Mastery," Bammer, a member of a professional class that sets her apart from most other women, looks at the selections that have been made in literary studies. Class, according to Bammer, is both an economic and a cultural category; academics, whatever our class origins, are economically middle-class and culturally upper-class. Nevertheless, in a society whose democratic ideology blurs the existence of class divisions, feminists and other academics are likely to experience our own circumstances as classless, even as we busily produce critiques of class. If we cannot speak from the lived experience of other women, we can, Bammer suggests, analyze the particularities of our own class experience. Accordingly, she considers the selections that we, academic feminists who have mastered learned as well as colloquial discourse, may make from literature *by* and *about* silenced classes.

In "Making Knowledge," Kathryn Pyne Addelson and Elizabeth Potter generalize to all academic feminists the situation Bammer delineates. They enjoin us to know our places — our several places as professionals in academe and as women in the community, as intellectuals and as activists. To understand professionalism is to understand what enables and constrains us in making knowledge. "Academic freedom" permits us to pursue inquiry but not to lead in making social change; "academic merit" legitimates women's studies programs but not political activism.

"Making Knowledge" broaches the position that opens and closes *(En)Gendering Knowledge: Feminists in Academe*: our professionalization has been gained at the cost of separating ourselves from a political movement that in the 1960s joined us with other women. Unless we manage to rejoin what we put asunder in the early days of the Second Women's Movement — intellectual inquiry and social activism — we shall find ourselves strung out between divided feminist purposes and divided feminist communities, inadvertently reproducing the system we once wished to alter.

Toward a Post-Phallic Science

Denise Fréchet

The Subject in/of Science

Science is an ideology of the
suppression of the Subject.
— Jacques Lacan, *Ecrits*

"These facts show that," "These observations confirm the hypothesis that"—the subject, the "I," rarely appears in scientific publications. The aseptic language of scientists tricks us into believing that science is a body of knowledge that produces itself almost without benefit of human intervention. What is at stake in the exclusion of the "I" of science? Edgard Morin, a French sociologist, claims that the exclusion of the scientific subject is a gigantic masquerade. The subject who pretends to be absent from his discourse is in fact in its center, identifying himself with "absolute objectivity." The unconscious, however repressed, is always in command.[1]

In this essay I wish to reestablish the connection between the object of knowledge and the knowing subject in science. Looking, on one side, at the genesis of modern science, its ideas and values, and, on the other side, at gender relationships in the family and their influence on the emergence of the human subject as a linguistic manipulator and manipulatee, I try to recover what is lost by their dissociation. I operate in the realm of privilege: science as we know it is done by men privileged by class and race as well as by gender. Science I discuss as an anthropo-social practice and, as such, an experience rooted in language.

Parallels between two developmental sequences, that of modern science and that of gender within the bourgeois family, suggest how the apparently neutral ideology of science follows a pattern that the unconscious associates with masculine modes of thinking. These associations, I argue, affect both the self-selection of scientists and their selection of research topics, methods, and rhetorics. My essay concerns many aspects of selection: those imposed by accepted thought processes and methods in science, and those imposed by childrearing practices among the privileged, from whom scientists are chiefly drawn; the congruity between established science and masculine traits, a congruity that perpetuates already entrenched selections; and the ways scientists defend these selections in their scientific practices as well as in their studies of gender-dependent differences. I then turn my attention to the social consequences of these reciprocal processes.

Although they have occurred only sporadically, I discuss the few (but nevertheless encouraging) blurrings, dilutions, and calculated theoretical revisions of these models of selection. Some of these "perturbations" offer hope for a more holistic science, less flawed because less exclusionary, at least of women; we have yet to envision fully inclusive scientific practices. Others offer hope for new social and psychic models, less faulty because they provide less dichotomously organized and less diminished possibilities from which to select.

The Conception of Science

We usually trace the origin of Western science to the seventeenth century. The work of Descartes and Bacon marks a turning point in the way we apprehend the world. Both break with the hermetic tradition and the animistic view of nature prevalent at the time. Indeed, nature, whether a nurturing mother or a wild and uncontrollable virago, was then believed to be endowed with supernatural powers, and the privileged though nonrational communication that nature carried on with witches was considered a proof of the existence of God.

For Descartes, nature is no longer organic and alive; it is a machine of matter and motion that obeys mathematical laws. He claims that, to understand a phenomenon, one must break it into simpler units and, starting from these, establish mathematical relationships that allow one to reconstruct the original. The essence of objectivity is reached through reason rather than through sense perception, "for as body, we are completely reactive and nondiscriminative, unable to make the most basic distinction between inner occurrence and an external event."[2] A clear delineation between mind and body and between inner self and outside world is a prerequisite to Cartesian knowledge. His "Cogito ergo sum" is not only the assertion of his own existential truth but also of truth in general.

To this mechanistic conception, Bacon brought the idea of manipulation, of using instruments to solve scientific problems: "The secrets of nature reveal themselves more readily under the vexation of art [i.e., artisanry, technology] than when they go their own way."[3] For the first time, a relation was established between the manufacture of goods and the pursuit of knowledge. Consequently, the purpose of science became not merely to know nature but also to gain power over it.

The marriage of rationalism and empiricism gave birth to modern science.

Far from being contradictory, these two approaches can be seen as complementary. They rest on a mechanistic world view in which every event, determined by initial conditions, is knowable with precision independently of the observer. Yet the world as it lies open to investigation is also sexualized: Bacon invites "true sons of knowledge" to join him in "passing by the outer courts of nature" that "we may find a way into her inner chambers."[4] Thus nature can be known and subdued by (male) penetration.

Indeed, investigating the world as though it were governed by a universal theoretical plan echoes the need of the scientist to dominate, to reduce the diversity of phenomena to a fundamental identity, to manage the uncontrollable by the promulgation of an all-encompassing law. The "validity" of such a scientific law is thought to be further reinforced by its expression in a flawless language, mathematics. In reality, the scientist also hopes that the beauty of mathematical relationships will cover up the tumultuous origin of the discovery. Aesthetics becomes a warranty of truth. The force of the mathematical model and its seductive glamour, then, may account for its present vogue in the humanities. Such mathematization can be seen as an effort to endow (sometimes uncertain) concepts with absolute certitude. Mathematics becomes a synonym for superpower and therefore is linked with the masculinity of those already privileged.

In order to grasp underlying principles and thus formulate laws, the scientist must distinguish between what is essential in a phenomenon and what is secondary. For example, when Newton discovered gravitation, he chose to neglect the friction of air when he framed his law. As such an omission was unthinkable for other physicists at that time, the new paradigm was therefore the result of a radical shift in values. Newton did not observe falling bodies in nature as Aristotle did, but rather a "purified" phenomenon that he staged to accord with his expectations—falling bodies in a vacuum. He questioned nature until it revealed the law it obeys.

Those in a position to discriminate between the significant and the insignificant, to have scientific judgment, are those whose social position warrants their making decisions all around; those barred from discriminating, who have only opinions, are the socially disempowered. For example, the curative powers of several "home remedies" may never be acknowledged, despite evidence of their efficacy, because their discoverers did not have access to medical laboratories. Similarly, the ability of water diviners was considered a mystification in the scientific community until recent studies correlated it with hypersensitivity to variations in the magnetic field.[5]

Those who discriminate between the significant and insignificant also discriminate between "neutral" scientific information and its evaluation and application. The scientist is often presented as an ascetic, motivated by a desire to withdraw from the world. As Einstein wrote:

A finely tempered nature longs to escape from personal life into the world of objective perception and thought; this desire may be compared with the townsman's irresistible longing to escape from his noisy, cramped surroundings into the silence of high mountains, where the eye ranges freely through the still, pure air and fondly traces out the restful contours apparently built for eternity.[6]

If this image accurately describes scientists like Einstein, others describe scientists like Frankenstein, the madman interested above all in personal power and glory. Freeman Dyson, for example, says of the scientists involved in the Manhattan Project: "Nuclear explosives have a glitter more seductive than gold to those who play with them. To command nature to release in a pint pot the energy that fuels the stars, to lift by pure thought a million tons of rock in the sky, these are exercises of the human will that produce an illusion of illimitable power."[7] This illusion made the creators of the atomic bomb blind to the social and political contexts of their research. Indeed, if officially most of them admitted to be motivated by their fear of Nazi Germany's nuclear potential, they intensified rather than decreased their efforts after the Nazi surrender. "What I did immorally," recalls Richard Feynman, "was not to remember the reason why I was doing it. So when the reason changed, which was that Germany was defeated, not a single thought came to my mind that it meant I should reconsider why I was continuing to do this. I simply didn't think."[8]

The border between the ascetic and the mad scientist may be more tenuous than it seems. Both subjects are constituted by the same current of ideas, ideas structured by an emphasis on separation: separation between subject and object, between those who know and those who don't, between "pure" science and its "impure" applications. We may well wonder what type of people are drawn to such a separatist ideology.

The Social Construction of Masculinity

Modern scientific ideals of objectivity, based on a clear delineation of the boundaries between self and world, on detachment and renunciation of a libidinal investment in the object of study, and on control and mastery of nature, can be identified with masculine modes of thinking. Nancy Chodorow and Evelyn Fox Keller trace the origin of these pervasive associations to the sexual division of labor within the family and its consequences for early childhood development. Women in almost all societies are the primary caretakers and nurturers of children, their mothering taken for granted because of female capacities for childbearing and lactation. This nurturing behavior, Chodorow claims, is not primarily the product of biology or of intentional role training, but of social, structurally-induced psychological processes. Her account of gender, deriving from object-relations psychology, is vulnerable because it depends on a schema of family relations in which childrearing is unmodified by social, economic, and political contexts: it takes the gendering of power relations within the family as paradigmatic for power relations in society as a whole.[9]

Nevertheless, among the privileged from whom scientists are drawn, gender fundamentally discriminates women from men and nonscientists from scientists. These discriminations begin with the earliest relationship, that of mothers and infants. In the first few weeks of life, Chodorow argues, infants probably do not perceive the boundaries between themselves and the external world. When a need arises, it elicits the memory of satisfaction. If the mother provides this satisfaction, a perceptual identity is established. Sometimes the mother's attention is diverted from the infant and frustration results. Through successive experiences of frustration and satisfaction, infants begin to see their mothers as separate entities and discover the pleasure of autonomy. On occasion, however, anxiety arouses in young children the desire to regress to the original symbiosis. In this process, merging becomes associated with "mother" and separation with "not mother." At the same time, children turn to their fathers for protection from the fear of losing their separate identity. "Father" therefore comes to stand for objective reality, "mother" for subjective intimacy. These early relationships instill in young children the *structure* of gender stereotypes; they will come to associate activities in which the subject-object division is accentuated (such as science) with masculinity and those in which it is blurred (such as art, love, or religion) with femininity.

These associations are reinforced by the asymmetrical resolution of the Oedipus complex, as described by Freud and his followers.[10] Because mothers are of the same sex as their daughters, they tend to consider their daughters as less separate than their sons. Fighting for their autonomy, girls typically come to wish they had been born "different," like their brothers and their fathers, who have penises. At the same time, they notice that their mothers have more sexual interest in the opposite sex, and, frustrated, turn to their fathers for symbolic sexual gratification.

Because fathers are less available and less emotionally involved, however, girls never completely break their maternal attachment. Their relationship-ships to their fathers are less intense and less threatening to their other sexual relationships than are boys' relationships to their mothers. Inasmuch as girls maintain their relationships to their mothers, they are unlikely to fear maternal retaliation and lack powerful motives to undo them.

The sexual development of "normal" boys follows a different path. Mothers perceive their sons as more separate and more different than their daughters, and their affection for them is likely to have sexual overtones. These relationships can be intense, especially when fathers are often absent from the family. For their part, the sons want to have their mothers all for themselves and see their fathers as rivals, whom they wish to kill or castrate. Because of the intensity of their wishes, they fear parental revenge and, sensing their fathers' greater strength, they are afraid for their own safety. This fear leads them to repress their sexual attraction to their mothers.

In consequence, repudiation of the desired parental figure is more complete and more severe in boys than in girls. Freud considers this repudiation to be the basis of a scientific world view, a world view that allows "no sources of knowledge of the universe other than the intellectual working out of carefully scrutinized observations . . . and alongside of it, no knowledge derived from revelation, intuition and divination."[11] The persistence of strong family links, on the other hand, favors a religious world view, since "all who transfer the guidance of the world to Providence, to God, or to God and nature arouse the suspicion that they still look upon these ultimate and remotest powers as a parental couple in a mythological sense and believe themselves linked to them by libidinal ties."[12] This Freudian story sends men to the laboratory, women to church.

The family structure in which women perpetuate relationships and men disdain this work is replicated by the organization of society along gender lines into domestic and public spheres. Because public institutions regulate the interaction among domestic units and because men are primarily involved in the public sphere, masculinity becomes the norm for social relations. As Simone de Beauvoir remarked, the terms masculine and feminine are used symmetrically only in certain formats, as for example in legal papers. She points out that in actuality the relation of the two sexes in social parlance is not comparable to that of two electrical poles, for "man" represents both the positive (male) and the neutral (in comon usage, the generic designation of human beings), whereas "woman" represents only the negative. Thus "woman" is defined by limiting criteria and without reciprocity: "He is a Subject, he is the Absolute, she is the Other."[13] Because masculinity is attained through a radical denial of the mother, males come to devalue nurturing attitudes and activities. They also feel repressed hostility, which they may come to extend to the female sex in general. At the same time, they envy women's power to give birth and feel insecure about their own role in the reproductive process, since, as Freud puts it, "maternity is proved by the evidence of the senses, while paternity is a hypothesis."[14] Repressed uterus envy leads males to emulate women's reproductive capacities through exclusively masculine rituals and activities, while at the same time denigrating femaleness, "for it is not in giving life, but in risking life that man is raised above the animal."[15]

Both Brian Easlea and Carolyn Merchant view classical science as modern man's phallic ritual, its objective being to penetrate, reveal, and know the secrets of a decidedly female nature.[16] The congruence of science with masculine modes of thinking has consequences for women, for science, and for society.

Women and Science

> Masculinity . . . escapes the
> consciousness of its protagonists more
> easily than femininity. . . . For us,
> expressions of masculinity are easily
> elevated to the realm of supra-
> specific neutral objectivity and
> validity.
>
> — Georg Simmel,
> *The Relative and the Absolute*

The congruence between science and masculinity results in a double exclusion of women from the practice of science: first, it makes privileged women less likely than privileged men to be drawn to a scientific career; and, second, it predisposes privileged men to maintain science as an exclusively male territory. Several studies have shown that girls have a less positive attitude than boys toward science and a greater tendency to avoid taking math and science courses in high school.[17] When pressed to account for their attitudes, girls invoke the impersonality of science, the fierce competitiveness in the scientific community, and the divorce of science from its social contexts.[18] The authoritarian academic curriculum of the lower grades probably discourages students of both sexes, but it may reinforce the discomfort of the females. In most cases, science is taught as a mechanical pursuit that stifles individual creativity. Science permits only one good answer: either you get it or you fail. Children learn from uncontested sources. Teachers discourage unconventional approaches, countenance few questions, and rarely allow students to solve problems in collaboration with their peers. The grading system encourages competitiveness instead of cooperation. Moreover, the steps leading to scientific discoveries, let alone their historical and social contexts, are seldom discussed in science courses. A different approach to science teaching, incorporating such values as cooperation and stressing relationships between science and society, would undoubtedly make science more appealing.

Men also have actively contributed to the exclusion of women from the study and practice of science. In particular, they have spent enormous amounts of time and energy doing research that aims to prove the "inborn" intellectual deficiences of women and thus to legitimate their exclusion. These studies, despite their questionable methodologies, receive significant media coverage. Anne Fausto-Sterling has analyzed a number of these so-called demonstrations of female inferiority.[19] Their most common flaw, she reports, results from the choice of observations that scientists consider significant. For example, Hilary Shuard reported sex-correlated differences in standardized mathematics aptitude tests.[20] He had two thousand ten-year-old schoolchildren take a 91-item test. Boys performed better than girls on 14, girls better than boys on 11 items. Although no differences were noted for the remaining 66 items, Shuard underplayed the importance of this consistency and focused on the variances. Indeed, Shuard concluded that boys perform better than girls because "the items on which girls did significantly better were easier." The logic of such a conclusion should be embarrassing to Shuard, for if the items were easier, why didn't the boys get them right? It is tempting to ask: "easier" for whom and under what circumstances? What biases are involved in the design of the tests, and have these been considered?

The fact that females obtain higher grades in all school subjects, including mathematics, is rarely publicized. When it is, the reasoning that attempts to discount this fact ironically goes awry. For instance, successes are presented as failures: "Those explanations that allow girls' success at all say that it is based on rule following, rote learning, and hard work, not on proper understanding. Hence, they negate that success at the moment they announce it: girls 'just' follow rules, they are 'good' compared with 'naughty' boys who can 'break set' (make conceptual leaps)."[21] Leprince-Ringuet used a related argument in his attempt to turn success into nonsuccess for those women who got the highest entrance examination grades when they were finally allowed to apply to the highly competitive Ecole Polytechnique. He claims, first, that concentration and hard work are important to be admitted to the Polytechnique, whereas creativity is not. Girls therefore have an advantage over boys, because they are more submissive and do not question the purpose of "brain-stuffing." He then suggests that the examiners, because they are men, are probably "seduced" by the young women; had the examiners been women, boys would have received better grades.[22]

People like Leprince-Ringuet usually argue that, while social factors enable girls to perform well intellectually and biological factors cause their deficiences, the reverse is true for boys. Indeed, sex-linked genetic or hormonal differences, or asymmetries in the lateralization of the brain, have been invoked as explanations for female "inferiority."[23]

Although differences in biology may influence male and female behavior, we cannot separate from biology the influence of social and cultural factors in interpreting our observations; human biology, the natural environment, society, and culture are inextricably meshed parts of a single dynamic system. In taking exception to the findings and trying to understand the attempts to establish female "inferiority," Valerie Walkerdine contends:

> This proof of the existence of the other, girl's performance as difference, is a constant reassertion that "woman" exists in her difference from and therefore deficiency in contrast to those rational powers of the mind that are constituent of "man." Female equivalence, or an absence of difference, therefore present a constant threat to the sexual difference and to the existence of "man" as supreme and omnipotent mathematician, the architect of reason's dream, created in the image of God, the divine mathematician.[24]

Such "proofs" of female inferiority are presented as "facts" in order to legitimate discrimination against women in science. From college admission to hiring into positions commensurate with their professional qualifications and finally to professional recognition, discriminatory practices reproduce sex-stereotypes. Moreover, women who think they have "inferior" mathematical ability will be afraid of mathematics, expect to do poorly, work harder to overcome their handicap or refuse to engage in mathematics at all, and thus perpetuate the myth that girls are either "incapable" of mathematics or simply hardworking while boys are natively brilliant.

A Matter of Style

> There are two equally dangerous
> extremes: to shut reason out, and to
> let nothing else in.
> — Pascal, *Pensées*

Masculine ideals of objectivity and detachment structure the rhetoric of science. Yet we may wonder how accurately this discourse describes the practice of science and how the discourse itself affects it. In articles or grant proposals, scientists present what they want to do not as their own intention but as rational necessity. They do not say: "I want to study this because it interests me." Instead they say: "This has to be studied." They present themselves as victims of the truth who have no choices. In practice, however, scientists are always making choices — and denying the interests, passions, and unconscious motives involved in those choices. These strategies transform individual perspectives and selections into absolutes.

Where do scientists hide their desires? In some cases, they may use work as an outlet or extension of their personal or social preoccupations. Anna Fels suggests that such a metaphor obtains in the case of Sir Peter Medawar, a Nobel Prize winner. In his early career, Medawar dabbled in various projects at the prompting of his mentor. Only later did he find a sense of direction that led him to his major discoveries. As he noted: "A scientist who wants to do something original and important must experience, as I did, some kind of shock that forces upon his attention the kind of problem that it should be his duty and will become his pleasure to investigate."[25] The "shock" to which he refers resulted from a plane crash near his house that subsequently exposed him to the problem of grafting skin over the burns of the young pilot. But, we might well ask, why did this problem engage him so intensely? Fels attributes the passion to the striking parallel between Medawar's social and scientific considerations. A recurrent theme in Medawar's autobiography is the difficulty of being a foreigner in Britain. It is significant that in his research he chose (perhaps unwittingly) an area of immunology that aims at reducing or abolishing the body's ability to recognize and reject foreign tissue.

In other cases, the predilections of scientists may surface in their styles of writing. Compare two statements. Nuclear physicist Ernest Rutherford makes this warlike pronouncement: "Many laboratories in the world are now being equipped for an attack on the atomic nucleus. . . . Several atoms succumb each week."[26] Oncological immunologist Anna Brito makes this empathic assertion: "Most importantly you must identify with what you are doing. If you really want to understand about a tumor, you have got to be a tumor."[27] These statements undoubtedly reflect different methodological approaches.

Scientists' psychological makeups and value systems also influence their choices of theory. Thomas S. Kuhn argues that such criteria as accuracy, consistency, scope, simplicity, and fruitfulness are insufficient to explain the determination an individual makes between two competing theories: "Every individual choice between competing theories depends on a mixture of objective and subjective factors, or of shared and individual criteria."[28] He believes that personal and social factors cause different theoretical choices that then give impetus to scientific advancement:

> Such a mode of development requires a decision process which permits rational men to disagree, and such a development would be barred by the shared algorithm which philosophers have generally sought. . . . What from one viewpoint may seem the looseness and imperfection of choice criteria conceived as rules may, when the same criteria are seen as values, appear an indispensable means of spreading the risk which the introduction or support of novelty always entail.[29]

Scientists' choice of theories will in turn affect their perception of reality. "It is theory which decides what we can observe," wrote Einstein.[30] Examples of theoretically inflected perceptions are commonplace in the history of science. The controversy concerning spiral nebulae serves as an illustration. Such nebulae actually are large clumps of stars that macroscopically take on a spiral configuration. For a time, scientists disagreed as to whether they were part of our own galaxy (and therefore relatively near) or represented other (distant) galaxies. The acceptance of the latter view, now judged to be correct, was retarded because of the manner in which one man, Adrian Van Maanen, treated his data. Only years later, a computer analysis of his photographic plates revealed perceptual errors of minute proportions (about 0.002 mm) systematically made in favor of his expectations, which yielded a distortion large enough to retard the acceptance of the alternate theory.[31] Such perceptual biases are fairly frequent, particularly when there are clear expectations on the part of scientists, ambiguity in the data, and heavy reliance on human beings as instruments of observation.

A scientist's beliefs also may inflect his interpretations. Newton, in an attempt to defend the static view of the universe, wrestled with the problem of symmetry in the distribution of stars. Since his original assumption of a linear relationship between stellar magnitude and distance from the sun yielded an infinite universe (something he was trying to avoid), he revised the magnitude-distance relationship to one that would support a uniform universe and then circularly applied this relationship to "prove" the uniformity of the universe.[32] Nobel Prize–winning geneticist Barbara McClintock, in an interview with Evelyn Fox Keller, characterized this particular flaw of scientific research as "inadequate humility." "Much of the work done is done," she explains, "because one wants to impose an answer on it. They have the answer ready and they know what they want the material to tell them. So, anything it doesn't tell them, they don't really recognize as there or they feel it is a mistake and throw it out."[33] McClintock's own research on transposition started with the observation of such a "mistake"— an aberrant pattern of pigmentation on a few kernels of corn. She committed her life to making this aberration understandable.

What the theories and beliefs of scientists have permitted them to perceive is reconfirmed by an overemphasis in scientific publications on positive results. As Stephen Jay Gould observes: "When scientists construct an experiment to test for an expected effect, confirmations are joyfully reported; negative results are usually begrudgingly admitted. But null results (the failure to find any effect in any direction) are usually viewed as an experiment gone awry."[34] Gould cites the example of a former student who completed a study proving that the color pattern of certain clam shells did not have the adaptive significance usually claimed. A leading journal rejected her paper with the comment, "Why would you want to publish such nonresults?" (It is tempting to view this equation — null results equal unworthy results — as a gender-laden metaphor for the common association, no penis or nothing to see equals nothing of worth.) This tendency leads to illogical modes of reasoning. The fact that theory X successfully predicts phenomenon Y does not necessarily mean that theory X is true; phenomenon Y is consistent with the truth of theory X, but does not prove it. Only *unsuccessful* predictions have conclusive implications; the disconfirmation of phenomenon Y does indeed demonstrate the invalidity of theory X — and even then, perhaps only in relation to Y.

Despite the irrationality of assuming that a theory's success in prediction confirms its truth value, technical journals tend to select manuscripts that report positive results. Researchers learn to formulate and pursue questions that yield positive results and selectively report only such studies. This practice leads to an epistemological discrepancy between the information content of "positive," "negative," and "null" results. Most studies of gender differences are examples of this type of bias: measured differences are reported prominently, but we have no idea of their relative importance, since, when no differences are found, the results simply are not published.

The practice of science is actually very different from the mechanistic view of it presented in textbooks. Since scientists' theories, beliefs, and values determine what they can and cannot see, it is obviously important to know as much as possible about their point of view and motives in order to evaluate the results of their research. A continuous interplay between what are usually termed "subjective" and "objective" types of knowing yields truths obscured by a rigidly conceived "objectivity." In this context, diversity of opinion, far from being an obstacle to the progress of science, becomes its impetus.

Evelyn Fox Keller, like me an advocate of a different kind of science, defines this interplay as

> a pursuit of knowledge that makes use of subjective experience (Piaget calls it consciousness of self) in the interest of a more effective objectivity. Premised on continuity, it recognizes difference between self and other as an opportunity for a deeper and more articulated kinship. The struggle to disentangle self from other is itself a source of insight, potentially into the nature of both self and other.[35]

Your Science or Your Life

Male science, male alchemy is
partially rooted in male uterus envy,
in the desire to create something

miraculous out of male inventiveness.
However, men in science have carried
us all to the brink of total
planetary, genetic and human
destruction. Repressed uterus envy is
a dangerous emotion. . . . Men created
civilization in the image of a
perpetual erection: a pregnant
phallus.

—Phyllis Chesler, *About Men*

The androcentric biases of high culture determine many values: for example, risking life outweighs giving life. Men are left, consciously or unconsciously, to convince themselves they are in fact superior to the inferior beings who brought them into the world. In prescientific societies, they attempted to deny women's creative role and to prove their greater worth by means of their "magical" powers or their demonstrable physical strength. Their will to dominate found even more efficacious expression in scientific discourse as it emerged at the beginning of the seventeenth century. They reduced nature to a dumb, passive entity governed by mechanical laws and subject to control and manipulation. In aggressive sexual metaphors, they demanded that nature be penetrated, revealed, tortured. The outcome of this depraved intercourse was Bacon's "masculine birth of time."[36]

The masculine objective of ever-increasing power over nature has found its most dreadful expression in the nuclear arms race. The first test of the atomic bomb was experienced by the physicists involved in its development as a kind of birth: "The baby is expected on such and such a date," stated the telegram Richard Feynman received to inform him of the test. "Doctor has just returned most enthusiastic and confident that the little boy is as husky as his big brother. The light of his eyes discernible from here to High-gold and I could have heard his screams from here to my farm," said the cable to President Truman announcing the results of the test.[37] These metaphors give us a clue to the motives of those who advocate nuclear power. For them, nuclear power is a scientific-technological mode of assuring immortality, unrelated to moral consequences. In order to defend his "baby," Edward Teller, a member of the nuclear elite, went so far as to deny the harmful effects of radiation. "Fallout might indeed produce genetic abnormalities which might be offensive at first sight," he explained, "but such mutations have always been necessary to the evolution of the human race."[38] Their rapture over the apparently illimitable power offered by the bomb made scientists psychically numb to the moral consequences of their discovery.

This pattern of excluding human concerns from the field of scientific inquiry can be traced to the seventeenth century. What is new, however, is that now science is truly efficacious and could lead to our annihilation. This threat brings about a greater awareness of the cost of domination, with respect both to nuclear war and to the environment in general. It leads many women, as well as ecologists and concerned scientists, to promote another view of science and nature, based not on domination but on interrelation, in the hope that we will not have to make the tragic choice: "Your science or your life."

Epilogue: Science Changing Gender Changing Science . . .

We have seen that gender constructions elaborated early in childhood can powerfully structure human activities. In particular, they affect our images of science as well as the selection of scientists, research topics, and methods. Ironically, scientific and technological advances have the potential to undermine these constructions. Reproductive technology may bring about a redefinition of maternity and paternity. "Giving life," a typically female activity, is becoming a more active process, while, in the shadow of nuclear warfare, "risking life," a typically male activity, is acquiring passive connotations.

The widespread availability of contraception, which now gives women reproductive choice, has broken the link between sexuality and procreation. Motherhood is no longer a biological fate but an active decision. The development of *in vitro* fertilization has shattered our old definitions of maternity. When several women share the "maternal process," who is the mother? the genetic mother? the child-bearing mother? or the caring mother? In these cases maternity is perhaps less certain than paternity, especially since gene-determinant typing now allows paternity to be ascribed. Whether, as Freud thought, the uncertainty of paternity is the motor of male creativity, we can nonetheless foresee profound psychic and social consequences resulting from these developments.

On the other hand, contemporary war no longer tests masculine heroism as ancient hand-to-hand combat did. A nuclear war requires neither courage, strength, nor endurance. "Pushing a button" can be done by anyone; it is a matter not of strength but of ethics. Face-to-face with this eventuality, men and women are equally helpless. Mastery will unavoidably be self-destructive.

Encouragingly, social functions are becoming less dichotomous, less tightly bound to the physiologies of those who perform them. More women are entering the public sphere, and more men are parenting. It is no longer aberrant for a father to take interest in his child during his wife's pregnancy, participate in the delivery, and help with the infant's care. In the law, these attitudinal changes are reflected by the increased incidence of shared custody in divorce cases. As the boundaries between so-called masculine and feminine activities become more tenuous, the values associated with both types of activities tend to equalize.

Science, as part of culture, affects and is affected by the evolution of gender and values in society. Scientific theories are beginning to incorporate values traditionally associated with femininity. In physics, for example, the concept of objectivity is taking on more subtle meanings. The rigid, mechanical views of Newtonian physics are mostly behind us. The theory of relativity puts the observer back into the system — the universe looks different depending upon where you stand within it — and therefore shatters the notion of separation between subject and object. Quantum mechanics revises the concept of knowability as it pertains to nature.[39] Light, for quantum physicists, has the dual properties of waves and particles, which are described probabilistically rather than causally. Heisenberg's Uncertainty Principle teaches us that the intrinsic properties of matter make it impossible to know the position and the velocity of a particle simultaneously. Natural phenomena are not completely predictable and therefore not easily controllable. Thermodynamics of irreversible phenomena provide a new concept of matter: open systems that are constantly exchanging matter and energy with the environment have unusual possibilities of self-organization.[40] Because nature is active, it has to be understood as a whole, not as an assemblage of isolated phenomena.

As cognitive styles that incorporate a fuller range of human possibilities become legitimate in science, views of nature change as well. Nature is alive, and whatever we can know of its laws will be revealed to us through interaction based on the presence, not the absence, of the knowing subject. Although strong resistance to these new paradigms of knowing exists, they suggest possibilities for a more inclusive science.

Notes

1. Edgard Morin, *La Méthode* (Paris: Points; Editions du Seuil, 1977), 1:24; translation mine.

2. Susan Bordo, "The Cartesian Masculinization of Thought," *Signs* 11, no. 3 (Spring 1986):448.

3. Francis Bacon, *The New Organon and Related Writings*, ed. Fulton H. Anderson (Indianapolis, Ind.: Bobbs-Merrill, 1960), 95.

4. Ibid., 36.

5. Ives Rocard, "Trente-cinq Millions de Sourciers," *Autrement* 82 (1986):96–98 .

6. Albert Einstein, *Ideas and Opinions*, trans. Sonja Bargmann (New York: Crown, 1954), 225.

7. Freeman Dyson, *Disturbing the Universe* (New York: Harper and Row, 1979), 91.

8. Brian Easlea, *Fathering the Unthinkable* (London: Pluto, 1983), 82.

9. Nancy Chodorow, *The Reproduction of Mothering: Psychoanalysis and the Sociology*

of Gender (Berkeley: University of California Press, 1978); Evelyn Fox Keller, *Reflections on Gender and Science* (New Haven, Conn.: Yale University Press, 1985). See Jane Flax's critique of Chodorow in *Thinking Fragments: Psychoanalysis, Feminism, and the Postmodern in the Contemporary West* (Berkeley: University of California Press, 1990), 159–68. Chodorow now acknowledges "multiplicities of gender(ed) experience which include varied axes of power and powerlessness and dimensions of gender that do not encode power." (Nancy Chodorow, *Feminism and Psychoanalytic Theory* (New Haven, Conn.: Yale University Press, 1989), 7.

10. Sigmund Freud, "The Dissolution of the Oedipus Complex," *Standard Edition*, ed. and trans. James Strachey (London: Hogarth, 1953), 19:172–79; "Some Psychological Consequences of the Anatomical Distinction Between the Sexes," *Standard Edition*, 19:243–58; Catherine Millot, "Le Surmoi Féminin," *Ornicar* 29 (1984):111–24. Here, like Chodorow, I stress what Elizabeth Spelman characterizes as "the more troubling aspects of Freud." Spelman, *Inessential Woman: Problems of Exclusion in Feminist Thought* (Boston: Beacon Press, 1988), 85.

11. Freud, "The Question of a Weltanschaung," *Standard Edition*, 22:159.

12. Freud, "The Economic Problem of Masochism," *Standard Edition*, 19:158.

13. Simone de Beauvoir, *The Second Sex*, trans. H.M. Parshley (New York: Knopf, 1952), xv–vi. Elizabeth Spelman provides a critical analysis of de Beauvoir's account in *Inessential Woman*, 57–79.

14. Freud, "Moses and Monotheism," *Standard Edition*, 23:114.

15. de Beauvoir, *Second Sex*, 95.

16. Easlea, *Fathering the Unthinkable*; Brian Easlea, *Witch-Hunting, Magic, and the New Philosophy* (Sussex, England: Harvester, 1980); Carolyn Merchant, *The Death of Nature* (New York: Harper and Row, 1983).

17. Lucy W. Sells, "The Mathematics Filter and the Education of Women and Minorities," in *Women and the Mathematical Mystique*, ed. Lynn H. Fox, Linda Brody, and Diane Tobin (Baltimore, Md.: Johns Hopkins University Press, 1980); Sheila Tobias, *Overcoming Math Anxiety* (Boston: Houghton Mifflin, 1980), 70–80. Elizabeth Spelman discusses the problems of isolating gender as a variable independent of class and race in *Inessential Woman*, esp. ch. 4.

18. Libby Curran, "Science Education: Did She Drop Out or Was She Pushed?", in *Alice Through the Microscope*, ed. Brighton Women and Science Group (London: Virago, 1980), 22–41.

19. Ann Fausto-Sterling, *Myths of Gender* (New York: Basic, 1985), 53–59.

20. Valerie Walkerdine, "Science and the Female Mind: The Burden of Proof," *Psych Critique* 1 (1985):1; see also Jon Beckwith and John Durkin, "Girls, Boys and Math," in *Biology as Destiny: Scientific Fact or Social Bias*, ed. Science for the People (Cambridge, Mass.: Science for the People Press, 1984), 37–42; Rebecca Ruth Struik and Roberta Flexer, "Sex Differences in Mathematical Achievement: Adding Data to the Debate," *International Journal of Women's Studies* 7, no. 4 (Sept.–Oct. 1984):336–42; Camilla P. Benbow and Julian C. Stanley, "Sex Differences in Mathematical Ability: Fact or Artifact?", *Science* 210 (1980):1262–64.

21. Walkerdine, "Science and the Female Mind," 5.

22. Louis Leprince Ringuet, *Science et Bonheur des Hommes* (Paris: Flammarion, 1973), 100–4.

23. Fausto-Sterling, *Myths of Gender*, 13–60.

24. Walkerdine, "Science and the Female Mind," 2.

25. Anna Fels, "Messing About and Growing Up" (review of *Memoir of a Thinking Radish*, by Sir Peter Medawar), *New York Times Book Review*, 15 June 1986.

26. Easlea, *Fathering the Unthinkable*, 60.

27. June Goodfield, *An Imagined World* (New York: Penguin, 1982), 226; see also Evelyn Fox Keller's account of an empathic method in *A Feeling for the Organism: The Life and Work of Barbara McClintock* (New York: Freeman, 1983).

28. Thomas S. Kuhn, *The Structure of Scientific Revolutions* (Chicago: University of Chicago Press, 1977), 325.

29. Ibid., 332.

30. Quoted in Michael J. Mahoney, "Psychology of the Scientist: An Evaluative Review," *Social Studies of Science* 9, no. 3 (Aug. 1979):351.

31. Ibid., 351–52.

32. Ibid., 356.

33. Keller, *Reflections on Gender and Science*, 162.

34. Stephen J. Gould, "Cardboard Darwinism," *New York Times Book Review*, 25 Sept. 1986.

35. Keller, *Reflections on Gender and Science*, 117.

36. Keller discusses Bacon's metaphors in ibid., 38–40.

37. Easlea, *Fathering the Unthinkable*, 95–96.

38. Robert Jay Lifton, *The Broken Connection* (New York: Basic, 1979), 428.

39. Keller, *Reflections on Gender and Science*, 139–49.

40. Ilya Prigogine and Isabella Stengers, *Order Out of Chaos* (Toronto: Bantam, 1984).

The Art Historical Canon:
Sins of Omission

Nanette Salomon

A s canons within academic disciplines go, the art historical canon is among the most virulent, the most virilent, and ultimately the most vulnerable.[1] The simplest analysis of the selection of works included in the history of western European art "at its best" at once reveals that selection's ideologically motivated constitution. The omission of whole categories of art and artists has resulted in a unrepresentative and distorting notion of who has contributed to "universal" ideas expressed through creativity and aesthetic effort.

The current official selection of great works of art owes much of its present composition to the ubiquitous standard college text by H.W. Janson, *The History of Art*, first written in 1962 and reprinted at regular intervals ever since.[2] Janson did not invent this list, although his personal selection from a limited number of possibilities is itself a text worthy of analysis. In fundamental ways, the art historical canon, as it appears in Janson (and in others who follow him with unembarrassed exactitude), ultimately and fundamentally is derived from the sixteenth-century book by the Florentine artist and writer Giorgio Vasari, *Le Vite De' più eccellenti Architetti, Pittori et Scultori Italiani*, first published in 1550 and reissued in a much enlarged edition in 1568.[3] This text is generally credited with being no less than the first "modern" exposition of the history of western European art, a claim that acknowledges its influence and privileges its constitution as the generative source.[4] Vasari introduced a structure or discursive form that, in its incessant repetition, produced and perpetuated the dominance of a particular gender, class, and race as the purveyors of art and culture.

Vasari's book was written at the moment when the accomplishments of the High Renaissance artists Michelangelo and Raphael, under the auspices of papal patronage, were being absorbed as both cultural heritage and Florentine history. Vasari's desire not only to construct that history but also to place Florence at its center motivated both the form and the content of his book.[5] While modern art historians concede that it is structured to place Michelangelo and his art at the very zenith of all artistic creation, above even the revered ancients, few have seen through the more insidious aspects of his project. This is true, no doubt, because the structural aspects of Vasari's book—ordering biographies chronologically by generations and making value judgments that stress innovation and influence—continue effectively to dominate the way art history is written today.

The most important premise of Vasari's book is his assertion that great art is the expression of individual genius and can be explicated only through biography.[6] The stress on individuals' biographies, announced in the book's title, encapsulates those individuals and presents them as discrete from their social and political environments. The inherent and manipulative limitations imposed by such a biographical system are clear. The most significant limitation is that, *as* a system, it at once ties the work of art to a notion of inaccessible genius and thereby effectively removes it from consideration as a real component in a process of social exchange that involves both production and consumption.[7] This constitution of art history as biography thus occludes an analysis of works of art as material objects and understanding their formulative role in the dynamics of ideological constructs.[8]

Here in Vasari's work we can identify the moment when the myth of the "artist" as a construct is born—that is to say, invented. This "artist" is identical to the author whose death is announced by contemporary theorists such as Roland Barthes.[9] Vasari inaugurates the idea that what is worth knowing about a work of art is explained only through knowledge of the artist. As Barthes wrote, "the Author" (for Barthes's "Author," read "Artist") when believed in, is always conceived as the past of his book:

> book and author stand automatically on a single line divided into a *before* and an *after.* The Author is thought to *nourish* the book, which is to say that he exists before it, thinks, suffers, lives it, is in the same relation of antecedence to this work as a father to his child.[10]

The individual whom Vasari describes as an artist is, socially, a free agent, and therefore is clearly gendered, classed, and raced; more specifically, he is a white upper-class male. Only such an individual is empowered by his social position successfully to stake a claim to the personal freedom and creative calling that Vasari's construct requires.

Moreover, we can identify here the moment when Vasari invents/produces the critic, or art historian.[11] He does so by giving individual works particular validity through his assertion of value judgments bearing the weight of his authority.[12] His basic strategies are intricately related. Great works of art are treated as the product of the life of an unfathomable genius. Yet, incomprehensible as they are, they can be retrieved and made accessible by the documentation and explanation of the art historian. In consequence, the art historian has the license and the authority to proclaim what has quality and is valuable. The power inherent in the art historian's position was quickly grasped and immediately made overt in the writings of Vasari's follower, Raffaello Borghini, in his book *Il Riposo*, published in 1584. What was new about Borghini's theoretical position — and soon to become the norm — is that he wrote from the position of a connoisseur rather than that of a practitioner, since he himself was not an artist. Of even greater significance is that he wrote for a new kind of reader, the art lover, the educated individual who wished to be cultured through the proper appreciation of art.[13] While Vasari implies this wider audience, Borghini emphatically says that he writes his biographies of artists not only for other artists but also for those who, though not artists, wish to be in a position to judge works of art.[14] This is, undoubtedly, the ultimate concern of Janson's *History of Art* as well.

The two most significant developments of Vasari's age that bear a complex relationship to the inception, conditions, and success of his formation of art history were the creation of an art academy and the proliferation of works of art through mechanical reproduction. The former event is directly tied to Vasari himself. His Accademia dei Disegno, created in Florence, was fostered by the joint authority of Michelangelo and the State of Florence through the person of Cosimo de Medici.[15] Just as Vasari's book became the model for histories of male artists for centuries to come, his academy became the model for art academies throughout the European continent up to and including our own century.[16] The art academy became a place where would-be artists could learn to privilege the formal qualities Vasari and his followers had described as great in Michelangelo's art. The academy institutionalized art instruction throughout Europe, and its promise was nothing short of empowering its students with access to divine genius.

As Linda Nochlin has shown, the conditions of the art academy, with its high priority on drawing from the live nude model, excluded women *qua* ladies from the possibility of creating "great art."[17] The art academy is at once a historical safeguard against women's entering the canon and a rationale for their exclusion, an exclusion that historically predated the institutionalized academy.

In addition, the mechanical reproduction of unique works of sculpture and painting in prints became popular in Vasari's age. The mass production in engravings of works by Michelangelo, Raphael, and Titian broadened the base of culturally literate consumers and gave a viability (one might say an urgency) to Vasari's programs in both the Academy and the *Lives*.[18] At this time, because the exclusivity and proprietorial possession of ideas expressed through representational images were threatened, Vasari's programs intervened to reassert control and management by determining selections.

Once conditions for value have been established, whole histories may be written in which art is ordered and ranked. Art critics or historians can determine the course of art history by establishing binary relationships in conformity with systems that in their turn reestablish their prerogative to establish them. Eleanor Dickinson's interview with Janson in 1979 is a case in point. When she questioned the exclusion of women artists from his textbook, Janson blithely replied that no woman artist had been "important enough to go into a one-volume history of art."[19] When asked what his terms of inclusion were, he said, "The works that I have put in the book are representative of achievements of the imagination . . . that have one way or another changed the history of art. Now I have yet to hear a convincing case made for the claim that Mary Cassatt has changed the history of art."[20] A critical reading of Janson's *History of Art* reveals that his notion of changing history is, like Vasari's, constructed on the ideas of innovation and influence. The internal logic that justifies his selection and thus inclusion in the canon is based on a reenactment of father/son relationships on various levels of the teacher/student project.[21] This kind of relationship is apparent in the structuring affinities that art historians create between the ancients and the Italian Renaissance, between Raphael and Poussin, between Manet and Degas, and ultimately between themselves, Vasari and Janson. The play set in motion here is a perpetual one, between submission to established authority and innovation within its preset terms. Artists thereby may "change the history of art" insofar as they can be located within this father/son logic. It is critical to analyze some of the practices that situate women outside this logic.

It hardly seems necessary to say that a fundamental condition of canonical selection as construed by Vasari and his followers, up to and including Janson, is that only male artists are taken seriously. Women are not simply omitted. Before the twentieth century, there is barely a history of art that completely omits women, and Vasari himself included some in the *Lives*—evidence of what must surely have been their undeniable presence in the art world that Vasari set out to chronicle.[22] These women artists remind us that women's participation in the somewhat rarified world of art, as in society in general, at some point in history was much greater than the accounts of modern historians suggest.[23] In fact, as Joan Kelly demonstrated, it was precisely in the period we call the "Renaissance" that the systematic diminution of social and personal options for women began.[24] In this context, Vasari's *Lives* may be seen as part of the apparatus that abrogated women's direct and unproblematical participation in cultural life. In discussing the creativity of women, Vasari strategically enhanced their marginalization by using patronizing and demeaning terms to explain their art and its oddity, their exceptional status as women artists. For example, his treatment of the Cremona artist Sophinisba Anguisola includes all of the by-now-clichéd references to women's creative abilities in childbirth, as well as astonishment at her exceptional abilities as a visual artist. The notion of the "exceptionál" woman artist may be one of the most insidious means of undermining the likelihood of women's entering the creative arts.

A primary strategy of Vasari/Janson is to establish a narrow focus through the imposition of a standard or norm. This standard is defined by classical art and by the recuperation of the achievement of classical culture as most perfectly realized in the art of Michelangelo.[25] The implications of this standard are complex and require dismantling on a variety of levels. I shall return presently to the inherent meaning of classical imagery and classicism for constructing notions of gender and sexuality. First, however, I discuss the more overt consequences of this standard. It functions to create a hierarchy of insiders and outsiders. The stigma of "otherness," as applied to the "outsider," can be bestowed equally on some male artists as it has been on female artists. The classical paradigm defines the "Renaissance" of central Italy as the art with the greatest value and successfully marginalizes all other artistic traditions.[26] Artistic traditions contemporary with the Italian Renaissance, no matter how diverse, are simply lumped together under the heading "art north of Alps." The rationale for discussing these complex and varied traditions as a single tradition can only be that their differences from one another are deemed irrelevant and their singular difference from Central Italian classicism crucial. For example, Vasari, discussing northern European artists, indiscriminately uses the term *fiamminghi* (that is, someone from Flanders), even when discussing the German artists Martin Schongauer and Albrecht Dürer.[27] In addition, he relegates his comments on these artists to his book on technical instruction rather than including them in the *Lives* proper, thereby locating them with the practical and manual aspects of art as craft, rather than with the more elevated position of art as an intellectual activity. It is true that some northern artists are discussed at the very end of the *Lives*, but in a section that has no name.[28]

Vasari/Janson's stated preference for classical forms as the basis of an absolute system of aesthetic evaluation enables them to judge all other European traditions according to how close they come to accepting classicism as a paradigm. Thus Janson writes: "Gifted though they were, Cranach and Altdorfer both evaded the main challenge of the Renaissance so bravely faced — if not always mastered — by Dürer: the image of man."[29]

The devaluation of "art north of the Alps," like the devaluation of the art of the "pre-Renaissance" Medieval period, can be seen as a strategy with a deeper import for us than might at first be suspected. Women in these cultures were more essential to, and better integrated into, the workings of economic and social life and thus, by extension, were better integrated into the production of works of art than women were in Italy.[30] Michelangelo's reputed comments on Flemish painting, reported by Francesca da Hollanda in 1538, recognize the importance of women in the constructs of Netherlandish painting: "Women will like it, especially very old ones, or very young ones. It will please likewise friars and nuns, and also some noble persons who have no ear for true harmony."[31] As late as 1718–21, Arnold Houbraken's book on the lives of the great Dutch painters not only includes both men and women artists but also acknowledges their joint contributions in its title, *De Groote Schooburgh der Nederlandtsche Konstschilders en Schilderessen.*[32] The decided prejudice in favor of Italian male artists and art therefore can be understood not only as a statement asserting the superiority of men over women but also as a prejudice in favor of whole systems that supported and made possible that superiority.

Between Vasari's *Lives* and Janson's *History of Art*, many variations of art history were written. Yet, despite the many versions produced by art historians of different nationalities at different times, fundamental constants can be discerned. We can attribute these constants to the unchallenged influence of Vasari, the orthodox source to whom writers returned again and again.[33] While Venetian, French, and Dutch art histories featured their own artists, they all adhered strongly to Vasari's structural prototype and maintained his classical bias. Vasari's structure itself took on canonical status. This characteristic structure emphasizes individual contributions, fixes the terms of a generational and stylistic development of the history of art, and provides standards for aesthetic judgments along classical lines. This structure is repeated in the art historical writing of Janson and most other contributors to this genre in the intervening four centuries. The project of the early art histories served nationalistic motives. Yet, clearly, more was at stake — that is, maintaining the control of culture for a privileged few. In the late seventeenth century, Joachim von Sandrart, Filippo Baldinucci, André Félibien, and Roger de Piles broke away from allegiance primarily to nationalistic motives and included an international array of artists in their texts.[34] Significantly, despite the tendency of art historians in the late seventeenth century to amplify their texts by adding artists of different nationalities, they systematically eroded and finally erased the presence of women.

In our own historical moment, women have fought for and regained the privilege and the responsibility of having a say in the ways culture gets produced and disseminated. Feminists have opened places within canonical discourse to allow for the inclusion of women as artists and women as critics. But at this juncture, inclusion alone is not enough. Feminist practice has produced several strategies for dealing with the academic field of art history and its canon. Primary among these is the archeological excavation of women as creators. The second is the appearance of women as critics and interpreters, receiving and inflecting works of art in ways meaningful for them. The implications of the two developments — women recovered as artists and women as critics — are vast, and they are, of course, not mutually exclusive.

Among the most useful consequences of the first strategy, the recovery of women artists, is bringing "normal" selection under direct scrutiny and thereby denaturalizing and politicizing it. What heretofore had appeared to be an objective account of cultural history, the "Western European Tradition," suddenly reappears as a history with a strong bias for white, upper-class male creativity and patronage. It is a history in profound support of exclusively male interests. Feminists' insistence on exposing exclusions reveals the ways in which works within the canon cohere with one another in terms quite different from those traditionally advanced. Rather than appearing as paradigmatic examples of aesthetic value or meaningful expression, or even as representative of major historical movements and events, canonical works support one another as components in a larger system of power relations. Significance and pleasure are defined as projected exclusively through male experiences. The simple corrective gesture of introducing women into the canon to create a more accurate picture of what "really happened" and to give them a share of the voice that proclaims what is significant and pleasurable does not really rectify the situation. Our understanding of the political implications of what is included and excluded from the repertoire of canonical works and, even more, our understanding of historical writing itself as a political act render this, at best, a tactic with limited effects. The terms of art historical practice themselves, whether formalist or contextualist, are so laden with ideological overtones and value judgments as to what is or is not worthwhile — or, as it was expressed in the past, "ennobling" — that questions of gender and class are designed to be irrelevant to its discourse. These crucial questions not only seem to be *beside* the point of traditional art historical questions; they are specifically *outside* the point.

Chronologically, in feminist art historical writing, the introduction of "great women artists" was the first real attempt at bringing women into the iconic system of the art historical canon.[35] A host of probing, but to my mind unanswerable, questions were asked. They remain unanswerable because they are wrought with essentially the same methodological tools that so restrictively govern the traditional art historical enterprise. For example, there is the question deriving from the Morellian tradition of connoisseurship: Can one tell from looking at a work of art that the artist was a woman? And one deriving from Panofskian iconology: Do women interpret themes differently than men? And from the Gombrich model: What are the social conditions that led women to paint and draw the way they did?

The uncritical insertion of women artists into the pre-existing structure of art history as a discipline tends to confirm rather than challenge the prejudicial tropes through which women's creativity is dismissed. Logically, the women artists who were hailed by the feminists of the 1970s were exactly the ones easiest to excavate, because their work most closely approximated that of traditional, mainstream movements as defined by academe. Yet, precisely because those women had achieved some measure of traditional success, they were by definition appropriate for comparison with the textbook male "genius" whose work their art most resembled. Like a knee-jerk reaction or a Pavlovian response, the device of "compare and contrast" was proffered to situate these new-yet-not-so-new entries into the canon. This device, the staple of art-historical analysis since the days of Wolfflin,[36] continually serves as an instrument for ranking value and establishing a hierarchy of prestige. The device compels its users to put "versus" between two artists. Thus, Artemisia Gentileschi is inevitably and detrimentally compared to Caravaggio; Judith Leyster, inevitably and detrimentally, to Frans Hals; Mary Cassatt, inevitably and detrimentally, to Degas. When the rules of the game are neither challenged nor changed, the very structure of such binary oppositions insists that one side be master, the other side pupil; one major, the other minor. These comparisons, in a disheartening way, seem to prove once and for all that women have not produced anything either innovative or influential. They were rather on the receiving end of the influence exchange, with all of the attendant anxiety assigned to that undesirable position in modernist discourse.[37] Their only form of retreat and solace comes in the ghettoized subcategory "women artists."

Whereas Vasari used the device of biography to individualize and mystify the works of artistic men, the same device has a profoundly different effect when applied to women. The details of a man's biography are conveyed as a measure of the "universal," applicable to all mankind; in the male genius they are simply heightened and intensified. In contrast, the details of a woman's biography are used to underscore the idea that she is an exception; they apply only to her and make her an interesting individual case. Her art is reduced to a visual record of her personal and psychological makeup.

No doubt the most egregious example is the seventeenth-century Italian artist Artemisia Gentileschi. Her rape by her "mentor," the artist Agostino Tassi, and the litigation brought against Tassi by her father Orazio Gentileschi, enter into every discussion of her art. Not to discuss it is to avoid it. The degree to which Artemisia Gentileschi's sexual history is the most discussed aspect of her persona contrasts sharply with the embarrassment about and denial of the equally documentable sexual histories that are an integral part of great male artists' biographies (the most obvious example being the homosexuality of Michelangelo and Caravaggio).[38]

Artemisia Gentileschi's history is brought to bear on her images of what Mary Garrard calls her "heroic women," particularly her paintings of *Judith*

Beheading Holofernes and *Susanna and the Elders*.[39] In the end, these paintings are reduced by critics to therapeutic expressions of her repressed fear, anger, and/or desire for revenge. Her creative efforts are thus compromised, in traditional terms, as personal and relative.

The fact that her father waited ten months before bringing charges against Tassi seems strange to modern-day researchers, as does her apparent consent to be Tassi's lover after the rape.[40] While the proceedings of the trial may or may not add to our understanding of Gentileschi's art, they can do so only when seen as part of the highly coded discourse of sexuality and the politics of rape in the seventeenth century. Perhaps more than anything, they emphasize the fact that Artemisia, body and soul, was treated as the site of exchange between men, primarily her father/mentor and her lover/rapist/mentor, but also between Tassi and Cosimo Quorli, orderly of the Pope, who, presumably because of his own jealous desire for her, asked Tassi not to marry her. Tassi complied with his request. The process of exchange began when she was "given" to Tassi as a pupil, and it continued when he violently "took" her, when her honor was "redeemed," and when she was given and taken again. The homosocial bonding ritual enacted and reenacted among these men render "Artemisia" a historically elusive construct. If the testimony of the trial reveals anything, it is a person with an obstinate sense of her own social and sexual needs. Her paintings thus look less like "heroic women" than like the nexus of a series of complicated negotiations between convention and disruption, between "Artemisia" and Artemisia.

Much writing on Artemisia Gentileschi and her art exemplifies the ways in which the conventional structures of art-historical discourse safeguard their deepest subtexts — those that preserve power for and endow with significance a privileged few. The motives behind this writing need not be seen as willful or even conscious. Their strength lies in their centuries-old history and in the mutually supportive, reciprocal relationship between that history and the ends such motives produce.

Mary Garrard's attempt to "heroize" Artemisia Gentileschi and the women she depicted reveals her desire to enroll Gentileschi in the canon as presently constructed. She wants for Gentileschi the status afforded to men who make "heroic" images and whose art, which is an extension of their biography, sets positive examples for others, in this case women. As most recently pointed out by Patricia Rubin, the aim of Renaissance biography in general and of Vasari in particular was to make heroes of exemplary men.[41] Yet we are rudely reminded that what can and has been done for men cannot simply and unproblematically be done for women. To cite Rubin again, our interest in Renaissance men "arises from the representative nature of these figures, taken to embody values that match and confirm basic themes which organize and characterize cultural understanding."[42] The hierarchical relationships established by Vasari are still intact and his preferences profoundly and successfully potent.

It may seem "natural" that Vasari put his fellow citizens above all others and that, within Italy, his Florentine bias was tolerated. It is less "natural" (that is, less understandable) that his heroes became the heroes of similar texts written by German, Dutch, French, English, and American authors, up to and including H.W. Janson.[43] The success of Vasari's canon with its classical bias must be accounted for on grounds more complex than its articulation of a proprietary turf for "men only." That canon creates a position of dominance for a certain kind of man who can understand and appreciate classical and classicist art as most perfectly embodied in the art of Michelangelo. The ideological value of the classical model in the constitution of power relations through the coding of gender and sexuality can be uncovered only by feminist analysis.

The art of Michelangelo and classical Greek sculpture, his primary source of inspiration, took as their ideal form the male nude youth, whom they viewed as equally the ideal of art and of "nature," predicated on a notion of beauty that they defined as specifically male.[44] For the Greeks and for Michelangelo, as in nearly all cases where the object of aesthetic admiration is the human form, the enjoyment of the male body is conjoined with homoerotic desire. For the Greeks this conjunction seemed a natural one, and surely that socially legitimate desire contributed to constituting the male nude as an ideal.[45] The conjunction for Michelangelo was far more problematical, yet not so problematical as to have been prohibitive.[46] Homoerotic desire and the artistic production of the idealized male nude youth clearly have a historical relationship. Yet, as important as that relationship is, it is equally meaningful and informative that there is no mention—in fact, can be no mention—of homosexuality in Vasari/Janson.[47] Their repression of homosexuality is facilitated by another fundamental principle of classicism, that a perfect body contains a beautiful spirit, that physical and moral beauty are inextricably united. This principle framed homosexual desire in a larger moral and aesthetic discourse. Art history, produced in patriarchal yet officially heterosexual Christian times, could use, and indeed embrace, the presumptive moral and aesthetic aspects of the desire that fostered the works of art, but only after severing them from any traces of sexual meaning. The erotic appreciation of artistic nudes was masked by the concept of pure aesthetic pleasure, unpolluted by either the sexual desires of the producers or the threat of corresponding sexual desires in the viewers.[48] The fiction created by this "purification" of the art object renders it sound currency in a heterosexual world that cannot bear to acknowledge homosexuality as anything but deviance.[49]

The form central to the art of Michelangelo and his Greek sources, the one heralded as the most brilliant of Western civilization by Vasari/Janson, is the freestanding sculpture of an idealized male nude youth. This form exhibits features worth considering in this context. It — or he — is characterized by the conflation of an athletic and a military iconography resulting in the "heroic." The nude stands unselfconsciously present, in the sense that he neither flaunts nor covers his penis. It is, rather, represented as is any other body part in the classical homoerotic system that sexualizes the youth as a complete and coherent being without fetishizing his genitals.

The male nude youth stands in startling contrast to the female nude youth, the other standard icon of the Vasari/Janson canon — whose portrayal, it must be said, is completely absent from Michelangelo's sculpted work. The fashioning of the female nude as it — or she — appears in ancient art and in the art of the Italian Renaissance (in, for example, the art of Botticelli or Titian) is also produced within the framework of sexual desire. That desire is also repressed in formal art-historical writing, despite recent attempts by some art historians to acknowledge it.

The history of the form raises interesting problems in evaluating the main subjects of the canon. The so-called "classical" female nude in monumental sculpture was, in fact, not introduced in Greek art until the postclassical period. It was invented by the fourth-century sculptor Praxiteles, whose life-sized sculpture of Aphrodite, entitled the *Cnidian Aphrodite* for the name of its ancient site, is known to us only through Roman copies.[50] This sculpture is the source for a massive number of works representing Aphrodite/Venus in the art of the Western world, not only because it is the first monumental female nude but also and more significantly because it is the first to be fashioned covering her pubis. This gesture is repeatedly interpreted as one of modesty, which the ancients called "pudica." Despite its name, the gesture signifies a great deal more than modesty. It is so endemic to our culture that its affect has been "naturalized"; that is to say, we no longer "connect" with the pernicious narrative of fear expressed by a woman shown trying to protect her pubis against violent assault. The "pudica" pose has become for us the epitome of aesthetics or artfulness. Nevertheless, looking at a naturalistically crafted sculpture of a woman who does not want to be seen cannot help but titillate, even if we react subconsciously. The gesture, with all it connotes, is more than an image of fear and rejection. Merely by placing the hand of the woman over her pubis, Praxiteles — and every artist since him who has used this device — creates a sense of desire in the viewer and constructs a Peeping-Tom response. This voyeuristic response is installed in all types of viewers, male and female, heterosexual or homosexual. However, it is clearly male heterosexuals who are encouraged to translate that desire into socially sanctioned acts. These acts, not to be confused with private acts of sexual behavior, are rather publicly displayed appreciation of the totally sexualized female form. As high culture, this appreciation is synonymous with the appreciation of a work of art signified by a female nude; as low culture, this appreciation is synonymous with lewd remarks made to women on the street by men in groups. In the end, the high and low forms of appreciation conditioned by the "pudica" pose create special opportunities for publicly shared male sexual experience without overt homosexual overtones. The female nude is the site of, and the public display of heterosexual desire the medium for, a male bonding ritual.[51]

The role of Vasari/Janson in promoting the heroic male nude and the sexualized, vulnerable female nude as paradigms cannot be underestimated. Historically, the two forms were created within the framework of constructing two male desires, one homosexual and the other heterosexual. The disparate erotic treatments of the male and female tell us a great deal about the different ways in which men and women were and are viewed as objects of sexual desire. Yet formal art historical texts like those of Vasari and Janson treat the male and female nudes in ways that prevent conscious consideration of them as dynamic components in establishing power relations that are expressed in sexual terms. Rather, more covert ways of giving the works their significance in structuring gender and sexuality become effective. In modern society, where heterosexual dominance has prevailed at least since the sixteenth century, the artistic fashioning of the male and female nude defines a cosmopolitan and international club of culturally literate heterosexual males whose ardent allegiance is to one another. The love and admiration of men for one another is thus made acceptable through the shared expression of their overt and irrepressible heterosexual drives.

Vasari's invention of the artist, the critic, and the canon is tied to the economic and social conditions of his moment in history. While these conditions have changed, the deeper stratifications of gender, race, and class continue to operate within the culturally expressed power relationships that he articulated. Vasari thus furnished the discursive forms that remain potent in Janson's moment—and ours.

Notes

1. I wish to thank Griselda Pollock, Keith Moxey, Flavia Rando, Ellen Davis, and the editors, Joan E. Hartman and Ellen Messer-Davidow, for reading earlier drafts of this essay.

2. Several articles have critically examined H.W. Janson, *The History of Art* (New York: Abrams, 1962): Eleanor Dickinson, "Sexist Texts Boycotted," *Women Artists News* 5, no. 4 (Sept.-Oct. 1979):12; Eleanor Tufts, "Beyond Gardner, Gombrich, and Janson: Towards a Total History of Art," *Arts Magazine* 55, no. 8 (Apr. 1981):150–54; and Bradford R. Collins, "Book Reviews of H.W. Janson and E.H. Gombrich," *Art Journal* 48, no. 1 (Spring 1989):90–95.

3. Editions of Vasari's book translated in all languages have appeared with regularity.

The edition most often cited is Giorgio Vasari, *Le vite de' più eccellenti pittori, scultori ed architettori italiani,* ed. Gaetano Milanesi, 9 vols. (Florence, 1865–79). See also the bibliography in T.S.R. Boase, *Giorgio Vasari: The Man and the Book* (Princeton: Princeton University Press, 1971), 341.

4. Vasari's *Lives* is "traditionally identified as the first art history" (W. Eugene Kleinbauer and Thomas P. Slavens, *Research Guide to the History of Western Art* [Chicago: American Library Association, 1982], 19, 88). While it clearly has been the most influential compilation of artists and art history, it was by no means the first. For the most complete history of the history of art, see Julius Schlosser, *Die Kunstliteratur* (Vienna: Anton Schroll, 1924). Vasari himself relied on a mixture of classical sources such as Plutarch and Pliny the Elder (Patricia Rubin, "What Men Saw: Vasari's Life of Leonardo da Vinci and the Image of the Renaissance Artist," *Art History* 13, no. 1 [Mar. 1990]:34).

5. Vasari's desire to relocate much of the credit for the achievements of the Renaissance to Florence under the Medicis is discussed by Anthony Blunt, *Artistic Theory in Italy, 1450–1600* (Oxford, England: Clarendon Press, 1940), 86–102, and T.S.R. Boase, *Vasari,* ch. 1.

6. See Griselda Pollock, "Artists Mythologies and Media Genius, Madness and Art History," *Screen* 21, no. 3 (Spring 1980):57–95, for a full discussion of how biography mystifies art in traditional art historical writing. For an early explanation of the myth of the artist and biography in psychological terms, see Ernst Kris and Otto Kurz, *Legend, Myth, and Magic in the Image of the Artist: A Historical Experiment* (New Haven, Conn: Yale University Press, 1979).

7. Griselda Pollock, *Vision and Difference: Femininity, Feminism, and the Histories of Art* (London: Routledge, 1988), esp. ch. 1.

8. Griselda Pollock, "Women, Art and Ideology: Questions for Feminist Art Historians," *Woman's Art Journal* 4, no. 1 (Spring-Summer 1983):39–48.

9. Roland Barthes, "The Death of the Author," *Image-Music-Text,* ed. and trans. Stephen Heath (London: Fontana, 1977), 142–47. The most recent application of Barthes's important essay to art history is Griselda Pollock, "Critical Reflections," *Artforum* 27, no. 6 (Feb. 1990):126–27.

10. Barthes, "Death of the Author," 145.

11. For the relationship of Vasari's *Lives* to the late 16th century as "the age of criticism," see Peter Burke, *The Renaissance* (London: Macmillan Education, 1987), 54–55.

12. E.H. Gombrich, *Meditations on a Hobby Horse* (London: Phaidon, 1965), 109.

13. Moshe Barasch, *Theories of Art: From Plato to Winckelmann* (New York: New York University Press, 1985), 206–9.

14. Blunt, *Artistic Theory,* 101.

15. For a history of the Art Academy and the seminal position of Vasari, see Nicholas Pevsner, *Academies of Art, Past and Present* (Cambridge, England: Cambridge University Press, 1940).

16. Ibid.

17. Linda Nochlin, "Why Have There Been No Great Women Artists?", rptd. in Nochlin, *Art, Women and Power and Other Essays* (New York: Harper and Row, 1988), 145–75.

18. Walter Benjamin, "The Work of Art in the Age of Mechanical Reproduction," rptd. in *Illuminations,* trans. Harry Zohn (New York: Schocken, 1969), 217–52.

19. Dickinson, "Sexist Texts," 12.

20. Ibid.

21. I am grateful for discussions with Griselda Pollock that clarified the ideas in this section.

22. Vasari's treatment of women has not, to my knowledge, been analyzed. There is a brief discussion of women artists in Netherlandish texts by Margarita Russell, "The

Women Painters in Houbraken's *Groote Schouburgh*," *Woman's Art Journal* 2, no. 1 (Spring-Summer 1981):5–12.

23. Rozsika Parker and Griselda Pollock, *Old Mistresses: Women, Art and Ideology* (New York: Pantheon, 1981), ch. 1.

24. Joan Kelly, "Did Women Have a Renaissance?", rptd. in *Women, History, and Theory: The Essays of Joan Kelly* (Chicago: University of Chicago Press, 1984), 19–50.

25. Hans Belting, "Vasari and His Legacy: The History of Art as Process?", in Belting, *The End of the History of Art?* (Chicago: University of Chicago Press, 1987), 73.

26. The reception of North Italian art was somewhat mixed, and it was approved only with qualifications. See, e.g., Vasari's treatment of Titian (Boase, *Vasari*, 277–79).

27. The case of Albrecht Dürer is particularly interesting, since much of his artistic project involved reconciling an Italianate mode with an essentially Northern iconography. His Italianate manner makes him a favorite non-Italian entry in the canon. Thus, in 1987, Hans Belting still could categorize the "other": "For the artist *north of the Alps* the journey to Italy became a voyage of discovery into the homeland of art. Albrecht Dürer . . . was among *the earliest of these pilgrims*" (emphasis added; Belting, "Vasari and His Legacy," 81). Certainly Dürer was not among the earliest artists "north of the Alps" to come to Italy, just among the first to attempt to paint in an Italian style.

28. Boase, *Vasari*, 197, n. 1.

29. Quoted by Collins, "Book Reviews," 92.

30. For the position of women in Germany, see Merry E. Wiesner, *Working Women in Renaissance Germany* (New Brunswick, N.J.: Rutgers University Press, 1986); in Germany and the Netherlands, Martha C. Howell, *Women, Production, and Patriarchy in Later Medieval Cities* (Chicago: University of Chicago Press, 1986). For the position of women in Italy, see Christiane Klapisch-Zuber, *Women, Family, and Ritual in Renaissance Italy* (Chicago: University of Chicago Press, 1985). See also Martha C. Howell's review essay, "Marriage, Property, and Patriarchy: Recent Contributions to a Literature," *Feminist Studies* 13, no. 1 (Spring 1987):203–24, esp. 209.

31. Charles Holroyd, *Michael Angelo Buonarroti* (London, 1903), 279. Svetlana Alpers attributes a slightly different significance to Michelangelo's remarks in "Art History and Its Exclusions," in *Feminism and Art History: Questioning the Litany*, ed. Norma Broude and Mary D. Garrard (New York: Harper and Row, 1982), 194–95.

32. Arnold Houbraken, *De Groote Schouburgh der nederlantsche konstchilders en schilderessen* [*The Great Theatre of Netherlandish Painters and Paintresses*] (1753; rptd. Amsterdam: B.M. Israel BV, 1976).

33. Schlosser, *Kunstliteratur*; Lionel Venturi, *History of Art Criticism* (New York: Dutton, 1964), 118.

34. Giulio Mancini and Carel van Mander, by considering artists on an international scale, may be considered precursors. Nevertheless, Mancini dealt only with artists active in Rome, and van Mander separated ancient, Italian, and Northern art by putting them in different books.

35. The list of books on women artists is by now quite long; see the bibliography in Whitney Chadwick, *Women, Art, and Society* (London: Thames and Hudson, 1990).

36. Heinrich Wölfflin, *Principles of Art History*, trans. M.D. Hottinger (1932; rptd. New York: Dover, 1950).

37. Harold Bloom, *The Anxiety of Influence: A Theory of Poetry* (London: Oxford University Press, 1973).

38. Michelangelo's homosexuality is discussed in James Saslow, *Ganymede in the Renaissance: Homosexuality in Art and Society* (New Haven, Conn.: Yale University Press,

1986). For Caravaggio, see Donald Posner, "Caravaggio's Homo-erotic Early Works," *Art Quarterly* 34, no. 3 (Autumn 1971):301–24.

39. Mary Garrard, *Artemisia Gentileschi: The Image of the Female Hero in Italian Baroque Art* (Princeton, N.J.: Princeton University Press, 1989).

40. Ibid.; Richard Spear, "Images of Heroic Women" (review of Garrard), *Times Literary Supplement* no. 4496 (2–8 June 1989), 603.

41. Rubin, "What Men Saw," 34–35.

42. Ibid., 34; 44, n. 1.

43. Venturi, *History of Art Criticism*, chs. 5–7; Kleinbauer and Slavens, *Research Guide*, 89.

44. John Boswell, "Revolutions, Universals and Sexual Categories," *Salmagundi* 58–59 (Fall 1982–Winter 1983):106–9.

45. For the history of homosexuality in ancient Greece, see K.J. Dover, *Greek Homosexuality*, 1978 (rptd. New York: Vintage, 1980), and, more recently, Michel Foucault, *The Use of Pleasure: The History of Sexuality*, trans. Robert Hurley, vol. 2 (New York: Pantheon, 1985).

46. Michelangelo's homosexuality was first discussed by John Addington Symonds in *The Life of Michelangelo Buonarroti*, 2 vols. (London, 1899), and most recently in Saslow, *Ganymede*, 17–63.

47. Saslow, discussing what he takes to be Vasari's lack of interest in sexuality, writes: "Vasari . . . is generally not much interested in his subjects' private lives" (Saslow, *Ganymede*, 14). This claim is difficult to sustain, looking at any two pages of Vasari's *Lives*.

48. The degree to which homophobia still distorts art history can be observed by the absence of "homosexuality" in David Freedberg's index to *The Power of Images: Studies in the History and Theory of Response* (Chicago: University of Chicago Press, 1989), despite chapters entitled "Arousal by Image" and "Senses and Censorship." Freedberg acknowledges only heterosexual responses to works of art, as if they are the only ones that exist.

49. Monique Wittig, "The Straight Mind," *Feminist Issues* 1, no. 1 (Summer 1980):103–11.

50. Praxiteles' sculpture is fully discussed in Chr. Blinkenberg, *Knidia: Beiträge zur kenntnis der Praxitelischen Aphrodite* (Copenhagen: Levin and Munksgaard, 1933).

51. Eve Kosofsky Sedgwick investigates homosocial bonding in English literature in *Between Men: English Literature and Male Homosocial Desire* (New York: Columbia University Press, 1985). Her ideas have stimulated my reading of the "pudica" pose. See also Susan Winnett, "Coming Unstrung: Women, Men, Narrative, and Principles of Pleasure," *PMLA* 105, no. 3 (May 1990):505–18, esp. 507.

Mastery

Angelika Bammer

If the position of mastery culturally comes back to men, what will become of (our) femininity when we find ourselves in this position? When we use a master-discourse?
> —Hélène Cixous and Catherine Clément, *The Newly Born Woman*

master.
1. The state of being master [one who has control, direction, or authority over someone or something, as over workers, a household, an animal, etc.] . . . To gain *mastery* of the entire world.
> —Funk & Wagnalls' *Standard College Dictionary*

"Selection," my *Funk and Wagnalls'* tells me, is "a thing or collection of things chosen with care." The select, I was taught in early Catholic girlhood, are the chosen, the special ones, those who will be saved, as opposed to those who have been rejected. Selection, I think, as I fill my basket with vegetables and fruits at the Saturday farmers' market, is deciding what we need at a given time, knowing what is available, and taking what is useful.

As the canon of "Great Books," of literary "master"pieces, is subjected to critical scrutiny by readers who no longer feel loyal to a civilization built on the hegemony of the Great White Fathers, the question of selection once again springs sharply into focus. What we *should* know ("those texts that a culture takes as absolutely basic to its literary education"[1]) and what we *must* know (about our culture, about power, about history, about our position in relation to these constructs as members of particular classes, races, and genders) are often, we find, disparate or even contradictory.

In her essay on "The Making of a Writer," Paule Marshall remembers her discovery of literature in the Macon Street Branch of the Brooklyn Public Library. It was a discovery that opened to her a culture that she, a young Black girl from Barbados, had not even known existed. Yet while reading the works of the nineteenth-century masters (Thackeray, Fielding, Dickens) satisfied her desire for learning, it also left her with a hungry sense of lack: "Something I couldn't quite define was missing." Only later, when she came across the works of Black—and especially Black women—writers, did she realize what it was that she had been missing: "What I needed, what all the kids . . . with whom I grew up needed, was . . . [to] read works by those like ourselves."[2] What was missing from the world of literature were people like herself. With this realization, Marshall learned the basic principle of cultural politics: power and culture are inseparable; the one sets the other in place. Those who hold power define what is "culture," what is to be included and what left out. Yet, couched in the formalist terms of aesthetic discourse, these politics of selection remain invisible. Indeed, that a process of selection—and rejection—has even taken place is seldom if ever acknowledged. Culture, such as the body of works that constitute the literary canon, is made to appear self-evident.

Marshall posits that we need a culture that includes the work of people "like ourselves." But who are they? How do we choose them? Is it a matter of choice or simply a matter of fact? This tangled relationship between identity (who we are) and identification (whom we ally ourselves with) is addressed by Virginia Woolf in *Three Guineas* (1938).[3] As the narrator looks down from her window at a procession of men bearing the weighty insignia of power, she suddenly realizes that "there, trapesing [sic] along at the tail end of the procession, we go ourselves." Decades of activism on the part of women, directed at gaining social equality, had erased many of the old distinctions between the men who had rights and power and the women who did not: "We too can leave the house, can mount those steps, pass in and out of those doors, wear wigs and gowns, make money, administer justice." As a result of these changes, proposes Woolf, we must ask ourselves some "very important questions . . . so important that they may well change the lives of all men and all women for ever." For, she explains, "we have to ask ourselves, here and now, do we wish to join that procession, or don't we? On what terms shall we join that procession? Above all, where is it leading us, the procession of educated men?" The answers to these questions have grave consequences, politically and personally. Therefore, she urges us to think carefully:

> Let us never cease from thinking—what is this "civilization" in which we find ourselves? What are these ceremonies and why should we take part in them? What are these professions and why should we make money out of them? Where in short is it leading us, the procession of the sons of educated men?[4]

As feminist scholars, critics, and teachers, we work within the context of academic institutions. Yet we define our inquiry in critical opposition to the structures on which the power of these institutions is based. Thus, Woolf's questions challenge us to ask: What do we read and to what end? What do we teach and why? What do we write about and for whom? What are "our" texts and what are we doing with them? Are our selections truly selections ("a thing, or collection of things chosen with care") or rather a display both of our familiarity with a body of works that has already been institutionally chosen and our willingness to legitimate it as if it were the product of our own choice?

A Matter of Taste

Some time ago a friend gave me a copy of Edith Wharton's *Summer*. "You can keep it," she said. "You like her; I don't." Her words and her gift referred to a conversation we had had several weeks earlier. We had been talking about literature and feminism, about books we had read that had given us pleasure or spoken to us in memorable ways. We had found, as we talked, that even though we were both feminists and had similar academic training, our tastes were, in fact, quite different. I, for example, loved *The House of Mirth*; she did not like Edith Wharton at all. She loved *Daughter of Earth*; I had not much liked it. We tried to articulate reasons for our differences, searched for criteria we could use to legitimate that curious mixture of desire and need we often, for lack of more rigorous scrutiny, simply call "taste." She found Wharton effete and condescending; I found Agnes Smedley boringly self-absorbed. We each found the other's writer tedious. Unable either to agree or to muster convincing arguments in support of our respective choices, I proposed that perhaps it really was, in the end, simply a matter of taste. But then what *was* "taste," and what did our personal aesthetics have to do with our feminist politics? Finally, my friend put into words what we no doubt already knew but had avoided speaking of: "Don't you think," she said, "that class might have something to do with it?"

What *does* "class"—as a historical construct and as a lived experience—have to do with our work as feminist critics? How does it shape our literary pleasures and aesthetic values? How does it influence our selections and stances? As my friend and I set out to explore the specifics of difference—i.e., of class difference—between us, we took as our starting point our differing reactions to the texts of Smedley and Wharton. We examined our choices, both as feminists and as literary critics, in light of the environments that had shaped us: the neighborhoods we grew up in, the places we called home, the families that raised us, the friends and heroes we had, the education we received. The more we talked, the more we realized that, once acknowledged as a factor, class came into focus everywhere: it affected our attitudes toward work, money, security, and status, as well as our choice of, and preference for, particular authors or works. This essay grew out of those talks.

That race, gender, ethnicity, sexual affiliation — both what we experience and how we are categorized — affect what and whom we read, whether for personal or for professional reasons, no longer needs to be argued. That class is as important a factor has of course been posited. Not only is it much less often acknowledged, however, but *how* it is a factor remains largely unexamined. These, then, are the issues I propose to take up here.

We can begin with the definition of "literature" itself. Already, as the young Paule Marshall discovered, the very criteria by which we determine whether something qualifies as "literature" or not, the standards by which we distinguish "good" writing from "bad," reflect the means and aspirations of a particular class.[5] In an illuminating study of the evolution of American literary history between the 1920s and the 1950s, Paul Lauter examines why and how, within the space of a few decades, "black, white female, and all working-class writers [were eliminated] from the canon." Works by the very writers who, in the early part of the century, had been both popular and influential, by mid-century had virtually disappeared. One important reason, Lauter argues, was the "professionalization" of literary studies taking place during precisely this time. In order to validate and upgrade the status of the profession, aesthetic theories were fashioned that favored those works appealing primarily to a culturally privileged audience. Everything else was ruled culturally inferior. Standards of excellence that emphasized such qualities as complexity, ambiguity, and irony not only valued the high art of modernism more than the popular art produced for a mass audience; in the same move, they also placed "a premium on the skills of the literary interpreter."[6]

In "The Politics of Bibliography," Deborah Rosenfelt provides yet another example of how literary critics function as custodians of the status quo. With respect to women writers, she shows, not much has changed since the 1950s. While feminist challenges to the white, middle-class male tunnel vision of literary history have produced some changes (notably the inclusion of a few select women in the canonical list of men), Rosenfelt maintains that the biases of mainstream literary scholarship continue more or less unbroken. In fact, she notes, feminist gains in one place are taken back in another: while concessions to the existence of a few "great women" writers are made, in retaliation "'minor' women writers are perceived as *more* minor than their male counterparts."[7] Aesthetically and politically, she concludes, the old hegemonies prevail. The criteria that expunged from literary history whole bodies of work by women (such as nineteenth-century domestic and sentimental poetry and fiction) or entire genres (such as "memoirs, diaries, personal essays, letters — forms in which women writers have excelled"[8]) are still operative. The old claim that women writers are not only fewer but also not as good as men is once again confirmed.

In "The Leaning Tower," a paper presented to the Brighton Workers' Educational Association in 1940, Virginia Woolf reflects on the class implications of writing from within the ivory tower of "middle-class birth and expensive education."[9] From this position, she notes, one's view of the world is dangerously distorted: everything is seen from the perspective of a top-down gaze. In "Democratizing Literature: Issues in Teaching Working-Class Literature," Nicholas Cole demonstrates both how this perspective works and how to counter it.[10] His example of the former is Rebecca Harding Davis' *Life in the Iron Mills* (1861).[11] For rather than seeing the steel mills she writes about as evidence of the reality of industrial labor in the America in which she is writing, she filters what she sees through her perspective as an educated "daughter of the privileged class" (Tillie Olsen) and "reads" it metaphorically as images of a Dantesque inferno. Rebecca Harding Davis, writes Cole, "*looks* into the mills of Wheeling, West Virginia, but *conceives what she sees* there within the aesthetic categories available to her class position" (emphasis mine).[12]

Matters of taste are always also matters of class. Our training as literary critics is a perfect example. To learn to read, understand, and appreciate literary texts characterized by complexity and ambiguity, replete with erudite and arcane references to other texts that already have been canonized by the cultural custodians, calls for a class that not only can afford the extensive and expensive training, but also considers such an investment of time and money to be worthwhile. Our intellectual "tastes"— the texts we read, the criticism we write, and the theories we espouse — thus inevitably, and inadvertently, reflect values that are class-specific. For, despite the challenges of a number of contemporary critical theories to the concept of a canon of great books written by the masters, the "basic class distinction between Literature and other writing and between Criticism and other reading remains in force in the structures of our departments and curricula."[13] Since, whatever else we do, we also represent the institutions that employ us, our textual choices are never a simple matter of preference or taste: "questions about criticism and the canon — about what gets taught and in what ways — are finally questions about institutional power and the maintenance of privilege."[14] In short, the literary canon is "a means by which culture validates social power."[15]

In the rarified atmosphere of currently fashionable theoretical discourses, such bluntness has almost the same old-fashioned ring as terms like "class" and "struggle." Nevertheless, the claim of cultural critics on the Left that "literature" has always meant "writing which embodied the values and 'tastes' of a particular social class,"[16] has been accepted as a premise in most discussions of aesthetic values and canon formation. The realm of culture is recognized as a privileged one, based on and constitutive of class power. "Culture" is an attribute of those who, as the saying goes, "have class."

Feminism does not provide immunity to the multiple seductions of power. Moreover, since most feminist critics, scholars, and teachers work within the context of educational institutions, we are bound in very real ways to the concept of culture upheld by those institutions. The fact that it is Virginia Woolf rather than Harriet Arnow, Emily Dickinson rather than Pat Parker, Jacques Derrida rather than Sheila Rowbotham, who appear in courses on women and literature, in works of feminist criticism and feminist theory, does not simply indicate the inherent worth of these particular writers. These selections also demonstrate the degree to which we, too, trade in the dominant currency. What we in theory reject, we often unwittingly find ourselves reconstituting in our own practice.

As people living in a class society, we are all inescapably shaped by the material and ideological realities we sum up as "class." Yet this is not a process of which we are, for the most part, conscious. We experience class — ours and others'— most often viscerally and unconsciously. Particularly in academia, where we learn to think of ourselves as generators of ideas rather than as receivers of paychecks, class consciousness ranges from ephemeral to nonexistent. Awareness of class as a factor in our professional actions and interactions is rare. It is perhaps experienced, briefly and fleetingly, as a touch of scorn, a flush of embarrassment, a feeling of unease or estrangement in relation to someone of a different class, but rarely does this feeling surface to become conscious thought. Thus, we talk of class as an abstract concept; as an experience, it remains intangible.

The degree to which the reality of class is felt but tends to remain unconscious brings our feminist politics into conflict with the exigencies of an academic career. For our political agenda does not always fit comfortably with some of the choices dictated by our professional interests and desires. As feminists, we want to attend to and include women of different classes, we want to avoid regarding or treating any one experience as normative, and we want this multiclass perspective to inform our selection of materials as scholars and as teachers. As professionals, on the other hand, in the employ of bourgeois cultural institutions, we want to prove that we are deserving of membership in the company of educated men. And since we know that it is from their perspective that our choices will be judged, we learn to choose judiciously. Reading Edith Wharton or Virginia Woolf will be seen approvingly as a sign of culture; reading Agnes Smedley or Pat Parker will be seen unfavorably as a political act. If our choices are congruent with the expectations of those in power — i.e., if we "want" to do what we are, in fact, supposed to do — these choices appear self-evident and need no explanation. Only when they do not conform do the politics of our choices become visible. Then suddenly we are called upon to explain, justify, and defend. Class consciousness, feminist politics, and academic status — can we "have it all"? And what do we do when these interests, as they inevitably will, diverge?[17]

In 1985, Lillian Robinson began a review of a new book on working-class women by reflecting on the fact that, even in feminist circles, class was a reality that continued to be denied. *Class*, she noted, was still treated as if it were a dirty word: "From the timorous way it's applied and the many places it isn't even whispered, you'd certainly get the impression that it is not in decent usage."[18] By the mid-1980s, when Robinson was writing this review, feminist scholars in history and the social sciences already had made significant contributions to a class-specific understanding of gender issues, from sexuality to housework to the politics of development in the so-called "Third World." In the field of *literary* scholarship, however, the class dimensions of feminist theory and practice (in the United States, at least) had not been sufficiently addressed. Nor, I would argue, have they yet.

This is not to say that nothing, or nothing of importance, had — or has — been done. Important — indeed, groundbreaking — work was already being done in the early 1980s by American feminist literary scholars such as Lillian Robinson, Judith Lowder Newton, Jane Marcus, Sheila Delany, Janice Radway, Nancy Armstrong, Mary Poovey, and Florence Howe.[19] Moreover, in the work of those women whose thinking was already informed by the conscious experience of socially defined "otherness"— women of color, lesbians, women in or from the "Third World"— the reality of class as a factor shaping women's lives was often sharply delineated.[20]

Traditionally, class-consciousness and the use of class as a category of critical analysis have been the domain of Marxist scholars. The best-known and most influential typically have been men, from the forefathers, Marx and Engels, on down to our contemporaries. Obviously, this does not mean that they are unfeminist. Indeed, as the work of Marxist literary scholars such as Paul Lauter, Richard Ohmann, Michael Ryan, Fredric Jameson, or Terry Eagleton amply proves, in principle, and even in practice, such men often have been not only receptive, but responsive, to the challenges of feminism.[21] What is for the most part missing from their work, however, is the kind of feminist perspective that treats gender as a category of analysis significant in itself and not subordinated to class as a "secondary contradiction."

Given the fact that in Europe class historically has been much more "explicitly negotiated in consciousness and culture,"[22] it is not surprising that some of the most important work on class as a factor in cultural history has been and is being done there. This is true within the context of feminist scholarship as well. Women such as Sheila Rowbotham, Juliet Mitchell, Catherine Belsey, Michèle Barrett, and Cora Kaplan in England; and Simone de Beauvoir, Monique Wittig, and Christine Delphy in France;[23] and journals such as the British *Feminist Review* or the French *Questions féministes (Feminist Issues)* initially provided and continue to elaborate an analytical framework that is informed equally by a consciousness of class *and* by women's history. Particularly interesting in this respect is the work of women in the socialist part of Germany (the former German Democratic Republic), such as Christa Wolf, Irmtraud Morgner, Maxie Wander, Helga Königsdorf, and Monika Maron, who, from about the mid-1970s on, combined an acute awareness of class with an increasingly strong feminist perspective.[24]

In the mainstream of American feminism, scholarly and otherwise, the combination of an often unconscious and thus unacknowledged universalism with a well-intentioned but uncritical liberal pluralism all too often has blurred the critical edge of feminist analyses. "Class" became a category, among others, that feminist critics learned to invoke in the litany of oppressions we recited. Yet too frequently this litany functioned more as a ready-made checklist than as a sign of serious attention to the lived diferences among us. Reciting the "isms" enabled us to "deal with" the issues by virtually abstracting them out of existence. In the process, the material reality of something like class — the schools we had attended, the language we used, the clothes we wore, the books we read — lost any meaningful specificity. Class was part of our concept of a correct feminism; but it was not recognized in our experience as women. We dealt with it best, it seemed, when we most carefully ignored it.

This left us, once again, with the contradiction between our theory and our practice: in theory, class was a critical feminist issue; in practice, we rarely acknowledged it. This inability (or reluctance) on the part of feminist critics to recognize class as basic to an understanding of where we stand has led to an avoidance of the issue, which is all the more curious as our own positions within the institutions of bourgeois culture are clearly shaped by class realities: the jobs we have, the pay we get, the social status we enjoy as professors. In short, we are paid — and paying — members of a cultural elite.[25] And although we think of ourselves as "professionals," even professional work is work. Moreover, while we may have offices in ivory towers, we have to live in the real world. We, too, worry about such things as money, job security, health insurance, work hours, and whether our office has a window or an air-conditioner. These are the realities of our working lives. To pretend that class issues do not concern us because we are "intellectuals" is a silly and dangerous myopia.

In the field of literary criticism, traditional and feminist alike, avoidance of the issue of class generally has taken two superficially different and contradictory forms. Those whose critical stance is based on the assumption that one kind of experience (namely, that of the educated class) is the only kind valid, universal, or interesting enough to be written into public discourse generally ignore the issue of class altogether. Most of the standard works and anthologies of feminist literary criticism exemplify this stance. If class is mentioned at all, it is merely in passing, as an incidental rather than a central factor in women's social and cultural history.

Another form of avoidance—more noble, perhaps, but no less problematical—is what I call self-blind altruism: "we," full of liberal benevolence, address our attention to the problems experienced by "them." As the objects of this well-intentioned but nonetheless reifying gaze, "they" (e.g., women of the working class) become the subject of liberal feminist analyses. An example from my own teaching experience can serve as illustration. An early (1976) version of Women's Studies 101, taught at the University of Wisconsin, included, toward the end of the semester, a separate unit on "class" in a cluster with two other units on "race" and "lesbianism." These special sessions had a compensatory function: they provided a chance for "us" to look at and talk about "them."[26] "Class," of course, meant "working class," just as "race" essentially meant "Black." Under the guise of acknowledging difference, "we," full of good intentions, were actually reenforcing the dominant norms. For "class," like "color" in "women of color," referred to those who deviated from the racial and class-based norm. That we who were white and middle-class were also of a race and class was a fact that remained unspoken. From the normative perspective of the empowered, only "they" were seen as an issue.

We inevitably see from our own centers, from the categories that constitute the identities we have learned to call our selves. Rejecting the perspectives of those men (and women) whose privileged positions blind them to the realities of gender, race, and class, feminists have insisted on the need not only to be conscious of these realities but also to understand the ways in which our affiliations, chosen or imposed, constitute significant differences among us. Particularly those of us whose identities happen to be congruent with what has been established as normative have to understand how *we* are different from others and what that difference means. Yet, despite the struggle toward a heightened consciousness of difference, a struggle which has shifted the very ground of feminist theory and practice, our perspectives remain far too one-sided. We are conscious of "them," yet remain comfortably unconscious of ourselves.

Why has feminist criticism, when talking about class, mostly talked about working-class women as the "they" to our "us"? Why have "we," individually and collectively, been so unwilling or unable to take a good look at ourselves? Turning the lens of class on ourselves as feminist critics almost inevitably produces anxiety. To begin with, it means that we must acknowledge the fact that, regardless of our family backgrounds, economic status, or politics, our work as scholars and teachers within academic institutions marks us as products and proponents of bourgeois culture. Obviously, "we" too have our share of difference. While some of us contemplate the universe from special chairs, most of us labor under heavy workloads of required service courses. Yet, regardless of where, whom, or what we are teaching, our work is pressed into service for the cultural enhancement of a bourgeois class. We need only think of whose sons and daughters we are teaching and what we are expected to teach them, of who our Trustees and Regents are, of who sets the policies and who gives the monies, to realize the extent to which we are implicated in the very structures we are hoping to transform. Our dilemma is how to go about the business of dismantling the masters' houses while we are trying to get computers for the offices we have set up inside them.

Part of the difficulty of understanding what class, on a personal level, actually means is that its meaning is equally unclear on a conceptual level. For "class" is both an economic and a cultural category. It refers, on the one hand, to how much money one has and, on the other, to what kind of culture one possesses. But what it means exactly (how, for example, class affects my selection of texts for a "Women and Literature" course or of works to cite in a piece of feminist criticism) is not at all clear. Whether as a concept or as an experience, the meaning of class is particularly difficult to grasp. It seems nebulous and intangible. And no wonder. For, officially, in our society, class does not exist.

This denial of the existence of classes and thus of the differences or conflicts between them is, of course, basic to the ideology of a class society. This ideology requires a concept of culture that transcends such mundane realities as money, training, or work. And so we have Culture (literature and art made for the educated class) opposed to the commercialized and mass-marketed popular culture consumed by common people. As academics, teachers, and critics, we are appointed to be purveyors and custodians of Culture. Our task is to legitimate these distinctions, proving that some have class and culture, while others clearly do not.

As feminists in academia, we are thus forced into a class affiliation about which most of us, no doubt, are ambivalent. Moreover, given the nebulous quality of "class," our affiliation with one class is experienced as vague and insubstantial. This uncertain and uneasy relationship to our actual class identity is not unique to either feminist intellectuals or professionals. It is, rather, symptomatic of a deeply felt yet barely conscious identity crisis experienced by the American middle class in general. If everyone is more or less part of one all-encompassing "middle" class, then "class" as a defining and distinguishing factor becomes meaningless. "We" have been dissolved into an amorphous plurality. As a result, the middle class can only be defined negatively: neither "upper" nor "lower," it finds itself somewhere in between. Hoping to rise and trying not to fall, the social status of its members is always tenuous; torn between resentful envy toward those above them and patronizing guilt toward those below, their self-concept is always uncertain. The "middle" class, it seems, is unwilling or unable to say who or what they are. "But what, you may ask, is a middlebrow?" writes Virginia Woolf:

> That, to tell the truth, is no easy question to answer. They are neither one thing nor the other. They are not highbrows . . . nor lowbrows. Their brows are betwixt and between. . . . They do not live in Bloomsbury . . . nor in Chelsea. Since they must live somewhere presumably, they live perhaps in South Kensington, which is betwixt and between.[27]

The very class that historically had presumed to speak for those it had defined as Other thus ironically has become unable to speak in a voice of its own; in trying to make this Other invisible, it has become invisible to itself. For who, concludes Woolf, would want to admit to being such an utterly nondescript, "betwixt and between" nonentity: "If any human being, man, woman, cat, dog, or half-crushed worm dares call me 'middlebrow,' I will take my pen and stab him, dead."

In a Manner of Speaking

If in thinking about women we lose the specificity of class, while in thinking about class we blur the specificity of women, then we need a position from which both gender *and* class can be brought into focus. An obvious place is the perspective of language. For language is at once a class and a feminist issue.[28] In *Woman's Consciousness, Man's World*, Sheila Rowbotham describes the oppressiveness of a "language [which] is part of the political and ideological power of the rulers":

> In the making of the working class in Britain the conflict of silence with "their language" . . . has been continuous. Every man who has worked up through the labor movement expressed this in some form. The embarrassment about dialect, the divorce between home talking and educated language . . . is intense and painful.[29]

In "The Laugh of the Medusa," Hélène Cixous describes the relationship of women to the master language in strikingly similar terms:

> Every woman has known the torment of getting up to speak. Her heart racing, at times entirely lost for words, ground and language slipping away. . . .
> Listen to a woman speak at a public gathering (if she hasn't painfully lost

her wind). She doesn't "speak," she throws her trembling body forward; she lets go of herself, she flies. . . . She lays herself bare.[30]

Language has always been a central issue for feminists. We saw how women had been excluded from and oppressed by what Adrienne Rich termed "the oppressor's language"; we also saw their attempts at subversion. Yet our concern with language has not adequately addressed its class dimensions.

As feminist critics, our relationship to language is a particularly complex one: on the one hand, it is a source of empowerment, the means and product of our work; on the other hand, we have recognized (and experienced) it as a tool of oppression. What, then, do we do? If the language of the masters confers power, then an obvious strategy is to gain mastery over it. We can learn to command language masterfully, just as we can learn to "dress for success." Yet, like every issue involving power and its transfer—or its transformation—the process is not without risk. The line between cooptation and subversion is hard to draw and easy to cross.

The consequences of learning to master language are worth considering carefully. As Gayatri Spivak notes, "What one might think of as a political 'privilege'—knowing English properly—stands in the way of a deconstructive practice of language—using it 'correctly' through a political displacement, or operating the language of the other side."[31] If Spivak is suggesting that "operating the language of the other side" is, *eo ipso*, "a deconstructive practice," a revolution in language through which we displace the social privilege our education and professional-class status confer, then we might think that to use working-class texts in our classrooms and our scholarship would be a revolutionary act.

Yet to the question implicit in Spivak's proposal—namely how to bring together the culture "of the other side," the texts and language of the working-class, and the dominant culture of an educated class in a politically effective, deconstructive practice—there is, unfortunately, no simple answer. To begin with, how do we define "working-class text"? Is it a matter of who wrote it or of what it is written about?[32] Must it be written in "working-class language"? And what, exactly, is that?

Cole illustrates the complexity of this latter question through the story of Stephen Duck, an early eighteenth-century poet who began as a farm laborer. As Cole tells it,

> Duck cast his dissent from pastoral idyllicization of agricultural labor in the heroic couplets of the day, adapting the language of Pope to a critique of Pope's social assumptions, because it was both the language of his own self-education and moreover the only language in which he could be heard by a literate audience.[33]

But Duck's story was not to end triumphantly, with the common man creating literature in his own voice. Instead, "once he had been lionized and given a sinecure at court, [it was fatally easy] for Duck to turn out exactly the kind of verse against which his earlier work had been set." The master's tools, in this case, turned against the hapless intruder: having achieved the approbation of the courtly class whose power he had set out to challenge, Stephen Duck drowned himself in a fit of despondency.

If we recast Spivak's contention that "operating the language of the other side" is an act of political displacement, then from the perspective of a Stephen Duck, the problematic equation of linguistic and political action becomes particularly apparent. Adopting the language of the other side does not necessarily change anything in the actual configurations of power.

That the selection of texts "of the other side" does not function as an inherently deconstructive practice was brought home to me when I was teaching at Bryn Mawr College in 1983. In a course called "Women in the Arts," the unit on literature included a short story by a working-class writer, Sharon Isabell. The students' reaction to "Twenty Days,"[34] a first-person narrative of a woman sentenced to twenty days in jail for writing bad checks, was emphatic and virtually unanimous: they were angry, resentful, offended. These feelings, then, became the focus of our discussions that entire week, as we struggled to understand the reasons for and the implications of such a reaction. It was not the "content," they said, that bothered them. What they objected to was the "form," or rather what they saw as the offensive and inexcusable *lack* of it. Isabell used bad language, or, from the perspective of my students, she used language badly. Challenged by me with Judy Grahn's arch reminder that "Murdering the King's English is a crime only if you identify with the King,"[35] the students attempted to make their case for what was wrong with the language of this story. It was not the expletives (if James Joyce could use them, so could Sharon Isabell), nor the misspelled words and incorrect grammar (Faulkner's Dilsey didn't speak in standard English, either). What was wrong was that her language was inauthentic. This couldn't be how she "really" talked; the poor grammar and misspelling were deliberate. This text, they concluded, was an act of cultural provocation. And indeed they felt provoked.

The response of my Bryn Mawr students to "Twenty Days" inadvertently came right to the heart of the issue that both Isabell and Grahn were addressing: the cultural politics of language. For, from the vantage point of the students' class culture, Isabell's use of a working-class woman's language was not an affirmation, but an apporopriation. Take Katherine Mansfield's "The Garden Party" for comparison, they argued. She too talks about working-class experience, but she does not try to talk *like* them. Rather, she writes respectfully about working-class people and their culture without denying or rejecting the values of the bourgeois class culture within those formal conventions she produces her texts.

Mansfield commanded my students' respect because she had mastered the language so artfully; she earned their admiration because she had done so as a woman. Where Isabell was disturbing, Mansfield reassured; like the students, she was well and genteelly educated,[36] and her elegant language affirmed their own cultural experience and class values. Literature was art and should not be politics. Yet, as they themselves displayed their mastery at wielding the language of aesthetic formalism, they proceeded to articulate a position that was clearly and unabashedly political. For they finally concluded that what they most liked about Mansfield was that she maintained the proper distance between "us" and "them."

Mansfield (like Wharton) maintains the proper distance; Isabell (like Smedley) does not. Mansfield takes us across the "broad road [that] ran between" the big, white mansion of the Sheridans and the "little mean dwellings painted a chocolate brown," where washer-women lived and children swarmed and where the Sheridan children "were forbidden to set foot . . . because of the revolting language and of what they might catch." Mansfield takes us to this place that "was disgusting and sordid" because it is part of our education to "go everywhere . . . [and] see everything."[37] But, in the end, she returns us safely home to the Sheridans, uncontaminated by "revolting language" or any other kinds of revolt.

Isabell, meanwhile, brings us into intimate contact with the very people the Sheridans find so mean and revolting. And indeed they are, although not in the sense of the words as used in "The Garden Party." For, as the narrator of "Twenty Days" remembers her treatment at the hands of a judge whose "face was hidden behind the paper mask of authority," she confronts us with her class rage: "The hate flowed through me and I felt the strength of it."[38] Hers is a world in which "life was angry words. No one was shocked. . . . No one held their hands over my ears."[39] Isabell does not hold her hands over our ears, either; she makes us listen to the feelings of those who are "made . . . [to] feel so low" because they are poor and do not have a "proper" education. She makes us listen to what they have to say, refusing to explain or to mediate. And in the process, she makes us realize that to a woman who is treated disrespectfully "because she was not upper class and did not dress in there cloths and speek there perfect English,"[40] we with our middle-class values and our "higher" education, we whose faces also are often hidden behind paper masks of authority, "we" constitute the "they."

The Question of Mastery

"The question is," said Alice, "whether you *can*
make words mean so many different things."
"The question is," said Humpty Dumpty, "which
is to be master—that's all."
— Lewis Carroll, *Through the Looking Glass
and What Alice Found There*

The question for us as feminist critics is how to find a language that is true to "those like ourselves," a language with which we can live, professionally and politically. How can we avoid merely appropriating language from one side or the other, either to assert a position of dominance by acquiring the language of the masters or to make a political statement by adopting working-class language? Can we use language in ways that will enable us to effect changes in the existing hegemonies of class, race, and gender? If we are "trained for appropriation,"[41] (how) can we go against our training? And, moreover, (why) should we?

I will address these questions by referring to two literary texts that not only raise them in particularly urgent and compelling ways, but also suggest directions for pursuing possible answers. They were written in different times and different contexts, yet they are informed by a strikingly similar consciousness. Rebecca Harding Davis lived in a house with servants and was raised to appreciate the so-called "finer" things in life. Yet, in 1861, she wrote *Life in the Iron Mills*, a deeply sympathetic account of the life of millworkers in a small Pennsylvania steel town. In 1978, with the financial help of grant monies, Marianne Herzog, a West German writer and freelance documentarist, worked with Vera Kamenko on *Unter uns war Krieg* [There Was War Between Us],[42] the story of Kamenko's life, first in rural Yugoslavia, then as an immigrant factory worker in West Germany. Both Harding Davis and Herzog approach the writing of these texts with an acute and pained self-consciousness of the class politics of language and of their own contradictory relationship to their class cultures. They write against their cultures even as they acknowledge and use their privileged status within them. Since we, their readers, also bear responsbility for the terms of this dilemma, they engage us indirectly.

Harding Davis addresses her projected middle-class readers at the very beginning of her narrative: "Stop a moment . . . I want you to hide your disgust, take no heed to your clean clothes, and come right down with me . . . I want you to hear this story . . . I want to make it a real thing to you."[43] The story she wants to make us hear, and in the process "make real," is that of the working-class men and women whom she watches from the comfort of her father's house, "the slow stream of human life creeping past, night and morning, to the great mills."[44] Their lives and stories had been muted by the cultural categories of a class that presumed the right to speak *for* them, without bothering to speak or listen *to* them.[45]

In her foreword to Kamenko's autobiography, Herzog acknowledges the inevitable and unresolvable contradiction in which she, like Rebecca Harding Davis, finds herself. As one who masters the language and has access to the means of text production, she wants to share her power with another who is disempowered as an immigrant working-class woman. Ironically, she can do so only by speaking *for* the other, in her stead, by taking away Vera Kamenko's language and replacing it with her own: "I had to create new sentences because they were incomprehensible, and I could only write them in my language, and not in broken German."[46]

In "The Making of a Writer," Paule Marshall describes how she came to a consciousness of herself as poor and Black and female by seeing herself through the eyes of those for whom she represented the Other. Rebecca Harding Davis and Marianne Herzog describe a similar process. As these writers' views of themselves are refracted through their growing awareness of those whose class, race, and culture are different from their own, they come to understand not only the meaning of difference, but also their role in its construction. They understand, above all, that historically and materially "we" and "they" are fatefully linked.

We can learn from their experience. For their critical doubled vision — at once self- and other-conscious — provides a perspective from which to deal with issues of difference such as class, without falling into a detached and reifying manner of speaking about "them."

Herzog and Harding Davis acknowledge the power attendant upon their ability to use language correctly. They also acknowledge the class imbalance of power inherent in the established standards of correctness. They acknowledge, in other words, that the issue of language and power is an extraordinarily complex one, in which privilege also functions as a form of limitation. As a strategy for disrupting this bind, they suggest that we see our way of speaking as only one of many ways. Difference, then, may mean diversity: different languages that can — and should — be used differently. Diversity offers us a way out of the class-bound double-bind of either mastering language or being mastered by it: mastery could be redefined as multilingualism.

From such a perspective, we might be more attentive to the different ways people speak. We might learn to listen more carefully to the meanings of language among us. To recognize that, whenever we use language, we are making a statement about our place in and our relationship to the existing configurations of power is, I believe, to regain a critical sense of choice and control. It is a sense that can embolden us: to strive for mastery even as we speak in or with a vulgar tongue.[47] For if "vulgar" means "of, pertaining to, or characteristic of the people at large,"[48] then our use of vulgar tongues not only places us in an eminent tradition of interventions into the politics of language, but also brings the utopian "dream of a common language" a step closer to reality.

My initial questions (what are "our" texts and what are we doing with them?) thus need to be recast. For if we recognize that "we," in fact, are multiple, speaking in many languages and writing in different ways, then all texts are, in a sense, "our" texts. What matters is making them useful. *The House of Mirth* might be useful in one way because it confirms my sense of decorum, because it give me aesthetic pleasure and integrates me into a culture of which I am proud. Yet *Daughter of Earth* or "Twenty Days" might be useful in another way, because they challenge my narrowly middle-class sense of decorum, because they force me to confront the class prejudice of my aesthetics and the exclusivity of my culture.

Other questions need to be added to the ones we were trained to ask, questions not just about literary merit or philosophical sophistication, but also about passion, purpose, and politics. We might ask of a text where it stands in class terms: does it reinforce, perpetuate, or challenge prevailing standards of what is worth writing about and how it should be written, standards that privilege the culture, experience, and language of one class over that of another?

Our dilemma as feminist academics in relation to class politics is that our professional investment in the institutions of a bourgeois culture is in tension with our political opposition to those same structures. We can't get out and don't want to sell out. Our challenge, therefore, is to live with as much integrity as possible, using the tension—not against ourselves, but to sustain the balance we need. After all, the very contradictions that cause us trouble are also what cause us to make trouble when we act on our political consciousness.

To become more conscious of class dynamics and of the ways they are operative in our work as feminist scholars and teachers can only lead to change for the better. We can begin by looking at the choices we make and at their consequences: Which texts do we use, what do we value, and what does this have to do with a class-specific set of values? How do we use language?

In a sense, this last question is the most important, because it extends far beyond our work into the very texture of our relationships. It is basic both to who we are and to who we become in communication with others. Therefore, we should be particularly conscious of our acts of selection in relation to language. When are we using language that is difficult? Are we using it because it is appropriate to the complexity of our analysis? Can we make complexity accessible in order to permit communication with others who can learn from us and from whom we can learn? In other words, when is our language a means of exchange, and when is it a tool of domination?

Our professional work is shaped in myriad ways by the economic and ideological exigencies of the institutions that employ us. This sobering discovery is a necessary step toward realizing a feminist politics that is able and willing to face reality. Only by facing the fact of our class positions as intellectual workers in academic institutions can we acknowledge the ways in which we are instruments paid to serve these institutions. It is no shame, then, to acknowledge that, while we may refuse this service in theory, in practice we are vulnerable to its threats and its seductions. The shame or honor comes from what we choose to do next.

To own our contingencies is merely to acknowledge that we are human. Contingencies are defined as weaknesses only in the language of the masters. If we are able to live with a consciousness of them, then perhaps the question of how we can reconcile a feminist politics with the professional use of a master-discourse can at least partially be answered: we can occupy positions of mastery as long as we don't treat others as if we were masters over them.

Notes

1. See Charles Altieri, "An Idea and Ideal of a Literary Canon," *Critical Inquiry* 10, no. 1 (Sept. 1983):37–60.

2. Paule Marshall, "The Making of a Writer: From the Poets in the Kitchen," in Marshall, *Reena and Other Stories* (Old Westbury, N.Y.: Feminist Press, 1983), 1–12; quotation, 10.

3. Virginia Woolf, *Three Guineas* (New York: Harcourt Brace Jovanovich, 1966), 61–63.

4. Ibid., 63.

5. See the first chapter ("What is Literature?") of Terry Eagleton, *Literary Theory: An Introduction* (Minneapolis: University of Minnesota Press, 1983), 1–17.

6. Paul Lauter, "Race and Gender in the Shaping of the American Literary Canon: A Case Study from the Twenties," *Feminist Studies* 9, no. 3 (Fall 1983):450.

7. Deborah S. Rosenfelt, "The Politics of Bibliography: Women's Studies and the Literary Canon," in *Women in Print I: Opportunities for Women's Studies Research in Language and Literature*, ed. Joan E. Hartman and Ellen Messer-Davidow (New York: Modern Language Association, 1982), 16. See Barbara Christian's powerful and polemical essay, "The Race for Theory," *Cultural Critique* 6 (Spring 1987):51–63, for an analysis of a similar process in relation to race.

8. Rosenfelt, "Politics," 21.

9. Virginia Woolf, "The Leaning Tower," in *The Moment and Other Essays* (New York: Harcourt Brace Jovanovich, 1948), 128–55.

10. Nicholas Cole, "Democratizing Literature: Issues in Teaching Working-Class Literature," *College English* 48, no. 7 (Nov. 1986):671.

11. Rebecca Harding Davis, *Life in the Iron Mills, or The Korl Woman* (Old Westbury, N.Y.: Feminist Press, 1972). See also Tillie Olsen's afterword, "A Biographical Interpreta-

tion," in Davis, *Life in the Iron Mills*, for an excellent discussion of the class and gender issues this text raises.

12. Cole, "Democratizing Literature," 671.

13. Ibid., 664.

14. Ibid., 665.

15. Lauter, "Race and Gender," 435.

16. Eagleton, *Literary Theory*, 17.

17. I am indebted to Ellen Messer-Davidow for her incisive summary of this dilemma.

18. Lillian Robinson, "Poverty, Purpose, Pride" (review of *Dignity: Lower Income Women Tell of Their Lives and Struggles*, oral histories compiled by Fran Leeper Buss [Ann Arbor: University of Michigan Press, 1985]) in *Women's Review of Books* 3, no. 3 (Dec. 1985):1–4. Quotation, 1.

19. See, e.g., Lillian Robinson, *Sex, Class, and Culture* (1978; rptd. New York: Methuen, 1986) and "Treason Our Text: Feminist Challenges to the Literary Canon," *Tulsa Studies in Women's Literature* 2, no. 1 (Spring 1983):83–98. Judith Lowder Newton, *Sex and Class in Women's History* (London: Routledge and Kegan Paul, 1983). Judith Lowder Newton and Deborah Rosenfelt, eds., *Feminist Criticism and Social Change* (New York: Methuen, 1986). Jane Marcus, "Storming the Toolshed," in *Feminist Theory: A Critique of Ideology*, ed. Nannerl O. Keohane, Michelle Z. Rosaldo, and Barbara C. Gelpi (Chicago: University of Chicago Press, 1982), 217–37, and "Still Practice, A/Wrested Alphabet: Toward a Feminist Aesthetic," in *Feminist Issues in Literary Scholarship*, ed. Shari Benstock (Bloomington: Indiana University Press, 1987), 79–98. Sheila Delany, *Writing Woman: Women Writers and Women in Literature, Medieval to Modern* (New York: Schocken, 1983). Janice Radway, *Reading the Romance: Women, Patriarchy, and Popular Literature* (Chapel Hill: University of North Carolina Press, 1984). Mary Poovey, *The Proper Lady and the Woman Writer: Ideology as Style in the Works of Mary Wollstonecraft, Mary Shelley, and Jane Austen* (Chicago: University of Chicago Press, 1984) and *Uneven Developments: The Ideological Work of Gender in Mid-Victorian England* (Chicago: University of Chicago Press, 1988). Nancy Armstrong, *Desire and Domestic Fiction: A Political History of the Novel* (New York: Oxford University Press, 1987). See also the class- (as well as race-) sensitive analyses of literary texts in the work of the feminist historian Elizabeth Fox-Genovese. Florence Howe, finally, as the editor of the Feminist Press, has played a critical role in shaping a class-conscious feminist culture in the United States; see her "Those We Still Don't Read," *College English* 43, no. 1 (Jan. 1981):12–16.

20. In addition to the rich body of fictional work produced in the United States in the 1970s and 1980s by women of color and lesbians, the theoretical and critical writings of feminist writers/theorists/activists such as Barbara Smith, Audre Lorde, Alice Walker, bell hooks, Cherríe Moraga, Adrienne Rich, Charlotte Bunch, Minnie Bruce Pratt, and Tillie Olsen have been consistently sensitive and attentive to class issues. Cherríe Moraga and Gloria Anzaldúa, eds., *This Bridge Called My Back: Writings by Radical Women of Color* (Watertown, Mass.: Persephone Press, 1981), was a landmark text in this regard. For feminist and class-conscious analyses from a postcolonial, "Third World" perspective, see, in particular, the work of Gayatri Chakravorty Spivak, e.g., *In Other Worlds: Essays in Cultural Politics* (New York: Methuen, 1987) and "Can the Subaltern Speak?" in *Marxism and the Interpretation of Culture*, ed. Cary Nelson and Lawrence Grossberg (Urbana: University of Illinois Press, 1988), 271–317. See also Chandra Talpade Mohanty, "Under Western Eyes: Feminist Scholarship and Colonial Discourses," *Boundary* 2, vol. 12, no. 3/vol. 13, no. 1 (Spring-Fall 1984):333–58.

21. One of the distinguishing marks of work defined as "new" (as opposed to "old") Left

is precisely its acknowledgement of the historical importance of feminism and its willingness to draw on feminist insights and methodologies. In this respect, see, e.g., Paul Lauter's already cited analysis, "Race and Gender in the Shaping of the American Literary Canon," or his "Working-Class Women's Literature: An Introduction to Study," in Hartman and Messer-Davidow, *Women in Print I*, 109–35. Also see Terry Eagleton's conclusion, "Political Criticism," in Eagleton, *Literary Theory*, or his reflections on the historical significance of feminist criticism in Terry Eagleton, *Walter Benjamin, or Towards a Revolutionary Criticism* (London: Verso, 1981), 98–100. In Fredric Jameson's work a feminist perspective tends to form the critical subtext rather than being articulated consciously. In Michael Ryan's work, this perspective is more fully formulated historically (see, e.g., his *Marxism and Deconstruction: A Critical Articulation* [Baltimore, Md.: Johns Hopkins University Press, 1982], esp. the concluding chapter on "Postleninist Marxism — Socialist Feminism and Autonomy").

22. Cole, "Democratizing Literature," 667.

23. Among the work that laid the groundwork for class-conscious feminist analyses was that of Simone de Beauvoir, *The Second Sex*, trans. by H.M. Parshley (1949; New York: Knopf, 1953); Juliet Mitchell, *Woman's Estate* (New York: Random House, 1971); and Sheila Rowbotham, *Woman's Consciousness, Man's World* (Harmondsworth, England: Penguin, 1973). For more recent analyses of the intersections of class and gender, see, e.g., Christine Delphy, *Close to Home: A Materialist Analysis of Women's Oppression* (Amherst, Mass: University of Massachusetts Press, 1984). See also articles in *Feminist Issues*; Janet Batsleer, Tony Davies, Rebecca O'Rourke, and Chris Weedon, *Rewriting English: Cultural Politics of Gender and Class* (London: Methuen, 1985); Catherine Belsey and Jane Moss, eds., *The Feminist Reader: Essays in Gender and the Politics of Literary Criticism* (London: Macmillan Education, 1989). Cora Kaplan's *Sea Changes: Essays on Culture and Feminism* (London: Verso, 1986), esp. her essay, "Pandora's Box: Subjectivity, Class and Sexuality in Socialist Feminist Criticism," 147–77, is a fine example of class-sensitive feminist scholarship and writing.

24. Unfortunately, most work by East German women has not (yet) been translated. Available in English and of likely interest to feminists are Christa Wolf, *The Quest for Christa T.* (New York: Farrar, Straus and Giroux, 1971); Christa Wolf, "Self-Experiment," in a "Special Feminist Issue" of *New German Critique* 13 (Winter 1978):109–33; Christa Wolf, *Cassandra: A Novel and Four Essays* (London: Virago, 1984); Monika Maron, *Flight of Ashes* (London: Readers International, 1986); Monika Maron, *The Defector* (London: Readers International, 1988); short prose pieces by Irmtraud Morgner and Helga Königsdorf in a "German Issue" of *Slavic and East European Arts* 3, no. 3 (Fall 1985); and selections by Wolf, Morgner, and Maxie Wander in Edith Hoshino Altbach, Jeanette Clausen, Dagmar Schultz, and Naomi Stephan, eds., *German Feminism: Readings in Politics and Literature* (Albany: State University of New York Press, 1984). An anthology of texts in translation, edited by Dorothy Rosenberg and Nancy Lukens (working title: *The Daughters of Eve: Contemporary Women Writers of the German Democratic Republic*) is scheduled to appear soon.

25. Many of the essays in Richard Ohmann's *Politics of Letters* (Middletown, Conn.: Wesleyan University Press, 1987) address the implications of this point directly and precisely.

26. This "we/they" perspective, determined by and embedded in our discourse, is held regardless of our actual, personal identities. Whether "we" were white or women of color, lesbian or heterosexual, the "they" we referred to were those who deviated from the predetermined social norm.

27. Virginia Woolf, "Middlebrow," in Woolf, *The Death of the Moth and Other Essays* (New York: Harcourt Brace Jovanovich, 1942), 204–5.

28. A particularly illuminating illustration of the link between class as an economic category and class as a cultural one is the history of voting-right qualifications in the United States: the property requirements that were standard throughout most of the 19th century had, by the early 20th century, for the most part given way to literacy requirements. Until the Jacksonian age of the "common man," only landowning gentlemen could vote; by the 1920s this right was based on a person's ability to read and write "proper English." The requirement of mastery, in other words, shifted from proof of property ownership to evidence of mastery of the language of those now in power.

29. Rowbotham, *Woman's Consciousness, Man's World*, 33.

30. Hélène Cixous, "The Laugh of the Medusa," in *New French Feminisms: An Anthology*, ed. Elaine Marks and Isabelle de Courtivron (Amherst: University of Massachusetts Press, 1980), 251.

31. Gayatri Spivak, "Translator's Foreword" to Mahasveta Devi's "Draupadi," in *Writing and Sexual Difference*, ed. Elizabeth Abel (Chicago: University of Chicago Press, 1982), 271.

32. Cole, "Democratizing Literature," suggests that the concept "working-class literature" should be based on both class position *and* subject matter, i.e., "writing by working-class people . . . that deals substantially with working-class life" (667).

33. Quotations from Cole, "Democratizing Literature," 674.

34. Sharon Isabell, "Twenty Days," in *True to Life Adventure Stories*, ed. Judy Grahn (Oakland, Calif.: Diana Press, 1978), 1:15–22.

35. Judy Grahn, "Murdering the King's English," in Grahn, *True to Life Adventure Stories*, 1:6–15.

36. Mansfield attended Queen's College in London from 1903 to 1906, then studied music in New Zealand before returning to London in 1908.

37. Quotations from Katherine Mansfield, "The Garden Party," in *Women and Fiction: Short Stories By and About Women*, ed. Susan Cahill (New York: New American Library, 1975), 68–69.

38. Isabell, "Twenty Days," 15–16.

39. Ibid., 20.

40. Ibid., 17.

41. Hélène Cixous, "Poetry is/and (the) Political," unpublished essay read at the "Second Sex" Conference, New York, 1979.

42. Vera Kamenko (with Marianne Herzog), *Unter uns war Krieg: Autobiografie einer jugoslawischen Arbeiterin* (Berlin: Rotbuch, Verlag, 1978). This text is not (yet) available in English; I have translated it, but it has not yet been published.

43. Davis, *Life in the Iron Mills*, 13.

44. Ibid., 12.

45. The concept of "mutedness," as a term with which to describe the cultural disempowerment of women, has been used and developed by several groups. Anthropologists include Edwin and Shirley Ardener (see, e.g., Shirley Ardener, ed., *Perceiving Women* [London: Malaby Press, 1975]). Sociologists include Dorothy Smith, "A Peculiar Eclipsing: Women's Exclusion from Man's Culture," *Women's Studies International Quarterly* 1, no. 4 (1978):281–97. Feminist theorists include Dale Spender, "The Dominant and the Muted," in Spender, *Man Made Language* (London: Routledge and Kegan Paul, 1980), 76–106. Within the context of discussions of the relationship between class and language, the concepts of "restricted" and "elaborated" codes, developed by the British sociolinguist Basil Bernstein, *Class, Codes and Control*, 3 vols. (London: Routledge and Kegan Paul, 1971–75), to describe working-class and middle-class language, respectively, are, albeit controversial, much more commonly employed. Bernstein's principle — as Richard Ohmann summarizes it in

"Reflections on Class and Language," the concluding chapter of Ohmann, *Politics of Letters* — is one of social continuity: "The class system sorts people into elaborated and restricted code users; the codes perpetuate the class system" (281).

46. Marianne Herzog, "Foreword," in Kamenko, *Unter uns war Kreig*, 6 (my translation).

47. Lillian Robinson plays and experiments with such deliberately vulgar uses of language in *Sex, Class, and Culture*, particularly in "Criticism: Who Needs It?" (1975). Robinson demonstrates the potential of working-class language and perspectives to scrutinize what we as academic literary critics do; she also demonstrates that mixing languages and thus crossing established class boundaries in our acts of literary criticism is not only possible but critically effective.

48. *Funk & Wagnalls' Standard College Dictionary*, 1505.

Making Knowledge

Kathryn Pyne Addelson and Elizabeth Potter

It is in the knowledge of the genuine conditions of our
life that we must draw our strength to live and our
reason for acting.
— Simon de Beauvoir, *The Ethics of Ambiguity*[1]

When contributors to this volume describe ourselves as feminists, we use a word that has many meanings. "Feminist" carries the political meaning it had in 1970: we are members of the women's movement. It carries a professional meaning: we are academic feminists who do research within disciplines and work in professional organizations. It carries one or another theoretical meaning: for example, we are self-conscious members of the class of women under patriarchy. And it carries practical meanings: for example, we are members of NOW, or we fight *for* the ERA and abortion rights, or we open our homes to shelter battered women, or we live our lives as lesbian separatists.

The initial meaning of "feminist" in this volume on feminist restructuring of knowledge is the professional meaning: we are feminist academics. This is the intial meaning but not the final meaning; we do not separate this meaning from the others in our lives or our work. The relations of these different meanings must somehow be understood as we set about restructuring knowledge by rethinking the dominant intellectual traditions, by integrating the work of feminist scholars and by resturcturing the institutions that make knowledge. In this section of the book, our concern is with selection within academic disciplines, in the sciences and the humanities. It includes selecting the languages and styles, as well as the canons and texts, that define disciplinary fields. It includes selecting research problems and solutions — what Thomas Kuhn called our "paradigms."[2] In the broadest sense, it includes the social organization of knowledge in the United States, and the place of academic feminists within it.

Feminist approaches can best be understood by contrasting them with traditional, "objective" approaches to the production of knowledge. In the traditional approaches, there is one knowledge, valid for everyone and biased in no one's favor. Objectivity is supposed to be guaranteed by proper criteria and methods, continually corrected for gender, class, racial, and other biases. Behind the feminist critiques lies our recognition that traditional selections are not independent of the values of those who make them. The selections that feminists criticize are made by people who have the authority to make them and thus to produce the knowledge their selections shape. Feminist critiques ultimately point to the hierarchical structure of cognitive authority that allows the perspective of some to determine the shape of knowledge for all.

Feminist transformations of scholarly knowledge have followed in large measure from new criteria and methods of selection, as the articles of Fréchet, Salomon, and Bammer show. Recently, however, feminist academics have begun to examine their own class and race biases. These biases pose a particularly acute problem, because academic feminists share their class positions, as professional producers of knowledge, with the males they criticize. Philosophers Maria Lugones and Elizabeth V. Spelman point out this problem in feminist theory[3]: while feminist philosophers have uncovered the upper-class androcentrism of traditional philosophical theories, they have often failed to recognize the upper-class, white "Anglo" perspectives represented in their own theorizing. Just as upper-class, heterosexual, white male perspectives dominate traditional knowledge, so too upper-class, heterosexual, white female perspectives dominate feminist inquiry. A concern for what Micaela di Leonardo refers to in this volume as the "feminist metonymic fallacy"—our habit of portraying white, middle-class, Western women's experiences as the experiences of all women—has increased our appreciation for methods allowing feminist inquirers to be sensitive to power differentials in their interactions with the people they study.[4] As feminist scholars, we must continuously correct in ourselves what we have criticized in others.

Over a decade ago, Dorothy Smith spoke to feminist sociologists of the need for a "reflexive" sociology for women.[5] She argued that the academic professions are part of the capitalist superstructure. Social scientists, she said, support bourgeois ideology when they construct abstract theories of society. She criticized sociologists' efforts to place themselves, as knowers, on an "Archimedean point" outside society and thereby to turn women (and others) into objects, not subjects. In the "reflexive" sociology she called for, the knowers are situated in the society they study, and women and others appear not as objects of the professional knowers' study but as knowers themselves. Thus do the theorizers become subjects of study and the subjects of study become potential theorizers.

The authors of the essays in this section of *(En)Gendering Knowledge* have followed the first half of Dorothy Smith's recommendation: they have reflexively turned their disciplinary lenses on professional knowers. They have examined those who select and make knowledge from a variety of feminist standpoints: as members of the class of women under patriarchy, as marginalized members of academic disciplines, and as members of a professional class that produces knowledge.

Denise Fréchet makes her critique from her place as a woman, an intellectual: a member of the revolutionary class of women under patriarchy. She attempts to make scientists reflect about the origins of gendered practitioners and practices. She examines the differences gender makes in scientific agency and selection. Linking scientific objectives to Western childrearing practices, she suggests that in childhood the psyches of the founders of modern science were constructed with sharp boundaries between the self and the other. Fréchet speculates that their objective framing of scientific agency and selection was an intellectual abstraction from these early social relations. The methods they devised to constitute objective science served to constrain the individual subjectivities of scientists and to unite them in their quest for universal truths about a nature apart from themselves. In this way, individualism was subsumed by universality: a chorus of male scientists shared an objective approach, produced a single, authorized version of knowledge, and declared it everyone's knowledge.

Nanette Salomon focuses on changes in agency and selection brought about by feminists in the academic disciplines of art history, including recovering lost women artists, demystifying the notion of the individual artistic "genius," and challenging the hierarchy of values that places Central Italian art of the Renaissance at the apex of art history. She reveals the impact that academic feminists can have on culture.

Angelika Bammer asks her students to consider how the texts that have been selected for them and how their responses to these texts are constituted along gender and class lines by those in power. Pointing out the class biases that infuse the literature they read and the evaluations they make of it, Bammer probes selection as simultaneously a personal matter—how feminists bring our own class affiliations into play, and as disciplinary matter—how literary studies have canonized literature, as Viriginia Woolf says, by and for educated gentlemen. Even as she takes her place in an academic discipline and a professional class, Bammer insists that we regard our work in literary studies as work done in a liberal, democratic, capitalist society. This work, like those who do it, is marked by a tension between privation and privilege, oppression and liberation, the reproduction of old structures and the creation of new ones.

These authors give us goals to strive for in making our research reflexive. From Fréchet, we have the goal of understanding our place as women and intellectuals in the sweep of human history. From Salomon, we have the goal of understanding feminist work within academic disciplines. From Bammer, we have one of the most difficult goals, for Bammer tells us that culture and power are inseparable. We would say that disciplinary knowledge and power are inseparable as well. Feminists working within disciplines exercise power — power that arises from their class positions — to bring about changes within our culture. Bammer insists that we come to terms withour class position. It is a position that both empowers us and separates us from other women. One of the main goals of this essay is to investigate our class position, the position of professionals who work within disciplines making knowledge.

Knowing That

Fréchet notes that modern science began with "a mechanistic view of the world, in which every event is determined by initial conditions, is knowable with precision independently of the observer." Current science, she says, questions the world "as though it were governed by a universal theoretical plan," an approach that echoes the need of the scientist to dominate, to reduce the diversity of phenomena to a fundamental identity, to manage the uncontrollable by promulgating an all-encompassing law. The "validity" of a scientific theory is thought to be further reinforced by its expression in a flawless language: mathematics. This reduction of complex phenomena to simpler laws requires a distinction between significant and insignificant aspects of phenomena, and a distinction between the people who are allowed to make judgments about scientific matters and those who are deemed only to have opinions. Yet another type of distinction, she adds, is that "between 'neutral' scientific information and its evaluation or application" in the outside world.

The model that Fréchet describes says that, ideally, knowledge is certified by reliable methods. For all their differences, the processes of certification in the humanities and the sciences have important similarities: both have disciplinary methods, canons, and modes of criticism or falsification designed to compel agreement. The abstract form of the knowledge they produce is quite similar. Among philosophers, the logical positivists offer the clearest example of this view of knowledge, although with a few modifications such knowledge persists among "post-positivists" (including some feminist philosophers).

In the logical-positivist view, the ideal sort of knowledge is essentially linguistic and propositional knowledge—"knowing that" rather than "knowing how" or "knowing a person or place." It is expressed in true propositions: truth, for the positivists, is a semantic concept inasmuch as it is a property of sentences. The sentences of natural science seem to offer the best (if not the only) examples of knowledge, so one of the positivists' major aims is to dis-

tinguish scientific propositions from the empirically meaningless pronouncements of metaphysicians, poets, moralists, and priests. The sentences of science
are deemed empirically meaningful because they can be confirmed or falsified by observations. In this model, metaphysics, poetry, morality, and the
Bible are not meaningless *tout court*; their words and sentences (can) have
emotive meaning, but they do not pass the scientific test of meaningfulness.
To be seriously meaningful, the terms in a proposition must have reference
to things in the world; and, to be true, a proposition must correctly describe
the things to which its terms refer. Moreover, to be meaningful, a proposition must be at least falsifiable; that is, we must be able to test it against
observations. "The dial registers 3.5" is meaningful because it can be verified
or falsified by looking at the dial, while "Abortion is permissible" fails to
have any but emotive meaning, since it is merely the expression of a positive
feeling about abortion.

The logical positivists selected definitions of meaning, truth, and knowledge, so as to exalt the products of scientists and downgrade the products
of poets, folk savants, and popes, to say nothing of mothers and fathers. But
it is the products that are exalted, not—except indirectly and at a great
distance—the work that professional scientists actually do. The appeal to
professional distinctions between philosophy as a "conceptual" endeavor and
sociology or anthropology as "merely empirical endeavors" allows positivists
to focus on abstract "scientific knowledge" or "scientific laws" rather than
on, say, the journal publications of workers in the hives of science departments, or their political struggles for tenure, grants, and prizes.

The positivist analysis is an abstract philosophical model that has had considerable influence among working scientists. It rests on two assumptions important to feminist inquiry. The first one is captured in the abstract method
of justification; according to the model, it doesn't matter who a scientist is.
Robert Merton refers to this rule as "the norm of universalism in science":
no one has special access to scientific truth. Given the proper training, any
individual—man or woman; white, black, or brown; worker, capitalist, or
aristocrat—can produce knowledge or know the truth produced scientifically.[6] The norm of universalism in turn assumes that all human beings are
epistemically alike, inasmuch as we all share the fundamental criteria of
truth and reason, as they are exhibited in Western science.

By portraying the justification of a scientific hypothesis as the work of the
individual scientist, the positivist model presents knowledge as an individual affair. This is "epistemological individualism," the view that knowledge
is a species of belief and that beliefs are states of individuals. It is an unexamined outcome of "methodological individualism," a theory that only individuals are real and suited for scientific observation. It naturally gives rise
to the view that scientific knowledge is advanced by the lone scientist duti-

fully following established procedures as he formulates his hypotheses, designs and performs his experiments, and publishes his results.[7] His gender, race, and class; his personal history; his values and politics; his position within the profession; and the place of the profession in society—all these appear to be irrelevant to the knowledge he "discovers." Agency is transformed into the mental activity of individual knowers grasping the one objective truth. The agent has propositional knowledge; he "knows that" something is true.

This notion of science was established and is maintained in our schools and colleges. In the schools, individual students listen, do their homework, and receive grades. The standard stories in the standardized texts support the individualistic model. For example, the satisfying story that often appears in introductory biology texts begins with Aristotle, moves on to Linnaeus, and describes the geologists who "far more than the biologists . . . paved the way for evolutionary theory." Inevitably, it mentions Lamarck and his "primitive idea" of evolution by inheritance of acquired characteristics; and almost inevitably it provides an accompanying picture of giraffes stretching their necks. After a few words on the economist Malthus and the great geologist Lyell, the story culminates with the "Darwin-Wallace" theory of evolution by natural selection. At this point, the pre-text of history stops and the text of science begins. For some years now, biology texts have been standardized within the publishing industry by using a characteristically wooden and impersonal language, pat formats, and strikingly similar styles of drawing and diagram. They are massive and weighty books, sewn-bound in hearty hardcover suited to "certified" knowledge and designed to last a lifetime (or to sell for the use of next year's class).

These histories and the model they present of knowers and knowledge are not cynically constructed for the consumption of outsiders. Many scientists accept them, even brilliant ones who understand the importance of history, such as zoologist Ernst Mayr, who discusses why naturalists Charles Darwin and Alfred Russel Wallace found the solution to evolution while the great zoologists of the time failed.

> The naturalist . . . is constantly confronted by evolutionary problems. No wonder that this is what he is most interested in; no wonder that his constant attention to this problem places him in a much better position to ask the right questions and to find answers and solutions than the experimental biologist. Finally, Darwin and Wallace were not amateurs, but, as naturalists, highly trained professionals.
>
> This fails to answer, however, why great systematists and comparative anatomists of the nineteenth century were so blind. There are probably multiple reasons for their failure. In the case of Owen and Agassiz, it was unquestion-

ably too strong a conceptual commitment to alternate interpretations; in the case of leading German zoologists like J. Muller, Leuckart, and so on, it might have been a conterreaction to the unbridled speculation of the Naturphilosophen.[8]

Mayr's procedure here is interesting. He makes a natural event of scientific discovery itself. That is, the events occur as discovery events: they originate in the psychological or mental processes that precede the discoveries, and they conclude in the revelation of objective regularities in nature. Darwin and Wallace face nature in a way that leads them to ask the "right questions." The failure of Owen and Agassiz, Muller and Leuckart, is explained by their irrationality — their commitments and counterreactions.

Mayr of course picks out Darwin and Wallace in retrospect; they are the figures who wrote treatises that later investigators took to be important to their own work. Mayr explains their success in terms of a scientific rationality that he reifies. He understands this rationality in a fairly subtle way, but he reifies it and contrasts it with the nonrational procedures that are responsible for others' failures. Mayr reifies nature as well, when he distinguishes Darwin and Wallace's work from that of others in terms of how well their words captured reality and approached the truth. Thus, their discovery counts as a step in the scientific progress toward truth, and today's professional scientists continue this task, as it has been figured, of drawing the veil from the face of Nature.

These histories of discoveries subsume the work of individual scientists as part of the work of members of an abstract community engaged in extending human knowledge. The scientific community crosses cultures and periods, to join together Bacon, Newton, Darwin, Einstein, and Watson and Crick. For this community of scientists, nature is *there*, as if nature is the same for all people in all times, as if the properly scientific questions asked of nature would be questions anyone would ask to find the truth, as if our relationship to nature were only cognitive, as if we were individuals sharing ideas and propositional knowledge. Disciplinary distinctions, let alone social and personal ones, are epistemologically irrelevant because scientists merely divide the work of knowing the great mosaic of nature.

Denise Fréchet offers a feminist criticism of the traditional construal of science. She argues, quite compellingly, that the paradigm of objective knowledge is male biased. But in doing so, she retains the usual roster of "great men" and "great ideas" by which science traditionally has been defined in the West. Although she rejects any simple version of universalism, she seems to retain the premise that the fundamental forces in making knowledge lie in individual thought and emotion. Ernst Mayr attributes the failures of individual scientists to their irrational commitments and reactions. Fréchet attributes the gender biases of individual scientists to the self-structures created in them by childrearing practices in which only women mother. Thus she conceives of male scientists as members of an abstract class of males, characterized by the internal structure of the essential self they share. Here we find not the traditional assumption of androcentric universalism, but a dualistic universalism of two norms—male and female. Although this analysis allows feminist academics to take our places as members of the class of women under patriarchy, it allows us, nevertheless, to ignore crucial differences among women and among men.

The central fault of the traditional approach was that it obscured upper- and middle-class male dominance—indeed, concealed it—by ignoring the concrete social and historical places of the groups of people who made knowledge. Fréchet's criticism allows us to ignore our own social and historical places as makers of knowledge. And yet Fréchet's sort of criticism, and the mothering theories on which is it based, have opened the eyes of many women—they express what many of us intuitively feel. But they retain aspects of the traditional model which have been seriously criticized by feminists and which, for scholarly and political reasons, must be overcome.

Feminist scholars (as well as others) have been moving away from the traditional paradigm of knowledge toward a more sociological, historical, and political approach. In doing so, we face squarely the contradiction Bammer points out: academic feminists are, after all, academically trained, and we share our class positions, as professional knowledge workers, with the predominantly white, upper- and middle-class men we criticize. Self-reflective work, in its fuller sense, requires a deep understanding of that class position. It requires us to understand the social organization of professions in the United States, the historical process of professionalization through which knowledge came to be produced as it is, and the process of training through which we come to know how to produce it.

Knowing How

In *The Death of Nature*, Carolyn Merchant pictures the rise of modern science as a movement away from viewing our world as an organism and toward viewing it as a mechanism. The dominant metaphor binding cosmos, society, and self changed from organism to machine. No longer an active teacher and parent, Nature became a mindless, submissive body.[9] Nature was known. Nature was manipulated. Nature was managed. The knower, manipulator, and manager was Man. Using science and technology, Man came to know how to do these things.

The death of nature that Merchant describes was a long, slow process changing the ways many people lived and worked. Out of this process came our present ways of doing both sciences and humanities: intellectual work became employment, and, in the academy, it was divided into disciplines with special content and methods. This relationship to nature and the human world through the sciences and humanities is a way of making knowledge and a way of knowing how to do it — a social organization of knowledge. Professions and disciplines are important to that social organization of knowledge.

As we use the term, disciplines are social worlds organized around subjects and methods of inquiry, and, roughly speaking, a social world is a group of people sharing forms of communication, symbolization, activities, sites, technologies, and organizations. Through disciplines, we divide intellectual labor and organize work on research problems. Disciplines are sources of skill and technology for other organizations, including businesses, universities, and the professions.[10] Our concern here is with academic disciplines in which members make their livings as members of professions.

The notion of a profession has been widely debated. Howard Becker has identified some of the normative characteristics: a profession is an occupation having a monopoly on a difficult and important body of knowledge, in part by requiring lengthy training to master that knowledge and certification to practice it. While the training and certification are organized across the profession, the body of knowledge is specialized within the discipline. Elliot Freidson says that a profession offers ways of building, controlling, and regulating markets for a class of technical services: a way of organizing an occupational labor market.[11] The main way that we organize knowledge in the United States is through professions.

The academic professions were born and the modern departmental structure of colleges and universities was made after the Civil War, as the United States became an industrialized, urban nation. The new view among some of the elite was that what the nation needed for leadership was not the old-style gentlmen who shared social and moral values in a stable society, but trained experts who could guide social change. The new men of learning were not so much men of culture as specialized experts.[12]

At the turn of the century, there ocurred a proliferation of scholarly professions, a birth of multiple disciplines that eventually became the sciences, social sciences, and humanities. Discussing "the plural organized worlds of the humanities," for instance, Laurence Veysey recounts how the humanities underwent "intellectual segmentation" between 1865 and 1920, dividing into the several fields of classics, modern languages, history, philosophy, art, and music, each in turn subdivided into specialties. The same process occurred in the natural and the social sciences. Although we might in all cases mark some differences in subject matter, the similarities in these processes of specialization indicate that disciplinary content was not the main source of the divisions. Doing intellectual work in particular kinds of workplaces required standardization. As Veysey observes,

> Here one encounters all the phenomena linked to the much discussed concept of professionalization, and indeed the arrival of firmly planted notions of structural hierarchy and bureaucratic procedure in all respects. The kingdoms may have been separate and diverse, but nearly all of them came to be governed by the same kind of rules.[13]

The rules were those of the professional organizations, professional media, and academic departments. In the beginning, Veysey explains, those who "professed" in academic work were "members of a single, quite well defined, cultivated elite," but as the twentieth century wore on, this profession became more a career than a calling.

Nevertheless, from the start, an important feature of this new social organization of knowledge was the autonomy of those who made knowledge, produced knowledge, trained other knowers, and taught students. Normatively, professionals were free of lay control (except through licensing and regulating laws) and were supposed to be self-policing according to their codes of ethics. Within disciplines, researchers were autonomous, in the sense that they were supposed to be free to do research on any topic, subject to the criteria of their disciplines. Until recently, many of the academic disciplines were predominantly male, and the knowledge produced was androcentric. Autonomy has been a source of gender bias in research, but it also has proved to be a source of feminist power to overcome gender bias.

In *Advocacy and Objectivity*, Mary Furner traces the development of the social sciences as professions, achieving job security, academic freedom, and influence on the laws and policies affecting peoples' lives. These gains were made, Furner argues, at the price of limiting academic freedom to dissent from an authorized range of views and forfeiting the right to advocate controversial social policies. In reviewing academic freedom in economics, Furner points out that

> In order to survive professionally, economists had to find ways of repressing partisanship and presenting an appearance of unity and objectivity to the public. Gradually moderates forged a kind of working alliance that sacrificed extremists . . . to scholarly values that highly self-conscious professionals considered more important: professional security and the orderly development of knowledge in their disciplines.[14]

Perhaps one of the most celebrated cases in the history of the struggle to define academic freedom was that of Edward Alsworth Ross, fired from Stanford University in 1900, at the demand of Mrs. Leland Stanford herself. Ross was, Furner tells us, career-minded, but he was involved in leftist politics. Although he did not join any socialist organizations, he was the friend of laborers and socialist politicians and publicly expressed his support for free silver and public owernship of monopolies, including the railroads. Since Leland Stanford's fortune derived from his railroad investments, Ross's views were directly at odds with the Stanford family's interests.

Ross's dismissal set off a spate of resignations by those social scientists at Stanford "who could afford the gesture" (and by Arthur Lovejoy in philosophy), as well as a furor in the academic world. Despite strong support from the profession, immediate efforts to find Ross another equally desirable position resulted only in a "five-year detention" at the University of Nebraska. At last, in 1906, Ross took a chair in sociology at the University of Wisconsin and held it for thirty years. Academic freedom cases such as this one produced mixed results, as Furner reports. Academics gained more autonomy and relief from external pressure to tailor their knowledge to the demands of interested parties, but they forfeited the possibility of legitimately advocating radical social change, as this would be viewed as behaving unprofessionally. The definition of knowledge that developed in response to these academic freedom cases concerning advocacy is one that selected "objectivity" as the appropriate stance for professionals. But the case histories themselves reveal that, in no small part, the term "objective" means "nonadvocating." An objective scholar is one who does not advocate controversial views; in fact, he is not supposed to advocate any views at all. Selecting objective scholarly work means suppressing the agency of the scholar. We find this suppression in the social sciences, the natural sciences, and the humanities. Philosophy provides a good example.

The author disappears from the philosophy text, leaving, in the words of Arthur Danto, "a noble vision of ourselves as vehicles for the transmission of an utterly impersonal philosophical truth."[15] These impersonal reports sacrifice the identities not only of the philosophers but also of the people whose "positions" the philosophers debate. Instead of taking seriously what people mean in their social contexts, philosophers construct "positions" (the skeptic's position, the liberal feminist's position) or arguments (the empiricist argument on the foundations of knowledge, the pro-life argument). The professional benefits of mastering these impersonal literary forms include presenting papers, winning tenure, and perhaps even serving as president of the American Philosophical Association.

In fact, few philosophers are able to devote the major part of their time to writing papers for journals; instead, nearly all academic philosophers devote most of their time to teaching. The existence of a philosophy profession depends on the existence of philosophy departments that, in turn, depend not only on teaching but also on courses that set the subject matter of the field, serve as introductions and prerequisites, and offer standard questions for preliminary examinations as well as definitions of competence for job applicants.

Foundational to philosophy course offerings are the roughly matched pair, History of Ancient Philosophy and History of Modern Philosophy. These two are among the most canonical of canonical courses in philosophy departments in the United States; they are required of undergraduate majors and covered in graduate qualifying examinations. Bruce Kucklick has traced the construction of the modern canon in his paper, "Seven Thinkers and How They Grew." The selection of these masters allowed philosophers to professionalize their discipline; they enabled philosophy to define a subject matter, claim a history, and conceive of itself as an independent field of knowledge suited for departmental status in institutions of higher education. Kucklick refers to this history as "victors' history" and claims that elevation to the canon "depends on disorder, on luck, on cultural transitions . . . on scholarly power plays, and on the sheer glacial inertia of the institutions of higher education."[16] In fact, "the canon has been frozen in conjunction with the relegation to the university of the learning of all philosophical material." It is the canon that sets problems for scholarly discussion and fundamentally structures the content of philosophy by selecting contrasting "tropes" such as rationalism versus empiricism and monism versus dualism. The cultural "dualisms" that feminist philosophers criticize were installed by this canon as well: mind versus body and culture versus nature. The canon persists in many departments, courses, and introductory texts. Severely criticized over the past generation, the canon now shares the stage with other approaches — as citations in this section show.

The construction of a canon is a process of selection by the few for the many, and it occurs within a complex set of practices. Even as they join together to restructure knowledge within the academy, feminists work within these practices. In this situation lie our opportunities as well as the dangers we face.

Despite the conservatism of the disciplines, the practices of autonomy and authority have allowed feminist art historians to take advantage of the women's movement and a political climate against sexism to make changes in art history and art criticism. Salomon shows us how feminists have revealed that standards of "universality" for art are relative to men. She argues that the inclusion of women artists in the historical canon must be accompanied by a revolution in the very terms of art historical analysis, since these terms were constructed in a way that makes issues of gender and class irrelevant to the understanding and evaluation of art. By analyzing the use of the heroic nude male and the sexualized, vulnerable female nude, Salomon shows us that feminist art historians are taking on a homosocial, homoerotic world of male artists, critics, and connoisseurs.

Across the academic disciplines, feminists have shifted from an investigation of "reality" to an investigation of the ways "reality" is constructed, and they have shown that gender is a crucial category of analysis. Feminists have used the practices of their disciplines to make this change in focus and in some of the practices themselves. For example, the field of women's studies cuts across the "separate and diverse" disciplines, and women's studies' programs, courses, journals, anthologies, and professional organizations are multidisciplinary. The field of women's studies offers an intellectual community and an institutional site for feminists who still must do most of their work within disciplines; it legitimates courses, journals, conferences, research, and funding for projects that use gender as a category of analysis.

We have ourselves had our successes in the academic professions, but how have we fared in changing the role they play in making knowledge? Angelika Bammer's essay leads us to raise this question and, raising it, to ponder some dilemmas of academic feminism.

Knowing Our Places

Angelika Bammer poses a familiar feminist dilemma: How are we to go about the business of dismantling the masters' houses while we are trying to get computers for the offices we have set up inside them? This dilemma faces all those who work for social change by boring from within institutions. To dismantle from within requires us not only to locate ourselves within institutions but also to wield their forms of power and authority for our purposes. But to dismantle institutions from within also requires us to maintain our feminist relationship to all women. Can we, who reside in them, use these institutions to transform patriarchal hierarchies? The danger is cooptation. The danger in using the masters' tools is that we may do to other women what we have accused men of doing to all women.

The danger exists because, as feminist academics, we have a class position—we work within the professional classes charged with making knowledge and educating the populace in a society marked by class, race, age, ethnic, religious, and other differences. Bammer fears that class has become merely "a category, among others, that feminist critics learned to invoke in the litany of oppressions we recited." She asks us to consider what class, as a historical construct and a lived experience, has to do with the work of feminist literary critics—or indeed with the work of feminists in any discipline. How can we feminist academics create and maintain a sisterly relationship to all women when our relationships to many women are marked by class dominance — and by racial, age, and ethnic dominance as well? Our dilemma can only be resolved in political action, by making new relationships in a revitalized women's movement, one in which feminists move together to reshape the institutions of society, including the academy.

But as we await that historic moment, there are questions that concern our work and our places now. What is our place as feminists among the academics? What is our place as academics among the feminists? And a wider question: What is our place as feminist academics among women?

Each woman's answers to these questions differ, according to whether she lives in Cambridge, Massachusetts; Shreveport, Louisiana; Las Vegas, Nevada; Pierre, South Dakota; or Los Angeles, California. They differ according to whether she works in an elite women's college, a Catholic university, a technical school, or a prestigious research institution. They differ according to the community she lives in, her family and neighborhood, her town or city, county and state. They differ according to a multitude of demographic markers — race, class, age, marital status, single parenthood, sexuality. Women's answers differ because the opportunities open to us differ. "Our place" is both a historical construct and a lived experience. But some circumstances are shared by all of us. As academics, we have institutional warrant to produce knowledge and to engage in professional practices. But as feminists, we need to reaffirm and recreate the political warrants that governed our work in earlier years.

What is our place as feminists among the academics?

The essays in this volume show the places we have made for ourselves in the disciplines. In this section, Salomon shows us places women have made in disciplinary research. The history of women's studies shows the places we have made, not only in research but institutionally in departments, programs, institutes, and academic organizations. But to call ourselves academic feminists indicates that we have political connections and responsibilities. What is the warrant for calling this work feminist? Who defines what makes some academic work feminist and other work not feminist (or even antifeminist)? We know who grants our authority to speak as academics. Who grants our authority to speak as feminists? We are led to the second question.

What is our place as academics among the feminists?

Some feminist academics believe it is their responsibility to articulate a feminist theory that will serve as a basis for a feminist revolution, just as Marxist intellectuals believe it is their responsibility to make theory for a socialist revolution. Because feminist academics are, as women, members of the revolutionary class, the question of our place as academics among the feminists seems moot. For example, Sandra Harding argues that the condition of women who are feminist inquirers just is the condition of women. She asserts:

Women feminists remain women no matter what they do. . . . Thus the "problem of intellectuals" and of "vanguardism" . . . should be less probable within feminism, or at least less intense than in these other scientific movements for social change. Does it make a difference to the path a revolution takes if the social group that articulates revolution and the group that is to make the revolution are the same?[17]

Harding notes that, given the crucial differences among women, we cannot expect a unified feminist theory at this time. But the question of our place as academics among feminists might be rephrased: Should we think of ourselves as theorists of revolution at all? Are we, sitting at our computers in our offices, the ones to articulate how to dismantle the masters' houses?

Once upon a time, less than a generation ago, the place of feminist intellectuals was in the movement. When we worked with activist groups in the 1960s and 1970s, we were part of a mass political struggle. We helped to write position statements that analyzed the historical moment in which a revolutionary group found itself and that set forth strategies to bring about social change. When the authors of these position statements wrote of "all women," they were making rallying calls for political unity and defining the directions that strategy and reform should take. They were not making statements about "objective knowledge of true propositions about all women." They addressed a constituency to be organized, not a category to be described. They wrote in the mode of "knowing how," not "knowing that"; they had political know-how, not simply academic knowledge.

In those times, feminist intellectuals, including academics, were accountable to others in the groups with whom they formed political alliances, and that accountability enabled us to take our stands within our institutions. The knowledge we helped to produce did not arise from our activities as professionals but from our participation in a mass struggle for social change. We could work in the tension between advocacy and objectivity because we were responsible to and supported by the feminists with whom we worked in the movement. Our analyses could be tested by their success in the political struggle, and our relationships to other feminists were made within the political alliances. Relationships to other women (not simply feminists) were made within this political context.

What is our place as feminist academics among women?

The feminist insistence on a connection with all women signaled that, politically, feminism was not simply an alliance of organizations fighting for the interests of their members (as, for example, the reproductive rights or consumer rights alliances are). It was a mass movement based on the premise that women's liberation requires self-determination for all women. It was committed to dismantling patriarchal oppression, so that women could

gain self-determination. More important, perhaps, it was committed to using only means that respect other women and their varied experiences. Sisterhood was the model for the double commitment, moral and political, of this
movement. The model and the commitment give us a way, even today, to
test our places and our work.

Certain intellectual analyses that have been influential among feminists
inside and outside the academy are problematical. In this volume, for example, Denise Fréchet explains traditional knowledge in terms of the socially constructed selves of the male founders of modern science. Female
selves are said to be constructed differently. This theory sets out the essential
characteristics that women share and thereby sanctions female academics
to make knowledge in the name of all women. One serious difficulty faces
academic feminists, because gender is not the only significant category in
the construction of our selves. Can women of one age, race, class, ethnicity,
and so on, speak for women who are different from them in these ways? The
question is a very serious one, if we believe theory provides a basis for politics.

The difficulty of this question has been widely recognized, particularly
with regard to racial or ethnic difference. Consider Maria Lugones, who
speaks in a Hispanic voice from "the viewpoint of an Argentinian woman
who has lived in the U.S. for sixteen years, who has attempted to come
to terms with the devaluation of things Hispanic and Hispanic people in
'America.'"

> None of the feminist theories developed so far seem to me to help Hispanas
> in the articulation of our experience. We have a sense that in using them we
> are distorting our experiences. Most Hispanas cannot even understand the
> language used in these theories — and only in some cases the reason is that the
> Hispana cannot understand English. We do not recognize ourselves in these
> theories. They create in us a schizophrenic split between our concern for our-
> selves as women and ourselves as Hispanas, one that we do not feel otherwise.
> Thus they seem to us to force us to assimilate to some version of Anglo culture,
> however, revised that version may be. They seem to ask that we leave our com-
> munities or that we become alienated so completely in them that we feel hollow.[18]

Lugones' complaints would be echoed by many other women — including
women of non-Anglo races, pro-life women, senior citizens, businesswomen,
religious women, children, women recently immigrated, physically disabled
women, teenagers, working-class women, and even academic women who
by some miracle come from the lower classes to be knowledge workers in
the professional classes.

The "litany of oppressions" Bammer criticizes selects the categories on the
basis of an abstract rather than a lived politics of oppression. As a litany,
"gender, class, race" is recited *a priori* from unassimilated political struggles.

The essays in this volume indicate that, as feminists among academics, we must struggle to find appropriate methods of selection within our disciplines, methods that overcome not only gender bias but all the other biases that distort the knowledge we make. In all of the disciplines, this endeavor requires us to understand historical construction and lived experience. It requires us most of all to see that, through our sisterly actions, we must continually make our political connections to feminists and to all women.[19]

Few of us today write position papers. Many of us teach new bodies of knowledge that feminist academics have made. In the process, some new ties have been made between women in the academy and women outside. For example, the National Institute for Women of Color and the Institute for Women's Policy Research have offered ways for academic women to serve other women. But, for the most part, we have had to leave the mass movement for a professional individualism that embodies the "epistemological individualism" and the "universalism" of the old model. This professional individualism guides us as we select and teach what our students will learn. Too often, we present papers at meetings using the male forms of address that we criticized in years past and an academic language that most women cannot understand. Academic survival forces us to pursue success in our individual careers. In the crush of duties, we often are pushed to treat other women in the workplace as secretaries, custodians, cooks, waitresses, or students rather than as sisters. Times have changed, and sisterhood is not as powerful as it once was in the academy. The change in our place is due to the successes and the failures of the women's movement — we may make history, but, as Marx said, we do not make it in circumstances of our own choosing.

We make history, but we also have a history. Our past is one of mass movements, including the recent Second Women's Movement. Our past history shows in our research — the essays in this volume attest to it. If we are to be self-reflective, we must be so in our academic work and in our lives outside the academy. Feminist practice can render permeable the boundaries between classrooms and communities, research and lived experience, academic and everyday knowers. Feminist inquiry must be based on understanding our own places in our communities and societies. It is a heritage we must enact in our lives so we may pass it on to those who will make history when we are gone.

Notes

We thank the editors of this volume for their literary, intellectual, and scholarly help. We also thank the participants at our talk at the New England Women's Studies Association meeting in May 1976 at Trinity College, Hartford, Conn. Portions of the introduction on Dorothy Smith are taken from Addelson, "Introduction," *Women and Politics* 3, no. 4 (1984).

This essay appeared in Kathryn Pyne Addelson, *Impure Thoughts: Essays on Philosophy, Feminism, and Ethics* (Philadelphia, Pa.: Temple University Press, 1991).

1. Simone de Beauvoir, *The Ethics of Ambiguity* (New York: Philosophical Library, 1948), 9.

2. Thomas Kuhn, *The Structure of Scientific Revolutions* (Chicago: University of Chicago Press, 1970).

3. Maria Lugones and Elizabeth V. Spelman, "Have We Got a Theory for You! Feminist Theory, Cultural Imperialism and the Demand for 'The Woman's Voice,'" *Hypatia: Journal of Feminist Philosophy* 1, no. 1. Also published in a special issue of *Women's Studies International Forum* 6, no. 6 (1983):573–81.

4. The point is that, as academic feminists, we all would do well to follow the example of feminist ethnographers, who recognize that they occupy the more powerful position and need to appreciate the characteristics of their female subjects that are antipathetic to their own white, middle-class, feminist sensibilities.

5. Dorothy Smith, "A Sociology for Women," in *The Prism of Sex*, ed. Julia A. Sherman and Evelyn Torton Beck (Madison: University of Wisconsin Press, 1979), 135–87.

6. Robert K. Merton, *Social Theory and Social Structure* (Glencoe, Ill.: Free Press, 1949).

7. Naomi Scheman, "Individualism and the Objects of Psychology," in *Discovering Reality*, ed. Sandra Harding and Merrill B. Hintikka (Dordrecht, Netherlands: Reidel, 1983), 225–44.

8. Ernst Mayr, *The Growth of Biological Thought* (Cambridge, Mass.: Harvard University Press, 1982), 424–25.

9. Carolyn Merchant, *The Death of Nature: Women, Ecology, and the Scientific Revolution* (San Francisco: Harper and Row, 1980), 190.

10. See Adele Clark and Elihu Gerson, "Symbolic Interactionism in Social Studies of Science," in *Symbolic Interactionism and Cultural Studies*, ed. Howard Becker and Michael M. McCall (Chicago: University of Chicago Press, 1990); and Anselm L. Strauss, "A Social Worlds Perspective," in *Studies in Symbolic Interaction*, ed. N.K. Denzin, vol. 1 (Greenwich, Conn.: JAI Press, 1978).

11. Elliot Friedson, *Professional Powers: A Study of the Institutionalization of Formal Knowledge* (Chicago: University of Chicago Press, 1986); and his "Occupational Autonomy and Labor Market Shelters," in *Varieties of Work*, ed. Phyllis L. Stewart and Muriel G. Cantor (Beverly Hills, Calif.: Sage, 1982), 39–54.

12. Douglas Sloan, "The Teaching of Ethics in the American Undergraduate Curriculum, 1876–1976," in *Ethics Teachings in Higher Education*, ed. Daniel Callahan and Sissela Bok (New York: Plenum Press, 1980).

13. Laurence R. Veysey, "The Plural Organized Worlds of the Humanities," in *The Organization of Knowledge in Modern America*, ed. Alexandra Oleson and John Voss (Baltimore, Md.: Johns Hopkins University Press, 1979), 51ff.

14. Mary Furner, *Advocacy and Objectivity: A Crisis in the Professionalization of American Social Science* (Lexington: University Press of Kentucky, 1975), 7.

15. Arthur Danto, *Narration and Knowledge* (New York: Columbia University Press, 1985), 67.

16. Bruce Kucklick, "Seven Thinkers and How They Grew: Descartes, Spinoza, Leibniz, Locke, Berkeley, Hume, Kant," in *Philosophy in History*, ed. Richard Rorty, J.B. Schneewind, and Quentin Skinner (Cambridge, England: Cambridge University Press, 1984), 137. The great thinkers covered in Ancient Philosophy include the Presocratics, such as Thales, Parmenides, the Pythagoreans, Plato, and Aristotle.

17. Sandra Harding, *The Science Question in Feminism* (Ithaca, N.Y.: Cornell University Press, 1986), 242.

18. Lugones and Spelman, "Have We Got a Theory," 576.

19. Addelson argues that the methods of finding the categories should be both empirical and political. See Kathryn Pyne Addelson, "Why Philosophers Should Become Sociologists (and Vice Versa)," in Becker and McCall, *Symbolic Interactionism and Cultural Studies*, 119–47.

Part V

Academic Knowledge and Social Change

14

Know-How

Ellen Messer-Davidow

For the past twenty years, feminists have been writing an academic success story—sort of. Armed with equal opportunity laws, we have forced departments to admit, graduate, and hire more women—substantial numbers in literary studies and history, though still inconsiderable ones in chemistry, physics, mathematics, and economics.[1] We have supplied academic presses and journals with literature for steadily growing markets. We have established women's studies programs and conducted curriculum transformation projects.[2] During the past year alone, over five hundred women's studies programs offered certificates, minors, majors, and degrees[3]; a dozen new feminist journals commenced publication[4]; and a national network was founded to consolidate some two hundred women's caucuses, committees, and commissions.[5] These and other developments have constituted the extensive apparatus we now use to produce and disseminate feminist knowledge.

This knowledge is the result of a feminist inquiry, whose advances and limitations have been well documented.[6] Using such techniques as archaeology, critique, and theory, feminists have altered the disciplines. We have written histories of women's experiences, deciphered gender codes, mapped sexualities, criticized disciplinary constructs, and founded such fields as women's history, psychology of women, and feminist literary criticism, to name a few. Yet we have not transformed the disciplines, which, however much enlarged and corrected, have retained their traditional structures. At the same time, we are pursuing cross-disciplinary inquiry into the systems of multiple oppressions—gender, race, class, sexuality, ethnicity, nationality—that structure various societies. This inquiry has stimulated a lively debate, particularly among black, poststructuralist, and other feminists, about the viability of gender as an analytical and a social category.[7] Notwithstanding the problems, the success of feminist inquiry has been acknowledged in all quarters.

In the flush of this success, however, feminists have begun to ask whether, in institutionalizing ourselves, we have reproduced the academic organization and production of knowledge we once sought to change. By securing for the next generation of feminists the educational opportunities that we wanted for ourselves, Joan E. Hartman worries, we may have depoliticized them.[8] How, Angelika Bammer asks, do we "go about the business of dismantling the masters' houses while we are trying to get computers for the offices we have set up inside them?"[9] Have we, Kathryn Pyne Addelson and Elizabeth Potter wonder, become more attentive to our professional advancement than to our political alliances?[10] How can we return to activism at a time when many academics are preoccupied with discourse? How can we not return to activism at a time when many politicians are repealing our gains?

In pondering the institutionalization of feminist inquiry, we must avoid characterizing universities and colleges as we did in the 1960s. We envisioned them as social structures that "housed" people and believed that we, as agents for change, had to position ourselves on their margins. If we were inside them, movement leaders warned, we would be co-opted. So we met for criticism and coffee in basement rooms, took to the quadrangles and streets, banged down the doors, and liberated the administrative offices. By the mid-1970s, when those of us in the New Left had departed for academic feminisms of our own, we realized the ineffectuality of confrontational modes and developed other ways to get institutional resources. By then we were situated precariously inside universities and colleges, where we negotiated women's studies programs with our administrations and litigated tenure-discrimination cases against them.[11] Still caught up in an us/them model of politics, we did not recognize that our institutions were not exactly functioning as *containers* of us/them, the metaphor we used to think about them.[12] Rather than being in them, I want to suggest in retrospect, we were becoming them.

Universities and colleges are in a strange way us, and we are them. They constitute our behaviors and desires, and we academics, through our daily practices, constitute their structures and processes. Thus feminists do not have the opportunity we thought we had in the 1960s to liberate these institutions or to set up counterinstitutions. We have the opportunity to use them even as they use us, to change them even as they change us. Universities and colleges, because they educate, perform structuring mediations between those who constitute them and the system of multiple oppressions that orders our culture. They can, for the same reason, perform restructuring mediations between ourselves as feminist agents and the system we want to change. As I see it, our goal, especially in this conservative era, is not "merely" to reconceptualize knowledge and transform curricula, but to find ways *to use* educational institutions to create feminist social change.

What I am going to argue is that institutionalization has placed us in a paradoxical situation. We have been existing both in the disciplines and in opposition to them. We have increased academic knowledge even while we have been led by our political interests to counter the academy by calling into question its organization of that knowledge. We have built an academic apparatus that has enabled *and* constrained feminist inquiry. It has given us the capacity to think and act: to form subjects, deploy methods, and devise justifications, and also to embody them in individual practices and institutional processes. At the same time that this apparatus has allowed us to produce knowledge, it inevitably has divided us into disciplines and separated us from other feminist communities.

Constituting Academic Feminism

The decision merely to produce feminist knowledge in the academy, even without the political and cultural differences among women that we discovered there, would have divided us, because academic knowledge is organized by three structures that, I believe, necessarily lead to division: disciplinarity, professionalism, and institutionalization.

Contemporary disciplines may be defined as fields of knowledge and practice that are monopolized by their practitioners. "The notion of a field of study," James J. Sosnoski explains, is one of those metaphors inherited from the nineteenth century. It suggests "a factual ground" which, through the application of "special disciplinary techniques," will "yield a harvest" of "truths."[13] Practitioners seek objects and techniques that make their discipline distinct from other disciplines and an ideology that proclaims it distinguished for its capacity to know "truths," as in the sciences, or "enduring values," as in the humanities. Hence distinction is both ontologically necessary and epistemologically useful in constituting disciplines; a discipline must be sufficiently distinct from other disciplines in order to exist and sufficiently distinguished in order to have authority. Practitioners can accumulate these distinctions by controlling the sites of publishing, curricula, and accreditation where they are produced — sites that may be envisioned collectively as nodes in the disciplinary organization of knowledge.[14]

This organization, Foucault reminds us in *Discipline and Punish*, was achieved in the eighteenth century through the use of distribution and seriation (or the partitioning of space and time) to categorize and discipline individuals and information. Spatially, Foucault writes, "Each individual has his own place; and each place its individual." As in a classroom divided into rows of desks, the individual place is a compartment and the aggregate a grid. The purpose of partitioning is to locate and enclose individuals, to initiate or interrupt communications, to monitor and judge. When this spatial configuration is transposed to the conceptual dimension of inquiry, "discipline organizes an analytical space."[15] The structure of inquiry in the contemporary academy is a grid of proliferating disciplines and, within them, specializations in subjects, methods, rhetorics, and theories.[16]

Nationally, Burton R. Clark envisions the U.S. professoriate distributed in a giant matrix: "To pin down professors by both specific institution and specific discipline would require a scheme containing over 3,000 rows to represent institutions and 100 or even 200 or more columns to depict major disciplinary specialities and formal professional school segments."[17] Clark's image vividly catches not only the fragmentation of contemporary knowledge but also the dispersal that causes academic knowers to feel conceptually isolated from colleagues at their own institutions who practice different specialties and geographically distanced from colleagues at other institutions who share their specialties.[18]

Temporally, the structure of discipline is a seriated routine: performance of daily tasks at regular intervals, for instance, or passage through levels. When this temporal configuration is transposed into a professional register, it becomes a course for training and certifying disciplinary knowers. Courses vary in terms of difficulty of access (the prerequisites and competition), elaborateness and stringency of the training sequence, and barriers thrown up along the way to eliminate students,[19] but they perform similar functions. Paradoxically, each course limits the number of would-be practitioners while reproducing the discipline. It reproduces the discipline by certifying the chosen practitioners in that discipline while implicitly decertifying them in others, so that they are compelled to produce disciplinary work and protect disciplinarity.[20]

A course also socializes future practitioners into the "culture" of the discipline, imbuing them with *its* perspectives and values, which they may experience as *their* motives for disciplinary reproduction. Thus practitioners declare science an exciting quest for truth about nature or literary studies the propagation of the best that has been known and thought.[21] Socialization into a disciplinary culture, according to Ladd and Lipset's *The Divided Academy*, the most comprehensive empirical study of correlations between disciplines and political attitudes, is a more important determinant of professors' political attitudes than are their gender, race, class, age, or religion. Although the authors acknowledge that disciplines selectively recruit social groups and ideological types, they miss the convergence that feminists have noticed: traditionally those who became professors were preselected for their "similar class, gender, and racial backgrounds" before they were socialized into disciplinary cultures.[22] If the preselections are narrow, the political attitudes associated with certain cultural affiliations become those associated with certain disciplines.

Finally, discipline is not merely an accumulation of lessons taught and learned, but processes and practices institutionalized in the form of departments. Some of the processes are the resources that flow through an institution and congeal in departments: human (faculty and students); financial (budget lines); informational (curricula and decision making); and physical (space and equipment allocations). They enable the routine practices of individuals that also constitute departments: hiring, promoting, and dismissing faculty; teaching and graduating students; holding meetings and even gossiping in the halls. Discipline is a structured way of life.

In short, disciplinarity partitions the academy intellectually and institutionally, selects the practitioners, and standardizes them "culturally" in three senses of the word: it constitutes social groups, cultivates individuals, and produces characteristic perspectives and values. Thoroughly overdetermining practitioners' identities, the disciplinary features of partitioning, selection, and socialization also have a social consequence. They block the formation of groups that might oppose disciplinary regimes and their local institutionalization.

Modern professionalism, another structure of academic knowledge, can be defined critically as a way of organizing an occupation that constructs a distinctive identity for professionals, places them in a status economy, and gives them the wherewithal to gain a virtual market monopoly.[23] Although academic professionalism in the United States allows for particular disciplinary identities, it bases them on the principles of liberal individualism. According to these familiar principles, all individuals who have the capacity and desire to learn can have access to professional training and employment. Through this training and employment, they acquire cognitive property — the theoretical and practical knowledge that gives them the authority to produce additional knowledge, train professionals, and serve clients.[24] These activities allow for a measure of control, which gives academics the impression that their knowledge and authority are qualities they possess rather than a state created for them by their profession.[25] Perceiving knowledge and authority as belonging to an individual, they likewise perceive merit as a quality of that individual's work. But as Foucault reminds us, a piece of work is not good; it is "in the good" that is authorized by the discipline.[26] Just so, an academic is "in the knowledge" constructed by his discipline, but to the extent he believes this knowledge is "in him" he will not see how disciplines, professions, and institutions have constructed it and how he might change them.

The identity constructed by academic professionalism is a possessive one, for professionals not only acquire expertise but also work in an academy thoroughly imbued with status. Profession by definition claims a higher status than "ordinary" employment, professions jostle one other for regard, and institutions compete for rankings. In the accrual of status, institutional ranking and individual merit interact: the higher ranking the institution where scholars train or teach, the more merit they are presumed individually to possess; and, conversely, the more merit they demonstrate, the higher the ranking assigned to their institution. Similarly, the status (not to mention the wealth) of professions and of individual careers interact. The prestige economy of academic professionalism functions like a monetary one. It not only marks the value of disciplinary practitioners, but also acts synergistically with disciplinarity to both incite and limit the production of knowledge.[27] Desire for and decisions about professional status (e.g., tenure, promotion, consulting), which accrue through disciplines, incite academics to produce more knowledge, as well as limit the kind they can produce to that which is authorized by disciplines.

The cognitive property and the status acquired by academics are perceived by the public as expertise; and expertise is what gains them public consent to monopolize a field of knowledge and service. Or, as Dietrich Rueschemeyer puts it, academic professionals "'strike a bargain with society' in which they exchange competence and integrity against the trust of client and community, relative freedom from lay supervision and interference, protection against unqualified competition as well as substantial remuneration and higher social status."[28] Although the public may dismiss esoteric knowledge, as in the expression, "Oh, that's academic," it does not necessarily by this means diminish professional power. Control of an apparatus and some public recognition of expertise give academics a virtual monopoly to produce knowledge and services in their fields and to reproduce their profession.

Although professionalism is a transdisciplinary form of academic organization, it accentuates the divisions not only among academic institutions but also between the expert knowledge of academe and the everyday knowledge of other communities. Accentuating these divisions, professionalism moderates them with ideology. To the extent that they believe the professions afford equal opportunity and determination by merit, academics will be blinded to the structures that categorically disadvantage people. To the extent that they believe in expertise, they will discount what others know. To the extent that they focus on professional goals and criteria — the enhancement of professions and careers, the merit of institutions and individuals — they will be distracted from the social contexts and consequences of the knowledge they make. Engaged in professional practices, academics miss some of the action.

Constituted by disciplines and authorized by professionalism, academic knowledge is produced and transmitted in institutions. Institutionalization appears to insulate the production of this knowledge from the world. But is it really insulated? The disciplines have diverse relations with the world.

Professional schools have long had a dual mission — the academic one of research and teaching, and the social one of serving clients — and therefore tend to respond to both institutional and social pressures. Colleges of education have struggled for years to produce research respected by their universities and also to improve primary and secondary schools. Medical colleges, traditionally academic, now grapple with the operation of huge health care organizations. Endowments, consultancies, and graduate placements have become "strong incentives for business [schools] . . . to gear academic programs to perceived corporate interests," but academic credentials determine their "standing in the university."[29]

For some natural sciences, this influence is also reciprocal. Chemists, physicists, and biologists routinely leave academe to work for corporations that manufacture pesticides, drugs, electronics, and computing devices.[30] Genetic engineering, at the cutting edge of academic research, is becoming "commercialized into one of the fastest growing segments of the economy."[31] For military-related research and development, academic sciences now receive some $40 billion annually, a sum that represents over two-thirds of the federal funds for academic and other research laboratories.[32] When much of the knowledge scientists produce is used for commercial and military purposes, and when funding sources orient them toward its production, the range of scientists' research choices is hegemonically determined. Moreover, the flow of scientists and their research into the commercial and military sectors and the flow of commercial and military resources into scientific fields thoroughly permeate the boundaries that "insulate" academic sciences from the world. Peter T. Manicas describes this relationship as a "symbiosis of [positivist] science, business, industry, and the state."[33] "Symbiosis," however, is a misleading figure. By analogizing this relationship to an organismic process that lacks an ethical dimension, it joins these sciences to the world while obscuring their responsibility for the negative consequences. Not only are these sciences influenced by a presently dangerous and endangered world, but they have been instrumental in creating it.

Social scientists, faced with the problems of urbanization, immigration, and poverty in the late nineteenth century, seized the opportunity to provide solutions by distinguishing their expertise from the dilettantism of social reformers. To professionalize themselves, they scientized their disciplines: political science, economics, and later sociology turned to quantification and prediction, psychology to experimentation and control. The relationship these disciplines have established to a socially troubled world is one of expert to client, but not to just any client. They target policy as the object of scientific management rather than social experience as a field for explanation. Their clients are more often governments and businesses than people.

The humanities have been far more insular than the professions and sciences, but not by choice. Suffering a long decline that began with the establishment of research universities in the nineteenth century and the adoption of empirical research by other disciplines, humanists have tried to recover their status. Literary scholars invoked great literature for its capacity to cultivate gentlemen and, later, criticism for its capacity to professionalize them. Philosophers declared their discipline foundational and their analytics productive of truth. Attacking these claims, deconstructionists, pragmatists, and hermeneuticists have proposed replacing traditional literary and philosophical study with polysemy, practice, or conversation. The intellectual skirmishes conducted over these issues have distracted scholars from impacting experience, so that the social consequences of the humanities are negligible.

Not surprisingly, the ideologies of these disciplines misrepresent their relations with the world. Natural scientists, avowing objectivity, have conspired with the goals of the military-industrial complex to bring us near to ecological and nuclear destruction. Social scientists advise the world in languages few understand. "Political scientists," David J. Sylvan reports, "take pride in the development of arcane quantitative methods. . . . Graduate students in political science are drilled for hours on statistics or game theory, but never taught how to talk with people about politics."[34] Literary and cultural critics employ political hyperbole but have virtually no impact even on those systems of mass culture (e.g., pornography and television) about which they claim expertise. The social consequences of academic knowledge have ranged from catastrophic to negligible, but many practitioners steadfastly deny such effects and insist that the academy, through its insulation from the world, can and should guarantee their free pursuit of knowledge. Steve Fuller makes the point the other way around: "A growing body of empirical research suggests that as disciplines pursue their internally defined problem areas, their practitioners become less inclined to pool together their inquiries in addressing a problem of general public concern."[35]

Academic knowledge is a historical phenomenon. We should approach it, Donald M. Scott cautions, "as a changing social and cultural construct, encompassing different meanings of the idea of profession and different institutional arrangements at different times."[36] Feminist inquiry, too, is a historical phenomenon. Heretofore, it has used disciplinarity and professionalism to establish itself in the academy, but it has also turned on these structures to criticize them. Nevertheless, disciplinarity, professionalism, and institutionalization affect feminist inquiry in ways that must concern us.

First, the traditional disciplinary cleavage between materiality and ideation, natural and social objects, empirical and hermeneutic methods[37] rends part of our inquiry into cultural categories and oppressions. With regard to gender, for instance, this cleavage is expressed as the feminist distinction between sex as materially manifested and gender as socially manifested. The emphasis on gender reflects our hope that the sex-gender system is tractable; we fear it is not if we base it on biological sex.[38] The intractability of biological sex is an idea enforced by the powerful disciplines—life sciences, physical sciences, technologies, and some schools of philosophy — that assert the intractability of materiality.[39]

Moreover, disciplinarity fragments whatever we study — gender, race, class, sexuality — so that we locate it everywhere and, as it seems, significantly nowhere. Gender, for instance, is played out in the behaviors of people at work and the policies that structure that work. It resides in the poem, the author, and the reader. It appears in the tilt of a child's chin and in a nation's history. The questions we understandably ask about coherence (do we have a subject?) and location (where do we locate it?) are the effects of disciplinarity — as are the answers. A psychologist "finds" gender in persons, a sociologist in social systems. A micro-theorist "finds" it in a gesture, a macro-theorist in a *longue durée*. Notwithstanding the cross-disciplinary tradition in women's studies, specialized findings are invited daily by the newest disciplinary feminist journals and conferences (the specialized ones!), and women's studies programs now (or still!) offer separate social science and humanities minors.

Politically, this intellectual and institutional partitioning divides academic feminists in a familiar way. The disciplinary grid is like the domestic grid that, we discovered in the 1960s, disempowers women. Isolated in a compartment (a specialty or a home), each woman is prevented from knowing the structures of oppression and acting to change them. Paradoxically, we may have escaped from our domestic enclosures only to find ourselves two decades later ensconced in disciplinary ones. Twenty years ago, movement critique told us our separation would be our downfall; now professional ideology tells us specializations are the places to seek academic success.

Finally, although our use of participatory structures in feminist teaching and women's studies program governance breaks down barriers within the academy, disciplinarity, professionalism, and institutionalization erect barriers between us and other communities of women. We may have forgotten that the organizational purpose of consciousness-raising groups in the late 1960s was to separate women from Left political movements and from male-centered households, in order to integrate them as an independent women's movement. Necessarily emphasizing the similarities among women — the categorical oppression they suffered and their common interest in opposing it — the process constituted, at once, a "sex class" and a feminist consciousness about it.[40] Thus, movement publications integrated literature, criticism, journalism, scholarship, and personal narrative into the political struggle. The editors of *Women: A Journal of Liberation* were typical in stating that "art is *social* expression. As we struggle to change society now, our art is part of that struggle and expresses that struggle in such things as political posters and guerrilla theater."[41]

The twenty-year separation of academic feminists and other women makes it difficult for us to reconnect academic knowledge to social change. To ask some rude but revealing questions: Besides a handful of feminist public policy centers and friends of women's studies organizations, what structures have feminists built to span academic and other communities? How many women's studies programs have courses that treat social change historically, theoretically, or practically? What difference does our knowledge of discourse make to child incest victims whose stories are discredited in court because they don't meet the judicial criteria for valid discourse? Clearly we need to move beyond these forms of disengagement — the division of our inquiry, our isolation from others, the separation of academic knowledge from social change — if we are even to *think* about a feminist inquiry in and for the world, let alone try to change that world.

Thinking About Feminist Inquiry and Action

At the very least, we need a framework that overrides these forms of disengagement — a cross-disciplinary framework that accommodates multiple identities and oppressions and that suggests connections between academic inquiry and social action. Structuration theory, I shall argue, offers such possibilities. This theory is concerned with human agents, who make decisions and take action; their social systems, which enable and constrain them; and the dynamics of their mutual constitution.

Structuration theory was developed in response to a problem that exists in disciplines — such as sociology, economics, political science, and history — that attempt to explain social life with reference both to individuals as purposeful and effective actors and to their social system as the template for action. This problem is the dualism of social life. On the one hand, individuals have identities, projects, and hopes, and, on the other hand, society has economies, politics, and culture. The dualism of social life is "central to our very existence in modern society" and consequently "to all the forms of thought and work which articulate our experience of that society."[42] However, theories about social life have tended to privilege one entity to the virtual exclusion of the other; they highlight either the powers of human agents "as active, purposeful, self- and socially-created beings" or the determinative force of the social system in providing agents with "definitions of their situations, relationships, purposes, and lives — their subjective meanings — and their consequent action and interaction."[43] These disjunctive types of social explanation, agent-centered and system-centered, may also comprise fallacies — individualism, if actions are completely determined by agents, or social determinism, if they are completely determined by the social system;

voluntarism, if social processes are created by human agency, or reification, if they are independent of human agency.[44]

Devised to transform the dualism of social experience and explanation, structuration theory postulates that human agents and social systems are mutually constituted. The routinized practices of the agents maintain and transform the social system, and the social processes enable and constrain the agents. Each dimension of social existence — the agentic and the systemic — is seen to some extent as a function of the other, as well as in terms of structuring dynamics. "Agency," Anthony Giddens explains, "refers not to the intentions people have in doing things but to their capability of doing those things in the first place."[45] Agents act and act *otherwise*. To act means to engage in practice — "to intervene in the world, or to refrain from such an intervention, with the effect of influencing a specific process or state of affairs."[46] Actions are what constitute social systems when, Giddens writes, they "are organized as regularized social practices, sustained in encounters dispersed across time-space"[47]:

> Human societies, or social systems, would plainly not exist without human agency. But it is not the case that actors create social systems: they reproduce or transform them, remaking what is already made in the continuity of *praxis*. . . . In general (although certainly not universally) it is true that the greater the time-space distanciation of social systems — the more their institutions bite into time and space — the more resistant they are to manipulation or change by any individual agent. This meaning of constraint is also coupled to enablement. Time-space distanciation closes off some possibilities of human experience at the same time as it opens up others.[48]

Thus, practice results both in production and in reproduction (or transformation) of the social conditions of production; and society is both the ever-present outcome and the ever-present condition of human practice.[49]

Giddens hypothesizes that relations and resources, which bring about the structuration of agents and social systems, usually have been manifested as domination and power. In turn, domination and power work on and through cultural categories familiar to feminists — gender, race, class, and sexuality. That they operate both agentically, through identities and interpersonal relations, and systemically, through social institutions, was an organizing concept of early feminist analyses. This "dual nature of oppression" was acknowledged almost irrespective of feminists' theoretical orientations — in, for instance, Betty Friedan's *The Feminine Mystique* (1963), a liberal feminist analysis; Shulamith Firestone's *The Dialectic of Sex* (1970), a radical feminist treatise; Kate Millett's *Sexual Politics* (1970), a literary-cultural study; and Juliet Mitchell's Marxist-feminist companion pieces, *Woman's Estate* (1971) and *Psychoanalysis and Feminism* (1974). Structurationally, then, domination and power are relations that obtain among agents, among the components of the social system, and between the agents and the social system. The agentic and social relations can reproduce each other in the way suggested by Nancy Chodorow's *The Reproduction of Mothering*: a particularly gendered social structure (i.e., families where mothers mother) creates gendered boys and girls, who become the agents that maintain these social structures and thereby the conditions of reproduction for this rendition of gender.

Structuration theory has been criticized in social science and Marxist circles[50]; unmodified, it is not a wholly satisfactory framework for thinking about feminist inquiry and action. Although it was developed partly in reaction against inadequate concepts of agency — at one extreme, the liberal individualist subject in all *his* fixity and typicality, and, at the other extreme, the antihumanist reduction of subjects to the functions they serve in a social structure — it does not now provide an adequate explanation of agentic structuring.[51] Second, most structuration theorists believe that class furnishes the structural properties of agents and social systems, but do not regard gender, race, and sexuality in the same light. Moreover, they are disposed by their disciplinary affiliations (social scientific and/or Marxist) to deal with class, state, and world systems rather than with local practices, constituencies, and institutions. Finally, theorists need to develop a fuller account of the functions of ideology in the reproduction (and transformation) of agents and social systems. But these modifications can be made.

As a framework for feminist inquiry and action, structuration theory has several advantages that result, I believe, from its counterdisciplinary possibilities. It does not fragment what we seek to investigate and change, systems of multiple identities and oppressions, but accommodates them in some important ways. It allows us to recast the taxonomically and historically conceived categories of gender, race, class, and sexuality as the dynamic structuring of agents and their social systems. It accommodates explanations, as theories of subject positions do not, of the capacity of agents to act *otherwise* and of institutional mediations in the reproduction or transformation of relations. Additionally, a structurationist framework reorients us analytically to practice and process. But analyses of practice and process can provide only one kind of knowledge about feminist social change; they can indicate *where* we might effectively intervene for such change. Reengagement in practice can provide another kind of knowledge; it can teach us *how* to intervene for social change.

Knowing About Feminist Social Change

The making of feminist social change in the early years was and arguably still is the primary goal of the women's movement. But the *making* of social change does not exist as an academic inquiry. It is not yet an ensemble of processes and practices that we can learn and teach in the academy. As a subject of study, it too is fragmented by disciplines and specializations. Important kinds of social change — as exemplified by the French Revolution, Japanese-style management, the resurgence of the Christian Right, and the urban renewal drive of the Southeast Baltimore Community Organization — are studied discretely in history, sociology, organization development, speech-communications, and community planning. The usual way to study such change, and particularly social movements, is to study *what* gets changed and *when* it gets changed, but not *how* it changes: for example, the changes brought about by the Suffrage movement and the events marking those changes, but not how constituencies mobilize, organize, and strategize and how institutions are used to facilitate these processes. Studies that do focus on these processes often are regarded as "popular" rather than scholarly and thus dismissed by the academy. The literature on community organizing, much of it authored by people with organizing experience, is often so regarded.[52] Although the practices of making social change may be observed by academics, their actual performance is left to revolutionaries, managers, evangelicals, and community activists. Finally, important kinds of feminist social change are reviewed in women's studies courses, as well as in feminist courses offered in some disciplines. Common topics are history of the Second Women's Movement, women and public policy, sexism and the schools, and psychotherapy for women; uncommon ones are the practices of making change.[53] In other words, insofar as the making of social change is an academic subject, it is divided by disciplines and is taught intellectually, not practically. But learning about the *making* of social change from explanation and learning about it from practice are not the same ways of knowing, nor even the same things known. In the discussion that follows, I use structuration theory and my experience as a feminist activist to think about models for making social change and, more particularly, to find strategic points of intervention.

Agent-centered models of change represent powerful people and passive objects. Creating change is like playing pool: you stand outside the play and drive the cue ball in a direction that activates other balls, which in turn are slowed by the felt surface and the rim of the pool table. In this situation, the agent acts on objects (people, institutions, procedures), causing them to change, while the social structure minimally constrains the action. This model, which represents change as unidirectional and forceful, informs particle physics, linear causality, ego psychology, and traditional histories of great men and events.

Engineered change, a variant of this model, is the figure employed in some management literature and practice. As Bennis et al. explain in *The Planning of Change*, the classic textbook on this subject, "Plans are made by the experts to meet the needs of the people affected by the plan as the experts interpret these needs, as well as relevant objective technical and economic conditions and requirements. After the plan is made, the consent of those affected to the plan is engineered by effective means of monologic persuasion."[54] Engineered change is the process often used in corporate reorganization, colonial rule, and welfare reform. The rhetoric enlisted to support it flows in one direction and is usually embellished by statistics, charts, diagrams, and other expert paraphernalia, if not subtle coercion. The figure of engineered change privileges the agents; it combines liberal individualist philosophy, the professional service ideal, and the technological fix.

Democratic change, the variant preferred in the academy, is also an agentic model, but here the agents work to achieve change by a consensus that may, however, elude them. They employ dialogic persuasion, the rhetoric of academic equals, trusting that dialogue, embellished by argument, explanation, and evidence, is the way to change the minds of their colleagues and of the public as well. Even those who never dreamed of engineering change still believe in compelling it by reasoned explanation and supporting evidence. The rhetorical manner may be dialogic rather than monologic, but the agentic mode is the same.

Social-system models of change represent powerful systems and passive people. Creating change is like playing bumper-cars at the amusement park: you drive an electric car inside a bounded field, chasing and chased by other cars, and, if your reflexes are good, smacking into them or swerving out of their way. When the system is on, the cars are powered; when it's off, they stop. In this situation, the structure generates the impulses to which the agents respond; change is the conformity of agents to the demands of the system. In a more deterministic version of this model, people exercise virtually no agency. Change is operant conditioning: by the administration of electric shocks or food pellets at each turn, people are taught to run the maze. This model of change informs Thomas Hardy's "chance," behaviorist psychology, some Marxian economics, and the sociobiological version of sex.

Feminist models of change tend to bring agents and their social system into a mutual relation. Catherine Belsey, for instance, attempts to moderate the social determinism of Althusserian change.[55] She begins with his premise that the subject is created in discourse and, since the symbolic order in its discursive use is closely related to ideology, in ideology. . . . Ideology suppresses the role of language in the construction of the subject. As a result, people "recognize" (misrecognize) themselves in the ways in which ideology "interpellates" them, or in other words, addresses them as subjects, calls them by their names and in turn "recognizes" their autonomy. As a result . . . they "willingly" adopt the subject-positions necessary to their participation in the social formation. . . . Ideology interpellates concrete individuals as subjects, and bourgeois ideology in particular emphasizes the fixed identity of the individual.[56]

If we accept the notion of a fixed identity, Belsey asks, "How is it possible to suppose that, even if we could break in theoretical terms with the concepts of the ruling ideology, we are ourselves capable of change, and therefore capable both of acting to change the social formation and of transforming ourselves to constitute a new kind of society?"[57] The answer she gives is based on the Lacanian concept of the double "I," the gap created between the one who is represented and the one who represents. Through the ensuing contradictions, as well as shifts in discourse, the subject can occupy a range of positions, thereby becoming not a unitary identity but a process of change. In process, she concludes, "lies the possibility of transformation."[58]

The figure of positioning, as a linchpin concept in the analogizing of discursive and social frameworks, is unsuited to convey what happens in the making of social change. Theoretically speaking, if all positions are discursively (or ideologically) determined, the process of changing subject-positions is no answer because it too is determined by discourse(s) as a closed and determining system. Under these conditions, it does not follow that, by changing the subject-position, one changes the discursive system; nor does it follow that, by changing discourses and thereby the subject-position, one changes the construction of the self. Practically speaking, two equations seem unwarranted to me: processes do not necessarily hold out the possibility of transformation (that is, of changes in form), nor are changes in discourse synonymous with changes in other social structures. Finally, the changes of subject-position Belsey describes, even if we consider them initiated by agents rather than by discourse, also do not necessarily entail agentic purpose with regard to social structure; but such purpose is integral to a feminist movement dedicated to social justice. In other words, feminist agents do consider the desirability and feasibility of the changes they might undertake (though not always accomplish) in light of their goal of social justice. If they did not or could not, then there would be no point in having a goal or, for that matter, a movement.

Teresa de Lauretis, long concerned with the making of feminist social change, chooses the term "op-position" to figure resistance to institutions, which, as she points out, can mean — and has meant historically — rather diverse things, translating into different practices and strategies that must be assessed and developed each in its concrete sociohistorical situation. Resistance has been armed or unarmed, for instance (though never disarmed, if it was really resistance). It can be socially organized in group action or lived subjectively as a personal commitment, and often is both. But by the very nature of power and of the mechanisms that harness power to institutions, rather than individuals, resistance tends to be cast as op-position, tends to be seen as locked in an opposite position, or what the media call an "opposing viewpoint." Thus, it is not just accommodated but in fact anticipated, and so effectively neutralized, particularly by democratic institutions.[59]

The figure of opposition is particularly unsuited to convey what happens in the making of social change. To oppose suggests *two* entities, sides, or positions that are set against each other, each withstanding, resisting, combating, hindering, or obstructing its opposite. Of the assumptions entailed by the figure of opposition, three are especially problematical. First, as in the passage above, this figure leads us to believe that two kinds of entities — agents and institutions — exert force against one another. But the entities are, in fact, *ensembles* of agents, practices, and processes, albeit with different resources to employ. Second, the radical dichotomizing of this side and that, of actions and counteractions, prevents us from thinking about change as a much more complicated process. We need a rhetoric that conveys the complexity of what in my experience is a virtual force-field of diverse routines and interventions, initiatives and responses, that even as they "neutralize" some processes may spark others, both intended and unintended. Finally, in opposition, the agents resist, combat, or hinder but do not transform the institutional structure. Without this change, the template that enables and constrains them remains exactly the same.

As heuristics, feminist models that bring agents and their social system into mutual relation do not necessarily highlight the possibilities for social transformation. A better heuristic, I believe, is the structurationist model. If agents and their social system are mutually constitutive, then the critical point of intervention, according to this model, would be the constituting itself — the daily practices and processes that occur in "mediating institutions." Local social units — families, schools, churches, neighborhoods, voluntary associations, and subcultures — that stand between individuals and the megastructures of the modern state are what Peter Berger calls "mediating structures." He believes that public policy not only should foster them but should use them as its agents.[60] By "mediating institutions," I mean the larger structures that have transformative power in our socity: educational institutions and the media. They are not so distanciated that we cannot experience our constitution of them and their constitution of us. This combination of features, transformative power and manageable distanciation, makes them effective places to intervene for social change. Nationally, for example, the New Right has targeted schools, colleges, and universities, because these institutions shape agentic practice, and has used other structures to leverage changes in these educational institutions. It has organized citizen-action groups to police schools, libraries, and textbook publishers; redirected federal funding of public and higher education; and used government agencies, courts, and legislatures to regulate (or deregulate) educational activities. What it wants to change in these institutions are the texts, curricula, and research that form the hearts and minds of the citizenry who have access to education. In other words, the Right is attempting to initiate a transformation of society by making changes in educational processes that in turn will (re)form the agentic practices which constitute that society.[61] As a means of leveraging those changes, the Right has chosen the resources (human, informational, and financial) flowing to and through educational institutions.

To cite an example, the National Endowment for the Humanities (NEH) is an agency that the Right is using to create academic change by directing the flow of resources. The conservative goals of Lynne V. Cheney, the chairman of the NEH, are clear. In a recent speech she declared, "When I become most concerned about the state of the humanities in our colleges and universities is not when I see theories and ideas fiercely competing, but when I see them neatly converging: when I see feminist criticism, Marxism, various forms of poststructuralism, and other approaches all coming to bear on one concept and threatening to displace it." What she fears will be displaced is the traditional "concept of Western civilization, which has come under pressure on many fronts, political as well as theoretical. Attacked for being elitist, sexist, racist, and Eurocentric, this central and sustaining idea of our educational system and our intellectual heritage is being declared unworthy of study."[62] Feminism, Marxism, and poststructuralism, according to Cheney, are joined in a struggle against the Western cultural heritage that has been preserved and disseminated in the academy, and they must be disarmed. Their disarming is proceeding financially and rhetorically.

The pattern of awards made by several NEH programs from 1985 through 1987, as well as published criticism of the agency, suggest that its budget is being used to strengthen the "intellectual heritage" its chairman believes is under siege. No more than 10 percent of the awards, in numbers and in dollars, support projects on women, gender, or feminism, while most of the awards support traditional academic research on religion, classical and canonical texts, and patriotic subjects, as well as comparable subjects of public programming.[63] Moreover, the NEH has awarded at least $1.4 million to radical Right projects that promulgate original-intent approaches to the nation's founding documents; that theorize conservative Christianity; or that attack affirmative action, abortion, aid to the poor, homosexuality, the American Civil Liberties Union, and the Critical Legal Studies movement.[64] The NEH does not publish full and accurate data on its awards. The projects receiving funding are listed briefly in the annual reports, but the projects in the applicant pool are not. Thus the public cannot tell whether projects on women, gender, or feminism are disproportionately eliminated during the selection process or are underrepresented in the applicant pool. These two problems suggest very different superficial remedies: the first that the NEH needs a more equitable selection process; and the second that it needs to invite applications for support of such projects.

Although facts are lacking on the process of selection, we do know that the criteria used in the process have changed during Cheney's tenure. In her biennial report, *Humanities in America*, she declared her opposition to specialized knowledge, politicized knowledge, theory, and cultural pluralism requirements. She contends that "viewing humanities texts as though they were primarily political documents is the most noticeable trend in academic study of the humanities today. Truth and beauty and excellence are regarded as irrelevant; questions of intellectual and aesthetic quality, dismissed. . . . The key questions are thought to be about gender, race, and class."[65] And again, perturbed by the debate about the "classics," Cheney exclaims against her "opponents who argue that those works, mostly written by a privileged group of white males, are elitist, racist, and sexist. If students are to be taught works by writers like Plato and Rousseau at all, it should be to expose and refute their biases. Teaching becomes a form of political activism."[66] Academic specialization she equates with narrowness and insignificance, and public programming (which the NEH also funds) with broadness and significance. Specialization prevents scholars from talking with the general public, whereas "television enlarges opportunity, making the arts and humanities available to millions."[67] In 1987, the NEH National Council devoted several meetings to discussing policy changes that would shift "NEH-supported research toward broad and synoptic topics as opposed to more narrowly drawn and specialized subjects."[68] A suggested modification in the guidelines would require the applicant to address the question, "Does this project lead to something enduring and significant?"

In 1988, the NEH Division of Research Programs adopted guidelines on "significance." These guidelines are aimed, I believe, at shifting funding toward conservative humanities research and its dissemination to the public. The strategy is a familiar one: by invalidating the categories of specialized knowledge, politicized knowledge, theory, and cultural pluralism, one need not consider the projects that exemplify them. "Insignificance" is the justification for disenabling not only the new inquiries into gender, race, and class, but also most critically reflective inquiries. Conversely, the "signifi-

cance" now attached to conservative humanities research and its dissemination to the public categorically enhances the potential for funding projects
of this sort. As a criterion for funding decisions, "significance" becomes a
powerful determinant of the organization and production of knowledge in
the humanities.

The rhetorical assault on the humanities is widely known; it has been
mounted by former NEH chairman William J. Bennett and present NEH
chairman Lynne V. Cheney, as well as by such humanities scholars as E.D.
Hirsch, Jr., and Allan Bloom. These critics of the humanities have had easy
access to the media and the public, while the academics who have responded
to the assault on their disciplines have had to reply mainly in academic
forums.[69] With few exceptions, these respondents have scrutinized the terms
of debate far more carefully than they have the patterns of funding.[70] The
discourse that we felt must be engaged has kept us distracted from the action: the flow of resources away from critical inquiries and into traditional
ones, away from the humanities and into military-related research, away
from feminist visions of social justice. Recently, Congress has reviewed the
practice of regranting by the National Endowment for the Arts and the National Endowment for the Humanities — that is, the awarding of block grants
to arts and humanities groups (for instance, the American Council of Learned
Societies), which then redistribute the funds in the form of individual awards
and fellowships. Among the proposed restrictions are that the Endowments
reduce the regrants made to groups and assume the authority to approve individual awards and fellowships. While representatives of the arts and humanities groups have observed that a reduction in grants would force a reduction in their programs, they have not argued that the shift in approval gives
the Endowments the power to determine what kinds of projects get funded.[71]
To direct the flow of resources in the way that the Right appears to be doing
is to make a strategic intervention into the practices and processes that structure knowledge — and not only academic knowledge but also knowledge
produced by other institutions, for the Endowments also fund projects sponsored by the media, libraries, historical associations, museums, and similar
public organizations.

Meanwhile, some academics are doing what academics do. We are studying the theory upon which the New Right is acting: those who can direct
the flow of resources to and through mediating institutions — at present, the
financial sponsors, the federal regulators, and the ideologues on the Right —
have the power to change the production of knowledge, of agents, and thereby
of social realities. What may interest us in theory, however, may intimidate
us in practice. The practice that most immediately concerns us, the production of knowledge, now appears likely to involve a protracted struggle. If
the New Right has the capacity to use institutions to instate their beliefs, then

we all will have to fight to maintain our beliefs. This fight will not take place in print among colleagues who have an agreement to disagree and a protocol for doing so, but in the political arena against those who repudiate the ground rules. And this is what I think we fear — not only the enormous struggle for control of knowledge production, but also our confusion when our ground rules are repudiated.

Faced with such a struggle, academics may find "pure truth" more attractive than politicized knowledges, but we cannot have it both ways. If we cannot face the consequences when academic authority dissolves into ideology and the production of knowledge recedes into political arenas, then we had better stop producing critiques. If we continue to argue that academic knowledge is a system of ideas, values, and practices shaped by ideological, material, and social forces, then the pertinent question is: can we merely choose among knowledges, or will we have to struggle?

I have chosen "know-how" for my title because I think a struggle is inevitable. I want to emphasize the *making* of social change and urge us to make academic change, both intellectual and institutional, instrumental to this goal. "Know-how" is something more than technical expertise. Technique, from the Greek word *techne*, an art, and from the base *tekth-*, to build, is procedural knowledge, the knowledge of how to accomplish something in an art, a science, a profession, a craft. Know-how completes our knowledge of such a process by giving us the capacity to expedite it. I have chosen this colloquial term deliberately, because I want to valorize in my definition a traditionally denigrated kind of knowing. Know-how, then, is both a term and a capacity that feminists must reclaim in order to rejoin inquiry and social change.

To reclaim the term, we as academic feminists need to value everyday knowing as well as esoteric; practical knowing as well as theoretical; skilled knowing as well as elegant and intellectual; and useful knowing as well as pure. Some traditionalists have objected that know-how violates the principles of intellectuality, such as scholarly "objectivity" and "commitment," and some feminists have objected that it entails a coercive or fraudulent use of power over others. Indeed, know-how has been deeply implicated in endeavors that feminists criticize — commerce, technology, militarism, expert science, and engineered change — which is why it needs revaluation.

To reclaim the capacity, we as academic feminists need to admit know-how into the realm of academic inquiry by increasing our understanding of social change and our ability to make it. We have several opportunities. First, we can join with other feminist communities to relearn the practice of social change by making it, once again, for the movement. But this time, we must be chastened by the observation bell hooks made in 1981: although academic feminists "probably know less about grassroots organizing than many poor and working class women, they were certain of their leadership ability, as well as confident that theirs should be the dominant role in shaping theory and praxis."[72] Second, we can teach the practice of feminist social change in the academy, as does the women's studies program at Mankato State University. "Collective Action/Analysis," a typical course, is described as: "An examination of a current feminist issue in terms of both theory and practice. The course will include an action component that will provide practical experience in the praxis of social change."[73] An internship in feminist organizations, paired with a weekly seminar, is required of women's studies majors at the University of Massachusetts in Boston. This "course" integrates the development of academic skills (research methods, critical analysis, and writing), personal work skills, and organized social change by teaching these ways of knowing in theory and practice.[74]

Finally, we can do social research that is equitable and change-oriented. The contributors to *A Feminist Ethic for Social Science Research,* for instance, describe research that is liberating for women. By involving the researchers and subjects collaboratively in all aspects of a project, including design, data gathering, and presentation of results, this research changes the participants. Moreover, by presenting this research to the public, to other affected women, and to those who make decisions about the lives of these women (e.g., policy makers, judges, medical workers, agency staff), it attempts to change social contexts. Research, these social scientists realize, has "the potential to affirm or negate realities, to be consciousness raising or consciousness denying."[75] Each of these examples reconnects feminist inquiry and action; each puts know-how to work for feminist social change.

Academic feminists now occupy a paradoxical position. By locating ourselves "in" academe, we have made remarkable gains at a remarkable cost. Our work — developing women's studies programs and producing feminist knowledge — has given us new skills, but has not exercised us in the old political and strategic ones. Indeed, many academic feminists have not worked as social activists since the early 1970s, and some not at all. To get out of our paradoxical position "in" the academy, feminists must look to the academy. The apparatus we have built will constrain us *if* we allow it to absorb us in traditional academic activities; or it will empower us during this conservative era, *if* we use it to amplify feminist social change. We must amplify that change not only in classrooms and in print, but also in and for the world. Conservatives already have begun to use educational instutitions to make social change. If they succeed, we will find ourselves "in" an academy ever more permeated by a conservative culture. Occupying a paradoxical position "in" this academy, we had better start using what we have.

Notes

I am grateful to Michael Hancher, Joan E. Hartman, Barbara Laslett, Bruce Lincoln, June Reich, and Larry T. Shillock for their patient and helpful readings of this essay in its many versions; and to a Grant-in-Aid of Research from the Graduate School, University of Minnesota, which was awarded in part to support my work on this essay.

1. For percentages of women as students and faculty in the sciences, see Linda Dix, ed., *Women: Their Underrepresentation and Career Differentials in Science and Engineering* (Washington, D.C.: National Academy Press, 1987); and *Changing America: The New Face of Science and Engineering*, Interim Report of the Task Force on Women, Minorities, and the Handicapped in Science and Technology, Sept. 1988 (330 C Street S.W., Washington, D.C. 20201).

2. The development of women's studies is detailed in: Christine Grahl, Elizabeth Kennedy, Lillian S. Robinson, and Bonnie Zimmerman, "Women's Studies: A Case in Point," *Feminist Studies* 1, no. 2 (Fall 1972):109–20; Marilyn Boxer, "For and About Women: The Theory and Practice of Women's Studies in the United States," *Signs* 7, no. 3 (Spring 1982): 661–95; Paula R. Holleran, "The Feminist Curriculum: Issues for Survival in Academe," *Journal of Thought* 20, no. 3 (Fall 1985):25–36; and Maxine Baca Zinn, Lynn Weber Cannon, Elizabeth Higginbotham, and Bonnie Thornton Dill, "The Cost of Exclusionary Practice in Women's Studies," *Signs* 11, no. 2 (Winter 1986):290–303. Information on curriculum transformation is provided in: Bonnie Spanier, Alexander Bloom, and Darlene Boroviak, eds., *Toward a Balanced Curriculum: A Sourcebook for Initiating Gender Integration Projects* (Cambridge, Mass.: Schenkman, 1984); Betty Schmitz, *Integrating Women's Studies into the Curriculum: A Guide and Bibliography* (Old Westbury, N.Y.: Feminist Press, 1985); Marilyn Schuster and Susan Van Dyne, eds., *Women's Place in the Academy: Transforming the Liberal Arts Curriculum* (Totowa, N.J.: Rowman and Allanheld, 1985); Margaret L. Anderson, "Changing the Curriculum in Higher Education," *Signs* 12, no. 2 (Winter 1987):222–54; and Susan Hardy Aiken, Karen Anderson, Myra Dinnerstein, Judy Lensink, and Patricia McCorquodale, "Trying Transformations: Curriculum Integration and the Problem of Resistance," *Signs* 12, no. 2 (Winter 1987):255–75.

3. An exact count is not available. PMLA 103 (Sept. 1988) lists approximately 500, while the new *Women's Studies Program Directory* (College Park, Md.: National Women's Studies Association, 1989) lists 519. Beth Stafford, ed., *Directory of Women's Studies Programs and Library Resources* (Phoenix, Ariz.: Oryx Press, 1990) promises to list nearly 600 women's studies programs.

4. According to the *Media Report to Women* 15, nos. 1–2 (Jan.–April 1987):7, the number of entries for 1987 had increased over 1986 by 13 for U.S. periodicals and 21 for foreign periodicals. Of course, the number of entries may not accurately indicate the number of journals started, because it includes newsletters and depends upon requests to list. The following is a sample of new feminist journals from late 1987 to early 1989: *African Woman* (Akina Mama Wa Africa, London Women's Centre, Wesley House, 4 Wild Court, London WC2B 5AU); *Desde el Feminismo*, a journal of theory, analysis, and criticism (Partado de Correos 9.084, 28080 Madrid, Spain); *Differences: A Journal of Feminist Cultural Studies* (Indiana University Press, 10th and Morton Streets, Bloomington, Ind. 47405); *Diva: A Quarterly Journal of South Asian Women*, focusing on Canada, USA, Europe, and South Asia (253 College Street, Unit 194, Toronto, Ontario M5T 1R5, Canada); *Gallerie*, a woman's art quarterly (Gallerie Publications, 2901 Panorama Drive, North Vancouver, British Columbia V7G 2A4, Canada); *Gender and Education* (Carfax Press, P.O. Box 25, Abingdon, Oxford OX14 1RW, England); *Gender and History* (Basil Blackwell,

108 Cowley Road, Oxford OX4 1JE, England); *Gender and Society* (Sage, 211 West Hill-crest Drive, Newbury Park, Calif. 91320); *Genders* (University of Texas Press, P.O. Box 7819, Austin, Tex. 78713); *Journal of Feminist Family Therapy* (Haworth Press, 10 Alice Street, Binghamton, N.Y. 13704); *Journal of Women and Aging* (Haworth Press); *La Parole Mé-teque*, a journal of art, culture, music, literature, feminist studies, and sociopolitical issues (Service des Abonnements, 5005 Coté Sante-Catherine, Suite 12, Montréal, Quebec H3W 1M5, Canada); *NWSA Journal* (Ohio State University Press, 1050 Carmack Road, Colum-bus, Ohio 43210); *Reproductive and Genetic Engineering* (Pergamon Press, Maxwell House, Fairview Park, Elmsford, N.Y. 10523).

5. The National Network of Women's Caucuses and Committees in the Professional Associations (Sara Delano Roosevelt Memorial House, 47–49 East 65th Street, New York, N.Y. 10021).

6. See Ellen Carol DuBois, Gail Paradise Kelly, Elizabeth Lapovsky Kennedy, Car-olyn W. Korsmeyer, and Lillian S. Robinson, *Feminist Scholarship: Kindling in the Groves of Academe* (Urbana: University of Illinois Press, 1985); Teresa de Lauretis, ed., *Feminist Studies/Critical Studies* (Bloomington: Indiana University Press, 1986); and Christie Farn-ham, ed., *The Impact of Feminist Research in the Academy* (Bloomington: Indiana Uni-versity Press, 1987).

7. Black feminists long have insisted that multiple-category models are needed. See, e.g., Frances Beale, "Double Jeopardy: To Be Black and Female," in *The Black Woman: An Anthology*, ed. Toni Cade (New York: Mentor/NAL, 1970), 90–100; Kay Lindsey, "The Black Woman as Woman," in Cade, *The Black Woman: An Anthology*, 85–89; Barbara Smith, "Toward a Black Feminist Criticism," *Conditions Two* (1977):25–32; bell hooks, *Ain't I A Woman: Black Women and Feminism* (Boston: South End Press, 1981); Bonnie Thornton Dill, "Race, Class, and Gender: Prospects for an All-Inclusive Sisterhood," *Fem-inist Studies* 9, no. 1 (Spring 1983):131–50; Deborah K. King, "Multiple Jeopardy, Multiple Consciousness: The Context of a Black Feminist Ideology," *Signs* 14, no. 1 (Autumn 1988): 42–72; and Patricia Hill Collins, "The Social Construction of Black Feminist Thought," *Signs* 14, no. 4 (Summer 1989):745–73. Poststructuralist feminists have insisted on the in-stability of identity. See, e.g., Jane Flax, "Postmoderism and Gender Relations in Feminist Theory," *Signs* 12, no. 4 (Summer 1987):621–43; Linda Alcoff, "Cultural Feminism Versus Poststructuralism: The Identity Crisis in Feminist Theory," *Signs* 13, no. 3 (Spring 1988):405–36; and Leslie Wahl Rabine, "A Feminist Politics of Non-Identity," *Feminist Studies* 14, no. 1 (Spring 1988):11–21. Navigating the claims of these two constituencies, Susan R. Bor-do argues for the retention of gender as an analytical category. See her "Feminism, Post-modernism and Gender-Skepticism," in *Feminism/Postmodernism*, ed. Linda J. Nicholson (New York: Routledge, 1990).

8. Comment to the author at a panel on "Generational Shifts in Feminist Politics and Thought," sponsored by the MLA Commission on the Status of Women, Modern Lan-guage Association Convention, 28 Dec. 1987.

9. Angelika Bammer, "Mastery," in this volume.

10. Kathryn Pyne Addelson and Elizabeth Potter, "Making Knowledge," in this volume.

11. See Athena Theodore, *Campus Troublemakers: Academic Women in Protest* (Hous-ton, Tex.: Cap and Gown Press, 1986); and George R. LaNoue and Barbara A. Lee, *Aca-demics in Court: The Consequences of Faculty Discrimination Litigation* (Ann Arbor: University of Michigan Press, 1987).

12. For a discussion of the "container" metaphor and metaphorical systematicity, see George Lakoff and Mark Johnson, *Metaphors We Live By* (Chicago: University of Chicago Press, 1980), esp. 29–32, 46, 52–53, 56–60, 97–105.

13. James J. Sosnoski, "Literary Study as a Field for Inquiry," *Boundary 2* 7 (1985–86):94.

14. Steve Fuller declares that "a discipline is 'bounded' by its procedures for adjudicating knowledge claims"; Fuller, *Social Epistemology* (Bloomington: Indiana University Press, 1988), 191. I would add that *who* deploys the procedures is intimately related to *what* the procedures are and *where* the boundaries are drawn.

15. Michel Foucault, *Discipline and Punish: The Birth of the Prison*, trans. Alan Sheridan (New York: Random/Vintage, 1979), 143.

16. See John Higham, "The Matrix of Specialization", 3–18; and Laurence Veysey, "The Plural Organized Worlds of the Humanities," 51–106; both in *The Organization of Knowledge in Modern America, 1860–1920*, ed. Alexandra Oleson and John Voss (Baltimore, Md.: Johns Hopkins University Press, 1979). For a more detailed study of specialization in relation to one discipline, see Gerald Graff, *Professing Literature: An Institutional History* (Chicago: University of Chicago Press, 1987).

17. Burton R. Clark, *The Academic Life: Small Worlds, Different Worlds* (Princeton, N.J.: Carnegie Foundation for the Advancement of Teaching, 1987), 42.

18. "A professor will often know members of his field at universities across the country better than he will know most people in other departments at his own university" (Everett Carll Ladd, Jr., and Seymour Martin Lipset, *The Divided Academy: Professors and Politics* [New York: McGraw-Hill, 1975], 56). I want to point out that the connection and distance felt by professors may vary by type of institution and institutional culture. A professor at a small college, for instance, may feel closer to local colleagues than to disciplinary ones elsewhere, but that closeness may be experienced as comfortable or stifling.

19. Burton R. Clark, *The Higher Education System: Academic Organization in Cross-National Perspective* (Berkeley: University of California Press, 1983), 39.

20. Betty Jean Craige points out that "specialists in literature served their own interests . . . by preserving the separateness of a literary canon from other social discourse; they could hardly do otherwise for they generally believed themselves incapable of speaking or writing authoritatively on matters outside their discipline, being specialists in literatures alone"; Craige, *Reconnection: Dualism to Holism in Literary Study* (Athens: University of Georgia Press, 1988), 75.

21. See Graff, *Professing Literature*, 63; and Craige, *Reconnection*, 28–29.

22. Patricia Hill Collins, "The Outsider Within: The Sociological Significance of Black Feminist Thought," in this volume. In 1970, the "American academic profession" was "roughly 80 percent male" and "well over 90 percent white." Women were "heavily concentrated in nursing, social work, and education," and they "remained far behind men in appointments to prestigious institutions, tenured positions, and high-rank departments" (Walter P. Metzger, "The Academic Profession in the United States," in *The Academic Profession: National, Disciplinary, and Institutional Settings*, ed. Burton R. Clark [Berkeley: University of California Press, 1987], 155). Studies are needed to show the extent to which future practitioners arrive with or are socialized into disciplinary perspectives and values, and particularly the extent to which those who have acquired their perspectives and values as a result of gender, race, or class oppressions resist or disrupt this disciplinary socialization.

23. Eliot Freidson, "The Theory of Professions: State of the Art," in *The Sociology of the Professions: Lawyers, Doctors and Others*, ed. Robert Dingwall and Philip Lewis (New York: St. Martin's Press, 1983), 23. Freidson reviews several definitions in order to point out the difficulty of defining professionalism. For a brief review of the Parsonian, capitalist, and ideological models in the literature on professionalism, see Gerald L. Geison, "Introduction," in *Professions and Professional Ideologies in America*, ed. Gerald L. Geison (Chapel Hill: University of North Carolina Press, 1983), 3–11. "Professionalism," which in sociological literature designates a particular kind of occupation and a sense of mission

about it, should not be conflated with "discipline," which in Foucault's work designates particular structures and technologies of knowledge and power. For an analysis of the differences, see Jan Goldstein, "Foucault among the Sociologists: The 'Disciplines' and the History of the Professions," *History and Theory* 23, no. 2 (1984):170–92.

24. Magali Sarfatti Larson, *The Rise of Professionalism: A Sociological Analysis* (Berkeley: University of California Press, 1977), 222.

25. "Downgrading all external controls," Clark writes, "the culture of the profession everywhere emphasizes personal autonomy and collegial self-government" (*Higher Education System*, 91).

26. Michel Foucault, "The Order of Discourse," in *Untying the Text: A Poststructuralist Reader*, ed. Robert Young (Boston: Routledge, 1981), 60–61.

27. See David R. Shumway, "Discipline and the Genealogy of Knowledge," paper presented at "Disciplinarity: Formations, Rhetorics, Histories," Seventh Annual Meeting of the Group for Research into the Institutionalization and Professionalization of Literary Studies (GRIP), 20–23 Apr. 1989, Minneapolis, Minn., p. 9. Distributed in *The GRIP Report*, vol. 9. Available from the GRIP Project, Department of English, Carnegie Mellon University, Pittsburgh, Pa. 15213.

28. Dietrich Rueschemeyer, "Professional Autonomy and the Social Control of Expertise," in Dingwall and Lewis, *Sociology of the Professions*, 41. I want to point out that professionalism as a transdisciplinary form of social organization is enormously complicated by particular institutional circumstances. At those institutions where the chief activity is teaching, where students receive primarily employment training, where demographic changes force the consideration of social issues, or where faculty have unionized, professional ideology may be under attack and professional practices may be displaced by other labor practices.

29. Sydney Ann Halpern, "Professional Schools in the American University," in Clark, *Academic Profession*, 309.

30. The involvement of science and commerce has a history that begins in the 18th century. See Peter T. Manicas, *A History and Philosophy of the Social Sciences* (Oxford: Basil Blackwell, 1987), 203.

31. Ruth Doell, "Whose Research Is This?: Values and Biology," in this volume.

32. According to Franklin A. Long, professor emeritus of chemistry and of science and society at Cornell University, "Federal funds constitute roughly two-thirds of the total support for university research, with mission-oriented federal agencies supplying the major funding." By "mission-oriented," Long means that the Departments of Defense, Energy, Health and Human Services, and Agriculture, as well as others, fund research and development essential to their functions and goals. From the Defense Department alone, "Federal funding for military R & D amounts to some $40 billion per year — roughly 12 percent of the total U.S. military budget"; Long, "Government Dollars for University Research," *Bulletin of the Atomic Scientists* 42, no. 3 (March 1986):45.

33. Manicas, *History and Philosophy*, 201.

34. David J. Sylvan, "The Qualitative-Quantitative Distinction in Political Science," paper presented at "Disciplinarity: Formations, Rhetorics, Histories," Seventh Annual Meeting of the Group for Research into the Institutionalization and Professionalization of Literary Studies, 20–23 April 1989, Minneapolis, Minn., p. 12; to appear in *Poetics Today* 12, no. 2 (Summer 1991), forthcoming.

35. Fuller, *Social Epistemology*, 282.

36. Donald M. Scott, "The Profession That Vanished: Public Lecturing in Mid-Nineteenth-Century America," in Geison, *Professions and Professional Ideologies in America*, 14; and Stanley Fish, "Anti-Professionalism," *New Literary History* 17, no. 1 (Autumn 1985):89–108.

37. For a discussion of these two traditions in the social sciences, see Roy Bhaskar, *The Possibility of Naturalism* (Atlantic Highlands, N.J.: Humanities Press, 1979), 1–30.

38. See, e.g., Helen H. Lambert, "Biology and Equality: A Perspective on Sex Differences," *Signs* 4, no. 1 (Autumn 1978):97–117; Stephanie A. Shields, "The Variability Hypothesis: The History of a Biological Model of Sex Differences in Intelligence," *Signs* 7, no. 4 (Summer 1982):769–97; Joseph S. Alper, "Sex Differences in Brain Asymmetry: A Critical Analysis," *Feminist Studies* 11, no. 1 (Spring 1985):7–37; and Londa Schiebinger, "The History and Philosophy of Women in Science: A Review Essay," *Signs* 12, no. 2 (Winter 1987):305–32.

39. We need a history of the materiality-ideation dualism, including the sex-gender dualism, that suggests alternative models — a continuum, a system, a process. For one such model, see Marian Lowe, "The Dialectic of Biology and Culture," *Woman's Nature: Rationalizations of Inequality*, ed. Marian Lowe and Ruth Hubbard (New York: Pergamon Press, 1983), 39–62.

40. The overriding purpose of feminist theory and action was to consolidate women as a politicized "sex class." See Ti-Grace Atkinson, "Radical Feminism," in *Notes from the Second Year: Women's Liberation*, ed. Shulamith Firestone (New York: n.p., 1970), 32–37; Shulamith Firestone, *The Dialectic of Sex: The Case for Feminist Revolution* (New York: Morrow, 1970); and Kate Millett, *Sexual Politics* (Garden City, N.Y.: Doubleday, 1970).

41. *Women: A Journal of Liberation* 2, no. 1 (1970):1.

42. Alan Dawe, "Theories of Social Action," in *A History of Sociological Analysis*, ed. Tom Bottomore and Robert Nisbet (New York: Basic, 1978), 365; also see 363–69 and elsewhere. For an explanation of the agent/structure problem in Marxist thought, see Alex Callinicos, *Making History: Agency, Structure and Change in Social Theory* (Ithaca, N.Y.: Cornell University Press, 1988). For a programmatic article reviewing structuration theory literature, see Alexander E. Wendt, "The Agent-Structure Problem in International Relations Theory," *International Organization* 41, no. 3 (Summer 1987):335–70.

43. Dawe, "Theories of Social Action," 367.

44. Wendt, "Agent-Structure Problem," 361.

45. Giddens, *The Constitution of Society* (Berkeley: University of California Press, 1984), 9.

46. Ibid., 14.

47. Ibid., 83.

48. Ibid., 171.

49. Bhaskar, *Possibility of Naturalism*, 43.

50. Alex Callinicos criticizes Giddens for the inadequacies of his theory at this macrolevel and, in a related move, for overemphasizing agents and capitulating to interpretive sociology ("Anthony Giddens: A Contemporary Critique," *Theory and Society* 14, no. 2 [March 1985]:133–66). Roger S. Gottlieb claims that Giddens's distinction between resources of allocation and those of authorization is unworkable; Gottlieb, *History and Subjectivity: The Transformation of Marxist Theory* (Philadelphia, Pa.: Temple University Press, 1987), 10–11.

51. Giddens, for instance, combines Erik H. Erikson and Erving Goffman to explain consciousness and presentation of self. While Goffman has done illuminating work on practice, Erikson's work seems to me less insightful than the following approaches to self-structuring. For self-psychology approaches to self-structuring, see Heinz Kohut, *The Analysis of the Self* (New York: International Universities Press, 1971); Heinz Kohut, *The Restoration of the Self* (New York: International Universities Press, 1977); Heinz Kohut, *How Does Analysis Cure? Contributions to the Psychology of the Self*, ed. Arnold I. Goldberg and Paul Stepansky (Chicago: University of Chicago Press, 1984); Heinz Kohut and Ernest S. Wolf, "The Disorders of the Self and Their Treatment: An Outline," *International Jour-*

nal of Psycho-Analysis 59, no. 4 (1978):413–25; George E. Atwood and Robert D. Stolorow, *Structures of Subjectivity: Explorations in Psychoanalytic Phenomenology* (Hillsdale, N.J.: Analytic Press, 1984); and Judith Kegan Gardiner, "Self Psychology as Feminist Theory," *Signs* 12, no. 4 (Summer 1987):761–80. For an approach to self-structuring in preverbal infancy that combines psychoanalysis and developmental psychology, see Daniel N. Stern, *The Interpersonal World of the Infant* (New York: Basic, 1985). On the structuring of erotic domination, see Jessica Benjamin, *The Bonds of Love: Psychoanalysis, Feminism, and the Problem of Domination* (New York: Pantheon, 1988).

52. An example is the tradition of radical urban politics based on the work of Saul D. Alinsky and the Industrial Areas Foundation. See, e.g., Alinsky, *Reveille for Radicals* (New York: Random House, 1969) and *Rules for Radicals: A Practical Primer for Realistic Radicals* (New York: Random House, 1971); Robert Baily, Jr., *Radicals in Urban Politics: The Alinsky Approach* (Chicago: University of Chicago Press, 1972); Harry C. Boyte, *The Backyard Revolution: Understanding the Citizen Movement* (Philadelphia: Temple University Press, 1980); Heather Booth, Harry C. Boyte, and Steve Max, eds., *Citizen Action and the New American Populism* (Philadelphia: Temple University Press, 1980); Harry C. Boyte, *Community Is Possible: Repairing America's Roots* (New York: Harper and Row, 1984); John McKnight and John Kretzmann, "Toward a Post-Alinsky Agenda," *Social Policy* 14, no. 3 (Winter 1984):15–18; Greg Delgado, *Organizing the Movement* (Philadelphia: Temple University Press, 1986); Robert Fisher, *Let the People Decide* (Boston: Twayne, 1986); Harry C. Boyte and Frank Riessman, eds., *The New Populism: The Politics of Empowerment* (Philadelphia: Temple University Press, 1986); Jim Gittings, "Churches in Communities: A Place to Stand," *Christianity & Crisis*, 2 Feb. 1987; and Harry C. Boyte, *Common Wealth: A Return to Citizen Politics* (New York: Macmillan/Free Press, 1989).

53. I have surveyed the curricular offerings of two dozen women's studies programs which were selected because they are large, radical, community-oriented, and/or prestigious programs (years of bulletin in parenthesis): University of Arizona (1989–91), Barnard College (1988–89), Brown University (1987–89), University of California, Berkeley (1989–90), University of California, Los Angeles (1989–90), California State University, Long Beach (1989–90), Carleton College (1988–89), University of Cincinnati (1989–90), Cornell University (1988–89), George Washington University (1988–89), Hunter College (1988–90), University of Illinois (1988–90), Mankato State University (1988–89), University of Maryland (1989–90), University of Massachusetts, Boston (1987–89), University of Michigan (1988–89), University of Minnesota (1988–90), New School for Social Research (1988–89), State University of New York, Albany (1988–90), State University of New York, Buffalo (1987–89), Ohio State University (1988), Rutgers University (1987–89), San Diego State University (1989–90), and University of Washington (1988–90). According to bulletin descriptions, the courses that treat social/personal change are those on gender, race, and class; the Second Women's Movement; public policy; counseling or psychotherapy for women; sexism and schools; and women's work. They are offered at California-Berkeley, Cincinnati, Cornell, George Washington, Illinois, Minnesota, SUNY-Buffalo, Rutgers, San Diego State, and Washington. Only four programs emphasize social/personal change and in some way teach practice. (1) California State–Long Beach offers a half-dozen courses focusing on changes brought about by the Second Women's Movement and by feminist community agencies; from its inception, this program involved community activists as well as academics. (2) Massachusetts-Boston has, beside courses on feminist public policy and therapy, a semester-long field placement in feminist agencies, organizations, and institutions (8–15 hours per week) and a concurrent seminar to deal with related theoretical issues (3 hours per week). (3) Michigan has a half-dozen courses on practical

feminism, group process, social organization, and women and communities. (4) Mankato State's program specifically teaches the practice of making feminist social change.

54. Warren G. Bennis, Kenneth D. Benne, Robert Chin, and Kenneth E. Corey, eds., *The Planning of Change*, 3rd ed. (New York: Holt, Rinehart, and Winston, 1976), 17.

55. For a different approach, see Callinicos's modification of Althusserian interpellation (*Making History*, 155–57).

56. Catherine Belsey, "Constructing the Subject: Deconstructing the Text," in *Feminist Criticism and Social Change: Sex, Class and Race in Literature and Culture*, ed. Judith Newton and Deborah Rosenfelt (New York: Methuen, 1985), 49.

57. Ibid., 49.

58. Ibid., 50.

59. Teresa de Lauretis, "Feminist Studies/Critical Studies: Issues, Terms, and Contexts," in de Lauretis, *Feminist Studies/Critical Studies*, 3.

60. Peter Berger, *Facing Up To Modernity: Excursions in Society, Politics, and Religion* (New York: Basic, 1977), 130–141 and elsewhere; and Peter Berger and Richard John Niehaus, *To Empower People: The Role of Mediating Structures in Public Policy* (Washington: American Enterprise Institute, 1977).

61. See Ellen Messer-Davidow, "The Right Moves: Conservatism and Higher Education," in *Literature, Language and Politics*, ed. Betty Jean Craige (Athens: University of Georgia Press, 1988), 55–83. For social change on the Left that uses mediating structures to organize, see n. 52, above.

62. Lynne V. Cheney, "Scholars and Society," a speech to the American Council of Learned Societies, New York, N.Y., 15 April 1988. Printed in *ACLS Newsletter* 1, no. 3, 2nd series (Summer 1988):6.

63. Ellen Messer-Davidow, "Monitoring the National Endowment for the Humanities," paper presented at the Annual Meeting of the National Network of Women's Caucuses and Committees in the Professional Associations, Washington, D.C., 20–23 Feb. 1989. For this report, I tabulated the awards for the years 1985, 1986, and 1987 in several NEH programs, including Fellowships for University Teachers, Fellowships for College Teachers, Summer Seminars, Museums and Historical Organizations, Media, Editions, Translations, Interpretive Research Projects, and Regrants-Conferences. In each program, I compared the total awarded, in numbers and dollars, for projects on women, gender, and feminism with the total awarded for all projects. I also reviewed the awards made in such subjects as religion, classical civilizations, modern literatures, and history, noting which projects were canonical and which were not. For copies of report: Ellen Messer-Davidow, Dept. of English, University of Minnesota, Minneapolis, Minn. 55455. Also see *National Endowment for the Humanities Twentieth Annual Report – 1985* (Washington, D.C.: U.S. Government Printing Office, 1986); *National Endowment for the Humanities Twenty-First Annual Report – 1986* (Washington, D.C.: U.S. Government Printing Office, 1987); and *National Endowment for the Humanities Twenty-Second Annual Report – 1987* (Washington, D.C.: U.S. Government Printing Office, 1988).

64. See Jamie Kitman and Ruth Yodaiken, "Celebrating (Yawn) the Constitution," *The Nation*, 2/9 July 1988, pp. 1, 14–16, 18–21.

65. Lynne V. Cheney's discussion of this issue is in *Humanities in America: A Report to the President, the Congress, and the American People* (Washington, D.C.: U.S. Government Printing Office, 1988), 11–12.

66. Ibid., 12.

67. Ibid., 9.

68. John Hammer, National Humanities Alliance Memorandum, 1 Oct. 1987. Available

from National Humanities Alliance, 1527 New Hampshire Avenue, N.W., Washington, D.C. 20036.

69. For criticisms, see William J. Bennett, "The Shattered Humanities," *Wall Street Journal*, 31 Dec. 1982; William J. Bennett, *To Reclaim a Legacy* (Washington, D.C.: U.S. Government Printing Office, 1984); E.D. Hirsch, Jr., *Cultural Literacy* (Boston: Houghton Mifflin, 1987); Allan Bloom, *The Closing of the American Mind* (New York: Simon and Schuster, 1987); Lynne V. Cheney, *American Memory: A Report on the Humanities in the Nation's Public Schools* (Washington, D.C.: U.S. Government Printing Office, 1987); Lynne V. Cheney, *Humanities in America* (Washington, D.C.: U.S. Government Printing Office, 1988); and Lynne V. Cheney, *50 Hours: A Core Curriculum for College Students* (Washington, D.C.: U.S. Government Printing Office, 1989). Among the replies from humanists are articles in *Salmagundi* 72 (Fall 1986); *Profession 88* (New York: Modern Language Association, 1988); *ADE Bulletin* 89 (Spring 1988); *ADE Bulletin* 90 (Fall 1988); and Betty Jean Craige, ed., *Literature, Language and Politics* (Athens: University of Georgia Press, 1988); as well as Peter Brooks, Jonathan Culler, Marjorie Garber, E. Ann Kaplan, George Levine, and Catharine R. Stimpson, *Speaking for the Humanities* (New York: American Council of Learned Societies, 1989). Also see Ellen K. Coughlin, "Scholars in the Humanities are Disheartened by the Course of Debate Over Their Disciplines," *Chronicle of Higher Education*, 13 Sept. 1989, A1, A14–15.

70. An exception is Catharine R. Stimpson, "Politics and Academic Research," in Craige, *Literature, Language and Politics*, 84–98.

71. See Christopher Myers, "Humanities Endowment Weighs Closer Supervision of Organizations that 'Re-Grant' Its Funds," *Chronicle of Higher Education*, 14 June 1989, A19, A21; Myers, "Ban Proposed on Arts and Humanities 'Re-Grants,'" *Chronicle of Higher Education*, 28 June 1989, A1; and "Washington Update," *Chronicle of Higher Education*, 5 July 1989, A20.

72. bell hooks, *Ain't I A Woman*, 53.

73. Mankato State University Bulletin, 1988–89, p. 169.

74. Material on Women's Studies 490/490A Internship in Women's Studies, as well as other courses, from Professor Ann Froines, Department of Women's Studies, University of Massachusetts—Harbor Campus, Boston, Mass. 02125.

75. Ann R. Bristow and Jody A. Esper, "A Feminist Research Ethos," in *A Feminist Ethic for Social Science Research*, ed. Nebraska Sociological Feminist Collective (Lewiston, N.Y.: Edwin Mellen Press, 1988), 74.

Contributors

Kathryn Pyne Addelson, B.A., Indiana University; Ph.D., Stanford University; professor, philosophy and history of science, Smith College. She is the author of *Impure Thoughts: Essays on Philosophy, Feminism, and Ethics* (Philadelphia, Pa.: Temple University Press, 1991) and is a past executive secretary of the Society for Women in Philosophy.

Angelika Bammer, Vordiplom, University of Heidelberg; M.A., Southern Methodist University, French; Ph.D., University of Wisconsin, Madison, comparative literature; assistant professor, German studies and Institute for Women's Studies, Emory University. She has written *Partial Visions: Feminism and Utopianism in the 1980s* and published articles on women writers, film-makers, and the politics of theory.

Patricia Hill Collins, B.A., Brandeis University; M.A.T., Harvard University; Ph.D., Brandeis University, sociology; associate professor, Afro-American studies, University of Cincinnati. She is the author of *Black Feminist Thought* (Boston, Mass.: Unwin Hyman, 1990).

Micaela di Leonardo, B.A., M.A., Ph.D., University of California, Berkeley; associate professor, anthropology, women's studies, and American studies, Yale University. She has written *The Varieties of Ethnic Experience* (Ithaca, N.Y.: Cornell University Press, 1984) and edited *Gender at the Crossroads of Knowledge: Feminist Anthropology in the Postmodern Era* (Berkeley: University of California Press, 1991). She is engaged in fieldwork among working-class Black women in New Haven, Connecticut.

Ruth G. Doell, B.A., Ph.D., University of California, Berkeley, biochemistry; professor, biology, San Francisco State University. She has published articles in biochemistry and cancer research as well as feminist criticism of science.

Denise Fréchet, B.Sc., Université Laval (Québec, Canada); M.Sc., Ph.D., Université Louis Pasteur (Strasbourg, France); senior research scientist, Rhône-Poulenc Santé (Vitry-sur-Seine, France). She has managed the Nuclear Magnetic Resonance Facility at Hunter College, City University of New York, taught Women and Science courses there, and published in professional journals.

Kathryn J. Gutzwiller, B.A., Marshall College; M.A., Bryn Mawr College, Latin; Ph.D., University of Wisconsin, classics; associate professor, classics, University of Cincinnati. She has published *Studies in the Hellenistic Epyllion* (Meisenheim, Germany: Beiträge sur klassischen Philologie, 1981), *Theocritus' Pastoral Analogies: The Formation of a Genre* (Madison: University of Wisconsin Press, 1991), and articles.

Sandra Harding, B.A., Douglass College; Ph.D., New York University; professor, philosophy and sociology, and director of women's studies, University of Delaware. She has written *The Science Question in Feminism* (Ithaca, N.Y.: Cornell University Press, 1986), which won the Jessie Bernard Award of the American Sociological Association; and *Whose Science? Whose Knowledge? Thinking from Women's Lives* (Ithaca, N.Y.: Cornell University Press, 1991). She has edited five collections of essays, including *Discovering Reality: Feminist Perspectives on Epistemology, Metaphysics, Methodology, and Philosophy of Science* (with Merrill Hintikka; Dordrecht, Netherlands: Reidel, 1983); *Sex and Scientific Inquiry* (with Jean O'Barr; Chicago: University of Chicago Press, 1987); and *Feminism and Methodology: Social Science Issues* (Bloomington: Indiana University Press, 1987).

Joan E. Hartman, B.A., Mount Holyoke College; M.A., Duke University; Ph.D. Radcliffe College; professor, English, College of Staten Island, City University of New York. She has edited *Women in Print I* and *Women in Print II* (with Ellen Messer-Davidow; New York: Modern Language Association, 1982); and *The Norton Reader* (with Arthur M. Eastman et al.; New York: Norton 1980, 1984, 1988). She has published articles on seventeenth-century English literature, women's studies, and professional issues.

Joyce A. Joyce, B.A., Valdosta State College; M.A., Ph.D., University of Georgia; professor, English, University of Nebraska. She has published *Native Son: Richard Wright's Art of Tragedy* (Iowa City: University of Iowa Press, 1986), edited *Cavalcade: An Anthology of Afro-American Literature* (with Arthur P. Davis and Saunders Redding; Washington, D.C.: Howard University Press, forthcoming), and published articles on African-American literature.

Ellen Messer-Davidow, B.A., M.A., Ph.D., University of Cincinnati; McKnight-Land Grant Associate Professor, English, University of Minnesota. She has edited *Women in Print I* and *Women in Print II* (with Joan E. Hartman; New York: Modern Language Association, 1982) and edits a book series, *Knowledge: Disciplinarity and Beyond* (with David R. Shumway and David J. Sylvan; Charlottesville: University Press of Virginia). She has written articles on English women's literature, literary and feminist theory, and higher education, and is completing a book on feminist inquiry.

Ann Norris Michelini, B.A., Radcliffe College; Ph.D., Harvard University; professor, classics, University of Cincinnati. She has published *Tradition and Dramatic Form in the Persians of Aeschylus* (Leiden, Netherlands: Brill, 1982), *Euripides and the Tragic Tradition* (Madison: University of Wisconsin Press, 1987), and articles.

Elizabeth Potter, B.A., Agnes Scott College; M.A., Ph.D., Rice University; associate professor, philosophy, Hamilton College. She has published articles on mainstream epistemology but recently has turned to feminist approaches to epistemology and philosophy of science; she is currently exploring gender politics in seventeenth-century science. She has been executive secretary of the Society for Women in Philosophy, Eastern Division, and is a founder of the Kirkland Historical Studies of Science and Technology conference series.

Nanette Salomon, B.A., Queens College, City University of New York; M.A., Ph.D., New York University; assistant professor, art history, College of Staten Island, City University of New York. She has published articles on seventeenth-century Dutch and Spanish and nineteenth-century French painting, and a book, *Jacob Duck and the Evolution of Dutch Genre Painting* (Doornspijk, Netherlands: Davaco Press), is forthcoming.

Naomi Scheman, B.A., Barnard College; M.A., Ph.D., Harvard University; associate professor, philosophy and women's studies, University of Minnesota. She has published articles on the epistemological implications of the social construction of gender and other systems of privilege.

Bonnie Zimmerman, B.A., Indiana University; Ph.D., State University of New York, Buffalo, English; professor, women's studies, San Diego State University. She has published articles on George Eliot, on women's studies, on lesbian literature, and a book, *The Safe Sea of Women: Lesbian Fiction, 1969–1989* (Boston: Beacon Press, 1990).

(En)Gendering
Knowledge